STALIN AND THE INEVITABLE WAR
1936–1941

The Cummings Center for Russian and East European Studies
The Cummings Center Series

STALIN AND THE INEVITABLE WAR, 1936–1941

Silvio Pons

THE CUMMINGS CENTER
FOR RUSSIAN AND EAST EUROPEAN STUDIES
TEL AVIV UNIVERSITY

The Cummings Center is Tel Aviv University's main framework for research, study, documentation and publication relating to the history and current affairs of Russia, the former Soviet republics and Eastern Europe. The Center is committed to pursuing projects which make use of fresh archival sources and to promoting a dialogue with Russian academic circles through joint research, seminars and publications.

THE CUMMINGS CENTER SERIES

The titles published in this series are the product of original research by the Center's faculty, research staff and associated fellows. The Cummings Center Series also serves as a forum for publishing declassified Russian archival material of interest to scholars in the fields of history and political science.

EDITOR-IN-CHIEF
Gabriel Gorodetsky

EDITORIAL BOARD
Michael Confino
Igal Halfin
Shimon Naveh
Yaacov Ro'i
Nurit Schleifman

MANAGING EDITOR
Deena Leventer

STALIN
AND THE INEVITABLE WAR
1936–1941

SILVIO PONS

FRANK CASS
LONDON · PORTLAND, OR

First published in 2002 in Great Britain by
FRANK CASS PUBLISHERS
Crown House, 47 Chase Side
London, N14 5BP

and in the United States of America by
FRANK CASS PUBLISHERS
c/o ISBS, 5824 N.E. Hassalo Street
Portland, Oregon, 97213-3644

Website: www.frankcass.com

Copyright © 2002 S. Pons

British Library Cataloguing in Publication Data

Pons, Silvio
  Stalin and the inevitable war, 1936–1941. – (The Cummings Center series)
  1. Stalin, I. (Iosif), 1879–1953 – Views on foreign policy
  2. World War, 1939–1945 – Soviet Union – Causes 3. Soviet Union – Foreign relations – 4. Europe – Foreign relations – Soviet Union 5. Soviet Union – Politics and government – 1936–1953
  I. Title II. Cummings Center for Russian and East European Studies
  327.4'7'04'09043

ISBN 0-7146-5198-2 (cloth)
ISSN 1365-3733

Library of Congress Cataloging-in-Publication Data

Pons, Silvio,
  [Stalin e la guerra inevitable English]
  Stalin and the inevitable war: 1936–1941 / Silvio Pons.
    p. cm. – (Cummings Center series)
  Includes bibliographical references and index.
  ISBN 0–7146–5198–2 (cloth)
  1. World War, 1939–1945–Diplomatic history. 2. World War, 1939–1945– Causes. 3. Soviet Union–Foreign relations–1917–1945. I. Title. II. Series.
  D754.S65 P6613 2002
  940.53'2–dc21

2002024195

All rights reserved. No part of this publication may be reproduced, stored in or introduced into a retrieval system or transmitted in any form or by any means, electronic, mechanical, photocopying, recording or otherwise, without the prior written permission of the publisher of this book.

Typeset in 10/12pt Garamond by FiSH Books, London
Printed in Great Britain by
Creative Print and Design (Wales), Ebbw Vale

Contents

Preface	ix
List of Abbreviations	xvi
Prologue: Stalin and the Threat of War	1
1. The Western Crises: The Rhineland	5
2. The Western Crises: Spain	42
3. The Internal Crisis	77
4. The Eastern Crises: Czechoslovakia	126
5. The Eastern Crises: Poland	150
6. The War Crisis	186
Epilogue: Stalin and the War	216
Bibliography	225
Index	235

Preface

This book is a study of how the Soviet Union responded to the European crises which led to World War II. Chapters 1, 2, 4 and 5 focus on Soviet and communist policies during the main international crises that transpired from 1936 to 1939 (the Rhineland, Spain, Czechoslovakia, Poland). Chapter 3 is devoted to the interaction between the domestic context of the Great Terror and Soviet conduct in foreign affairs during 1937 and 1938. Chapter 6 is an assessment of the main guidelines of Stalin's foreign and security policy as they emerged in the aftermath of the pact with Hitler in 1939 and 1940.

The book is intended to convey how influential the doctrine of the inevitability of war was for Soviet policy-making during the second half of the 1930s, and how the collapse of the Versailles system in the face of Hitler's foreign policy contributed to invigorating this doctrine. Seen from this perspective, Soviet foreign policy appears to have been less a reaction to Western appeasement towards Nazi Germany (as historians have often understood it) than the outcome of a specific political culture, interacting within foreign and domestic contexts. Contrary to a widely accepted image of policy-making under Stalin, this interaction provided more ground for conflict and contradictions than for planning. Accordingly, any attempt, following a traditional polarity that continues to divide historians, to specify either ideology or realism as the primary source of Stalin's foreign and security policy proves unconvincing. The alternatives overlapping and opposing each other in the Soviet Union on how to respond to the Nazi threat – whether with confrontation (i.e., anti-fascism and a 'collective security' approach) or appeasement (i.e., the anti-Versailles tradition and an undifferentiated approach to the 'capitalist world') – involved varying doses of ideology and realism. The combination that eventually emerged at the time of the pact with Hitler reflected more closely than any other the traditional Soviet vision of the outside world.

When World War II broke out in September 1939, the USSR's rulers appeared to have foreseen the conflict. Beginning a year earlier, Soviet propaganda had been proclaiming that a 'second imperialist war' was on its way. For over three years, the most influential Soviet and communist authorities had been speaking of the impending threat of war. Even before such talk had begun, Stalin himself had been predicting that Europe and the world were heading for disaster. However, these prophecies arose only in part thanks to political awareness and clear-sightedness. They sprang not so much from an appraisal of the European situation after Hitler's rise to power, as from Lenin's doctrine on imperialism and from the original experience forged in the cycle of wars of 1914–21. The concept of war as the inevitable consequence of inter-capitalist conflicts became firmly embedded in the Bolshevik mentality, and it exercised a longstanding influence on Soviet foreign policy and on the communist movement. As long as Stalin held the reins of power, he would cling to this axiom.

This vision of a catastrophic modernity perpetuated an inextinguishable perception of danger and prompted feelings of insecurity. Foreign intervention during the Russian civil war became the archetype of an undifferentiated, hostile outside world. This was to be the principal image in the Soviet concept of foreign affairs, the basis for the isolation and antagonism of the Soviet world. Stalin's 'revolution from above' of the late 1920s reinforced the strategic choice to separate the Soviet Union from the chaotic, conflict ridden capitalist world. Accordingly, the survival strategies outlined by the Bolsheviks during their discussions of *Weltkapital* continued to serve as the backbone of security policy in Stalin's Russia. Only by exploiting and encouraging 'inter-imperialist contradictions' could the Soviet Union avoid conflicts among capitalist states spreading to the socialist state. Soviet policy-makers continued to devote the greater part of their energies to frustrating an alliance among the major capitalist powers.[1]

Faced with the drastic international changes brought about by Hitler's rise to power in Germany, the Soviets found that such a political tradition needed revision. They had to make a substantial distinction between Nazi Germany and Western democracies. They realized that the days when Germany and the USSR had enjoyed a special bond based on their joint exclusion from the Versailles system were now over. And they redefined the international role of the USSR as a stabilizer of the European order by joining the League of Nations in 1934. Soviet diplomacy under Maksim Litvinov stressed the principles of 'collective security' and of an 'indivisible peace'. Contemporaneous Comintern policies under Georgi Dimitrov also stressed the new importance of a 'defence of peace' and of political alliances for the communist parties. These were the components of an anti-fascist foreign-policy line and bespoke a serious effort to cope with the security dilemmas of the USSR by a multilateral approach.[2]

PREFACE

However, the legacy of isolationism had not been entirely shaken off. Beneath the surface, but occasionally apparent, was an orientation aimed at separating the fate of the USSR from the European order, and at maintaining the tradition of unilateral security, divisive diplomacy, and pure anti-imperialist ardour. The old survival strategies were not abandoned, and recurrent doubts emerged among the Soviet leaders about the prospects of rebuilding and defending the post-war international system. This continuity persisted even though the Soviet Union had sufficient military and industrial potential by the mid-1930s to reclaim its role as a great power in Europe. Thus, building the bases of Soviet power did not mean a complete reversal of the tendency to isolation from the outside world. Such a tendency was reinforced by Western distrust of the Soviet Union and by the hostility of authoritarian states in central and eastern Europe to the USSR. But more than anything else the isolationist approach sprang from a cultural heritage and from a structural bent in Soviet policy, an obsessive concern about encirclement. In other words, Soviet international policy took two divergent and contradictory paths, which cannot be regarded as the classic confrontation between ideology and realism.[3]

This twofold approach became apparent during the succession of crises in Europe, giving expression to an underlying conflict. Especially after the outbreak of the Spanish civil war, Litvinov's policy of actively countering aggressive Nazi foreign policy by means of international alliances yielded to a sort of crisis-management mechanism, aimed at avoiding serious involvement in international conflicts. The political tools wielded by the Soviet leadership became more and more inadequate to the task of resolving the European crises; furthermore, each successive crisis acted to justify political pessimism. Domestic events also left an impact, as the Great Terror of 1937–38 interacted with Soviet foreign and security policy. The regime's internal crisis was accompanied by the return to an undifferentiated view of the outside world and by a revived obsession with domestic and foreign threats to state security. The impact of the purges forced the USSR to retreat into itself, and as it did so it revived the old psychology of a Soviet state separated from the rest of the world. The web of continuity was woven by Stalin's closest collaborators, Viacheslav Molotov, head of the government who became commissar for foreign affairs in Litvinov's place in May 1939, and Andrei Zhdanov, chief of the Leningrad party organization. Molotov yearned nostalgically, even after Hitler's rise to power, for the cooperation Moscow and Berlin had enjoyed during the 1920s; Zhdanov was spokesman for the fundamentalist wing of the regime, which was radically anti-Western and xenophobic.

The vision of an outside world dominated by permanent conflict was pervasive in the political culture of Stalinist communism. Whatever conflicts sprang up over the USSR's foreign policy as various currents and components of the regime collided, they did not affect the cultural premises of Soviet politics. Even those most consistently opposed to isolationism, namely Litvinov and his diplomats, observed these limits, though their thinking implied cultural change. At the same time, Stalin was not fully committed to any of the various foreign policy options, whether 'moderate' or 'radical'. His personal power was highly pragmatic, devoid of visible political coherence, ready to support different orientations at different times and legitimized by terror even as the exercise of this power gave rise to deep contradictions. Over the course of the purges, revisionists and catastrophists, Germanophiles and Westerners disappeared or were reduced to impotence. Stalin's sole rational objective seemed to be that of avoiding a situation in which a structured set of political alternatives might limit his autonomy in policy-making over international affairs. This ruthless and unprincipled realism sprang directly, if paradoxically, from an ideological and political vision, based both on Leninist doctrine and on bitter experience in the field of international politics – again, Western intervention in the Russian civil war and the exclusion of the USSR from the Versailles order.

Although the Soviet political élites were as likely to react to imaginary conditions as to real ones, the psychosis of encirclement was not simply an instrument cynically adopted to consolidate central control; rather, it was the extreme expression of a peculiar political culture. Soviet leaders saw themselves as predestined protagonists in an age of civil and world wars. The culture of permanent conflict legitimized Stalin's regime as the heir to 'war communism' and as a means by which to cope with external threats; things were not seen as having substantially changed since the time of the Revolution and the civil war. But historians should take for granted the Soviet self-representation in Stalinist dress. Bolshevism and Stalinism were an autonomous component of the 'European civil war', not a simple reaction to an external menace. The Soviets' fatalistic perspective destroyed the ability to distinguish clearly between a state of war and a state of peace. Their dogmatic logic was even more blindly promoted in the 1930s by a regime in crisis, which, after waging ferocious class war against the peasants in peacetime, was incapable of establishing a real principle of national unity. Thus was sharpened a longstanding sense of internal fragility and of inability to meet the challenges of world politics. It may be said that a vicious circle emerged between the doctrine of the inevitability of war, the appeal to the war experience, and the definition of the USSR's security interests. This was the aftermath of a complex interaction between Soviet Russia's internal and international contexts, as far as political culture was concerned.[4]

PREFACE

The point largely missed by historians is that the concept of security assumed a specific meaning under Stalin. While the violent suppression of any residual oligarchic practices cleared the way for the definitive concentration of foreign policy in the hands of Stalin, the abnormal politicization of security factors gave rise to an extreme notion of Soviet security, with aggressive implications. Such a 'total security state' hardly fits the classic images of totalitarianism. Even as late as the end of the 1930s, Soviet foreign policy was not based on uncontainable expansion resulting from innate factors, but rather on a security concept, distorted by its entanglement with the internal regime and by an ideological perception of the outside world.[5] This was no longer a revolutionary ideological thrust, nor was it consistent political planning based on a coherent set of ideas and aimed at the expansion of socialism in Europe.[6] It was also quite different from the foreign policy tradition of Imperial Russia, in spite of the persistence of strategic features and of the similarities destined to emerge in the course of the definition of geopolitical interests.[7]

The pact with Nazi Germany must be appraised in the light of all these considerations. Contrary to the prevailing historical interpretations, the pact was not imposed on the USSR by an unresolvable international situation in the spring and summer of 1939, nor was it the result of a carefully premeditated design in which all talk of 'collective security' had been nothing but a propagandistic expedient. To understand the end of 'collective security' and the Soviet decision to join in the pact requires a more complex approach.[8] The pact with Hitler was the outcome of Stalin's priority to avoid entanglement in the European war at all costs. Stalin saw an opportunity to take advantage of frictions between the capitalist powers and improve security for the USSR. This policy was the result of a combination of ideology and realism in Soviet political culture: an ideological view of the outside world centred on the idea that historical events would repeat themselves on the pattern of World War I; and a realistic approach to great-power policy essentially following the blueprint of the nineteenth-century struggle for mastery in Europe.

From August/September 1939 onwards, Stalin was committed to appeasing Hitler and to exploiting the conflict between the Western powers and Nazi Germany to create a territorial 'security system' involving expansion into eastern Europe. He expected the 'war of attrition' between the two blocs of 'capitalist powers' to precipitate the collapse of the 'old order' in Europe, creating favourable conditions for the USSR. But the quest for unilateral security ended in failure as a sharp contradiction emerged between Soviet appeasement towards Hitler and Soviet security objectives.[9] The abandonment of anti-fascism and the application of the ideological label 'inter-imperialist conflict' to the European war prevented Stalin from understanding the effects of Hitler's racist and anti-communist ideology on his war objectives. Then, weakened by the devastating effects of purges and mass violence, the USSR would face a brutal war aimed at its annihilation. Thus, Stalin's commitment to the theory of the inevitability of war influenced Soviet policy both before the outbreak of World War II in Europe and in its aftermath – it was a sort of self-fulfilling prophecy. Accordingly, the effect of the pact with Nazi Germany on Soviet policy should be understood both in terms of continuity with the isolationist tradition and of the turn towards imperial expansion in eastern Europe.[10] Territorial acquisitions and spheres of influence were based on a security notion that uniformly identified the 'capitalist powers' as a threat to the Soviet Union. The old Bolshevik survival strategy was thus reshaped into an antagonistic strategy – a perspective crucial to Soviet foreign policy under Stalin.

This book is a revised and updated English version of my *Stalin e la guerra inevitabile, 1936–1941* (Turin: Einaudi, 1995). I have drawn heavily on a body of documents (both published and unpublished) that has become accessible to scholars since the opening up of former Soviet archives in 1992. In Moscow I have consulted the archives of the Comintern and of the CPSU at the Russian State Archive for Social and Political History (Rossiiskii gosudarstvennyi arkhiv sotsialno-politicheskoi istorii – RGASPI) and the diplomatic archives at the Archive of the Foreign Policy of the Russian Federation (Arkhiv vneshnei politiki Rossiiskoi Federatsii – AVP RF). I have been able to enrich my study with documents from the Public Record Office (PRO) in London and from the Historical Archive of the Italian Ministry of Foreign Affairs in Rome.

Archives in Russia are now far more accessible than in the past, but unfortunately some, such as the Archive of the President of the Russian Federation, are still off-limits. Moreover, the Archive of the Foreign Ministry of the Russian Federation does not make available the indices and catalogues of archival material prepared by archivists over the years. These limitations make it difficult to get a complete picture of the way in which political decisions were made in the Soviet Union. And unfortunately, the access to archival documents in Russia is generally becoming more and more limited in recent years, especially as far as foreign policy is concerned.

Nevertheless, the available documentation has enriched our knowledge of 1930s Soviet foreign policy to an extent that only a few years ago would have been unthinkable. Historical scholarship on this subject has been assisted, not only by the new openness of former Soviet archives, but also by the recent publication of archival documents, both in Russia and in the West. It seems likely that new historical

PREFACE

interpretations will gradually take shape thanks to a growing body of scholarship, and if my book can in some measure contribute to this, then it will have fulfilled its purpose.

This English edition of my book has been made possible thanks to the financial support of the Gramsci Institute Foundation in Rome and of the University of Bari. I am sincerely grateful to Gabriel Gorodetsky for offering kind encouragement and invaluable advice as I prepared this edition. Thanks are due to Giuseppe Vacca for his friendly support; to Francesco Benvenuti, Franco De Felice, Anna Di Biagio, Francesca Gori and Giuliano Procacci, for their critical comments; to Jonathan Haslam, R. Craig Nation, Geoffrey Roberts and Robert Service, for kindly discussing various issues with me; to Alexander Chubarian and Mikhail Narinsky for their important help; and to all the Russian archivists who have made my research possible.

NOTES

1. See J. Erickson, 'Threat Identification and Strategic Appraisal by the Soviet Union, 1930–1941', in E. R. May (ed.), *Knowing One's Enemies: Intelligence Assessment between the Two World Wars* (Princeton, NJ: Princeton University Press, 1984). A. Di Biagio, *Le origini dell'isolazionismo sovietico. L'Unione sovietica e l'Europa dal 1918 al 1928* (Milan: Angeli, 1990).
2. J. Haslam, *The Soviet Union and the Struggle for Collective Security in Europe, 1933–39* (London: Macmillan, 1984).
3. For discussion on the character and significance of different Soviet foreign policy and security policy orientations during the 1930s, see J. Haslam, 'Litvinov, Stalin, and the Road Not Taken', in *Soviet Foreign Policy 1917–1991*, G. Gorodetsky (ed.), (London: Frank Cass, 1994); and T. Uldricks, 'Soviet Security Policy in the 1930s', in *Soviet Foreign Policy 1917–1991*.
4. See S. Pons and A. Romano (eds), *Russia in the Age of Wars, 1914–1945* (Milan: Annali Feltrinelli, 35, 2000).
5. On the historical origins of the image of the Soviet Union as an implacable totalitarian expansionist power, see A. Gleason, *Totalitarianism: The Inner History of the Cold War* (Oxford: Oxford University Press, 1995).
6. Such a view is held by R. C. Raack, *Stalin's Drive to the West, 1938–1945: The Origins of the Cold War* (Stanford, CA: Stanford University Press, 1995).
7. On persistence and similarities between Russian and Soviet foreign policy, see A. J. Rieber, 'Persistent Factors in Russian Foreign Policy: An Interpretative Essay', in H. Ragsdale (ed.), *Imperial Russian Foreign Policy* (Cambridge: Cambridge University Press, 1993).
8. See T. Uldricks, 'Debating the Role of Russia in the Origins of the Second World War', in G. Martel (ed.), *The Origins of the Second World War Reconsidered* (London: Routledge, 1999).
9. On this contradiction, see G. Gorodetsky, *Grand Delusion: Stalin and the German Invasion of Russia* (New Haven, CT, and London: Yale University Press, 1999).
10. For opposing views about the significance of the relationship with Nazi Germany to Stalin's foreign policy, stressing respectively either defence or expansionist factors, see G. Roberts, *The Soviet Union and the Origins of the Second World War: Russo-German Relations and the Road to War, 1933–1941* (London: Macmillan, 1995); and A. M. Nekrich, *Pariahs, Partners, Predators: German–Soviet Relations 1922–1941*, ed. G. L. Freeze (New York: Columbia University Press, 1997).

List of Abbreviations

ASMAE   Archivio storico del Ministero degli Affari Esteri (Historical Archive of the Ministry for Foreign Affairs, Rome)
AVP RF   Arkhiv vneshnei politiki Rossiiskoi Federatsii (Archive of the Foreign Policy of the Russian Federation, Moscow)
Comintern   Communist International, world organization of communist parties; existed 1919–43
CPSU   Communist Party of the Soviet Union
d.   *delo* – file
DBFP   Documents on British Foreign Policy
DDF   Documents Diplomatiques Français
DDI   Documenti Diplomatici Italiani
DGFP   Documents on German Foreign Policy
DVP SSSR   Dokumenty vneshnei politiki SSSR (Documents on the Foreign Policy of the USSR)
f.   *fond* (record, group)
GARF   Gosudarstvennyi arkhiv Rossiiskoi Federatsii (State Archive of the Russian Federation, Moscow)
IKKI   Ispolnitel'nyi komitet Kommunisticheskogo Internatsionala (Executive Committee of the Communist International)
Komsomol   Kommunisticheskii Soiuz Molodezhi (Communist Youth League)
Narkomindel   Narodnyi komissariat innostrannykh del (People's Commissariat for Foreign Affairs)
NKVD   Narodnyi komissariat vnutrennikh del (People's Commissariat for Internal Affairs)
op.   *opis'* – inventory
p.   *papka* – folder
PRO FO   Public Record Office, Archives of the Foreign Office, London
RGASPI   Rossiiskii gosudarstvennyi arkhiv sotsialno-politicheskoi istorii (Russian State Archive for Social and Political History, Moscow)
VKP(b)   Vsesoiuznaia kommunisticheskaia partiia (bol'shevikov) – All-Union Communist Party (Bolsheviks); name of Russian Communist Party from 1936 until 1952, when it was changed to CPSU

Prologue: Stalin and the Threat of War

Stalin's only clear denunciation of the threat that Nazi Germany posed to European peace was made in an interview of 1 March 1936 with the American journalist Roy Howard, published six days later. The Soviet dictator found it difficult to decide which of the two major military zones presented the greater threat, the 'Japanese zone' or the 'German zone'. Both were of concern to the USSR. However, Stalin maintained that Europe was likely to become 'the centre' of the future war.

He considered significant Hitler's attitude towards the pact signed by France and the USSR in May 1935. One of the 'symptoms' he noted was that even when Hitler spoke about peace, he could not 'avoid making threats'.[1] Stalin made an observation which had specific implications for the USSR: 'History tells us that when a state wishes to attack a state with which it does not share a border, it begins to create new borders until it neighbours the state that it wishes to attack.' This could happen in either of two ways: through force, as in the German attack on Belgium in 1914, or through the 'borrowing' of borders 'on credit', as Germany had tried to do in 1918 by enlisting the cooperation of Lithuania in order to threaten Petersburg. There could be no doubt, Stalin said, that Germany was in a position to find the 'on credit' borders it needed.[2]

He was alluding to Poland and implicitly acknowledging that the USSR could not feign indifference should there be a 'sudden eruption' of war in Europe. Poland had been the fiercest enemy of Soviet Russia since the war of 1920 between the two countries, and had acted as the linchpin of the Versailles system in central–eastern Europe. With Hitler's accession to power Moscow's greatest defence worry had become a reality, namely, an understanding between Germany and Poland. This rapprochement rendered meaningless the non-aggression pact signed by the USSR and Poland in 1932 and represented a much greater threat to the USSR than anything else that had occurred in the previous decade. At the same time, Stalin expressed satisfaction with the 27 February ratification of the Franco-Soviet pact by the French Chamber of Deputies, but he did not describe this pact in terms of what it seemed

STALIN AND THE INEVITABLE WAR, 1936–1941

to be: the basis of a system of security in eastern Europe which would isolate Nazi Germany and impose serious restraints on it.

Stalin did not give much credence to the factors that might prevent a new war. According to his pessimistic evaluation, even if the 'friends of peace' were consolidating their positions, the 'enemies of peace' might still undertake 'a war enterprise'. He did not even mention the concept of 'collective security', though it had been the main goal of Litvinov's foreign policy since December 1933, and a direct consequence of Hitler's rise to power.[3] This was a significant oversight, suggesting that even at the very moment when the Nazi regime was revealing its true intentions, the Soviet leadership was not vigorously enacting its diplomatic and political commitments. Stalin did not explicitly endorse an isolationist alternative – as Molotov had done only three months before – but that seems to have been his inclination.[4] With great care, he avoided any mention of the USSR's responsibility in the international field. In short, Stalin added nothing to the comments he had made about Soviet security at the 17th Party Congress in January 1934: 'We were not aligned with Germany before and we are not now aligned with Poland and France. In the past, we were aligned with the USSR and today we are aligned with the USSR and only with the USSR.'[5] Stalin's interview with Howard confirmed that Soviet foreign policy continued to be shaped by self-sufficiency. In other words, the Soviet Union clung to the isolationism that had dominated foreign-policy theory and practice in the years of the post-1929 'revolution from above'.

There were other continuities between the interview with Howard and the statements Stalin had made two years earlier. When asked what had led Europe to its current predicament on the brink of war, Stalin replied tersely that the causes were to be found 'in capitalism' and its imperialistic forms. The events of 1914 had to be kept in mind.[6] At the 17th Party Congress, he had expressed the strong conviction that 'once again, as in 1914, the parties of warmongering imperialism, the war and revenge parties, are on the alert'. He added that 'it is clear that we are heading towards a new war'.[7] There was nothing new about these affirmations: they referred to a question which had been central to the political battles of the previous decade, as well as to Stalin's own life.

In 1927 Stalin had played a leading role in the 'war scare' debate, using it to defeat Nikolai Bukharin and to set Soviet Russia on an isolationist course. Even then he had denounced the 'preparations' for a 'new war', identifying them as a device the capitalistic countries were using to emerge from their 'crisis'; he had declared the inevitability of new imperialistic wars.[8] But one must go back even further to find Stalin's first statements on this subject. At the 14th Party Congress, convened in December 1925, he proclaimed a 'state of armed peace'

PROLOGUE

(this was an allusion to the years preceding 1914) and spoke of a contradiction 'between the world of capitalism and the world of the Soviets'.[9] Earlier, during the 1925 plenum of the Central Committee, he had spoken of 'the warning signs of a new war', bound to erupt in a few years' time, and he had even begun to put together a code of conduct for the USSR in case of war. 'If war breaks out', he said, 'we must not twiddle our thumbs. We must intervene, but be the last to do so', in order to act as 'the deciding weight' on the scales.[10]

These precedents sketch out a political mentality and a strategic approach which were to be long lasting and in some ways permanent. This does not mean that Stalin's foreign policy was entirely predetermined and coherent, or that it would not evolve over the following decade. But as Hitler came to power and made war in Europe ever more likely, Stalin continued to see the world as it had been in 1914. He persevered to perceive German foreign policy mainly in terms of its tradition of imperialistic treatment of the East. Above all else, Stalin's thinking centred on the idea that with the growing instability of capitalism's international order, war would again manifest itself as the inevitable consequence of the clash of imperialistic interests. From the time of the Brest-Litovsk peace treaty in 1918 this Bolshevik precept was linked with the conviction that 'inter-imperialistic conflicts' would benefit the Soviet state.[11] In his address to the 17th Party Congress, Stalin outlined four different scenarios for war, only one of which directly concerned the USSR.[12]

During the interview of March 1936, Stalin did sound some new themes when the conversation turned to the link between war and revolution. The journalist wanted to know whether assurances that communism would not be broadcast to other countries meant a renunciation of 'plans' and 'aspirations' for a world revolution; Stalin replied: 'We have never had' such plans and the idea of their existence was a 'tragicomic misunderstanding'. He added that talk of exporting the revolution was 'nonsense'.[13] In 1934, Stalin had referred to the Marxist belief that the way to revolution would be opened by war. By choosing to go to war, the bourgeoisie would be hastening its own demise by sparking revolution, thereby risking 'the very existence of capitalism'. Such a scenario would be all the more likely if the bourgeois war were launched against the USSR, because then it would be fought 'not only on the enemies' front, but also behind their lines'.[14] In 1936 Stalin did not deny the connection between war and revolution, but simply kept quiet about it, emphasizing instead the Soviet Union's moderation and its efforts to 'normalize' its conduct in international affairs.

Stalin underlined the USSR's internal and international stability. This was something quite different from Lenin's formula that the fate of the

STALIN AND THE INEVITABLE WAR, 1936–1941

Russian Revolution depended on the world revolution – an idea which Stalin had begun to reverse as early as the 1920s.[15] Stalin's version of 'socialism in one country' seemed to make the USSR's inclusion in the community of states all the more likely. The USSR's new status as a major power, legitimated through indubitable industrial and military strength, might render ever more pressing the full adoption of the principle of national interest in the relations between the Soviet state and other states.

Nevertheless, the ideas which Stalin expressed in response to Howard's questions did not imply abandoning the basic concept of 'capitalistic encirclement'. Stalin did not foresee the USSR accepting any international responsibility, nor did he anticipate any modification to the Soviet isolationist tradition. Even the identification of foreign threats to national security remained highly indeterminate.[16] In Stalin's words we can see, as though preserved in amber, the essential features of the old concept of USSR security.

NOTES

1. I. V. Stalin, *Works* [Sochineniia], 3 vols, ed. R. McNeal (Stanford, CA: Hoover Institution, 1967), 1 [XIV], p. 119.
2. Ibid., p. 118.
3. M. Litvinov, *Vneshniaia politika SSSR. Rechi i zaiavleniia 1927–1937* (Moscow: Politizdat, 1937), pp. 74-96. On the impact of Hitler's rise to power on Soviet foreign policy, see Haslam, *The Soviet Union and the Struggle for Collective Security in Europe*, pp. 6 ff.
4. For Molotov's statement, see *Dokumenty vneshnei politiki SSSR* (hereafter: DVP SSSR), XIX, pp. 703-4.
5. I. V. Stalin, *Sochineniia* (Moscow: Politizdat, 1946–52), vol. 13, p. 302.
6. Stalin, *Works*, vol. 1, pp. 119–20.
7. Stalin, *Sochineniia*, vol. 13, p. 292.
8. Ibid., vol. 9, p. 323; vol. 10, p. 281.
9. Ibid., vol. 7, pp. 280–83.
10. Ibid., vol. 7, pp. 13–14.
11. See Di Biagio, *Le origini dell'isolazionismo sovietico*, pp. 15–27.
12. Stalin, *Sochineniia*, vol. 13, pp. 294ff.
13. Stalin, *Works*, vol. 1, p. 121.
14. Stalin, *Sochineniia*, vol. 13, p. 297.
15. See E. H. Carr, *A History of Soviet Russia: Foundations of a Planned Economy 1926–1929*, III, 1 (London: Macmillan, 1976) chap. LXVI.
16. See J. Erickson, 'Threat Identification and Strategic Appraisal', in E.R. May (ed.), *Knowing One's Enemies*, p. 391.

1

The Western Crises: The Rhineland

THE USSR'S TWO REACTIONS

Two days after the publication of Stalin's interview with Roy Howard, on 7 March 1936, German troops took possession of the Rhineland. Inevitably, Hitler denounced the 1925 Locarno agreements signed in the wake of the Versailles Treaty, in which Germany had agreed to the demilitarization of the region. The European tensions and dangers described by Stalin during his interview were suddenly much more obvious. This coincidence might appear to be a ringing confirmation of his concerns, but Stalin's foresight had not extended to war in Europe; he had spoken only of possible retaliation for aggression in the Far East. Now a more serious danger surfaced in the heart of Europe and the problem of finding an appropriate response necessarily involved the USSR and the communist movement.

The Nazi display of force did not take the Soviets unawares. It had been predicted by Mikhail Tukhachevskii, Deputy Commissar for Defence, during the Paris talks of January 1936.[1] Nevertheless, the USSR maintained a prolonged official silence. Only after the French Senate had rushed to ratify the treaty with the USSR (on 12 March) did an editorial appear in *Izvestiia*, expressing the Soviet government's condemnation of the invasion.[2] Litvinov, on the other hand, had responded immediately to French pressure. On 9 March he had charged Vladimir Potemkin, the Soviet representative in Paris, with the duty of accelerating ratification of the treaty between the two countries; Potemkin was also to inform the French foreign minister, Pierre Flandin, that he could 'count fully on my [Litvinov's] support in Geneva'.[3] On the same day Potemkin communicated to Ivan Maiskii, the Soviet representative in London, his opposition to entering into negotiations with Hitler – a move certain to 'diminish' international concerns about the Nazi danger and likely to 'encourage not only Germany but Italy and Japan as well'. Litvinov went further, declaring his readiness to support 'any action against Germany agreed upon

5

collectively in Geneva'.[4] Shortly afterwards, *Le journal de Moscou*, the official voice of the Narkomindel (Commissariat for Foreign Affairs), noted that the Rhineland crisis 'is perhaps the most serious political crisis since the end of the World War' and called on all 'friends of peace' to unite. Though the USSR had been excluded from the negotiations at Versailles and Locarno, it had come to support the principle of the 'indivisibility of peace'.[5]

Litvinov went to London on 12 March to attend the meeting of the League of Nations. France was demanding that German troops vacate the Rhineland and that sanctions be immediately imposed against Germany. But over the days of debate Litvinov realized that Paris would not win unanimous support; the British, in particular, believed that such an act would mean war.[6] Speaking in London on 17 March, Litvinov outlined the official Soviet position. He stated that it was not possible 'to fight for the collective organization of security without taking collective measures against the violation of international obligations', nor would it be possible 'to preserve the League of Nations if these violations were ignored and effective measures not taken against them'. Failure to insist on a set of basic principles would lead to assertions that 'such a league is unnecessary' and could 'indeed be dangerous'.[7]

Most of the points made in Litvinov's London speech were in response to German propaganda. He reasserted, for example, the defensive nature of the Franco-Soviet Pact and its compatibility with the Locarno Treaty. But Litvinov spoke of a longstanding Soviet concern: Germany's apparent drive to 'create hegemony' in Europe was a revival of an old longing 'to divide Europe into two or more parts, so that while one part enjoyed a truce, Germany would enjoy free rein in the other'.[8]

Litvinov's language was blunt:

> I have permitted myself, gentlemen, to express my thoughts candidly. This has been easier for me than for some other colleagues because the way in which Mr Hitler allowed himself to speak publicly about the state that I represent freed me from the restraint of diplomatic conventions. I had all the more right to do this, given that the entire purpose of Mr Hitler's intervention and of his stated views on international politics is the organization of an attack against the peoples of the country which I represent and the unification of the whole of Europe and of the world against it.[9]

However, in his closing remarks, Litvinov introduced a note of moderation. One should not assume, he explained, that the USSR acted more readily to condemn conflicts than it would to take measures for their peaceful resolution: 'peace is more sacrosanct for us than it is for others, not less. This is as true today as it will be over the coming decades and not only in one sector of Europe ... We are strongly against anything that can lead to war.' Litvinov thus linked firmness of principle to the strategic possibility of peace. At the same time, he left the door to diplomatic manoeuvres open by declaring that Germany's return to the League of Nations would be a contribution to the cause of peace.[10] Even after 7 March, 'collective security' meant the same thing for Litvinov that it had during the two previous years: avoiding conflict between different international alliances. Continuity and caution had become his watchwords.

Two days later Molotov gave an interview to the French newspaper *Le Temps*. From the outset, he offered an interpretation of European affairs and a prescription quite different from Litvinov's. Molotov recognized that the remilitarization of the Rhineland 'has undoubtedly endangered countries to the east of Germany, and particularly the USSR', but he specified that the German show of force was 'above all a threat to France and Belgium, the Rhineland's western neighbours'.[11] As he spoke with the French journalist, Molotov seemed to let down his guard, to allow himself one of his very rare moments of frankness. Asked whether the USSR's political inclinations would make it more likely than the states of western Europe to forge ties to Germany, he replied:

> Among a certain section of Soviet people there is extreme hostility towards the present rulers of Germany, particularly in response to the constant and repeated hostilities German leaders have manifested vis-à-vis the Soviet Union. Nevertheless, those primarily responsible for setting Soviet policy consider an improvement in German-Soviet relations possible.[12]

Molotov regarded Germany's re-admission to the League of Nations (a suggestion made by Litvinov) as only 'one of the better' proposals for ameliorating diplomatic relations between the two countries: clearly, he intended that Moscow might attempt something less ambitious than the building of a European security system in its quest for a *modus vivendi* with Berlin. Edging away from Litvinov's pet strategy, 'collective security', Molotov had begun to outline a different approach to Soviet security, that familiar ideal of 'peaceful co-existence' between the USSR and all the capitalist states. By presenting so publicly a picture of a foreign policy that differed from that of another Soviet leader, Molotov may have incurred Stalin's displeasure,[13] but he was, in fact, only repeating the traditional Soviet isolationist line, one that had been implicitly maintained by Stalin in his interview with Howard.

In any event, Molotov's apparent frankness was to a great extent instrumental. The unusual admission of different Soviet foreign-policy viewpoints was a signal to the Germans. The same admission also warned the Western powers that they were not the only ones who could play the German card, while at the same time making it clear that ideological differences would not keep the Soviets from making diplomatic overtures. On the other hand, Molotov's warning that the USSR considered the remilitarization of the Rhineland a direct threat to the Western powers was ambiguous. Did it refer simply to a common danger and the consequent need for alliances and instruments to guarantee security in Europe? Or did it imply (after all, there had been no explicit reference to 'collective security') that the Soviet Union was prepared to launch a unilateral gambit? If the latter, defence of the USSR's interests could radically diverge from the search for a system of general security.

There were significant precedents. A year earlier, in March 1935, immediately after the announcement of obligatory conscription in Germany, Stalin had personally censored an article written by General Mikhail Tukhachevskii on Nazi Germany's war strategy. The dictator had, in particular, crossed out the following words, 'upon achieving its vain goal of overwhelming Russia, German imperialism would certainly turn against France', and replaced them with the reflection that Hitler's 'anti-Soviet darts' were 'a useful screen for covering revanchist objectives in the West (Belgium, France) and towards the South (Poznan, Czechoslovakia, *Anschluss*)'.[14]

Clearly, Stalin did not feel that an important article written by one of the USSR's foremost military leaders was a suitable place for airing the theory that Germany would invade France only after attacking the Soviet Union, or for the suggestion that the Soviet Union was Germany's main objective.[15] Stalin proposed a very different interpretation of German military manoeuvres and of the Nazi regime's anti-Soviet propaganda. He even suppressed those concluding passages of Tukhachevskii's article devoted to lauding the strength of the Red Army and to the might of 'Socialist industry', whose 'peace policy' could never accommodate Germany's 'militaristic policy'. His obvious intention was to play down every important detail involving the USSR. The article finally appeared with an anodyne ending.[16]

It is worth noting that Tukhachevskii, in a speech given in January 1936, returned to the question of the German high command's strategic plans. On this occasion, he affirmed in no uncertain terms that 'given the present situation, in which states lying between ourselves and Germany enjoy a special relationship with Germany, the German army will probably gain access to the routes needed to invade our territory'.

THE RHINELAND

Naturally, he conceded, it was quite another matter to foresee 'how it would end'. He then spoke about Germany's meticulous preparations for war and stressed the need to take 'most seriously the defence of our western frontiers and organize the necessary level of defence'.[17] Unlike Stalin and Molotov, Tukhachevskii viewed a German attack on the Soviet Union as nearly certain.

Therefore, it would seem that Molotov's 'revelation' of March 1936 was not pure invention; in fact, the message may well have been intended for people inside the USSR as well as outside. Even after 7 March, he was saying, the Soviet government was unwilling to exclude bilateral relations with the German government. This recalled the Rapallo Treaty (1922) era, when a special relationship was established between Germany and the USSR.[18] We do not know whether the Soviet leaders then possessed specific information that pushed Molotov to take this stance. What is certain, however, is that a few months previously, at the end of November 1935, Stalin had ordered the Soviet ambassador in Germany, Iakov Surits, to make discreet enquiries among German political circles – the results had been keenly disappointing.

Surits had concluded that Hitler and his entourage were unlikely to change their position towards the USSR, at least in the short term.[19] In a secret memorandum dated 3 December 1935, Litvinov had informed Stalin that Surits was sure of Hitler's persistent hostility towards the USSR, and that this formed 'the basis for his tactical decisions in foreign policy'. Nor could one count on other members of the Nazi regime (e.g. Hjalmar Schacht) to work for internal change. In Litvinov's opinion, given the grim forecast for German–Soviet political relations, no attempts should be made to improve economic relations. He had also suggested increasing the volume of propaganda aimed at denouncing German fascism, and rooting out what he called the 'Tolstoyan attitude' of the Soviet press.[20] On 19 December, he confided to Surits his strong doubts about improving German–Soviet relations.[21]

The outlook sketched by Litvinov diverged from that of David Kandelaki, the Soviet commercial attaché in Berlin, who had not only looked favourably upon the German proposal for repaying long-term credit with raw materials, but had spoken of working to improve political relations and of signing an 'Eastern Pact agreement'.[22] The idea of joining with Germany in an 'Eastern Locarno' was not new, but it is curious that it was broached in such an unorthodox fashion by a lower official at a moment when the commissar of foreign affairs was seriously sceptical towards such a plan.

Economic talks had to proceed, notwithstanding Litvinov's unfavourable opinion. Such an orientation seems particularly significant when juxtaposed with the remarks made by Molotov in

March 1936. These remarks constituted a second foreign-policy line in a new 'twin-track' strategy for dealing with the European powers.[23] While Litvinov maintained that 'peaceful co-existence' was not enough for achieving security, Molotov suggested that it was and that the anti-fascist stance of 'collective security' might even be dangerous for the USSR. We may presume that Stalin had not yet decided between the two alternatives; the underlying conflict between them was not subsequently removed and became apparent only on the immediate eve of World War II.

Molotov's position also differed from that of Litvinov's deputy Nikolai Krestinskii. During the period chosen by Molotov and Litvinov to air their different positions, Krestinskii had denied that any elements within the Soviet leadership favoured *rapprochement* with Germany.[24] Krestinskii's evaluation sheds further light on Moscow's view of the international situation in March 1936. He assumed that Hitler would attack the USSR only if at the same time the Japanese attacked in the Far East. In this instance, Krestinskii was repeating an opinion already expressed by Litvinov in a conversation with Lord Chilston, the British ambassador in Moscow.[25] If Germany moved on France, it would of course be necessary for the USSR to enter into talks with France's European allies. Krestinskii felt 'that it would be difficult to count on Poland's help', and that Polish intervention against Germany was at best 'doubtful'. Warsaw would probably remain neutral and would deploy its armies along its eastern border.[26] The deputy commissar's words showed that Soviet leaders were well aware of the difficulty of achieving a unified stand against Germany. Krestinskii concluded by emphasizing a single point: he did not believe that the entry of German troops into the Rhineland had created 'a pre-war situation'.[27] This was a point hotly debated within the Soviet leadership.

When the League of Nations adjourned on 20 March 1936, it had offered only a general condemnation of Germany. The Franco-Soviet Pact was submitted for review to the World Court in the Hague; the German request for negotiations was accepted and the temporary introduction of an international force into the Rhineland was proposed. In all of these actions, and in the actions not taken, Great Britain had played a decisive role. Soviet diplomatic efforts had concentrated on avoiding the marginalization of the USSR through such means as a 'new Locarno Treaty' and a Western pact including Germany.

Litvinov sent a telegram to Stalin from London on 21 March, commenting on the agreement reached between the Locarno signatories and on their plans to negotiate with the Germans. He pointed out that the document contained 'no mention of eastern European security' and solicited advice regarding an appropriate response should the British

THE RHINELAND

and the French decide to support a non-aggression pact between the USSR and Germany.[28] The following day, the commissar received a communication from Krestinskii, who had presumably written at Stalin's behest: if the 'eastern European question' was not addressed, the very authority of the League of Nations would be seriously jeopardized. The Soviet Union would then be obliged to 'strengthen its own army and air force', an act that 'speaks for itself'. Krestinskii went on to recommend that Litvinov demand the establishment of an Eastern pact by bringing Germany into the Franco-Soviet pact. This would lead the Western governments themselves, possibly even the German government, to propose 'as a compromise' a non-aggression pact between the USSR and Germany. In such a case, the Soviet government would agree to the pact, with the caveat that such a pact would be nullified if either of the two contracting parties attacked a third.[29]

Krestinskii's guidelines had two dominant themes: the prospect of intensified Soviet isolation; and the possibility of an agreement between the USSR and Germany on security in eastern Europe that would be guaranteed by the Western powers, and might have to be imposed on Germany. Neither theme was new, and the first had been revived at the beginning of 1936. Obviously, remilitarization of the Rhineland had not put an end to Stalin's thinking about isolationism. The outlook for a bilateral treaty with Germany, whether in concert with the Western powers or not, was far from clear, particularly in light of Kandelaki's inconclusive mission of late 1935.

The first real display of Nazi aggression had prompted the Soviets to use the pact with France to conclude an agreement with Germany. But Soviet withdrawal from international politics remained a real possibility, and after 7 March 1936 Stalin seemed to envisage an orientation towards collective European security merely as a less attractive option. It should also be noted that the guidelines given to Litvinov made no mention of the wider and more lasting peace plan which he had described in London on 17 March.

Diplomatic prospects were not very promising. On 24 March Litvinov notified Potemkin that he had submitted to Joseph Paul-Boncour, the French representative, a series of points which included the proposal for an eastern European pact 'with the participation of Germany'.[30] The next day he made the same proposal to Anthony Eden, the British foreign secretary, who expressed grave doubts over whether Germany would back such an agreement.[31] While passing through Paris on his return to Moscow for the final ratification of the pact with France, Litvinov learned from the French premier, Pierre Flandin, that an agreement with Germany seemed 'unattainable'. Flandin did, however, assure Litvinov that France would not sign a pact that failed to provide for the security needs of eastern Europe.[32] Conversations with Foreign Minister József Beck of Poland, the key country for an Eastern pact, were not encouraging either and only confirmed the poor relations between the two countries.[33]

At the end of March, an editorial in *Le journal de Moscou* underscored the need for an Eastern pact that would be more far-reaching than extant bilateral pacts and would offer Germany and the countries in the east the same guarantees that the Locarno Treaty provided for countries in the west. Germany's opposition to such a treaty was not to stand in the way of its realization. The crisis of Locarno had shown that it was impossible to anticipate the form aggression might take and that any attempt to 'address' the aggression would endanger peace everywhere.[34] As early as 26 March, while Litvinov was still in Paris, Krestinskii voiced his own pessimism in a dispatch to Surits: prospects for a pact involving central and eastern Europe seemed to him 'very nebulous', and it was difficult to believe that the French government would abstain for long from undertaking direct negotiations with Germany.[35]

The events that unfolded after 7 March had paradoxically managed both to accelerate the ratification of the Franco-Soviet pact and to diminish its strategic significance in the eyes of both countries. Potemkin communicated from Paris that 'here they maintain that the USSR is too far away, that after all it does not share common borders with Germany, and that the Red Army is insufficiently prepared for a dynamic and aggressive war'. The French also insinuated that 'the USSR is deliberately pushing the European states towards war, and that it is continuing to prepare for world revolution'.[36] The Soviets, like the French, overestimated Hitler's military strength, despite the shrewd suggestion made to Surits by Attolico, Italy's ambassador in Berlin, that Hitler's dramatic military gesture was a bluff.[37]

The political significance of the pact with France was undergoing a metamorphosis. A product of Litvinov's policy, the pact yielded limited political results at the time of Europe's first international crisis. France's foreign policy ended by conforming closely to the English line, without significantly affecting relations between Great Britain and the USSR, which remained tenuous. Maiskii's 'peace front' speech in London had proved nothing more than a pipe dream.[38] As Litvinov himself had noted at the beginning of 1936, everything seemed to favour the isolationist tendencies in the USSR.[39]

POWER POLITICS AND CONFLICT BETWEEN 'SYSTEMS'

The first full analysis of the Rhineland crisis published in the Soviet press was by Karl Radek. Three years had already passed since Radek's rehabilitation, following his close association with Trotsky in

THE RHINELAND

the political struggles of the 1920s. Now he held the important role of commentator on international questions for *Izvestiia* and the journal of the Communist International (Comintern), having also taken over the foreign affairs desk in Stalin's personal secretariat.[40] In a semi-official capacity, he had played an important role in reorienting Soviet foreign policy from early 1934, becoming one of the most authoritative Soviet voices in international politics.

From the time of his political reappearance, Radek had called repeatedly for a careful assessment of Hitler's rise to power and his revisionist politics in international affairs. His own stance appears to have been close to the flexible posture described by Molotov in his interview in *Le Temps*.[41] But Radek vacillated. His admiration for the dedication and organizational zeal of Nazi youth (Gustav Hilger has described Radek's sentiments in his memoirs) can be interpreted both as part of the rivalry between the two totalitarian regimes, and as part of Radek's belief that there would be a revolutionary explosion in Germany.[42] Radek's opinions were far from unique, reflecting precise currents in Soviet and communist political circles; many believed that the Versailles peace treaty contained the germ of an inevitable future conflict. Such convictions seemed to have been strengthened by the 1936 Rhineland crisis when German forces entered the demilitarized buffer zone, which was also the last significant international issue in which Radek played a public part.

In an article published on 8 March, Radek tartly observed that the occupation of the Rhineland meant that yet another 'piece of paper' had been torn up. Was anyone surprised? After all, 'as soon as fascism was installed, Germany violated those points of the Locarno Treaty relevant to the demilitarized zone'. What Hitler really wanted from France was 'freedom of movement in the east'. The expectation that this would soon be granted had encouraged the Germans to move westward: whatever Hitler's true objectives were, if the Western powers did not rapidly correct their indecisive and uncoordinated posture, there would be war in the west.[43] Radek offered a grim picture of Germany's internal situation: after three years in power, Hitler had managed to alienate not only the working masses and peasants, but also the Catholics and important sectors of the middle classes: by now all were aware of the 'catastrophe' towards which the country was moving. By contrast, the USSR, 20 years after its founding, presented quite a different social picture in the wake of industrialization. Radek underscored the instability of the Hitler regime as an integral part of his analysis of the international situation.

Two days after his first article appeared, Radek published another, in which he returned to the 'collapse of Locarno'. He used the analysis drawn up by Soviet observers in 1925 to place the Locarno diplomatic agreement within a historical context. According to Radek, the agreement's principal effect was the division of Europe into two zones: 'the western zone and the eastern zone, whose borders were being challenged'. Over the ensuing decade, European power relations had changed, not only because Germany had ceased 'to be a political objective', but also because the influence of Great Britain had slackened. At the same time, the objectives of German foreign policy had undergone a revolutionary change, especially with regard to its eastern borders. Hitler's plans involved 'attacking the Soviet Union'. As soon as Hitler had realized that there would be no 'preventative war' against Germany he moved to dismantle the agreements made at Locarno. Now Germany could propose a 'new Locarno', one that would represent a great threat to France even as it left Eastern Europe without security guarantees. Radek concluded that a united front for European defence could be formed 'only through conflict' and that waiting for decisions from the League of Nations would be futile.[44]

On 14 March Radek sent a letter to Stalin, complaining he had received no instructions from him, nor from Litvinov, on the political line to observe after Germany's occupation of the Rhineland. His main point was the appeal for intervention against Nazi Germany in defence of peace, but not in defence of the Locarno Treaty. Should he receive no counter-instruction, Radek specified, he would continue to follow such a line.[45] We do not know whether Stalin replied, but undoubtedly Radek kept firmly to his purpose.

Radek exhibited a very negative opinion of Great Britain: the British looked incapable of repeating their past successes in quelling the agitated international waters.[46] Consequently, the course taken by Hitler was likely to meet no serious resistance and would lead Europe to disaster. Radek maintained that Nazism was incapable of wiping out mass unemployment and the attempt to do so through a policy of rearmament could only trigger 'bankruptcy' and 'catastrophe'. In other words, he insisted on viewing the economic problems generated by the Hitler regime on a social and political level; this led to his prediction that Hitler would accelerate preparations for war.[47] Not even the plebiscite on the Rhineland of 29 March 1936 shook Radek's conviction that Hitler's regime was shaky and Germany's internal situation explosive. He believed that there had been no tampering and that the numbers simply reflected a national desire for revenge, which the regime duly exploited. Votes for Hitler had been votes against Versailles, not for war, and when Stalin told Howard that 'in all the world there is not a people who wants war' he must also have had the German people in mind. The suggestion that the German masses desired fascism amounted, said Radek, to 'groundless pessimism'. But this generous assessment of the spirit of the German people did not lead him to underestimate the dangers posed by Nazism.[48]

Though Radek did not fully clarify his view of the significance of Germany's supposed internal instability, it is obvious that he considered this as an international factor bound to be largely uncontrollable given the crisis of the order of Versailles. There might even be a revolutionary outbreak in the country just as the Bolsheviks had always predicted. In Radek's view, there was little room for diplomatic manoeuvre and its very relevance was dubious.

At the beginning of April, Radek wrote that Hitler possessed a detailed strategic plan, complete with carefully formulated diplomatic manoeuvres. Hitler's objective was to divide western from eastern Europe and to create more favourable conditions for an attack against Russia. Radek believed the plan could work: France would be blackmailed by the threat of war and Britain would be prevented from adopting adequate countermeasures as long as it failed to provide any guarantee for European security. By now, it was clear to Radek that Germany 'does not wish to tie her hands with regard to the USSR and wants to be free to intervene against the USSR by crossing into a neighbouring state'. Radek was reiterating the concern which Stalin had expressed on the eve of 7 March, though he emphasized that the situation was by now much more critical. The Rhineland crisis was in fact 'a European problem' which 'significantly changes post-war power relationships', boosting 'the chances of German military aggression'.[49]

Radek closed by emphasizing the danger of war in the east. He expected nothing less than a cataclysm. A great deal had changed since Krestinskii had refused to foresee a 'pre-war situation' after 7 March. Radek's shift took place not only on the analytical level; it also included a change in how he saw the political consequences of the international crisis. During the month of March, he had remained faithful to the orientation prevailing in Soviet official circles. This had meant an allegiance to the idea that 'the guarantee of Soviet security lay, above all, in its own capacity to defend itself' – a capacity likely to be strengthened rather than weakened if 'the other powers cannot or do not want to take measures to reinforce collective security'.[50] Now Radek was declaring that, if Germany persevered in refusing to take part in any system of European security, 'then this system for maintaining peace must be created despite Germany's wishes'.[51] This new formulation confronted fascism more firmly and might have strengthened the Soviet Union's commitment to international politics. This was an apparent move away from an isolationist concept of security, and from the line of détente previously championed by Radek himself. But whatever the positive implications of the new formulation, it hardly amounted to a leap into diplomatic action.

A second commentator on the Rhineland question was the Hungarian economist Evgenii Varga, a commanding voice in the theoretical and political debates of the communist world. In 1936, he was close to Stalin and enjoyed considerable influence inside the Comintern (Communist International).[52] His article, which appeared in the international political review that he edited, placed recent European developments within the context of the general trends and contradictions to which capitalist economies were prone.[53] Far from original, Varga's thesis revolved around the sharpening contradictions between 'the highly developed monopolistic character of German capitalism and Germany's political position within the Versailles system'. Should Germany choose to abrogate the treaties and harness a revived economy to the needs of rearmament, the German standard of living might well plunge. In foreign affairs, the notion of Germany as the epicentre of 'imperialist contradictions' had sharpened. If in 1925 Great Britain had chosen to support Germany rather than France to ensure that no single hegemonic power on the continent achieved dominance, the time had now come to switch its support to France, but the success of such a move was far from certain. According to Varga, British policy amounted to 'substantial backing' for Hitler's actions. There could be no question that France's strategic position had worsened: in all probability, Hitler was thinking of a reinforced military position to the west as the basis for offensive rather than defensive tactics. In drawing up his formal conclusions, Varga stated the obvious: the Rhineland crisis was a 'serious threat' to the security of France and Belgium. But another conclusion could be drawn from his general discussion, based exclusively on the traditional view of 'inter-imperialist' conflicts. Occupation of the Rhineland had mainly inflamed conflicts between the capitalist powers, and the risks to USSR security had not escalated to the extent France's had. Consequently, the USSR could draw comfort from the sharpening of these conflicts rather than looking for collective security and defending the principle of 'indivisible peace'.

In sum, each of the two most influential Soviet commentators on international politics had taken as his interpretive tack a different element of traditional Bolshevik analysis. Radek emphasized the conflict between the socialist and capitalist 'systems', by now on the threshold of a showdown, while Varga underscored the inflexibility of power politics and 'inter-imperialist contradictions', which would hinder, he believed, a united front of capitalist powers opposed to the USSR – this was further substantiation of Molotov's earlier conclusions. But the two authors also presented some common features. For both, the USSR formed a 'third pole' in international politics, essentially distinct from the Western democracies and Nazi Germany. Neither doubted the inevitability of war, and neither offered any recommendation for a

THE RHINELAND

security policy that might serve as the basis for European peace. While Radek and Varga differed in their predictions of when war would come and whether the Soviet Union would avoid the initial outburst, both believed that Soviet security ought to rely on mass mobilization in the European countries and power strategies. Indeed it is probable that a limited confidence in diplomacy was allied to a limited belief in the chances for peace. In this light, the analyses of Radek and Varga might simply represent the two shifting poles of a single line of thought.

THE LIMITATIONS OF THE 'STRUGGLE FOR PEACE'

On 1 April 1936 the Comintern Executive Committee (IKKI) published one of the most significant documents issued by the Communist International on the question of war.[54] The resolution was drawn up at the end of a series of lengthy sessions of the Executive Committee's Praesidium, begun on 23 March. All of the principal members of the Praesidium and delegates sent from most of the Communist parties took part, and delegates from the Communist Party of the Soviet Union (CPSU) also seem to have participated.[55] Special meetings were convened during the crucial days of the Rhineland crisis, at a time when the League of Nations had already edged towards conciliation, but when the outcome of the crisis and its repercussions were still very much in doubt.

At a preliminary meeting held the day before the first official meeting of the Praesidium, Georgi Dimitrov, the Comintern's general secretary, presided over a review of the aftermath of the 7th Congress of the Comintern (July–August 1935). Among the topics discussed was the fate of the popular-front policy and the 'peacekeeping effort'. The verdict on the latter was essentially negative. Communism had been unable to develop a serious campaign in the wake of the 1935 Italian–Ethiopian war, and the same thing was now happening with the Rhineland crisis, which had to be considered a 'first step towards war'.[56]

Dimitrov pointed to what he saw as the main problem: though the communists were aware that war could break out at any moment (had not Stalin himself said so?) they still failed to draw the necessary political and organizational conclusions. Urgently needed was a 'single international policy against war', without which 'it's hard to say that what happened in 1914 won't repeat itself'. On the other hand, preparations for war had to begin immediately. According to Dimitrov, it was unlikely that any clash would turn 'into a world war overnight', but it was essential that each party prepare for such a contingency.[57] The Soviet delegate, Dmitrii Manuil'skii, exhorted the communist leaders present to explain, over the days that followed, why the anti-war campaign had been unsuccessful, and to devise and set forth new methods of fighting for peace, including the use of sanctions.[58]

On 23 March, Dimitrov presented his own report to the Praesidium, stressing the relationship between united front policy and international policy, demanding specific goals and concrete implementation of the 7th Congress' directives. In his view, the main objective ought to be 'achieving at all costs a unified opposition to fascism and to war'. He was convinced that Hitler's invasion of the Rhineland was, quite simply, 'preparation for war'. Suddenly, the threat, against which communists had been warning central and eastern Europe for some time, was upon them. For a communist it was axiomatic that, given the contradictions of imperialism, war could break out 'at any moment'; yet the communists continued to underestimate the 'profound dangers of war'.[59]

In spite of warnings from Dimitrov and Manuil'skii, communist leaders continued with business as usual. Maurice Thorez's speech was typical: when he addressed the issue of war, the French delegate simply admitted that mass mobilization would be difficult, despite the full assimilation of 7th Congress directives by French communists and the great popularity of Stalin in France.[60] If speakers who addressed the question were a bit vague, this was perhaps – as Dimitrov suggested – due to the formation of a specific commission to deal with the issue of war.[61] But the reaction also suggested uncertainty as to whether communism should present itself as an active peacemaker in Europe. The Praesidium never rose above a sort of exasperated iteration of the threat of war.

On 24 March a second meeting was held in Dimitrov's office. This time, Manuil'skii's suggestions were less moderate. He reminded those present that the existence of the USSR and the appearance of fascism had profoundly altered the international situation since Lenin's time.[62] Rather than limply moan about the coming war, which was an undeniable threat, communists would be wiser to start dealing with the immediacy of the threat. Recent events, Manuil'skii suggested, had given substance to the fear that sooner or later war had to come; it was time to take this very seriously. 'War is knocking at the door', he told the gathered officials.[63]

Manuil'skii wrote to the League of Nations and the British Labour Party: both had not only surrendered to fascism, they had abetted it. Fighting against war meant overthrowing the fascist governments, and Germany should be dealt with first, since its internal weaknesses were increasing. At the same time, he dictated the conditions for a uniform policy of the international workers' movement. The various socialist parties would have to do the following: dissociate themselves from the positions assumed by their countries' ruling classes; support the USSR's policy; fight

THE RHINELAND

against anything materially conducive to war; and achieve autonomy from the League of Nations.[64] A little reflection should convince them that such policies created many more obstacles than they removed. Compared with Dimitrov, Manuil'skii had added further hurdles to the 'struggle for peace'. Summing up his presentation with a single question posed at the end of the meeting, Manuil'skii asked: 'How can we forestall war when we can't rally millions of people?'[65] There was no denying the practical importance of this question, though taken rhetorically it belonged to the scepticism and pessimism often encountered in the communist movement and typical of Stalinist political views.

The speech delivered by Ercoli (Palmiro Togliatti), on the other hand, focused on practical means for the preservation of peace. He had already spoken on the subject at the 7th Party Congress, and now he was particularly insistent on the dangers of the fear of war; this fear could lead to passivity and even paralysis. His specific target was the British Labour Party, but it could just as easily have been the communists: taking a 'positive stance' meant asking the government to prevent war, and this had yet to happen. Neither the intervention of the British fleet, nor the abrogation of relations between Poland and Germany would necessarily lead to war. It was not up to the communists to call for intervention by the British fleet, but they should be aware that this sort of intervention could succeed in completely isolating Germany, if it was backed up by French defensive measures in the areas neighbouring the Rhineland.[66]

At this point Ercoli was interrupted by the second Soviet delegate, the NKVD secret police agent Moskvin, who declared 'This means war!' Clearly, the Stalinist leadership was concerned that deterrence measures might arouse rather than discourage the aggressor. This was not so different from the perspective Western governments were said to have adopted, and was also implicitly linked to Molotov's public statements. Ercoli replied that this might overturn Hitler's dictatorship.

> Even as we work to preserve peace, we must keep in mind the fear of war. In the present situation, certain people are making preparations for war. If one considers the balance of power within Europe, the chances of preventing a war are fairly high.[67]

Ercoli went on to outline his disagreements with Manuil'skii and Julian Lensky, the Polish delegate who had spoken at the Praesidium on the previous day. He reminded Manuil'skii that 'a distinction has to be made between Hitler and the German people', and that otherwise it was hardly possible to build a global coalition to stop war. Ercoli criticized Lensky for not discussing the danger of dividing up Poland,[68] a plan imputed to

Hitler, and for not defining the question of the Red Army's passage through Poland; after all, everyone had to be told 'what the Red Army is fighting for, that it is against dividing up Poland'. Interestingly enough, Ercoli did not pay the same attention to the 'national element' in Poland that he had in Germany. His main concern was the USSR's foreign and security policy.

Ercoli had come out as a strong supporter of efforts to prevent war and an advocate of a policy consistent with this goal. The Finnish leader Otto Ville Kuusinen began his speech by describing Ercoli's position as 'inadequate'. Kuusinen wanted to steer clear of the 'struggle for peace', which he felt led to confusion. Did not the Labour Party also talk about peace, while at the same time supporting 'Hitler's policy for localizing war'?[69] He had doubts about the effectiveness of the agreements among France, Czechoslovakia and the USSR. Particularly in France, socialists seemed poised to betray the pact, using the very fear of war described by Ercoli as an excuse, and it seemed likely that any future proposal of Hitler's to localize war in Europe would be successful. Kuusinen spoke about implementing a campaign 'against the invitation to join the League of Nations being extended to Hitler's Germany'. In response to Dimitrov's cautious objection ('I don't think that it is necessary to interfere with these diplomatic manoeuvres'), the Finnish leader replied that, in any case, the main goal was to create among 'aggressor countries' a movement 'for overthrowing the government'.[70]

Kuusinen also urged all communists to reflect on what would happen with the outbreak of war: 'The most likely thing is that at the beginning the war will be exclusively against us. Hitler does not want to start a war against everyone at the same time.' The 'struggle for peace' would have to be 'defined or refined'. At that point Manuil'skii spoke up, stressing the need to give even more attention to defending the USSR and 'unmasking' the League of Nations. Kuusinen agreed: 'If Hitler should attack the Soviet Union, and our parties have not already acquainted the masses with how things are unlikely to transpire, then the masses might be unprepared and could easily fall into the trap of glib fascist talk on neutrality.' He proposed that requests for sanctions by the League of Nations be assigned a merely tactical value, and that 'proletarian sanctions' be reintroduced.[71]

According to Kuusinen, the most pressing issues were how to hinder war, what the 'anti-war front' was supposed to do and how 'to end the war as soon as possible'. The 'struggle for peace' formula was double-edged, and could be turned against the communists – in short, it would have to be set aside.[72] Kuusinen admitted the existence of a certain amount of communist duplicity on this issue, and the means for getting rid of it he proposed were as completely in keeping with party tradition as they were hackneyed and pessimistic: to reinvigorate defeatist opposition to the war.

Dimitrov rejected Kuusinen's suggestions. In his opinion, the communist parties should essentially be asked 'to prevent or postpone war'. It was not necessary to 'get involved in the diplomatic relations between countries'; and yet it was impossible to be completely indifferent to the fate of one's country. Dimitrov felt that efforts ought to be made to win British public support for an agreement between Great Britain and the USSR; he also pushed for a non-aggression pact between the USSR and those countries 'who at this moment are against war'. It was advisable, the speaker continued, not to speak out against defence measures in Czechoslovakia, for example.[73] Dimitrov also maintained that pressure should be put on the League of Nations, even though 'we do not and cannot depend on the measures implemented by the League'. In any case, the centre of gravity would remain the 'autonomous actions' of the working masses.[74]

Dimitrov's speech revealed a pragmatic attitude, much closer to Ercoli than to Kuusinen and Manuil'skii. One might say that this reflected the 'duplicity' described by Kuusinen, whose suggestion that the 'struggle for peace' formula should be abandoned was completely ignored by Dimitrov. He admitted that communists should fight 'pacifism', but also insisted that 'fighting against war is not pacifism'. He did say, however, that preventing or delaying war was not the only option:

> If a crisis should arise, if war breaks out, then military forces will be one of the instruments used to bring peace, a stable, lasting peace, which will also mean destroying capitalism, because as long as capitalism exists there will always be war.[75]

On 26 March, when Dimitrov opened the meeting of the 'Commission on the United Front and on War', he once again stressed the need to establish 'more concretely' the basis of international communist policy. Some extremely important problems, such as what stance to take vis-à-vis the League of Nations, and what to do about sanctions and 'collective security', had yet to be satisfactorily resolved. Two months earlier, Dimitrov had spoken with Stalin about 'how to bring our attitude toward the League of Nations sanctions into accord with the so-called proletarian sanctions'.[76] Quite serious concern was now expressed at the eventual passage of the Red Army through 'a certain country' if war broke out. Dispelling all doubts about the identity of the country, Dimitrov specified: 'I mean Poland'.[77] Such an eventuality was being discussed quite seriously in Moscow; Ercoli had also mentioned it.[78]

Dimitrov also criticized the 'political passivity' of the Socialist

International, which he had already censured at the 7th Party Congress. In his opinion, the time had come to find a 'real platform from which the international proletariat can fight against war'. This fight needs not always be 'in agreement with diplomatic positions, or even with Soviet diplomacy'. On the contrary, Dimitrov said, 'our positions [those of the Comintern and of the Narkomindel] will not always be the same on every question of diplomatic policy'.[79] However, in Dimitrov's view, it was no less true that the Socialists' attitude towards the USSR was an impediment to good relations. How could the USSR be considered 'backward'? How could the difference of 'principle' between the USSR and capitalist countries be ignored? Dimitrov also felt that Socialist policy followed the lead of the League of Nations, whereas the guidelines of an international proletarian movement should come from the masses, and be 'independent of the middle classes'. In his opinion, the recent London summit held by the Socialist International and the International Federation of Trade Unions was exemplary.[80]

Dimitrov's plea for specificity grew out of his belief that no single 'yardstick' could be used to assess every country. Though communists believed that 'all imperialist states in one way or another are preparing the way for a future war', it had to be admitted that 'at every moment there is a country preparing for war'. Therefore, there had to be some discrimination in the analysis of the capitalist world. This was crucial to anticipate the main focus of the war. According to Dimitrov, the next war would start with an offensive launched against the USSR.[81]

As though determined to play the part of the prophet of doom, Dimitrov went on to paint a gloomy picture of the state of Soviet propaganda. He had already identified propaganda inadequacies on 23 March, and now he complained that the majority of workers in Europe had been utterly untouched by the communists' efforts. He wondered why there had been no mass demonstrations on the Rhineland issue in Paris or London. The masses in Germany should also have been involved, because without support from the workers in fascist countries, any mobilization would be one-sided.[82] In terms of propaganda, too, communists had yet to prove themselves a match for the social democrats. To illustrate his argument, Dimitrov quoted from the speech Hitler had given to the Reichstag on 7 March, noting that it was 'cleverly designed' to reach 'the average German'.[83]

Manuil'skii stressed, even more than Dimitrov had, the 'rising threat of war against the USSR'. However, he disagreed with the more alarmist views, stating that 'even if the threat were to become serious, we still don't think that war in central Europe could occur within as little time as a few weeks or months'. But the changes taking place on the international scene had to be acknowledged:

THE RHINELAND

The situation is now completely different from what it was, not just a year and a half ago but even three months ago. Now the fundamental problem is not war between France and Germany or between Poland and the Soviet Union: the fundamental problem now is war against the USSR. In the Far East, Japan already presents a concrete threat and now in central Europe the same threat is being posed by German fascism.[84]

According to Manuil'skii, the problem was being considered realistically by neither the League of Nations nor international socialism. The truth was that 'all of the League of Nations' efforts are directed against the Soviet Union, to achieve its isolation'; the time had come to face up to this unequivocally. The Soviet Union should use its every resource to maintain peace, and might legitimately continue to use the League of Nations to this end – though the organization had proved rather inadequate; on the other hand, the Comintern was not affected by diplomatic ties and could behave as it liked.[85] The communists might eventually have to 'criticize the decisions of the Second International in general', not only on single political issues.[86]

Manuil'skii thereby disposed rather brusquely of Dimitrov's limited acceptance of both the League of Nations and international socialism, and actually used old sectarian terms largely heard before the 7th Party Congress. His speech showed that all the new elements that the 7th Congress had brought in were weak-kneed and might well turn tail at the first sign of trouble. In coping with the threat of war, said Manuil'skii, the Narkomindel and the Comintern would need to divide up the work: the Comintern would deal with propaganda and denunciations, while the Narkomindel sought ways to avoid danger.

Kuusinen also stressed the danger of war to the USSR, reiterating his conviction that 'it would not immediately become a world war; rather it would begin as an anti-Soviet war' led by Hitler. The only real difference between the present and 1914 was that now a 'proletarian state' existed, and as a result those who favoured war would have additional room to manoeuvre. Kuusinen emphasized the limits of diplomacy:[87]

The Soviet Union now has mutual assistance pacts with France and Czechoslovakia. But who actually believes that if . . . Hitler were to attack the Soviet Union, France and Czechoslovakia would send their armies to assist us? These pacts are not yet a guarantee. They will last only until Hitler attacks.[88]

When he spoke of mobilizing the working classes and implementing 'international proletarian sanctions', Kuusinen revealed his attachment to a longstanding tradition, recently revived. During the 1935–36 war between Italy and Ethiopia, Manuil'skii had given precedence to the international activity of the masses instead of supporting diplomatic sanctions.[89] During his speech before the 'Commission on the United Front and on War', Manuil'skii did not fail to mention this distinction, urging his auditors to consider sanctions as a way of undermining an aggressive regime from the inside.[90]

Manuil'skii's arguments amounted to a direct attack on views expressed one day earlier by the British communist leader Harry Pollitt. Sanctions against Germany, Pollitt had said, were likely to strike the British public, which even among the working classes was heavily pacifistic, as provocative.[91] Kuusinen accused Pollitt of having set up a false dichotomy between the ideas of a 'struggle for peace' and a 'struggle against war' at the very moment when a real aggressor loomed on the horizon.[92] Actually, Pollitt had focused on a more general question: how to treat pacifism. He had requested that the USSR explain its own peace policy more clearly, remarking that 'the effect of our own propaganda against the League of Nations and the Versailles Treaty' had been underestimated. He went on to point out the contradiction between portraying the Versailles system as iniquitous while requesting, at the same time, that the German troops be withdrawn from the Rhineland.[93]

Manuil'skii and Kuusinen had set the tone for the debate that ensued. The main issues would be the increasing threat of war against the USSR, and concerns that diplomacy and the League of Nations would be of no help. Lozovskii, the leader of the Profintern (the Red International of Trade Unions), stated that not only would every diplomatic agreement reached in the London talks be damaging to the Soviet Union, but that even France was not to be counted on. Since both the retreat of the French government and a German war against the USSR were likely, why had the Communist Party failed to plan for such events?[94]

Perhaps the most earnest speaker at the debate was the French delegate, André Marty. His main contribution to the discussion was an emphatic reiteration of the notion that war originated from capitalism and that only a proletarian dictatorship could permanently suppress war. While there had been a time when this concept had been fundamental to communist propaganda, it had unexpectedly disappeared. 'While we do distinguish between aggressor and nonaggressor countries, I think that this is an excellent opportunity to show how imperialist capitalism functions as a permanent generator of war.'[95]

Lensky, the Polish delegate, was more realistic. In his opinion, the magnitude of the threat against the USSR was an 'elementary truth'. The thrust of communist propaganda still had to be the prevention of war,

THE RHINELAND

but that alone was not enough: 'The threat of war is so immediate that at this point we must communicate concrete war plans to the communist parties.' It was time to establish some 'basic practical measures', so that communist parties would not be 'caught off guard'.[96]

Compared with what he had said two days earlier, Ercoli's contribution to the debate was extremely cautious. He latched onto Dimitrov's appeal, saying that the masses had 'a much more realistic view of war than we give them credit for, more realistic than that of politicians or social democratic leaders'; the time had come to think about how to avoid war. Developing an international policy meant having a 'concrete goal' of defeating bellicose regimes and creating a mass movement. At the same time, this meant fighting against a common fallacy:

> Communists often think that they wouldn't lose much in a war. This is fatalism and therefore . . . no more than a feeling. It is not generally understood that vast segments of the population would be horrified if they realized that we are heading towards a catastrophe.[97]

The context of these emotional words was an argument with Pieck, whose speech at the Praesidium had included a generous assessment of the influence of Nazi propaganda on the German masses. The people of Germany, Ercoli believed, could respond positively to sanctions against Germany as long as they were emblazoned with slogans inciting class struggle; after all, 'the sanctions are aimed at Hitler, who is pushing us towards war, and not at the German people'.[98]

As far as the 'national element' was concerned, Germany was hardly the only place where communists had a difficult time producing effective anti-war propaganda. Lensky asserted that 'we Polish communists are entirely in favour of the Red Army entering Poland to defend it against fascist Germany, if the need should arise. This is indisputable.' But one can almost make out a certain embarrassment underlying Lensky's words: How were the Polish masses to be convinced that the Red Army would bring peace and national security with it? After all, most Poles believed that any sort of security agreement with the USSR 'would automatically mean allowing the Red Army to enter Poland and attack Germany', a prospect few relished.[99]

At the conclusion of his speech, Dimitrov repeated that he was quite certain that Hitler's policy was directed against the USSR, but this only made concrete preparations all the more imperative. He invited the assembly to consider that 'at this moment the threat of Hitler's fascism, when his troops are spread out along the Rhine, is directed towards Western countries'.[100] It was easier to mobilize the European masses to defend their own freedom, Dimitrov said, than to get them to fight for the USSR.[101] He also called for a more realistic approach to the League of Nations, insisting that it was necessary to criticize the league's passivity, but that repudiating it outright was not in the Comintern's interests.[102]

Dimitrov was outlining a position quite different from or even opposed to Manuil'skii's. Dimitrov did not believe that sanctions would provoke an immediate outbreak of war and declared that efforts to bring them about should be continued. In fact, he told the assembly that its members should not be embarrassed to talk of 'preserving peace', adding that 'this peace is a bad one, but peace is still better than war'.[103] This was far from nonsense. Nevertheless, most of those who spoke during the debate of 26–27 March 1936 preferred the 'struggle against war' to the 'struggle for peace'. For many of those present, the time had come to tear away all illusions from any doctrine of pacifism. This was seen as a way to grasp the essence of the communist tradition. Manuil'skii, whose political orientation was most closely identified with that of the Soviet leadership, denied that a European war implied Soviet involvement. However, he supported the idea of defending peace as a temporary goal, meant to delay the inevitable war as long as possible.

Dimitrov opposed this position, but his outlook was only slightly different. Both he and Ercoli used the threat of war to stress the need for prevention, a position no other speaker had taken. However, the Comintern general secretary presented peace and the defence of the international order as the lesser evil rather than as positive objectives. Although the debate failed to resolve the ambiguities in communist international policy and confirmed that Comintern leaders had different views about how to preserve peace, it also brought to light the essential characteristics of a common political culture.

THE PROSPECT OF WAR

In his 1 April 1936 speech summarizing the Executive Committee's concluding resolution, Ercoli emphasized that the 'enemies of peace', namely, the three fascist governments, were hard at work at 'a world catastrophe', whereas the 'peace forces' were weak and divided, and largely unaware of the 'universal danger' of fascism. Though the Socialist International would continue to be anchored to the attempt to tie the international workers' movement to the League of Nations, this was not an ideal situation. Ercoli concluded that 'the main task facing us today . . . is to overcome the weakness in the international workers' movement. This is, so to speak, our historic task at this moment.'[104] The resolution placed the general problem of maintaining peace at the core of communist policy: no doubt the Soviet Union would in time have to face a military aggressor, but this threat now concerned other European countries more directly and, 'in all probability, the aggression towards the east, towards the Soviet Union, will not be Hitler's first move'. His moves against other states could facilitate mass mobilization.[105] Thus, Ercoli sounded a note of realism, one already introduced by Dimitrov.

Strong opposition to fascism and open support for Soviet foreign policy marked the resolution. The French communists, for example, were ordered to mobilize against their indecisive government, 'which inclined towards an agreement with the German aggressor', while the Polish communists were to 'suggest a Polish security pact with Czechoslovakia and the Soviet Union'.[106] Ercoli emphasized that rejecting the League of Nations was in the interests of neither the Soviets nor the workers' movement ('Why should we play along with those who are against the League of Nations? For no reason whatsoever.'). Better to criticize 'the passivity' of the League and specifically denounce the role played by Britain.[107]

In all of these matters, Ercoli strictly adhered to the remarks made by Dimitrov in his report of 26 March. This was true also of his comments on sanctions: he denied that they would necessarily cause war, ignored the expression 'proletarian sanctions', and maintained that a 'bad peace' was always better than war.[108] This last point was not included in the resolution, which instead faithfully echoed the essential points Stalin had made in his interview with Howard, when he had been emphatic about the danger of war. The resolution stated that 'there has not been a time since 1914 when the world has stood so close to global conflict as it does today'.[109]

The report devoted ample space to the problem of defence. To begin with, Ercoli recalled that at the 7th Congress the Franco-Soviet Pact had been generally applauded. Now the situation had become more serious and needed further clarification. Communists could not remain indifferent to the fate of a country threatened by fascist aggression.[110] However, the drafters of the resolution had settled for a fairly weak formulation: 'Communists must not assume any political responsibility for the defensive measures' adopted by bourgeois governments though 'this does not exclude the possibility that in some cases the communists shall opt to abstain from defence measures aimed at preventing an aggressor's attack'. Communists were to throw their support behind a popular-front government, which would guarantee to 'defend the people against the fascist aggressor'.[111] It is fairly probable that the weak language of the resolution reflected Moscow's distrust of the French government and its military planning.[112] But it is equally likely that there was strong political and ideological resistance to a clearly outlined position on defence; in its first draft, the resolution contained the commandment that communists 'not vote for war credits', which had been suppressed at Dimitrov's instigation.[113]

Ercoli left to the last the point which had received most attention since Dimitrov's first speech on 23 March 1936: relations with the Socialist International and the verdict on the London Conference. His indictment of the right-wing component of the Socialist International, and particularly on the Labour leaders, proved harsh. Ercoli declined Manuil'skii's request to repudiate the position taken by the Socialist International, but his criticisms were no less scathing than those of the Soviet representative. The façade of unity would continue, but it would be only a façade – after all, the socialists had assumed a 'pro-Hitler position'. Though Ercoli reaffirmed the need to overcome sectarianism and to 'be concerned about politics', the distinction between politics and propaganda had largely ceased to exist in communist and Soviet circles.[114]

The resolution contained the propagandist conditions for the 'single international policy' proposed by Manuil'skii: a break with the 'imperialist interests of the bourgeoisie'; unconditional support for Soviet foreign policy; and the rejection of 'conspiracies' plotted by 'imperialist governments' in the League of Nations. And it attacked head-on the 'servility' of the British Labour Party's response to Hitler.[115] The words used to describe pacifist leanings were equally harsh.[116] Given Dimitrov and Manuil'skii's firm convictions that pacifism had to be uprooted, this part of the resolution contained no surprises,[117] although the Comintern secretariat had taken steps to promote a 'peace congress' just prior to the debate in the Praesidium.[118]

During the discussion of Ercoli's report, it was the Hungarian Communist Bela Kun who returned to the question of the 'struggle against war'. According to Kun, an anti-fascist war could only take place 'through a popular revolutionary war'. This sounded very much like a pure and simple update of Lenin's views on the transformation of the imperialist war into a civil war, and indeed Kun himself asked that propaganda promoting an anti-fascist war be modeled on 'Lenin's anti-war policy of 1914–18'.[119] In his closing comments Ercoli again expressed himself against such an approach. He did not approve of the belief that the 'maintenance of peace' was an objective already overtaken by events; the pendulum of history had not swung back to 1914. World War I was already part of the past, and could not be revived.

Yet, the significance of the resolution was described as follows:

What does the upholding of this resolution mean? For years we have spoken about the danger of war, and we have conducted international campaigns which, on occasion, were barely adequate . . . Where are we today? Where do we stand right now? What is new in the world today and what is demanded of us today? War is what is new. Let us make this clear in the resolution: war can break out at any moment in the East and in Europe.[120]

Ercoli made a point of adding that 'even at such a moment, we can still save peace, we can still fight for the maintenance of peace. But how? Only if we manage to involve the greatest number of the masses in the struggle'.[121] He insisted on the possibility of mass mobilization against Hitler's fascism and on the need to organize the 'peace front'. However, these words sounded weak and useless before the dire affirmation that 'there is war'. This was the one point where communists facing the Rhineland crisis found general agreement. Ultimately, the Comintern Praesidium gave more attention to the danger of war than to the possibility of peace. Likewise, isolationist tendencies moved forward, and the 'collective security' line retreated.

The resolution of 1 April 1936 was never published. In the April issue of the Comintern's theoretical review, *L'Internationale communiste*, a long editorial appeared in which sections of the resolution were quoted.[122] Then a public intervention by Dimitrov appeared in *Pravda* on 1 May, and was reprinted in the May issue of *L'Internationale communiste*.[123] Dimitrov returned to familiar themes: the danger of war came from fascism and affected both the West and the USSR. He assumed responsibility for the concept that a 'bad peace' was preferable to war, and contrasted it with 'fossilized and doctrinaire humbugs' who supported 'fatalistic ideas on the inevitability of war and the impossibility of maintaining peace'.[124] Dimitrov seems to have had in mind extremists from within the communist ranks who had come to the fore at the time of the Rhineland crisis. He also recapitulated an idea from the 1 April resolution that Ercoli had failed to emphasize in his report to the Praesidium: the 'maintenance of peace' was likely to provoke a crisis and bring about the defeat of fascism in Germany. If the workers' movement was able to block the outbreak of war, the resulting pressure would intensify, becoming not only 'a mortal danger' to fascism but also a threat to 'the foundations of the capitalist regimes'.

Dimitrov thus presented the 'struggle for peace' as 'a revolutionary struggle'.[125] This was not an original idea, and had been raised by Wilhelm Knorin in his speech at the 7th Congress.[126] The main point was to reconcile Soviet foreign policy with the prospects of the international communist movement. Revising a communist precept, Dimitrov suggested a link between the 'struggle for peace' and the struggle for socialism: now it was to be peace rather than war that led to revolution.[127] Clearly, this revision was born out of the need to provide a workable anti-fascist response to the Rhineland crisis, after so much inconsistency in Soviet reactions. At the same time, the situation in April was no longer what it had been in March, and the prospect of 'maintaining peace' seemed far better.

But setting up the 'struggle for peace' as a positive goal amounted to a basic contradiction of the prediction of an inevitable new imperialist war.[128] Nevertheless, as we have seen, Dimitrov's opening address of 26 March 1936 had included this same affirmation and had implicated all 'imperialist states' as equally responsible for the coming war. This weakened the anti-fascist (rather than anti-capitalist) focus of Dimitrov's ideas and endangered the entire structure of his argument. The Comintern leader let this contradiction ride. The break between the reformists and the revolutionaries he declared irreversible. As a result, Dimitrov's ideas on the revolutionary consequences of peace amounted to a political formula aimed at influencing the course of Soviet foreign policy, without changing its theoretical basis.

Simultaneously, the Soviet press also published the opinions of Radek, whose views on the 'struggle for peace' moved in a different direction. *Izvestiia* carried his intervention on the same day *Pravda* carried Dimitrov's.[129] Radek too made the comparison to 1914, but, contrary to Dimitrov, he emphasized similarities. He cited recent assessments from the British Ministry of Defence that the international situation was now even worse than it had been in 1914 (which he seconded) and that a war would mean the end of human civilization (which he rejected). In his opinion, far from leading to a collapse of civilization, the next war would undoubtedly possess 'even more revolutionary impact' than had World War I, given the crisis of the postwar capitalist system and the attraction exerted on the masses by the USSR. Much as reactionary imperialists might hope to join forces with fascism and so avoid

> the revolutionary consequences of a new world war ... we communists do not view the future of civilization so grimly ... After the day of the jackal will come the day of the lion.

This was Radek's interpretation of communism's catastrophic tradition. He saw in a second world war that lay just around the corner a new opportunity to beat the capitalist system. What did this mean for the Soviet Union? It had to be recognized that the main imperialist powers had already adopted a policy of 'each man for himself' and, in its own way, each had done 'everything to provoke war'. The anarchic tendency of capitalism was having a profound effect on international politics. The League of Nations was no guarantee against war and indeed the communists had never believed that it would be. How, then, could the League of Nations build 'a strong peace organization'? Those who had entertained the illusion that it was possible now had to recognize their error. It is not just whimsical to believe that Radek had Litvinov in mind. This dismissive verdict on the League of Nations (which recalled Manuil'skii's) was the reaffirmation of a principle which had never been abandoned, rather than the collapse of a genuine conviction. According to Radek, the USSR's criticism of the League of Nations was not only a lively response to the anti-Soviet policy of 'a significant number of powers', but also agreed with 'our estimate of the main forces of world development'. Was not the point of Soviet foreign policy to build 'the strength of its own state'? After all, 'the strength of peace will depend upon the strength of the USSR and should war occur, the destinies of all mankind will depend on a Soviet victory'.

Radek appealed to a prestigious precedent: the words with which Stalin had addressed the 17th Party Congress in 1934, according to which 'we were aligned with the USSR and today we are aligned with the USSR and only with the USSR' should be referred also to the relations between the USSR and the League of Nations. Everything that had happened since then confirmed Stalin's belief that war was imminent; only the strengthening of Soviet military power was keeping the dogs of war at bay. To 'struggle for peace' was to accelerate preparations for resistance. When Radek spoke of international developments he had little to say about the 'maintenance of peace'. His was an undifferentiated and catastrophic view of the capitalist world, and the only way to cope was isolationism. The USSR would benefit as revolution followed the war; as the global heartland of socialism the USSR would emerge from the chaos stronger than it had entered it. The moment had come to face the new inevitable cycle of war and revolution.

The opinions of *Izvestiia*'s political commentator still stimulate reflection. Did his article convey the opinions of Nikolai Bukharin, who at that time still held the post of editor of the government daily? Over the two previous years Bukharin had crept back into political life, though his new role was less prominent than Radek's. Several times he had raised his voice to denounce Nazi aggression, implicitly calling for Soviet opposition to fascism.[130]

Though Bukharin was not in the USSR at the time of the outbreak of the Rhineland crisis – he went on a tour of Europe between the end of February and the end of April 1936 to acquire the archives of the German Social Democratic Party – he took the opportunity provided by a scheduled talk in Paris on the 'problems of contemporary culture' to excoriate the Nazis publicly.[131] And during private conversations with Boris Nikolaevskii, Bukharin stressed the need for a united international movement against fascism. According to the account which Nikolaevskii gave months later in a well-known anonymous document, Bukharin is said to have disclosed during the same conversations the existence of a definite split between Soviet leaders, dating from late 1933, over how to deal with nascent fascist states.[132]

The July 1936 issue of the American journal *Foreign Affairs* carried an article by Bukharin on 'Imperialism and Communism', presumably written during his European tour.[133] Bukharin disputed 'geopolitical' theories and contended that 'the war of conquest is part of the social order'. Of course, Bukharin was simply repeating the Marxist interpretation of imperialism. The expansionist tendencies of countries such as Germany, Italy and Japan were aspects of the 'structure of contemporary capitalism', a structure in need of further 'scientific analysis'. Marxists who had ceased to apply this analysis were being asked to reconsider. When Bukharin declared that 'imperialist war is the expression of the expansionist policy of monopolistic capitalism', he was stepping away from his attempts of the late 1920s to revise the doctrine of the inevitability of war. His article supported the 'peace policy' he saw as innate in the Soviet social system and opposed the theory that if war represented a revolutionary occasion, then communists ought to encourage its outbreak. Bukharin believed that the only way revolutionary forces could overthrow the existing order at a time of impending war was by 'gathering the masses in the struggle against war'.[134] His article ended with the following words: 'We are and will be for peace, peace and more peace. This is why if the imperialists provoke war we will prevail.'[135]

This statement recalls Bukharin's old argument against the communist supporters of the *Kriegsprosperität* theory.[136] More broadly, such principles were not the legacy of communists alone but could be found, for example, in the thinking of the socialist Austrian leader Otto Bauer.[137] But there was a certain ambiguity to Bukharin's brand of anti-fascist intransigence, which could be reconciled both with a moderate position in defence of peace and with an extremist position; it could lead to the struggle against war, but could also lead down the road towards war. While Bukharin himself clearly favoured the first – after all, he had given the idea its original formulation – he may well have seen a war between Nazi Germany and the USSR as quite probable, even inevitable.[138] Bukharin's intervention constituted yet further proof that the prospect of war hung heavily over Soviet politics in the spring of 1936.

THE SECURITY DILEMMAS

On 1 April 1936, the German government presented a 'peace plan' that involved a non-aggression pact among Germany, France and Belgium, and broached the issue of Germany's possible return to the League of

Nations. The plan said nothing about the Rhineland. Soon the French government countered with its own plan, based on the principle of general European security, agreements about which would be made exclusively within the framework of the League of Nations. Reports in the Soviet press praised the French plan. An *Izvestiia* editorial described it as 'a serious starting point for those interested in bringing about peace'. While the German plan offered eastern Europe no guarantees and failed to so much as mention the USSR, the French plan raised 'questions fundamental to Europe's future' and would have forced the British government to take a stand.[139] The USSR reiterated its earlier proposal for an Eastern Pact which was still to include Germany, even after the presentation of the German 'peace plan', as Litvinov confirmed in a telegram to Ivan Maiskii on 5 April.[140] Maiskii noted in his diary that Moscow hoped to intensify Germany's isolation while joining with the other European powers in drafting a peace plan to present to Hitler.[141] His opinion, expressed in a letter to Litvinov, was that Great Britain was still not ready 'to participate seriously in a pan-European "peace front"'. On the other hand, if a front was formed within the League of Nations, Great Britain could be drawn in.[142]

On 14 April 1936, an article in *Le journal de Moscou* accused the League of Nations of underestimating the threat posed by Germany and expressed dismay that the British government should be so simplistic as not to see that behind the smoke-screen of Hitler's propaganda lay his preparations for 'the most bloody of tragedies facing the whole of Europe'. The journal added that 'it is impossible for the members not to see that if Hitler is ready to promise security to the West in order to obtain freedom of action in the East, he also imagines that, once he has isolated the USSR, he may dictate conditions allowing him to have freedom of action in the West'. The great powers proved unable to quench the fires ignited first in Ethiopia by Mussolini and now in Europe by Hitler. And the latter was 'incomparably larger' than the former.[143] It is worth observing that during this period the editorials that appeared in *Le journal de Moscou* were mostly written personally by Litvinov or at least based on outlines he prepared. The commissar himself had reminded Stalin of this only two months previously, in the context of calling for a more competent corps of editors capable of addressing a non-Russian public and of steering the journal away from the path taken by *Pravda*.[144]

Nonetheless, on 24 April Maiskii told Litvinov that Soviet foreign policy needed to become more forceful. By and large, Soviet policy of the last two to three years had been geared towards 'de facto support of the status quo', but this would no longer be adequate. Maiskii felt that 'if we do not wish to see our authority and influence over Europe's democratic elements seriously weakened' as more decisive criticism was leveled at Hitler's foreign interventions, 'we should develop some positive programmes, including a "peace plan" involving the mobilization of democratic and peaceful elements in both the West and the East'.[145] Maiskii felt that it was necessary 'to seize the initiative from Hitler'; just as the French had tried earlier – albeit with proposals that he judged inadequate and utopian.

Had the moment perhaps come, asked Maiskii, to present a Soviet peace plan to the League of Nations? Forestalling the possible objection that these were utopian visions, he reminded Litvinov of his own work on disarmament. If there was to be a conference of the League of Nations powers Maiskii wanted to know: 'Who should assume the leading role at this conference? England? France? Why should we surrender the initiative on this matter? Why shouldn't the USSR play a guiding role in a discussion of "peace in Europe"?' The ambassador went no further, noting that he did not know Litvinov's opinion on this matter. However, he did say that the plan he thought so crucial should not limit itself to regional pacts: only 'a pan-European mutual assistance pact' would lead 'England [sic] to become involved in the security of Eastern Europe'.[146] We do not know Litvinov's reaction to Maiskii's proposal, which sounded a bit like an indirect criticism of the USSR's cautious and wavering response to the Rhineland crisis. We can only observe that Maiskii's proposal was very much in keeping with what we know of Litvinov. But Litvinov's approval alone would not have been sufficient to launch a new foreign-policy initiative of the scope Maiskii outlined, and nothing came of it.

In April 1936, the Soviet government decided to approach Germany. A meeting between Litvinov and Germany's ambassador to Moscow, Friedrich von der Schulenburg, took place on 11 April but it was hardly a friendly event; when the ambassador denied that Germany was acting aggressively towards the USSR, Litvinov responded with passages from *Mein Kampf* and inflammatory speeches Hitler had given.[147] Despite such an inauspicious climate, a new trade agreement was concluded between the two countries on 29 April 1936, renewing the credits granted by the Germans in 1935. This meant that the negotiations broken off by the Soviets in the early days of the Rhineland crisis had been concluded.[148] It is difficult to believe that this was not a calculated political manoeuvre. When the Politburo gave its approval in early April of the agreement that would be signed later that month, its action amounted to the concluding move in a game that had begun on 7 March.[149] If so, then it was but one more instance of duplicity in Soviet foreign policy during the first European crisis.

The only public Soviet elaboration of Litvinov's London speech of 17

THE RHINELAND

March came in a speech Maiskii made before the Anglo-Russian parliamentary committee, also in London, on 15 May 1936.[150] Maiskii drew attention to the imminence of the storm: he believed that Europe – in fact the whole world – stood at a crossroads; the time had come to choose between 'collective security' and war. There was again talk of withdrawing from international affairs, thanks to the temptation of 'a false sense of security'. Though the USSR's matchless natural resources suited it better to isolationism than other countries, that option had been rejected because 'we appreciate fully the complexity of the modern world and the interdependence of different countries and states'. It was impossible 'to separate into static compartments' the security of the Soviet Union and that of other countries: this was the substance of the principle of the 'indivisibility of peace'. In other words, Maiskii took aim at the blindness of isolationism, which, as we know, was deeply rooted in Soviet politics. He also maintained that the League of Nations was not sufficiently 'prepared to run risks' – though this did not mean that it was utterly inactive. If the League was to be fortified – and it had to be – member states would have to enter into carefully negotiated mutual assistance treaties with military clauses. After all, the aggressor's ideal was an atomized Europe.

Maiskii's speech was not simply propaganda: he had expressed many of the ideas that went into his speech in a letter to Litvinov written a few days earlier.[151] The letter also revealed his doubts and fears: he agreed with Litvinov that the future was forbidding, saw no possibility of rapidly concluding a 'pact of three' with France and Great Britain, and was not convinced of 'the effectiveness of the Franco-Soviet pact', even after the victory of the popular front in France. After some serious thinking about European politics, 'one reaches the inevitable conclusion that in the immediate future one must expect war'. But, like Litvinov, he was not inclined to lose heart: 'There is still a little time (a little more than a year, I think) to try to prevent the outbreak of war.' Sounding the alarm of war did not necessarily mean lapsing into resignation and awaiting the inevitable.

As he made clear in a series of speeches, Litvinov was on the same wavelength as Maiskii. He spoke at the international conference held at Montreux on the question of the Turkish Straits in June and at greater length at the League of Nations on 1 July 1936. While speaking at the Straits Conference, he again deplored the 'fatalism' which he feared would foster a 'war ideology' in Europe.[152] During Litvinov's time in Geneva, the European response to the Ethiopian crisis convinced him that it was essential to strengthen the League of Nations as 'an instrument of peace'. He believed that the first steps should be the adoption of a more forceful definition of aggression, a more precise agreement about how to impose and generate compliance with sanctions and a clearly articulated process for the integration of regional pacts and the pacts agreed to by all members of the League of Nations. 'To a significant extent', said Litvinov, he concurred with the position presented in the same place by Léon Blum, the French prime minister, which affirmed the concept of the 'indivisibility of peace'.[153]

Maiskii's words and, more indirectly, Litvinov's, touched on a central question: national security. Maiskii had suggested an interpretation that differed considerably from Soviet tradition. For him, security was based neither on internal factors nor on the existence of 'inter-imperialist frictions', but instead on the recognition of 'interdependence' among states. Litvinov's reference to Blum's speech implied that war could be avoided. He took a step away from the determinist doctrines widespread in international socialism. However, the logical development of such a concept would have led to a revision of the concept of imperialism and might have poked some holes in the traditionally impenetrable barrier between the capitalist and Soviet worlds. But Comintern leaders and the leaders of the Soviet Communist Party never alluded to the possibility of such a revision. Even the most resourceful leaders, such as Dimitrov, saw the 'degenerative tendencies' of imperialism as the dominant phenomenon in international politics. As for Stalin and Molotov, they had never pushed for the assumption of responsibility invoked by Maiskii and had not abandoned the prospect of Soviet isolation. Molotov had even gone so far as to outline how the USSR might appease Germany.

Soviet political culture was largely inclined to perceive the Rhineland crisis as a demonstration that the capitalist world was a panoramic spectacle of massive chaos and that war was the basic capitalist activity. In such a world, 'maintaining peace' was nothing other than avoiding Soviet involvement in the conflict. Defending European peace became a meaningless objective. On the other hand, if 'inter-imperialist contradictions' could be exploited, the catastrophic vision of the capitalist world need not lead to an explosion between the 'socialist power' and the others. The Soviet concept of security was modeled on these foundations. By occupying the Rhineland, Hitler provided a testing ground for Soviet crisis management, following a transition period during which the USSR had gradually consolidated its position on the international scene. During the Rhineland crisis, political and diplomatic pressures towards 'collective security' failed to win the support of the country's leadership. Diplomacy was mainly employed to achieve the minimum objective of averting marginalization, and communist policy went no further than a propaganda campaign against an impending war. This sort of response to the German threat implied renewed attention to internal security.

Only the diplomats talked about the Soviet state as part of a larger, all-encompassing international system. But the dividing line that the Bolsheviks had always drawn between the USSR and the capitalist world was now more distinct and definite than ever. The tradition of isolationism was even strengthened by the relaunching of the concept of 'capitalist encirclement', which had important consequences for internal politics. In April 1936, Stanislav Kosior, a powerful member of the Politburo, speaking at the 10th Congress of the Komsomol, offered the following admonishment to young communists:

> We must always remind ourselves of the danger of war, remind ourselves that we are still surrounded by hostile forces and that sooner or later we will need to measure ourselves against our enemies. It must also be recalled that some of our enemies, the agents of hostile class forces, linger within the country.[154]

If there was to be war, the Soviet Union would need to attend first to internal solidity. But the growth of the police state in the aftermath of Sergei Kirov's assassination had exposed a contradiction between two apparently harmonious goals in Soviet politics: unity and stability. Over the spring and summer of 1936, the latter was finally sacrificed on the altar of monolithism – this was the advent of the Great Terror. At the end of March, Stalin pushed matters closer to the first Moscow trial, when he personally asked Genrikh Iagoda and Andrei Vyshinskii to apply greater rigour to the 'investigations' into the 'Trotskyites', a request which led the Politburo to ratify a secret resolution recommending the condemnation of those accused of Trotskyism. Shortly afterwards, the dictator issued a directive extending the scope of the trial to include 'Zinov'erists' among the accused.[155]

Addressing the Central Committee plenum held in June 1936, Stalin mentioned the international situation but only to stress that the USSR's new constitution contained language strongly opposing fascism. Fascism was described as an 'anti-social force', a political option worse even than that residing in the 'remains of bourgeois democracy'.[156] Not only was fascism the Soviet state's most dangerous enemy: democracy as it was known in capitalist countries was approaching extinction. Only 'Soviet democracy' could function as an alternative to the decline of the bourgeois world. Over two years earlier, at the 17th Party Congress, this concept had been linked to the new revolutionary crises in the capitalist world.[157] Even though fascism had been declared the main enemy, far more significant was the persistence of long-term vision of two utterly different and fundamentally opposed 'systems', a vision which implied an underlying undifferentiated view of the outside world.

STALIN AND THE INEVITABLE WAR, 1936–1941

NOTES

1. J. Erickson, *The Soviet High Command: A Military-Political History 1918–1941* (London: Macmillan, 1962), p. 412.
2. *Izvestiia*, 14 March 1936.
3. Documenty vneshnei politiki SSR (hereafter: DVP SSSR) XIX, doc. 70, p. 129.
4. Ibid., doc. 71, p. 130.
5. *Le journal de Moscou*, 17 March 1936.
6. DVP SSSR, XIX, doc. 79, p. 138; ibid., doc. 82, p. 142.
7. Litvinov, *Vneshniaia politika SSSR*, p. 140.
8. Ibid., p. 145.
9. Ibid., p. 146.
10. Ibid., pp. 146–7.
11. DVP SSSR, XIX, doc. 90, p. 166.
12. Ibid., p. 168.
13. See D. Watson, *Molotov and Soviet Government. Sovnarkom 1930–1941* (London: Macmillan, 1996), pp. 161–2.
14. *Izvestiia Tsk KPSS* 1 (1990), p. 169.
15. Ibid., p. 170–71. See also DVP SSSR, XVIII, doc. 161, p. 262.
16. *Pravda*, 29 March 1935.
17. *Pravda*, 16 January 1936.
18. See Di Biagio, *Le origini dell'isolazionismo sovietico*, Ch. 2. See also J. Jacobson, *When the Soviet Union Entered World Politics* (Berkeley, CA: University of California Press, 1994), pp. 96 ff.
19. DVP SSSR, XVIII, doc. 424, pp. 569–71.
20. *Izvestiia Tsk KPSS* 2 (1990), pp. 211–12.
21. DVP SSSR, XVIII, doc. 450, pp. 595–7.
22. See G. Roberts, 'A Soviet Bid for Co-existence with Nazi Germany, 1935–1937: The Kandelaki Affair', *International History Review* 16 (1994), pp. 466–90. On Kandelaki's missions, see also Roberts, *The Soviet Union and the Origins of the Second World War*, pp. 21–48.
23. On Stalin's 'double track' strategy of the first half of the 1930s, see T. Weingartner, *Stalin und der Aufstieg Hitlers. Die Deutschlandpolitik der Sowjetunion und der Kommunistischen Internationale 1929–1934* (Berlin: de Gruyter, 1970).
24. DVP SSSR, XIX, doc. 85, p. 150.
25. Public Record Office, London (hereafter: PRO FO) 371/20349, N910/307/38.
26. DVP SSSR, XIX, doc. 85, pp. 148–9. While he indicated that an improvement in relations between the two countries should 'come from Poland', Krestinskii nonetheless appreciated that the eventual militarization of the Franco-Soviet Pact would cause difficulties for the Poles. Molotov, on the other hand, limited himself to affirming that Soviet aid to France would be furnished 'in accordance with this pact and with the overall political situation'; cf. Ibid.
27. Ibid.
28. Ibid., doc. 95, p. 179.
29. Ibid., doc. 97, pp. 181–2.
30. Ibid., doc. 101, p. 186.
31. Ibid., doc. 102, pp. 186–7. See also DBFP, 2nd series, XVI, doc. 169, p. 226.
32. DVP SSSR, XIX, doc. 99, p. 734.
33. Ibid., doc. 100, p. 185.
34. *Le journal de Moscou*, 31 March 1936.
35. DVP SSSR, XIX, doc. 104, pp. 188–9.
36. Ibid., doc. 105, p. 194.
37. Ibid., doc. 92, p. 173.
38. *Izvestiia*, 21 March 1936.
39. In a conversation with Eden on 30 January 1936, Litvinov expressed dissatisfaction at the delay in the ratification of the pact with France and apprehension over the perplexing European situation. He specified that in the USSR 'many' were beginning

to doubt that the policy of collective security was the 'right one' (DBFP, 2nd series, XV, doc. 488, pp. 617–18).
40. See W. Lerner, *Karl Radek. The Last Internationalist* (Stanford, CA: Stanford University Press, 1970), pp. 156–7. On Radek's role as Stalin's personal secretary, see E. Gnedin, *Iz istorii otnoshenii mezhdu SSSR i fashistskoi Germaniei* (New York: Khronika 1977); W. G. Krivitsky, *J'étais un agent de Staline* (Paris: Champ Libre, 1979), p. 23.
41. See E. H. Carr, *The Twilight of Comintern, 1930–1935* (London: Macmillan, 1982), p. 96.
42. G. Hilger and A. Meyer, *The Incompatible Allies: A Memoir History of German–Soviet Relations, 1918–1941* (New York: Macmillan 1953), pp. 267–8.
43. K. Radek, 'Eshche odin razorvannyi klochok bumagi', *Izvestiia*, 8 March 1936.
44. K. Radek, 'Posle krakha Lokarno', *Izvestiia*, 12 March 1936.
45. Rossiiskii Gosudarstvennyi Arkhiv Sotsialno-Politicheskoi Istorii, Moscow (hereafter: RGASPI), f. 558, op. 11, d. 793, ll. 67–70.
46. K. Radek, 'Londonskie soglasheniia', *Izvestiia*, 22 March 1936.
47. K. Radek, 'Germanskoe khoziaistvo i politika voiny', *Pravda*, 22 March 1936.
48. K. Radek, 'Tragediia v komedii germanskikh vyborov', *Izvestiia*, 1 April 1936.
49. K. Radek, 'Strategicheskii plan Germanii', *Izvestiia*, 6 April 1936.
50. K. Radek, 'Londonskie soglasheniia'.
51. K. Radek, 'Strategicheskii plan Germanii'.
52. Cf. Z. Sheinis, *Maksim Maksimovich Litvinov: revoliutsioner, diplomat, chelovek* (Moscow: Politizdat, 1989), p. 352. See also Ia. Pevzner, 'Zhizn' i trudy E. S. Vargi v svete sovremennosti', *Mirovaia ekonomika i mezhdunarodnie otnosheniia* 10 (1989); and *Voprosy istorii KPSS* 8 (1989), p. 68.
53. E. Varga, 'Konets Lokarno', *Mirovoe khoziaistvo i mirovaia politika* 4 (1936), pp. 5–15.
54. See A. Agosti, *La Terza Internazionale. Storia documentaria*, III, 2 (Rome: Editori Riuniti, 1979), p. 943. The text of the resolution of 1 April 1936 has been published in ibid., pp. 999–1010.
55. See K. K. Shirinia, *Strategiia i taktika Kominterna v bor'be protiv fashizma i voiny (1934–1939gg.)* (Moscow: Politizdat, 1979), pp. 53ff.
56. RGASPI, f. 495, op. 73, d. 12, ll. 27–8.
57. Ibid., l. 29.
58. Ibid., ll. 31–2.
59. RGASPI, f. 495, op. 2, d. 215, ll. 6–7, 10.
60. Ibid., ll. 32, 39, 47.
61. Ibid., l. 10.
62. RGASPI, f. 495, op. 73, d. 12, ll. 49–50.
63. Ibid., l. 40.
64. Ibid., ll. 52, 55–6.
65. Ibid., l. 75.
66. Ibid., l. 62.
67. Ibid., l. 63.
68. Ibid.
69. Ibid., l. 64.
70. Ibid., ll. 64, 67.
71. Ibid., ll. 65–6.
72. Ibid., l. 68.
73. Ibid., ll. 69–70.
74. Ibid., l. 72.
75. Ibid., l. 73.
76. A. Dallin and F. I. Firsov (eds), *Dimitrov and Stalin 1934–1943: Letters from the Soviet Archives* (New Haven, CT: Yale University Press, 2000), p. 25.
77. RGASPI, f. 495, op. 60, d. 216, l. 3.
78. Dimitrov's and Ercoli's words confirmed rumours circulating in Foreign Office channels: PRO FO 371/20349, N1753/307/38 (24 March 1936); PRO FO 371/20349, N2290/307/38 (24 April 1936).

79. RGASPI, f. 495, op. 60, d. 216, l. 8.
80. At the London Conference of 19–20 March 1936 of the Socialist International and the International Federation of Trade Unions a cautious resolution was approved, which re-affirmed the principle of 'collective security' however inviting the League of Nations to undertake negotiations with Germany. See L. Rapone, *La socialdemocrazia europea tra le due guerre. Dall'organizzazione della pace alla resistenza al fascismo (1923–1936)* (Rome: Carocci, 1999) pp. 417–20.
81. RGASPI, f. 495, op. 60, d. 216, ll. 5–6.
82. Ibid., ll. 6–7.
83. Ibid., ll. 12–13.
84. Ibid., l. 15.
85. Ibid., ll. 16–17.
86. Ibid., ll. 19–20, 27.
87. Ibid., l. 77.
88. Ibid., l. 84.
89. See G. Procacci, *Il socialismo internazionale e la guerra d'Etiopia* (Rome: Editori Riuniti, 1978), p. 125.
90. RGASPI, f. 495, op. 60, d. 216, l. 26.
91. RGASPI, f. 495, op. 2, d. 219, ll. 70, 81.
92. RGASPI, f. 495, op. 60, d. 216, l. 85.
93. RGASPI, f. 495, op. 2, 219, ll. 66, 73.
94. RGASPI, f. 495, op. 60, d. 216, l. 120.
95. Ibid., l. 52.
96. Ibid., l. 103. Already at the meeting held on 22 March, Lensky had lamented the fact that too many communists 'still consider the war remote' (RGASPI, f. 495, op. 73, d. 12, l. 36).
97. RGASPI, f. 495, op. 60, d. 216, ll. 89–97. Togliatti's speech of 26 March 1936 has been published in P. Togliatti, *Opere*, IV, 1 (Rome: Editori Riuniti, 1979), pp. 114–19.
98. Ibid., p. 118. In the Praesidium session held on 23 March, Pieck had said that there was no way of guaranteeing that Hitler would not drag the German population into war (RGASPI, f. 495, op. 2, d. 216, ll. 90-93).
99. RGASPI, f. 495, op. 60, d. 216, l. 101. During the speech he gave at the Praesidium on 23 March, Lensky had already expressed his fear that the Polish middle class and peasant masses might see a pact with the USSR as a step towards war with Germany. This mounting fear of war had dramatic and grotesque implications, which Lensky also described. If war did break out, it was quite possible that 'national communism' might re-emerge. This danger had not yet been eradicated, Lensky said, and had to be avoided at all costs, for if it occurred during wartime, fascist demagogy might turn it to its own devices (RGASPI, f. 495, op. 2, d. 216, l. 70). It is easy to see the connection between this type of concern and the bloody purges which swept through the Polish Communist Party (and toppled Lensky, as well) two years later.
100. RGASPI, f. 495, op. 60, d. 216, l. 148.
101. Ibid., l. 149.
102. Ibid., l. 152.
103. Ibid.
104. RGASPI, f. 495, op. 2, d. 222, ll. 20–24.
105. Ibid., l. 26.
106. Agosti, *La Terza Internazionale* III, 2, p. 1002.
107. RGASPI, f. 495, op. 2, d. 222, l. 28.
108. Ibid., l. 30.
109. Agosti, *La Terza Internazionale* III, 2, pp. 999–1000.
110. RGASPI, f. 495, op. 2, d. 222, ll. 36–7.
111. Agosti, *La Terza Internazionale* III, 2, p. 1003.
112. Haslam, *The Soviet Union and the Struggle for Collective Security in Europe*, p. 102
113. RGASPI, f. 495, op. 60, d. 217, ll. 4 , 12.
114. RGASPI, f. 495, op. 2, d. 222, l. 41–3.
115. Agosti, *La Terza Internazionale* III, 2, pp. 1001, 1004–5.

116. Ibid., pp. 1006–7.
117. RGASPI, f. 495, op. 60, d. 216, ll. 4, 22.
118. RGASPI, f. 495, op. 18, d. 1082.
119. RGASPI, f. 495, op. 2, d. 222, l. 50.
120. Ibid., l. 113.
121. Ibid., l. 114.
122. *L'Internationale communiste* 4 (1936).
123. G. Dimitrov, 'Edinyi front bor'by za mir', *Pravda*, 1 May 1936; *L'Internationale communiste* 5 (1936), pp. 541–53.
124. Ibid., p. 543.
125. Ibid., p. 552.
126. *Rundschau*, 22 August 1935, p. 1882. Knorin was likely to oppose the new course launched at the 7th Party Congress; see Carr, *The Twilight of Comintern*, p. 411.
127. See G. Procacci, 'La lotta per la pace nel socialismo internazionale alla vigilia della seconda guerra mondiale', in *Storia del marxismo* III, 2 (Turin: Einaudi, 1981), p. 586.
128. *L'Internationale communiste* 5 (1936), pp. 542, 547.
129. K. Radek, 'Bor'ba za mir prodolzhaetsia', *Izvestiia*, 1 May 1936.
130. See S. Cohen, *Bukharin and the Bolshevik Revolution: A Political Biography, 1888–1938* (New York: Knopf, 1973).
131. *Novaia i noveishaia istoriia* 5 (1988), pp. 92–110. Bukharin gave his Paris talk on 3 April 1936.
132. See B. I. Nikolaevsky, *Les dirigeants soviétiques et la lutte pour le pouvoir* (Paris: 1969).
133. *Mezhdunarodnaia zhizn'* 4 (1988), pp. 127–37.
134. See Di Biagio, *Le origini dell'isolazionismo sovietico*, pp. 276–7.
135. *Mezhdunarodnaya Zhizn* 4 (1988), p. 137.
136. See Di Biagio, *Le origini dell'isolazionismo sovietico*, pp. 111, 199.
137. See O. Bauer, *Tra due guerre mondiali? La crisi dell'economia mondiale, della democrazia e del socialismo* (Turin: Einaudi, 1979), pp. 209–11. Bauer's book was first published in Prague at the beginning of 1936.
138. According to his wife, Bukharin maintained that 'I certainly am not ruling out the possibility of an attack by Hitler on the Soviet Union. I think a military conflict with Germany is unavoidable, and we must prepare for it not only militarily but also by inculcating an appropriate psychology in the rear'; see A. Larina, *This I Cannot Forget: The Memoirs of Nikolai Bukharin's Widow* (New York: Norton, 1993), p. 255.
139. *Izvestiia*, 10 April 1936.
140. DVP SSSR, XIX, doc. 117, p. 218.
141. Arkhiv Vneshnei Politiki Rossiiskoi Federatsii, Moscow (hereafter: AVP RF), f. 017a, op. 1, p. 1, d. 3, l. 27.
142. AVP RF, f. 05, op. 16, p. 117, d. 23, l. 110.
143. *Le journal de Moscou*, 14 April 1936.
144. AVP RF, f. 05, op. 16, p. 114, d. 1, l. 53.
145. AVP RF, f. 05, op. 16, p. 117, d. 23, l. 130.
146. Ibid., l. 133.
147. DVP SSSR, XIX, doc.125, pp. 223–4.
148. Ibid., doc. 143, pp. 250–3.
149. RGASPI, f. 17, op. 3, d. 976, l. 54.
150. PRO FO 371/20349, N2687/307/38. The text of the speech was sent by Maiskii to Litvinov in June; AVP RF, f. 05, op. 16, p. 117, d. 23, l. 215.
151. Ibid., l. 151–5.
152. Litvinov, *Vneshniaia politika SSSR*, pp. 154–5.
153. Ibid., pp.161–2. On Léon Blum's foreign policy towards central–eastern Europe, see N. Jordan, *The Popular Front and Central Europe. The Dilemmas of French Impotence, 1918–1940* (Cambridge: Cambridge University Press, 1992), pp. 98 ff.
154. *Pravda*, 17 April 1936.
155. *Izvestiia TsK KPSS* 8 (1989), pp. 83–4.
156. RGASPI, f. 17, op. 2, d. 572.
157. Stalin, *Sochineniia* XIII, pp. 293–4.

2

The Western Crises: Spain

THE 'BLOC FACTOR' AND LITVINOV'S STRATEGY

The outbreak of the Spanish civil war on 17–18 July 1936 returned Europe to a state of high tension just when the Rhineland crisis appeared to be over. It meant the end to the relative stability that had reigned in the Soviet Union's foreign relations since the conclusion of the Ethiopian question and the formation of the popular-front government in France. What made the Spanish crisis an international problem was the active and open support provided to the Nationalist leader General Franco by Germany and Italy. From the end of July, one could no longer doubt the existence of a new international crisis. And on this occasion the aggressiveness of the Nazis could not be justified according to traditional 'revisionism'. Moreover, events in Spain tended to unite Italy with Germany. So the crisis presented new ideological features. The fascist propaganda supporting the Spanish nationalist rebels suggested that Bolshevik revolution could erupt anywhere in Europe. The brutal campaign launched against the European left affected the popular-front government in France, and had obvious implications for the Soviet Union and the international communist movement.

As with the Rhineland crisis, the Soviet reaction was remarkably cautious. Measured by comments in the press and diplomatic steps, it was even slower in coming than before. In assessing the various reasons for this delay – Spain, of course, had provoked a far greater surprise – domestic factors need to be considered; the international strain caused by the Spanish crisis and the internal tensions that spilled over into the Great Terror aggravated one another. As they expressed hope for the speedy victory of the Republican forces and condemned Germany and Italy's military assistance to the Nationalist rebels, Soviet authors frequently compared the Spanish conflict with the Russian civil war. They called for a fusion of patriotic and revolutionary impulses: history and memory were to be the catalysts. At the same time, the war in Spain gradually came to be seen as just one more link in a chain of European wars.

SPAIN

On 1 August 1936, the anniversary of the outbreak of World War I, *Pravda* presented a picture of a perpetually agitated capitalist world. The military coup in Spain, abetted by the fascist powers, was seen as one more step towards the 'total war' glorified by Hitler. It was not suggested that the Spanish events might constitute the final step, nor did the article mention the position of the USSR in the new international emergency. Faithful to instructions calling for discretion and tact, the editors of the party organ limited their comments to a general denouncement of war.[1]

In an article in *Izvestiia* that appeared on the same day, Radek upheld more radical theories. A world war meticulously planned by the fascists was at hand, and all that stood between them and world domination was the masses. Among the capitalists, politicians and diplomats no longer spoke of 'whether it was possible to avoid war. Discussion is centred on when war will erupt.' There was no more time for debate: the war in Spain demanded an immediate response. As to 1914, 'today the situation is even more serious than in the months preceding the world war'.[2] As he had done three months earlier, Radek condemned the Nazi attempt to create 'a bloc of revisionist powers' isolating France and the USSR, and invited the Western powers to force Germany to choose 'between isolation and participation in collective peace'. But even as he discussed the options for dealing with a fascist Germany, he spoke hopefully of the revolutionary potential of mass movements 'throughout the capitalist world and primarily in fascist countries'.

For Radek, the weapons of revolution were fast becoming more relevant than the weapons of diplomacy and politics. After all, the USSR 'had never remained passive' when threatened, and with conflict just around the corner Radek believed that his theories of the 'proximity of war' equipped him best to diagnose the situation. Three days later, he linked the intervention of fascist regimes against the Spanish republic with preparations for a new world war. While Radek did not anticipate the installation of a proletarian dictatorship in Spain any time soon, he petitioned for an internationalist solidarity movement that would clearly go beyond the provision of funds and food.[3]

On 3 August a mass demonstration filled Red Square. This and similar demonstrations in other cities were organized to express support for the Spanish Republican government. By then the Soviet authorities had recognized the full significance of a bloody civil war backed by fascists. Nevertheless, none of the principal figures of the Comintern or the Soviet Communist Party took part in any of the demonstrations.[4] In Moscow, the main speech was entrusted to Nikolai Shvernik, the trade union leader, who confined himself to declaring that the fight for democratic Spain was 'at the same time a fight for peace' and that a fascist victory would mean more 'partisans of war'.[5]

The first diplomatic steps towards the isolation of the conflict and the policy that came to be known as 'non-intervention' were taken in the early days of August. Both domestic and international concerns led Paris to propose an agreement between the main powers on the question of Spain. The Blum government hoped to thwart any external interventions, which might provoke an expansion of the theatre of war.[6] Though gaps in the documentary record occur here, it is apparent that Soviet diplomatic action during this period was slow and clumsy. Western diplomats became aware of a real reluctance in Moscow to take a firm position.[7] The Soviet leadership appears to have opted for a 'wait-and-see' policy.

When the French sent enquiries on 5 August, they received assurances that, in principle, the Soviet Union supported their proposal.[8] In a note to Boris Shtein, the Soviet ambassador to Italy, Krestinskii justified this stance by pointing out that it would deprive Italy and Germany of their pretext for supporting the rebellion, namely Soviet interference in Spanish internal affairs; this was to become the standard explanation for the Soviet decision to join 'non-intervention'. In the same communication, Krestinskii reviewed recent events relevant to the war in Spain, pointing out that the French had failed to consult the USSR when they appealed to Britain and to Italy.[9] There was resentment on this score and a barely concealed uneasiness at the scant consideration shown the USSR by Western countries in general during this international crisis. By the same token, he recognized that the Spanish crisis was significantly compromising relations between the USSR and Italy, since the latter was fated to move closer and closer to Germany.

Le Journal de Moscou vacillated. In an article that appeared on the same day Radek's views on Spain were published in *Izvestiia* (4 August), the Spanish people's fight was declared important 'for the cause of peace in general', essential 'material and moral support' were appealed to and fascist calls for neutrality were described as hypocritical.[10] One week later, rather more prudently, the journal called for an end to the fascist intervention and explained that 'throughout the world there is a growing conviction that the great issues of history, including the possibility of a new world war, are being decided in Spain'.[11] On 18 August, it finally called for 'effective neutrality' and the speedy conclusion of an agreement among all powers to end the support being provided to the rebels by Italy and Germany.[12]

Later in the month, after both Germany and Italy had signed on to the French initiative, the USSR declared its own adherence to 'non-intervention'.[13] Litvinov had written to Lazar' Kaganovich on 22 August, suggesting that the Soviets join up.[14] No doubt the desire to avoid being marginalized in international affairs prompted this decision. Moreover, the Soviets believed that once foreign support had been cut off, the rebellion would soon collapse, permitting the revitalization of both the Spanish and French popular fronts. In any case, Litvinov saw a range of options besides non-intervention in the the repertoire of Soviet foreign policy.

When fierce anti-Bolshevik rhetoric spewed out of the Nazi congress held in Nuremberg, the Soviet press was forced to react. After denouncing Berlin's campaign for non-intervention as having been accompanied by increased covert assistance to the Spanish rebels, Soviet editorials predicted that the German misinformation campaign about Bolshevik politics would have no effect on the 'normal development of international relations'.[15] However, such measures failed to satisfy Litvinov, who had been maintaining a hard line during meetings with Schulenburg in late August.[16] In a letter to Kaganovich written on 2 September, he suggested the use of 'extraordinary measures' against Germany's propaganda: a note relayed to the governments of Great Britain, France, Italy, Czechoslovakia and other countries and perhaps even a note of protest to the German government itself. Litvinov had not forgotten an earlier snub and somewhat tartly observed that his 'previous suggestion for a government communiqué' had been rejected.[17] After the vacillating policy displayed by the USSR during the Rhineland crisis, Litvinov hoped to push policy-makers into firm positions as they faced the crisis in Spain and as they adjusted their stance vis-à-vis Germany.

At the beginning of August, Krestinskii had noted in a letter to Surits that Germany was unrelenting in its hostility towards the USSR, a hostility aggravated by events in Spain. Like Litvinov, Krestinskii saw little cause to court Germany – neither politically nor economically was there much to be gained. This was particularly true after the signing of the Anglo-Soviet trade agreement. If, as Krestinskii indicated, such a position coincided 'to a significant extent' with that of his superiors, then Litvinov's opinion would be in keeping with Stalin's.[18] It had begun to look as though Germany would soon cease to be seen as the key strategic player Molotov had made it out to be in March.

In a letter to Krestinskii written on 28 August, Surits supported Berlin's demotion, pointing out that Hitler had responded to the lowering of the conscription age in the USSR by extending Germany's mandatory military service to two years.[19] To judge from recent events and from German support for the non-intervention proposal, Hitler seemed unprepared for war. While Germany and Italy were clearly engaged in a sort of deep flirtation, there was as yet nothing that could be called a 'fascist bloc'. Surits concluded that 'even as German diplomacy works to clear a military path to the east, the complex manoeuvres required will take time, even in the west'. Nazi Germany's foreign-policy programme remained simple: 'the fight against the USSR'. But such a limited focus seemed likely to be a real liability to Germany since, as Surits remarked, 'its international and internal fronts are far from secure'.[20] By highlighting the delicacy of the international situation, he was suggesting the existence of wide margins for diplomatic manoeuvre. The one invariable element was Nazism's opposition to the Soviet Union.

In a letter to Stalin written on 7 September, Litvinov raised the question of Soviet foreign policy and the consolidation of European security. The moment had come for a 'great defensive bloc' and a push to isolate Germany. The extant pacts with France and Czechoslovakia seemed inadequate; they contained no military agreements – a glaring omission given the increasingly perilous position and the widespread feelings of 'capitulation' in these countries. Litvinov believed that only the conclusion of a general pact opposed to every sort of aggression, one signed by the USSR, France, Czechoslovakia, Romania, Yugoslavia and Turkey, could force Germany to back down. Such a bloc would certainly 'kindle the respect' of both Great Britain and Italy, who would approve the objectives of the agreement even if they did not sign. Poland too was likely to approve; only Hungary would side with Germany. Pursuing such a coalition was all the more pressing as Hitler moved to form 'an opposing bloc' dedicated to isolating the USSR; recent events suggested that he was making headway.[21] This last argument of Litvinov's had already cropped up in a press comment by P. Lapinskii, a former Comintern and Narkomindel associate.[22]

Faced with the Spanish crisis, Litvinov proposed a variation on the collective security theme not significantly different from the peace plan advanced by Maiskii some months earlier. The time had come, announced the Narkomindel, to introduce a more forceful attitude towards Germany. This posture was echoed by Surits. He believed that the Nazis' anti-Soviet campaign was a floundering regime's desperate attempt to find a rallying point, and in a letter to Krestinskii written on 13 September he called it 'a demonstration of its [i.e., Hitler's regime] relative internal and external weakness'. The anti-Soviet propaganda disseminated at Nuremberg had not had any effect on international opinion; rather, it had been greeted with reserve or outright disapproval. Surely a decisive move from Moscow would win the approval of the international community and do real damage to Germany's standing.[23] Writing to Kaganovich on 14 September, Litvinov backed Surits's request. The Soviet passivity of the past had, he felt, encouraged the Nazis to more and more open hostility; certainly it had not won the affection of other countries.[24]

But on the same day Kaganovich suggested to Stalin laying aside Litvinov's recommendation, since in his view 'the tactics you have

SPAIN

indicated of disallowing hysterics and observing aplomb and endurance has been completely justified'. Furthermore, Kaganovich maintained that the problem of a 'great united anti-German defensive bloc' had no 'direct sharp significance'.[25] On 20 September the Politburo decided to reject Litvinov's and Surits's pleas.[26] A day earlier, Krestinskii had notified Surits that the decision had been made not to voice an official protest over the vitriol spilled at Nuremberg; press commentary was deemed sufficient.[27] In other words, Stalin chose circumspection, following Kaganovich's advice. Litvinov's appeal had no impact on policy-making, and his proposed consolidation of collective security had been stillborn. There was to be no fundamental reformulation of policy towards Germany. Soviet foreign policy would not observe a resolute anti-fascist line in the near future.

INTERVENTIONIST PRESSURE

In his final and posthumous work, Edward H. Carr seems to have been inspired by the gossip exchanged in diplomatic circles during the Spanish civil war: he depicts a factional split between moderates and extremists in the Comintern and Soviet political circles. His 'moderates' would incline to positions closer to Stalin's, while his 'extremists' did all they could to bring about Soviet intervention in the Spanish conflict.[28] We now know that the political field was more intricate and that Stalin did not take sides. The outbreak of the Spanish civil war presented a series of difficult problems for Soviet and Comintern policy. Almost immediately the 'collective security' approach formulated during the Rhineland crisis proved feeble and useless. And thanks to the fragility of relations with France, Soviet foreign-policy options were severely limited; Litvinov hardly dared venture out on the thin ice of that relationship for fear it would give way under his feet.

No less important was the Soviet Union's domestic situation. Resistance to Litvinov's policy had already emerged during the Rhineland crisis. Faced with a new international crisis, the Narkomindel could not have felt stronger. No substantial support would come from the Comintern leadership; even those Comintern leaders who did not see revolution around the Spanish corner, like Dimitrov, seem to have looked upon the idea of prolonging a non-interventionist policy with mounting perplexity and unhappiness. They felt a contradiction between non-intervention and militant anti-fascism. In other words, non-intervention could be challenged both by those who predicted catastrophe and by those who still believed it was possible to prevent war by means of mass mobilization. After the outbreak of the Spanish war, even the supporters of popular fronts did not line up to sustain the Narkomindel.

At the same time, although preparations were under way to repress the more radical elements by charging them with 'Trotskyism', the Soviet leadership could not easily ignore the obligations incumbent on a self-declared socialist state. The consequence of such neglect would be a growing contradiction between Soviet foreign policy and the appeals routinely sent out to the downtrodden masses of capitalist countries. The Soviets took to declaring non-intervention nothing but the means to an end, at the same time practicing a more and more ambiguous brand of foreign and security policy. Litvinov's policy was gradually gutted over the course of the Spanish dilemma, a process we have seen in miniature in his foiled attempts to find a more determined course than non-interventionism, while preserving a relationship with the Western powers. The moment for orientation towards 'collective security' would soon expire.

After the installation of Francisco Largo Caballero as the head of a new Republican government in Spain – an achievement abetted by the Spanish communists – a solidarity movement arose in the Soviet Union, embracing the new administration. The Soviets believed that Caballero would be a strong military leader and a force for moderation in Spain's economic and social reforms. Marcel Rozenberg, the newly appointed Soviet ambassador to Madrid, had emphasized such qualities even before the formation of the new government.[29] Massive demonstrations in support of the republican cause were held in Moscow and Leningrad on 25 and 26 September.[30] At the same time a secret decision was made by the Soviet leadership to intervene in the Spanish civil war.

Narkomindel policy had failed to win support, and pressure to intervene came from within the Politburo and from Comintern circles. On 23 July, immediately after the outbreak of the war, the Comintern secretariat had received from Spain the first of what was to become a long series of communications. It was also at this time that Dimitrov began to underline the international consequences of the Spanish civil war. In fact, it was international policy considerations that led Dimitrov to advocate shelving domestic ambitions (specifically, the transition to a dictatorship of the proletariat) and focus all energies on defending democracy and republicanism in Spain. Did not all of Europe's communists (beginning with France) need to be provided with a sure political footing? Only after adequate political reflection and a sufficiently large popular base would it be possible 'to go further'. The communists were as interested in defending democratic regimes 'for a certain length of time' as they were determined to sway the masses in countries dominated by fascist regimes.[31] Stalin approved this approach and soon it had been communicated to the Spanish communists.[32]

As reported in Dimitrov's diary, on 14 September Molotov convened a meeting in the Kremlin to discuss Soviet aid to Spain.[33] On 16 and 17 September the Comintern Praesidium discussed the international situation during a meeting similar to the one that had been held at the end of March. In his report on the peace congress held in Brussels at the beginning of the month, Shvernik stated that, whatever their misgivings about Moscow's domestic policies, all the members of the trade union committee had denounced the role played by Germany in the Spanish civil war.[34] An organized movement had been empowered to pursue the four points that served as basic tenets for the congress: international treaties were to be universally recognized as inviolable; no pains were to be spared in reducing the world's storehouse of armaments; the League of Nations was to be strengthened so as to avoid wars and improve collective security; international disputes were to be referred to a special court constituted by the League of Nations.[35] However, Shvernik neglected to give a precise evaluation of the political outcome of the Brussels congress and his report was no less evasive than those published in the Soviet press.[36] This was hardly consistent with the hope earlier expressed by the Comintern secretariat, that the Brussels congress would unite 'the most varied defenders of peace' and 'explicitly single out the aggressor'.[37] Reporting on another peace congress held in Geneva, Aleksandr Kosarev, the Komsomol secretary, made clear that he had received instructions from Dimitrov to present 'the communist view of peace'.[38] Apparently this had been a fine policy, since Kosarev asseverated that the Soviet position had been quite influential. In his opinion, it was no exaggeration to affirm that opposition to fascism had been the order of the day in Geneva.[39]

However, the bright reports on the September peace congresses were out of all proportion to the general impact of the meetings. In Brussels, the topics to be discussed had been set in advance, and no reference to Spain was permitted.[40] In Geneva things were a bit different, and Kosarev had spoken of the Spanish conflict as a struggle 'in defence of peace and against war'. The Komsomol secretary nevertheless avoided any explicit mention of fascism and declared somewhat enigmatically that even German youth should play a role 'in the formation of a world youth front in the struggle against war ideologies'.[41]

Thus in spite of the reports of Kosarev and Shvernik, there was good reason to doubt that the international anti-fascist campaign announced by the Comintern at the beginning of April had been effective – events in Spain might be interpreted as a trial run. This failure was openly admitted by Maurice Thorez, who made an official report to the Praesidium about the situation in Spain and France. Any hope that the masses would spontaneously coalesce and trigger strong action by the social democrats had been throttled.[42] Things had changed since the height of the Rhineland crisis: then Hitler had spoken of national sovereignty; now he was interfering in the affairs of a sovereign state. Surely there was now a legitimate basis for demanding the withdrawal of the German fleet from Spanish waters, the convocation of an international conference and the expulsion of all diplomats representing states that had supported Franco. The Socialist International needed to be reminded that in communist parlance 'non-intervention' really meant 'combating fascist intervention'.[43] Ultimately, it was left to the representative of the French Communist Party to speak on anti-fascism – the Soviet speakers had almost completely ignored the issue.

Vittorio Codovilla, the fourth speaker at the Praesidium, reported on the military situation in Spain. Over the course of his summary he mentioned all the characteristics of a modern war. While the greater part of his speech was a sober account of the republican army, its organization and the role played by the Spanish communists, Codovilla did not limit himself to this. In his conclusion, he appealed for greater solidarity with the Republican cause: now that it was clear that the fight would not end soon, it was imperative that mass demonstrations and propaganda work be supplemented with 'something more tangible'. He was not referring to sanctions and humanitarian aid: 'The possibility of intervention is being discussed.' This was a tactful call for Soviet military support for the Spanish republic.[44] As early as mid-September the issue was being discussed in Moscow, though no decision was taken until the end of the month. Codovilla's appeal was not an isolated episode. 'The policy of remaining neutral does nothing but assist the fascists', declared the British communist Harry Pollitt in his vehement attack on non-intervention. He went much further even than Thorez, deploring the inadequacy of the communist response and insisting on the tremendous potential lying untapped in the widespread popular support for Republican Spain ('There is greater public sympathy for Spain than there was for revolutionary Russia'). He thought the French communists could have done far more, and as to the British: 'We have done nothing for fifteen days.'[45] Certainly, there was support for decisive action against the fascists – Pollitt gave a thorough summary of the spontaneous expressions of mass solidarity manifested since the beginning of the civil war – but speed was of the essence, and every day lost was a gift to the fascists. The world stood at a crossroads and Spain was the signpost. A fascist victory would impel many in that direction and civil war would break out in France. Communists could no longer put off mobilizing all their forces.[46]

When it was his turn to speak, Dimitrov agreed that some sort of intervention was overdue. He recognized that not enough had been done for the republican cause in Spain and proposed the adoption of more effective measures: 'Right now, as this international conflict, this conflict of international significance, enters a decisive phase in Spain, we must assemble all available forces to initiate a powerful international action which in the end will mean the victory of the Spanish republic, of the Spanish people.'[47] It is obvious that Dimitrov was referring to genuine military intervention. He also expressed concerns about the possible damage to the popular front in France and the need to follow up the congresses held in Brussels and Geneva with a movement 'based on the collaboration of all partisans of peace without distinction of political and religious beliefs'.[48] Dimitrov was intent on sweeping away the ambiguities that had blocked any explicit connection between support for the peace congresses and solidarity for Spain. He went on to shower abuse on a number of socialist leaders: both 'the reactionary side' of the Socialist International and 'the "left" – in quotes – people like Otto Bauer', had, in his opinion, 'sided with fascism against the idea of a single popular front'.[49]

No doubt the trial of Grigorii Zinov'ev and Lev Kamenev – the first of the Moscow show trials that were to become the symbol of the infamous Great Terror – and the subsequent campaign to 'fight against Trotskyism' contributed to raise the level of rhetorical animosity. Though the trial had taken place from 19 to 23 August, the political climate had begun its shift early in the month; a *Pravda* article calling for an intensification of 'class warfare' had set the tone. The article reflected the impact of a 'secret letter' of the Central Committee of 29 July in which former members of the 'united opposition' had been assigned direct responsibility for the assassination of Sergei Kirov.[50] The internal consequences of the trial were immediate; Radek, who had contributed to the anti-Trotsky campaign while he himself had been under investigation,[51] was removed from his post as semi-official commentator on international politics and disappeared from the scene. From this time onwards, the accusation of 'Trotskyism' would be fatal in the USSR and if not fatal, at least damning in Spain and in the international workers' movement.

The 'fight against Trotskyism' was the second item on the agenda of the 16–17 September 1936 Comintern Praesidium. Ercoli reported on the 'lessons' of the Moscow trial. The language used in his report did not differ greatly from that which had been used in public commentary.[52] Ercoli cited Dimitrov's description of 'the fight against Trotskyism' as an 'integral component' of anti-fascism.[53] He reiterated all the contradictory elements of Soviet propaganda, beginning with the accusation that 'terrorists' planned to defeat the USSR in war and to restore capitalism. National communist parties, with the exception of Spain's, foolishly indulged in an 'idyllic' idea of relations with socialists, but the creation of popular fronts led to growing friction in 'class relations and political struggle'.[54]

The gist of the report was that 'Trotskyism' could no longer be considered 'a current within the workers' movement'; it was now 'the vanguard of the counter-revolution'. Trotskyism could no longer be combated by taking on worrisome groups; instead, 'a drastic purging of class enemy agents from the workers' movement' itself was necessary.[55] And no longer could the Soviet Communist Party alone shoulder the responsibility of maintaining vigilance and producing propaganda. But the most sinister of Ercoli's warnings involved the supposed infiltration of the Comintern apparatus through German immigration to the USSR; he called on communist leaders to deal with this problem. He asked German communists 'to deduce from this element all the consequences which it brings in its wake'.[56] From that time on, no aspect of communist or Soviet policy was unaffected by the reaction against 'Trotskyism'.

By the end of the summer of 1936 the role of the Comintern had gone into eclipse. Its leaders instigated and approved a series of expressions of solidarity and of organizational measures for the struggle in Spain. But interventionist pressure in the Spanish civil war against diplomatic compromises was the last significant action undertaken by the Comintern leaders over the USSR's international policy. Their political function was now fated to have a rapid and irrevocable decline.

On 18 September the Comintern secretariat met to examine the Spanish question. We do not have any record of the talk given by Manuil'skii or of the interventions that followed, with the sole exception of Dimitrov's. He linked the political evaluation of the republic's internal situation to the international consequences of the civil war. The traditional alternatives, 'either capitalism or socialism; either the Soviet state or fascist dictatorship', lost their rhetorical efficacy as the USSR struggled with fascism.

Dimitrov later maintained that 'the question of the democratic-bourgeois state was no longer raised as before'.[57] This created new conditions for the Spanish republic:

> During the current vicissitudes in international relations, what with the existence of the Soviet state and Soviet democracy, bourgeois democracy exemplified by England and America and fascist dictatorship, this republic will be quite special, a state with full popular democracy.[58]

Dimitrov felt that the Spanish republic 'is unlikely to become a Soviet state, but may well become an anti-fascist state of the left'. The Soviet state ought to serve as a model, but there was a need for a transitional state, a democratic state in which the popular front was to play a decisive role. The mechanics of this transition would have to be carefully observed, since what was happening in Spain could very easily occur in France, Belgium and Holland.[59] The next day, the secretary of the Comintern reiterated that Spain's situation could be replicated in France and he reaffirmed, for the moment, communist support for Blum.[60]

At a meeting of the Comintern secretariat at the end of September, Manuil'skii opined that a 'pre-war situation' now existed; he was repeating the opinion voiced by Radek before his disappearance from the political scene. According to Manuil'skii, Spanish events showed that 'the world bourgeoisie and fascism, especially fascism, have now gone on the attack'; directly threatened were Belgium and Czechoslovakia, which, significantly, bordered on France and the USSR, respectively.[61] Kliment Voroshilov, the head of the armed forces, and a more powerful figure than Manuil'skii, expressed a similar fatalistic opinion. In a private conversation with a British military official, he affirmed his belief that very shortly Germany would start a war in Europe. He added that while some years earlier such a war would certainly have been instigated against the USSR, now that the latter had become a military power, Western states would become the German strategic goal.[62] To hear him tell it, war was imminent but the Soviets had shrewdly chosen an isolationist course that would allow them to avoid the worst possible fate.

THE BOUNDARIES OF COLLECTIVE SECURITY

On 28 September 1936, Maxim Litvinov gave a speech to the League of Nations on the question of 'collective security'. He began with a clear allusion to Nazism and observed that for the past four years the advocates of peace, of the unassailability of treaties and of an international order, had been on a collision course with those prepared to use war to get what they wanted. The former were weak because while they understood the importance of a joint defence they were mired in inertia. Litvinov stressed that if the nations that wanted peace stood united their joint strength would permit them to withstand any combination of aggressors; he declared that it was up to them 'to prevent the threat of war' and to force the aggressors to accept 'the general system of collective security'. Before the speech in Geneva *Le journal de Moscou* had underlined the importance of opposing Hitler through 'a common front subscribed to by those now being threatened and those who will be threatened in the future'.[63]

Since for some 'ultra-pacifists' the term 'new bloc' was a 'bugbear', Litvinov avoided possible finger-pointing by referring to 'the existing League of Nations bloc'.[64] His polemical targets were 'fatalism' and 'capitulation' and his declared objective was 'to avoid a catastrophe'. According to Litvinov, the Soviet Union opposed any step that increased the likelihood of war, whether it was war on its doorstep or war in distant lands. The non-intervention pact had been honoured 'only because a country friendly to the USSR wished to avoid international conflicts'.⁶⁵ If Litvinov did qualify the Soviet approach to non-intervention, he does not appear to have been sniping at the Committee for Non-intervention established in London. He was simply demanding greater authority and firmness in international security alliances and keeping the door open to discussions with Western democracies.

Litvinov had retreated a bit from the anti-fascist diplomatic scenario presented to Stalin on 7 September. He even stated that while the Soviet government viewed racism and national socialism as the 'sworn enemies of all workers and of civilization itself', it was committed to the maintenance of normal relations, even with states where such notions had triumphed. In all likelihood, this tactic had been determined by Stalin. Nevertheless, collective security was back on the table and would be used as a lever to force Germany to agree to a peaceful international order.

But in succeeding days events were to take a different turn. While in Geneva, Litvinov had meetings with both Eden and Blum, only to emerge deeply impressed by how much divided the USSR from Western democracies. The British foreign secretary had confirmed his government's intention to conclude a 'Western pact'.⁶⁶ As to Blum, Litvinov could only react to his words with sadness; the French prime minister was determined to 'wait and see', and seemed unlikely to take any steps before a new Locarno was convened.⁶⁷ The British and French responses to the proclamation of Spain's new Nationalist government under Franco then came as no surprise: Krestinskii told Samuil' Kagan, who was serving as the USSR representative to the London committee, that 'neither the English nor the French care to offer any assistance to the Madrid government'. He commented bitterly that non-intervention was nothing but a 'legal excuse' for this stance.⁶⁸ Three days later, on 7 October, Kagan dismissed the pact of non-intervention as 'useless' and announced that if fascist violations to international agreements did not cease immediately his own government would consider itself 'released from the obligations' it had taken on when it agreed to the pact.⁶⁹ The press immediately picked up this turnabout in Soviet policy. Of course, if all parties had respected the pact things would have gone well, but things had gone differently and reluctance to deal with transgressions had begun to foster a 'policy of connivance', if not a complete farce.⁷⁰

Meanwhile the Soviet military commitment to Spain was being consolidated. The ambassador from Republican Spain, M. Pascua, probably clarified the terms of military aid in his visit to Moscow at the beginning of October.⁷¹ Over the following days, massive shipments of arms left the Soviet Union for Spain, and by the middle of October technicians and military advisers were en route. They would be organized by Vladimir Antonov-Ovseenko, who had arrived in Barcelona at the beginning of the month to serve as consul general.[72] The Soviet Union's military commitment to Spain was by that date quite public, and it signalled a more general shift in Soviet foreign policy. This change was the result of careful calculations by Stalin and those around him. In a letter to G.K. Ordzhonikidze written on 12 October 1936, Kaganovich indicated that Stalin himself had laid out the shift in Soviet policy. Kaganovich spoke of 'deeds replacing words' and anticipated the upcoming Soviet announcements to the London committee.[73]

On 16 October 1936, Soviet newspapers published the telegram in which Stalin communicated to José Diaz, the Spanish communist leader, his belief that the liberation of Spain from fascists was not 'a private Spanish matter, but the universal responsibility of all progressive and developed mankind'.[74] Over the ensuing days, the tone of Soviet press coverage became significantly sharper. Articles affirmed that it was no longer possible 'to continue to tolerate' violations of the non-intervention pact.[75] The government daily took the French and British governments to task, asserting that in both nations the bourgeoisie had called the shots; the resultant 'capitalist world policy' was directly responsible for the current 'threat to peace in western Europe'. London had failed to provide any response to Soviet enquiries and consequently 'our agreement has ceased to exist'. The right of the Spanish government to take the steps necessary for self-defence could not be questioned and the USSR would act in accordance with 'the resolutions agreed upon by hundreds of workers' assemblies'.[76]

On 23 October 1936, just as Franco launched his massive offensive against Madrid, the Soviet government took a further step away from the non-intervention pact. In a letter to Lord Plymouth, chairman of the London committee, Maiskii complained that his country's attempts to stem violations of the pact 'have not been backed by the committee'. He concluded that the pact was dead and that the USSR had no more reason to adhere to it than did any other state.[77] But Maiskii was not slamming the door on further negotiations: if the other signatory nations were willing to accept the Soviet proposals made over the previous days, which were aimed at revitalizing the agreement through a system of detailed guidelines, there was still hope.[78]

This aggressive approach was Moscow's new strategy. On 25 October 1936 Maiskii received a note from Litvinov urging him to continue along his present course, to keep on the attack.[79] On 1 November Litvinov informed Maiskii that the Soviet leadership had decided that it would continue to participate in the work of the London committee only as long as 'some hope remains of asserting control in the future'.[80] The next speech Maiskii gave continued the theme of war versus peace – this was not about communism versus fascism, he declared.[81] The USSR did not withdraw its support from the committee. Though both the French and the British were upset by the Soviet intervention in Spain, an inflammatory act they viewed as likely to push the conflict beyond Spain's borders, relations between the Western powers and the USSR continued to be pursued in the name of European security. But this meant different things to different actors, and a serious decline in such relations had already occurred. While the non-intervention agreement continued to be given lip service for some time, the Soviet position had changed.

At the beginning of November 1936, *Le journal de Moscou* censured western European diplomacy, which had done little but 'sabotage the League of Nations and collective security, compromise and then capitulate to aggression'. Did France and England need to be told that a fascist victory in Spain would be a defeat for them far more than it would be a defeat for the Soviet Union?[82] *Izvestiia's* political commentator went further. In his opinion, the iniquitous system of international relations established at Versailles was fated to collapse: if revolution was not the cause, then inevitably counter-revolutionary forces would be. The laughably mendacious theories of 'organized capitalism' spouted by social democrats were wholly belied by fascist aggression. Most disquieting was the rise of 'the most transparent and gross class interests' in international politics, threatening not only peace, but 'what remains of democracy in capitalist countries'. The USSR made no pretense of thinking for any state but itself, but other states ought to know that should the Versailles system be superseded by a system 'even more inhuman and brutal', it would not be long before that system was eliminated through revolutionary efforts.[83]

Even Litvinov joined the fray. On 10 November 1936, at the ceremony honouring him with the Order of Lenin, the commissar gave a short address on foreign policy. 'Bankrupt' were the policies of states whose words had been hosannas to collective security but whose deeds had been the sappers of security. Much time and energy had been expended in the effort to convince Germany and Italy that collective security did not amount to the formation of a 'bloc';[84] now, of course, the aggressors had formed their own bloc. A little more than a month after his Geneva address, Litvinov's tone had changed considerably.

Nevertheless, he continued to hope that the 'pan-European pact' he had outlined to Stalin in September might be realized. This was his main argument in a letter to Maiskii of 4 November 1936, in which he emphasized the possibility of a new European balance of power, unfavourable to Hitler and Mussolini.[85] However, this would depend not only on the goodwill of Great Britain but on getting around the indisputable fact that the USSR had intervened in Spain. Besides the imperatives of international propaganda Litvinov's insistent proclamation of the Soviet commitment to peace satisfied another need: the defence of his own policies, which had little to do with sending weapons to Spain. In fact, there had hardly been unanimous support among Soviet leaders for the Spanish intervention. Litvinov held a seriously critical position.

A letter from Maiskii to Litvinov dated 11 November 1936 throws some light on the matter.[86] While he expressed solidarity with Litvinov on the question of a 'pan-European pact', Maiskii claimed to have read 'with great surprise' a letter from Litvinov to Rozenberg stating that 'our help to the Spanish government must cease as soon as possible'. Cessation of Soviet aid would no doubt be 'another step forward on the road to an Anglo-French-Soviet coalition, a significant event in the general consolidation of the forces of peace in the pre-war period'. But, for the time being, there was no plan to terminate aid to the Republicans. 'As you have rightly observed in your letter to Rozenberg', acknowledged Maiskii, involvement in the war in Spain 'has worsened our relations with England and France'. But this would all change once General Franco had been defeated, and the international prestige of the USSR had risen. If the Soviet Union now withheld all assistance, permitting a Franco victory, the international picture would be far, far worse than it now was. Logic dictated gambling on a Republican victory, but logic also dictated seeking the best odds; if the Spanish fascists were defeated, thanks in part to Soviet aid to their opponents, there would instantly be 'a bloc of peaceful states around us'.[87] Maiskii tended to think a few moves ahead. Just as he had earlier predicted that Blum would be influenced by the Socialist International's discussion of non-intervention,[88] so he now predicted that a joint effort by the Soviet government, the labourites, the Socialist International and the French communists could prod the British and French into action.[89]

Though there were very real differences between Maiskii and Litvinov, they did not affect the main thrust of foreign policy. The contrasting outlooks appear to have been linked to differing perceptions of public opinion in democratic Europe. But Litvinov was the more closely connected with Soviet politics and it is quite likely that his comments to Rozenberg grew out of existing tensions in Moscow and a concern to limit the international consequences of intervening in Spain. In any case, his words expressed a precise foreign policy priority. Rozenberg's own views may also deserve mention: he confided to the Republican Manuel Azaña that the single greatest obstacle to intervention was the need to maintain good relations with Britain.[90]

THE RETURN OF THE ISOLATIONIST OPTION

How would Germany react to the Soviet gambit in Spain? Soviet diplomats anxiously awaited the answer. Surits would not have been speaking only for himself when he expressed his fears to Krestinskii on 12 October: the arms shipments and Soviet advisers in Spain 'will only lead Germany to augment its own aid to the rebels and may even lead to the outbreak of open conflict between Germany and us'. On the other hand, 'today Germany benefits more than ever from the weakness of the forces working for peace. It is possible that by decisively intervening in Spain we will improve matters and help consolidate the anti-fascist movement.' This emphasis on the forces opposed to Germany permitted Surits to return to his theory of the internal weakness of the Nazi regime. He did not see Hitler at the brink of catastrophe, but he reckoned that German social and economic woes were such that the stiffened resistance of a coalition of peaceful nations might convince Hitler to back down.[91]

Then came the Rome–Berlin Axis pact of 24 October 1936, which established the basis for a military alliance. The Soviet response was cautious. During a meeting with the Italian ambassador to Moscow, Augusto Rosso, some days before the pact was made public, Litvinov had condemned Rome's increasing hostility towards Moscow and had remarked that it was getting harder and harder to distinguish the Italian from the German regime. Still, he went so far as to predict that no agreement between Germany and Italy could last.[92] Litvinov's later opinion of the pact remained firmly tied to this early position: the agreement would be temporary and existed largely to exert pressure on Great Britain.[93] Litvinov was probably less anxious than Surits; the important thing was to isolate Germany so that the fascist alignment already visible in Spain would occur nowhere else. But by the middle of November things showed no sign of stabilizing. On 16 November 1936 the governments of Germany and Italy officially recognized Franco's government, and on 25 November, Germany and Japan signed their 'Anti-Comintern Pact', a rather alarming turn of events from Moscow's perspective. After the Soviet decision to intervene in Spain, the situation had come to look more and more like Stalin's worst nightmare: encirclement.

A speech given by Litvinov on 28 November 1936, during the formal discussion of the new Soviet constitution, illustrated the Soviet reaction. The subject of the speech was European fascism and its global consequences. When Litvinov connected the fascist and proto-fascist infection of 'two-thirds of bourgeois Europe' to the economic decline and internal contradictions inherent in late-capitalist society he was only reiterating familiar clichés. The crisis in capitalism and the inability to resist fascism suggested little hope for Europe's democracies. The only question that remained to be answered was how long the democratic states would remain democratic.[94] If, as Litvinov believed and as the case of Spain seemed to confirm, 'militarist cliques' exerted powerful influence over the politics of democratic countries it was up to the USSR to take 'the banner of democratization' from the weak hands of the bourgeoisie and give it a 'Soviet imprint'.[95]

However, Litvinov was careful to specify that this did not necessitate the formation of an 'international anti-fascist bloc'. As we have seen he had long emphasized this point. This time he was more insistent and as justification he evoked the idea of a 'peaceful coexistence', with socialism and capitalism (including its subspecies, fascism) existing side by side. This approach erased much of the relevance of the supposed friction between democracy and fascism and revealed the purely rhetorical nature of the invocation of 'Soviet democracy'. At the same time, diplomatic action was released from the hobbling axiom of fixed political alliances. In other words, Litvinov was using the concept of 'peaceful coexistence' to play down the anti-fascist discourse, reviving longstanding Soviet doubts about any alliance with capitalist states.[96] This new approach would have surprised anyone who had followed Litvinov's statements up to that date and it definitely signaled a change in foreign policy.

Litvinov was wavering. As in his speeches to the League of Nations in 1936, he did insist on a 'show of strength' against Hitler, but he was backing away from his earlier talk of a European security alliance. As he presented a richly detailed summary of the non-intervention agreements he explained that the Soviet government had sincerely hoped that the agreements would be adequate to isolate the rebellion. And he recalled the repeated efforts to compel the London committee to take a stand, ending with the ironic comment that 'the London committee has, as we had feared, interpreted the term "non-intervention" to mean that it was not to intervene in the problem of others' interventions in Spanish affairs'. Given such an understanding of non-intervention, it had become necessary for the Soviet government to distance itself from the agreement. There was no talk of future plans for the London committee in Litvinov's speech, only of Soviet solidarity with republican combatants and with the defenders of Madrid.[97]

But the frustrating experience of working with the London committee was 'only the emotional aspect of the question'; yet to be discussed was the political aspect. One needed only to glance at the Spanish scene to see that 'the first massive fascist movement outside the borders of fascist countries' had materialized and that beyond the construction of a specific internal regime, fascism also entailed 'preparing for aggression for war against other states'. German actions in Spain confirmed the distinctive features of Nazism: unlike early Italian fascism the Nazis were compelled by an inner drive to move beyond the borders of their state. Only at this point did Litvinov mention recent international agreements between fascist states. He maintained that 'warmongering blocs' were being formed whose very existence constituted a threat to the 'general peace, security and interests' of many countries. However, he made a distinction between the fascist states, insisting on a basic difference between the German–Japanese agreement and any pacts involving Italy. Litvinov dismissed the public elements of the German–Japanese pact as 'meaningless', only a veil behind which lurked a secret military agreement 'in which the word communism does not occur once'. This agreement demonstrated 'the inclination to extend the war'.[98] Perhaps it was not really consistent to promote the idea of 'peaceful coexistence' while in the same breath condemning fascist states for forming blocs, but Litvinov had another point in mind. Conceding that the weapons of fascist states might not be turned against the Soviet Union, Litvinov insisted that while he was aware that 'everyone knows that dogs that do a lot of barking never bite', he was 'not sure that the dogs knew that'.[99]

At the end of his speech, Litvinov cast aside what little reserve had tempered his remarks up to that point and declared that the USSR counted not on 'talk of peace, but action that would bring peace'. As to blocs or alliances, the USSR wanted nothing to do with any of those and refused to be intimidated by the aggression increasingly common on the international stage – after all, 'other states are facing greater threats', and Soviet security was not founded on 'documents written on wastepaper or on foreign policy combinations'. 'The Soviet Union', declared Litvinov, 'is strong enough to take care of itself'; and he referred to the Soviet state as an 'impregnable fortress'. In addition to the self-sufficiency he insisted on, Litvinov also mentioned the 'millions and millions of workers' in capitalist states who believed in the USSR.[100]

The change in strategy evidenced by this speech was significant. Two months earlier Litvinov had made constant reference to the principle of 'collective security'. Not only had these appeals largely disappeared, but so had the talk of the 'forces for peace' and the need to unite these forces to prevent war. He had adopted an isolationist posture. Litvinov's address stressed a key aspect of the international situation as viewed from Moscow at the end of 1936: a fascist bloc had been formed, notwithstanding Italy's dubious position. However, the USSR had no plans to encourage or to join a defensive bloc. Without having formally repudiated the ideals of collective security the USSR did not seem interested in joining forces with anyone. The course Litvinov had recommended to Stalin in September, envisaging a firm response to the advance of fascism on the European scene, could hardly have been more different from the course he had begun to outline only a few months later. Isolationism had never been jettisoned from the vocabulary of Soviet foreign policy, and with the advance of fascism and war in Spain it emerged as the dominant strategy.

A few more months would pass before the full flowering of this revived policy. Litvinov had displayed a new commitment to 'peaceful coexistence', one inimical to the creation of antagonistic blocs. But perhaps events had already superseded all abstract principles, and it was now imperative that all countries interested in preserving peace band together in a defensive alliance. Never mentioned in public pronouncements, the issue nonetheless exerted an influence on Soviet foreign policy.

When, in early December 1936, Britain declared itself prepared to come to the defence of France and Belgium in case of war – a declaration soon echoed by France – Litvinov could not refrain from commenting (in a letter to Vladimir Potemkin written on 4 December) that had such assurances been made earlier, 'Hitler's position would be different.' Nevertheless, his scepticism was unchanged: after all, when Eden spoke about eastern Europe 'he does not necessarily include the USSR' and so a series of regional agreements would only emphasize the isolation of the Soviet Union.[101] The same scepticism marked relations with France. After a discussion with 'comrades in positions of authority' Litvinov informed the Soviet ambassador to France that Blum had earned their 'irritation' and that no efforts would be made to restrain the French communists in their struggle with the French government.[102] Unhappiness with how the League of Nations had handled the problems arising from the Spanish civil war led Litvinov to reiterate the position maintained since October: non-intervention ought to have been accompanied by 'effective controls' and Soviet preoccupation with Germany and Italy was due to their generally aggressive actions, not to anything related to non-intervention. As he had told Chilston, the USSR would not back censure of Italy and Germany at the meeting of the League of Nations in Geneva – Litvinov believed that such a move could not win broad support – if initiated by the foreign minister of the Spanish republic, Alvarez Del Vayo.[103] But the USSR would support the cause of the republican government and Litvinov also considered 'worthy of attention' the proposal for an armistice that Blum had informally described to Rozenberg.[104] On 7 December the Narkomindel asked for Stalin's approval of Blum's plan.[105]

During the first half of December 1936, slight advances were made by the Western powers, but it is not clear that they meant to influence

Soviet policy-makers. On 5 December, France and Britain proposed to serve as joint mediators for the Spanish question, and Germany, Italy and the USSR were asked not to intervene during the negotiations. On 14 December, in the face of the increase in German and Italian support to the Spanish rebels, Eden indicated that Great Britain would not tolerate such interference. Maiskii wrote to Litvinov on 10 December, stating that in his view a change in English public opinion was taking place. It also seemed to him that the outcome of the conflict in Spain, and in particular the battle for Madrid, would have a great impact on 'the prospects for peace in Europe and for our own international prestige as a great power'.[106] On 17 December he informed Moscow that, according to opinions circulating in London, 'Spanish events precipitated the approach of a very significant and perhaps decisive moment'. The military pressure of the Spanish fascists was increasing; the rebels seemed determined to push on to victory. But the activities of the Soviet Union in Spain could help halt the rebel push, and this might sway both British democratic circles and the British government. Maiskii referred here to a speech Eden had given on 14 December: though he did not specify a passage he must have been referring to Eden's comments about the 'indivisibility of peace'.[107]

Although the most one could expect from the British was 'moral and political support', that was not to be despised; in Maiskii's opinion, it could well serve as the crucial first step towards a new sort of international relationship, and surely the French would soon follow the British lead. This would only happen if the USSR became an 'active agent' and capitalized on the prestige it had accrued in European public opinion thanks to its intervention in Spain. In other words, the accrued capital now needed to be spent in foreign policy, and quickly at that. In the conclusion to his letter, Maiskii wrote dramatically that 'one thing is certain: one way or another, an extremely important change is boiling up in Spanish events'.[108]

On 19 December 1936 Litvinov expressed his agreement with Maiskii's assessment of the importance of Spain to the prestige and position of the USSR. 'This is', he noted, 'very clear, even to us', probably hinting at his own earlier hostility towards Soviet intervention: Maiskii had challenged him on this point, as we have seen. Nevertheless this did not convince Litvinov that the role of the USSR in Spain should be anything but 'limited'; after all, Moscow commanded no fleet in the Mediterranean and neither France nor Great Britain had offered anything more than moral support to the Spanish republic.[109]

Nor did Maiskii's talks with Eden or the Geneva meeting of the League of Nations change this picture. The latter turned out to be a low-key affair from which the most important diplomatic powers absented themselves. As to the British foreign secretary, he wanted mostly to be reassured about Soviet intentions in Spain and about the USSR's commitment to the re-establishment of a 'normal democratic order'. In additional comments, Eden reiterated the British commitment to regulating the admission of foreign volunteers to aid the Republican cause and expressed pessimism about a mediated ceasefire.[110] The issues discussed between Maiskii and Eden had all been raised before either by Potemkin, when he spoke on 11 December at the League of Nations, or by the public communication from Litvinov to the diplomatic representatives of Great Britain and France, wherein he proposed convening a conference to end the civil war.[111]

The Narkomindel doubted that the initiative for an Anglo-French mediation in Spain could succeed, and support for the proposal was tinged with scepticism.[112] On 19 December 1936 Litvinov had already confessed to Potemkin that 'as to the Spanish question, I expected nothing and I received nothing from the Council of the League'. In his opinion, as long as London and Paris insisted on maintaining a free hand, the League of Nations would be powerless.[113] Diplomatic matters had become quite stagnant.

On 28 December 1936 Litvinov advised Stalin to accept the Anglo-French proposal; he believed that it would redound to the benefit of the Spanish government.[114] The memorandum which the USSR submitted to the English and French governments on 29 December did not conceal a certain wariness: the Spanish situation had raised real concerns in the USSR, which hoped for the reduction and, possibly, the elimination of 'foreign elements' from the Spanish ranks and appealed for the speedy adoption of 'effective controls'.[115]

Maiskii appears to have been determined to improve the relationship between Great Britain and the USSR.[116] His description of the Spanish civil war as a turning point in British and European opinion might have been a rhetorical base for an attempt to revive collective security. At the beginning of January, he was still detailing to Litvinov the symptoms of change in British foreign policy, especially as illustrated in Eden's recent speeches.[117] However, this was not just Maiskii's personal view, since some press assessments were heading in the same direction; by mid-December Lapinskii was maintaining that 'over the past two or three weeks, a crucial shift has taken place' in western Europe. In fact, this author's observation took place prior to the speech by Eden so important to Maiskii's thinking – he cited previous statements made by Eden on the topic of British military aid to France and Belgium in case of aggression. Lapinskii pointed out that this was a sort of reciprocity lacking at the time of Locarno. And for the first time Western powers were making important international commitments without including

Germany in discussions. The change was due to German rearmament and to recognition of the 'aggressive nature of national socialism'.[118]

Lapinskii appears to have felt compelled to go beyond the picture of Europe as a locus for conflict between competing imperialist interests. Just ten days earlier, he had been talking about the determining role of 'class interests' in shifting British foreign policy away from peacemaking.[119] Now he was reversing his position: 'The basic and determining fact is that the Western powers, and especially England, are identifying the threat of war quite explicitly and are taking defensive measures against that threat.' In all likelihood, this new solidarity was a reaction to the Geman—Japanese pact. An additional motivation figured in British calculations: the fear of repeating 'the famous error' of 1914, when Britain failed to communicate to Germany how it would respond to war. This was not, Lapinskii decided, the classic case of intra-imperialist warfare, and the USSR could not sit smugly on the sidelines: 'Anything that can promote peace should be applauded by our country.'[120] But Lapinskii's particular response was not universal and Peri, one of the main commentators on international affairs in the Comintern press, compared the 'bloc of three' created at the beginning of December with the 'bloc of four of unhappy memory'; he saw a separate peace in the offing.[121]

Reactions to the pact between Germany and Japan also varied. The official interpretation held that fascism's anti-communist propaganda was a smokescreen concealing a drive towards European domination. Lapinskii ascribed to this theory but went on to claim that while the world could be perversely carved into ideological blocs, the more prevalent division was 'between countries that desire peace and countries that do not desire it'.[122] This was not the main focus of other authors. For example, Lemin specified the 'contradictions' within the fascist bloc. For him the German–Japanese pact was the work of the 'most foolhardy groups' in both countries, and marked the first time Hitler had proceeded with an international agreement without the full approval of Germany's élites.[123] Moreover, Italy had joined the German–Japanese alliance before the resolving its conflict with Germany over Austria and the Balkans. Every imperialist bloc was bound to generate internal contradictions, but the very evanescent quality of the fascist bloc, its lack of a general programme or of an explicit agreement about spheres of influence guaranteed that it would fall apart should war break out. Lemin emphasized the issue of internal contradictions in order to underline a resemblance between the present and relations among the major powers on the eve of the Great War. Lessons drawn from the Spanish civil war suggested that Germany would soon launch a major war against Great Britain and France.[124]

SPAIN

What was to be made of the deep crisis in the European system? Some said that it proved that the most salient line of demarcation ran between the imperialist powers, while others insisted that it demonstrated the basic difference between peaceful and aggressive states. Soviet opinion was divided between those who favoured continuity and those who favoured innovation, though both viewed the current state of Europe with a certain anxiety. This dimly reflected ambiguities and different orientations among the policy-makers.

At the beginning of January 1937 *Le journal de Moscou* took up once again the issue of bloc formation in international politics. One editorial described the efficient organization of Germany and fellow aggressor states in support of the nationalists in Spain, contrasting that with the Western powers, which dithered vaguely in the face of a war endangering 'the material and moral culture of mankind'. After that pessimistic assessment, the author launched into a surprising conclusion: it was time to form new alliances. The League of Nations was clearly unsuited to the task for which it had been created, since it faced not only the external challenge of the German–Japanese bloc but the internal challenge of member-states (read, Italy) acting as 'agents for the absent aggressors'. As long as the League embraced its own gravediggers, those who advocated collective security could only be 'a voice in the wilderness'. Yet the only possible unity could be among countries committed to collective security, countries that did not enter into neutrality by halves – by combining only those nations 'a firm and compact bloc of peaceful countries can be created'.[125]

This was a change in policy. Up until the end of December Narkomindel officials had insisted on a picture of Germany isolated in Europe, only tenuously and provisionally in league with Italy.[126] The January editorial, written or inspired by Litvinov, appears also to have reflected Maiskii's and Lapinskii's views. But this new position had yet to assume a systematic form; change appeared to be imminent, but change to what? Litvinov himself had noted something new in British and French foreign policy, but he had chosen to suspend judgement, and this editorial may have reflected that hesitation.

By the end of December 1936, Litvinov had grown very pessimistic about relations with Italy and he complained to Rosso that Italian involvement in Spain was growing.[127] There was, however, another reason to eye Italy with increasing distress: the rapprochement between England and Italy after the end of the war in Ethiopia, sanctioned by a 'gentlemen's agreement'. As though this was not enough, it also looked as though France and Germany might be moving towards some sort of alignment through talks about volunteers in Spain.[128] Taken together, the two events suggested to Moscow that a 'pact of four' might be in the air, an attempt to resolve the Spanish crisis through a compromise unfavourable to the Republican side.[129] Nevertheless, *Le journal de Moscou* was supporting an international anti-fascist bloc.

The reappearance of the bloc question in public Soviet forums was a symptom of a larger set of concerns. Which would better serve Soviet security: to assume that all capitalist states were likely to form a hostile undifferentiated grouping, although internally inconsistent, and so embrace isolationism, or, to assume that western European states were likely to oppose Hitler, and so conclude a defensive alliance with them? The latter course had been proposed by Litvinov at the beginning of the Spanish crisis, when no fascist bloc existed. But Stalin had not been convinced. Soviet policy-makers had not been talking recently about an alliance of peaceful states. The appearance of such proposals later attested that self-isolation was not yet fully re-established.

At the end of 1936, with fascism very much on the rise, Stalin again made an overture to Germany. Kandelaki was entrusted with the same mission he had undertaken the previous year, determining whether an extension of economic agreements could pave the way for a normalization of political relations. The results were identical. He met Hjalmar Schacht twice, in December 1936 and January 1937, but the talks soon ran aground.[130] This was more a consequence of Hitler's intransigence than it was the result of Moscow's instructions to Kandelaki. After the first meeting, Kandelaki returned to Moscow for briefing by Stalin, Litvinov and Molotov. They provided him with a written declaration to the effect that 'the Soviet government has never rejected the possibility of negotiations with the German government, and furthermore it has offered precise political proposals'. The declaration expressed the desire to improve relations between the two countries and to conduct negotiations between official representatives.[131]

Although instructions to Kandelaki appear to have been approved by Litvinov, it can be assumed that this mission had very limited objectives in the commissar's view. In fact, on 20 December 1936 Litvinov had sent Stalin an unpublished interview the *Daily Mail* had conducted with Hermann Goering, along with a secret note drafted by a former German foreign ministry official.[132] Both documents attested to deep German hostility towards the USSR. Goering was reported to have stated that collaboration with Russia would only be possible if the current regime was replaced. The Nazi leader maintained that a war between Germany and Russia was inevitable.[133] In the note Germany's chances of instigating and winning a war against the USSR were evaluated in light of the most recent international developments.

Though Germany would not be prepared to launch a war until 1938, said the report, at that time a war would certainly be initiated. Time would be required to cultivate favourable diplomatic relations – Poland's support and Britain's neutrality were both necessary – and to make improvements to the German war machine, not to mention the efforts required to weaken the Soviet state from within and foment a civil war (as we shall see, Stalin was not to forget this warning).[134] It should be noted that these two documents were sent by Litvinov to Stalin a few days after Goering himself had contacted Surits proposing an exchange of views: the Soviet ambassador had replied that this would have been possible only after the conclusion of the negotiations carried on by Kandelaki.[135]

There is evidence of Litvinov's mild enthusiasm for the German orientation. He believed that someone, especially in France, might be tempted to engage in economic collaboration with Germany without demanding assurances of peace in Europe in return – this sounded like the very sort of thing that Kandelaki was attempting in his contacts with German circles. As he had in the past, Litvinov spoke against such manoeuvres.[136] At the same time, Litvinov was sceptical about rumours that Hitler's policy in Spain had met with fierce opposition in German military circles, and that there had been talk of a coup d'état. In general he concurred with Surits that whatever economic troubles Germany had, no catastrophe lay just around the corner.[137] He did not foresee any significant changes in German policy. On 4 February 1937, after he had consulted Surits and after the second meeting between Kandelaki and Schacht, Litvinov sent a letter to Stalin proposing clear limits to the negotiations with Germany. Kandelaki ought not to return to Moscow for further briefing, since his sole task was to listen to German proposals. Both Surits and Kandelaki had known right from the start that any initiative had to be left to the German side. If the USSR decided to act on Schacht's proposal and publicize the content of the negotiations, three days would have to pass before the release of any communiqué so that both France and Czechoslovakia might be confidentially informed.[138] None of these conditions had been proposed in the directives sent to Kandelaki a month earlier.

Despite Litvinov's cautionary stance, there were signs that a 'parallel diplomacy' with Germany had been outlined. Even as a showdown was nearing in Spain between communism and fascism, and the world was still reeling from the German–Japanese pact, at that very moment the Soviets were holding a door open for Hitler. In many respects, the political factors affecting vast sectors of the European democratic public had ceased to have relevance to Soviet strategy.

STALIN AND THE INEVITABLE WAR, 1936–1941

THE FINAL BARRICADE, OR THE FIRST BATTLE

Perhaps the first significant sign that leading supporters of Stalin felt the time was right for a revival of isolationism was a speech given by Zhdanov to the Leningrad party committee at the end of October 1936. It was after the concerted attacks on non-intervention and the decision to provide military aid to Republican Spain that Zhdanov offered his blistering criticism of 'party experts' for forgetting that 'we live surrounded by capitalist states'. He warned that the events in Spain revealed 'an extraordinary exacerbation of class struggle' in the international sphere. This was the prelude to nothing less than 'the definitive and decisive clash of the world of communism and the world of capitalism'. The USSR would constitute 'the assault brigade in the vanguard of the world proletariat', whose fundamental objective was to bring 'the entire globe under the sway of the red flag of communism'.[139] This fanatical rhetoric marked a return to devices discarded in the wake of the Moscow trial, as if Zhdanov's phraseology took on the task of increasing ideological motivations as a component of Soviet policy. It is worth noting that Dimitrov had openly rejected the notion of an apocalyptic clash between socialism and capitalism. Zhdanov's rabid diatribe had obvious foreign policy implications: the emphasis on international 'class struggle' led to an undifferentiated view of the outside world.

One month later, on 29 November 1936, Molotov outlined the new orientation of Soviet foreign policy without so much as mentioning such issues as class and revolutionary struggle. In his view the German–Japanese pact was 'a mask concealing a conspiracy, an anti-Soviet conspiracy, aimed at conquest'; he declared that 'We will not ignore the aggressive nature of this pact.' But he did not go on to unfurl an anti-fascist plan. Molotov explained: 'We are wholly absorbed by our own internal affairs . . . In order best to defend peace and the peaceful enterprise of the peoples of the USSR, we must believe exclusively in our own strength.'[140] Although Litvinov, as we have seen, had also partially retreated from the collective security approach, Molotov gave the clearest and most authoritative affirmation of the isolationist option heard at this time.

It fell to Zhdanov to outline the Soviet position on Spain. His opinions about Blum were totally belligerent; when push had come to shove only the USSR, unlike the French government, had 'extended the hand of fellowship' and openly expressed solidarity with 'the heroic Spanish people'. In his view, fascism was preparing to attack the French popular front. But the real objective was the USSR: all the efforts of German fascism were directed towards the east, and racist propaganda was being used to lay the groundwork for an anti-Soviet war.[141]

Fear seemed to be spreading through the ranks of the Soviet leadership, spurred on by a deteriorating international climate. But the reactions to threat perception varied. Zhdanov believed that whatever setbacks the USSR suffered on the international scene could be made up for through retrenching and the support of the masses in the capitalist countries. He rejected the notion of looking for any assistance from the leadership of capitalist states, which had opted for 'a terrorist system of government'.[142] His attack on Blum was also a show of hostility towards Litvinov.

Zhdanov's association of isolationism and appeal to the masses articulated sentiments broadly shared by the top tier of Soviet leadership. No longer did Soviet aid to the Spanish republic have to figure in the debate among European socialists and communists on the subject of non-intervention or a lever to increase Soviet influence over the foreign-policy decisions of Western powers – now it could only be the prelude to division, separation, isolation. Such steps followed from the growing sentiment, widespread between the protagonists of the Republican resistance in Spain, that the events in Spain were but the first battle in a much larger world war. The early news of atrocities committed against the Spanish civilian population lent credibility to this apocalyptic vision. We know that by this time such ideas had become widespread in the Comintern; Manuil'skii himself had embraced them. Zhdanov too had signed on. Only Dimitrov held a divergent view.

In a *Pravda* article published 7 November 1936 Dimitrov underscored the urgency of the anti-fascist battle in Spain.[143] Later published in the Comintern press, the article was amended to indicate that the 'anti-Comintern pact' constituted proof that the struggle between fascism and the workers' movement had moved into the open.[144] Reiterating the arguments that had become familiar elements of his addresses to the Comintern, Dimitrov highlighted the international aspect of the conflict with fascism, now entering its final stage. Non-intervention had failed because it tried so hard 'not to irritate the beast' though the importance of 'taming the beast' was now clear. The progress of fascism had been impeded by the armed resistance of the popular front; clearly the time had come to 'defend democracy against the attacks of fascism through all available means, including the use of arms'. The international significance of the Spanish conflict meant that this was no less true for the defence of peace.[145] This goal could only be achieved by one force, namely the organized workers' movement. As to bourgeois democracy, it grew more fragile by the day and might soon succumb to reactionary attacks.[146] If Dimitrov was critical of non-intervention, his position nonetheless differed from Zhdanov's, since he continued to view the Spanish conflict as a means of retarding the spread of international fascism and of war.

Dimitrov had argued for active intervention in Spain, and on 10 October 1936 a communication from an alarmed Marty prompted the launch of a mass campaign to assist Republican Spain.[147] This was no trivial venture, and the selection of such prominent figures as Ercoli, Marty himself and Manuil'skii to lead the effort attested to its importance.[148] When Germany and Italy recognized the nationalists as the legitimate Spanish government, Dimitrov sent a dramatic telegram to the three leaders in which he demanded that the international workers' organizations be mobilized to deal with this new turn of events, suggesting his fear that the French and English might soon set aside their commitment to non-intervention. He also declared untenable the idea that non-intervention would permit the USSR to avoid greater international difficulties.[149] By the end of November Ercoli's office had drafted a memorandum on the defence of the Spanish republic: earlier thinking on the conflict had failed to grasp the essential truth that 'neutrality, instead of reducing the danger of war, will lead directly to a European war'.[150]

The thrust of Dimitrov's November article differed only slightly from the article he had published in May 1936. Both articles were written to rally support for Comintern campaigns and to influence Soviet foreign policy. However, the space accorded to the 'struggle for peace' in the later article had considerably shrunk. Dimitrov chose to keep silent about his own theory on the revolutionary nature of the fight for peace and did not revisit his own attacks on what he called the fatalistic view that war was inevitable – the latter had been one of the most significant aspects of his position in May.

The war in Spain had changed things. It was to have international repercussions and would decide, said Dimitrov, the fate of the workers' movement in Europe. And yet, if the conflict was the focal point for a more general struggle against fascism, it seemed as though the opening for a 'struggle for peace' might have expired. Armed resistance now seemed the only reasonable step, as the war threatened to escape Spain's borders and entangle all of western Europe. Was not the defeat of fascism now objectively and strategically distinct from the defence of peace? For Dimitrov, Spain was the last redoubt protecting Europe from a general outbreak of war. But, like many others, he began to blur the distinction between peacetime and war.

Before the end of the year, on 21 December, a letter signed by Stalin, Molotov and Kliment Voroshilov was sent to Largo Caballero, rejecting any comparison between the rebellion in Spain and the Russian revolution. The authors of the letter urged moderation in the Spanish government's internal policies, especially towards the peasants – the 'enemies of Spain' must not be provided with any pretext for criticizing the government. The Soviets would not contribute to the Republican war effort except through the military advisors already in Spain; implicit was the decision to bar Soviet volunteers from the International Brigades, which were being organized by the Comintern. Nevertheless, the Soviet leaders did emphasize the need to aid 'Spanish democracy' in its battle against the rebels backed by 'international fascist forces'.[151]

In the eyes of Soviet and Comintern leaders, the battle of Madrid was a turning point. On 27 December 1936 the Comintern secretariat prepared new measures to supplement aid to the Spanish Communist Party and the International Brigades.[152] The Spanish question was re-examined by the Praesidium on 28 December. The Hungarian Erno Gero, the speaker, noted the international significance of the defence of Madrid, but chiefly he introduced a note of realism: the last had not been heard from the enemies of the Spanish republic.[153] The future of the war depended on the interaction of many factors, both on the internal and international levels. The speaker did not fail to cite Stalin's personal role and the strength of the International Brigades, but he recognized that the solidarity shown to date was not enough to win the war, especially as the international situation continued to be very delicate.[154]

During the discussion that followed Gero's speech, Pollitt suggested that the Spanish government make efforts to exert pressure on the British government. Though Eden had not responded to the international campaigns, now that German troops had been deployed in Spain his apparent indecision might be turned to account.[155] Dimitrov observed that Britain's apparent flexibility had been due to Madrid's successful resistance, directly due to the efforts of the International Brigades.[156] He was insisting once more on the importance of independent mass initiative and armed resistance. These were for him the keys to changing international power relations, not diplomacy.

Varga publicly voiced a similar thesis. Even as he reminded his readers that war could easily spill out onto the broad stage of Europe, he revived an old idea and applied it to Spain: was not the Spanish civil war proof of the readiness of a global revolutionary proletariat to sacrifice itself to combat fascism and support the USSR? This meant that a war against the USSR would have threatened bourgeois dominion, a reflection that carved a chasm down the middle of the capitalist world – 'a significant portion of the ruling classes' was frightened by the thought of war. Varga was presenting an argument that the interventions Stalin had made in the course of 1936 had neglected. If the USSR possessed the unshakable support of the masses in capitalist countries, it possessed the security it needed in the wake of the Spanish crisis.[157]

But by the end of 1936 the hope that the Brussels congress would initiate a worldwide movement for peace had been replaced by great pessimism.[158] No organized peace movement had appeared in the wake of the congress. Furthermore, the support needed from trade unions and, in particular, the Amsterdam International, had not been consolidated.[159] The Comintern secretariat mourned the failure of 1936's campaign for peace. A wave of pessimism rolled over the press as well. The war in Spain, many were convinced, was pushing Europe beyond the threshold of a new world war. Lapinskii concluded that London was concerned only with finding a *modus vivendi* with Berlin, even though Hitler's plans had become quite apparent as Nazi Germany had deepened its involvement in Spain.[160] He asked bitingly whether the English might perhaps be members of an 'opium smoking club' and suggested that they had returned to 'the old methods of politics and drawing room diplomacy' – clearly when it came to foreign policy they were not inclined to take into account the wishes of the people involved.[161] On the anniversary of Lenin's birth, the same author suggested that the international situation was now dominated by 'the most primitive class instincts'.[162]

The strategic context of the Spanish civil war had significantly changed in a few months. The optimistic communist forecasts on the outcome of the civil war sounded less and less credible. As the fundamental strategies of both sides involved in the struggle shifted, military experts in the USSR began to speak of a 'new phase' of the war: this would lead to the success of the Republicans, but not before mid-1937, and possibly later.[163] The expectation that the war would last for at least another year meant that there would have to be continued vigilance to keep it from spreading outside Spain. At the same time such a forecast also implied that the geopolitical focus of the war threat would remain far from the eastern European theatre. This became a central goal of Soviet policy.

The choices made by the Soviets during the Spanish crisis had upset major aspects of their earlier foreign policy. Wedded to an attitude of judging the conduct of the European powers according to ideological schemes, Stalin was determined to succeed in a two-pronged approach: the latent conflict between international class solidarity and realism in foreign affairs must be eluded; in the wake of Soviet intervention in Spain both a break in relations with the Western powers and a confrontation with Nazi Germany must be avoided. This twofold approach coincided with isolationist retrenchment much more than with collective security. Soviet strategy in Spain had to be tentative, a policy of avoidance – the most sensitive parts of Europe were not to be put at risk. Ercoli was expressing this sort of view when, later, he told the Spanish communists that 'Russia regards her security as a most precious thing. A false move on her part could upset the balance of power and unleash a war in eastern Europe.'[164] These words were a plausible expression of Moscow's perspective.

SPAIN

NOTES

1. *Pravda*, 1 August 1936.
2. K. Radek, 'Dikhanie voiny', *Izvestiia*, 1 August 1936. Curiously, the version of the article which appeared in the Comintern press diverged from the *Izvestiia* text at this particular passage: according to the former, the parallel between the danger of the present war and that of 1914 could be accepted 'so long as one does not claim that the situation is more serious than in the final months before the world war' (*La correspondance internationale*, 8 August 1936). The episode cannot be considered accidental and appears at least to be a sign of serious uncertainty on the matter.
3. K. Radek, 'Podzhigateli voiny gotoviat interventsiiu protiv ispanskoi revoliutsii', *Izvestiia*, 4 August 1936.
4. *Documenti Diplomatici Italiani* (hereafter: DDI), VIII serie, IV, doc. 728, p. 798.
5. *Pravda*, 4 August 1936.
6. See H. Thomas, *The Spanish Civil War* (London: Penguin, 1990), pp. 387–99.
7. Documents on British Foreign Policy (hereafter: DBFP), 2nd series, XVII, doc. 78, pp. 83–5.
8. DVP SSSR, XIX, docs. 242 and 243, pp. 392–4.
9. Ibid., doc. 244, pp. 394–6.
10. *Le journal de Moscou*, 4 August 1936.
11. Ibid., 11 August 1936.
12. Ibid., 18 August 1936.
13. DVP SSSR, XIX, doc. 249, pp. 402–3.
14. AVP RF, f. 05, op. 16, p. 114, d. 1, ll. 160–62.
15. *Izvestiia*, 28 August 1936; *Pravda*, 31 August 1936.
16. DVP SSSR, XIX, doc. 248, p. 401; DVP SSSR, XIX, doc. 256, p. 415.
17. AVP RF, f. 05, op. 16, p. 114, d. 1, l. 174.
18. DVP SSSR, XIX, doc. 239, pp. 389–90. The Anglo-Soviet trade agreement had been concluded on 28 July 1936 (DVP SSSR, XIX, doc. 236, p. 388).
19. Ibid., doc. 253, pp. 408–12.
20. Ibid., p. 412.
21. AVP RF, f. 05, op. 16, p. 114, d. 1, ll. 195–6.
22. P. Lapinskii, 'Kak germanskii fashizm gotovit voinu', *Izvestiia*, 3 September 1936. On Lapinskii's role in the 1920s Soviet debates on international politics, see Di Biagio, *Le origini dell'isolazionismo sovietico*, pp. 153ff.
23. DVP SSSR, XIX, doc. 266, pp. 422–6.
24. AVP RF, f. 05, op. 16, p. 114, d. 1, l. 213.
25. RGASPI, f. 558, op. 11, d. 743, l. 56.
26. RGASPI, f. 17, op. 162, d. 20, l. 78.
27. DVP SSSR, XIX, p. 762.
28. E. H. Carr, *The Comintern and the Spanish Civil War* (London: Macmillan, 1984), p. 15.
29. *Izvestiia*, 1 September 1936.
30. *Pravda*, 16 September 1936; *Leningradskaia pravda*, 26 September 1936.
31. RGASPI, f. 495, op. 18, d. 1101, ll. 14–15.
32. *Dimitrov and Stalin 1934–1943. Letters from the Soviet Archives*, p. 46.
33. G. Dimitrov, *Dnevnik 9 mart 1933–6 februari 1949* (Sofia: Universitetsko izdatelstvo 'Sv. Kliment Okhridski', 1997), p. 114.
34. RGASPI, f. 495, op. 2, d. 232, ll. 205, 216, 220.
35. Ibid., l. 221.
36. B. Grigor'ev, 'Mezhdunarodnyi kongress mira', *Bol'shevik* 19 (1936), pp. 72–82.
37. RGASPI, f. 495, op. 18, d. 1099, l. 28.
38. RGASPI, f. 495, op. 2, d. 232, l. 52.
39. Ibid., ll. 47–8.
40. *Pravda*, 5 September 1936.
41. *Leningradskaia pravda*, 5 September 1936.
42. RGASPI, f. 495, op. 2, d. 232, ll. 112–13.
43. Ibid., l. 115.

44. Ibid., ll. 164–5.
45. Ibid., ll. 13–14.
46. Ibid., l. 23.
47. Ibid., l. 230.
48. Ibid., l. 232.
49. Ibid., ll. 233–4.
50. *Pravda*, 7 August 1936.
51. *Izvestiia*, 21 August 1936.
52. *L'Internationale communiste* 9 (1936).
53. RGASPI, f. 495, op. 2, d. 234, l. 4.
54. Ibid., ll. 17–18.
55. Ibid., ll. 33–4.
56. Ibid., ll. 62–4.
57. RGASPI, f. 495, op. 18, d. 1135, l. 7.
58. Ibid., l. 8.
59. Ibid., ll. 8–9.
60. Ibid., l. 24.
61. Ibid., l. 159.
62. PRO FO 371/20349, N4796/307/38 (21 September 1936).
63. *Le Journal de Moscou*, 15 September 1936.
64. Litvinov, *Vneshniaia politika SSSR*, p. 165.
65. Ibid., p. 170.
66. DVP SSSR, XIX, doc. 287, p. 454.
67. Ibid., doc. 294, pp. 461–2.
68. Ibid., doc. 292, pp. 459–60.
69. Ibid., doc. 296, pp. 463–4. On the London committee, see D. Cattell, *Soviet Diplomacy and the Spanish Civil War* (Berkeley and Los Angeles, CA: University of California Press, 1957).
70. *Izvestiia*, 11 October 1936.
71. PRO FO 371/20568, W14218/2254/41.
72. Archivio del Ministero degli Affari Esteri, Rome (hereafter: ASMAE), Affari politici: Urss, 1936, b. 12, fasc. 2.
73. *Stalinskoe politbiuro v 30-e gody. Sbornik dokumentov* (Moscow: AIRO-XX, 1995), p. 151.
74. Stalin, *Works*, vol. 1, p. 135.
75. *Pravda*, 18 October 1936.
76. *Izvestiia*, 18 October 1936.
77. DVP SSSR, XIX, doc. 327, pp. 513–14.
78. Ibid., doc. 303, pp. 470–71; Ibid., doc. 311, pp. 485–6.
79. Ibid., doc. 329, pp. 515–16; Ibid., doc. 330, p. 516.
80. Ibid., doc. 340, pp. 530–31.
81. Ibid., doc. 360, pp. 570–71.
82. *Le Journal de Moscou*, 3 November 1936.
83. P. Lapinskii, 'Teni "Sviashchennogo soiuza" i prizrak voiny', *Izvestiia*, 7 November 1936.
84. Litvinov, *Vneshniaia politika SSSR*, pp. 172–3.
85. AVP RF, f. 05, op. 16, p. 116, d. 22, ll. 29–32.
86. AVP RF, f. 05, op. 16, p. 117, d. 24, ll. 47–51.
87. Ibid., l. 51.
88. DVP SSSR, XIX, doc. 333, p. 519.
89. Ibid., doc. 342, pp. 533–4.
90. Fondazione Istituto Gramsci, Biografie memorie testimonianze, fasc. Palmiro Togliatti, 4 April 1938. Rozenberg's words were revealed by the same Azana, according to Togliatti's notes from a meeting held on 4 April 1938.
91. DVP SSSR, XIX, doc. 305, pp. 473–6.
92. Ibid., doc. 320, pp. 499-500; ASMAE, Affari politici: Urss, 1936, b. 21, fasc. 1 (21 October 1936).
93. DVP SSSR, XIX, doc. 366, p. 579.

SPAIN

94. Litvinov, *Vneshniaia politika SSSR*, pp. 174–5. GARF, f. 3316, op. 8, d. 16, ll. 25–68.
95. Litvinov, *Vneshniaia politika SSSR*, p. 177.
96. See G. Procacci, 'La coesistenza pacifica. Appunti per la storia di un concetto', in *La politica estera della perestrojka*, edited by L. Sestan (Rome: Editori Riuniti, 1988), p. 42.
97. Litvinov, *Vneshniaia politika SSSR*, pp. 178–81.
98. Ibid., pp. 186–7. In a conversation with Chilston, on 1 December, Litvinov said that he had concrete evidence that a secret agreement had been concluded between Germany and Japan (DVP SSSR, XIX, doc. 390, pp. 621–2).
99. Litvinov, *Vneshniaia politika SSSR*, p. 184.
100. Ibid., pp. 187–8.
101. AVP RF, f. 136, op. 20, p. 167, d. 828, l. 27.
102. Ibid., ll. 27–8.
103. DVP SSSR, XIX, doc. 390, p. 622. DBFP, 2nd series, XVII, doc. 424, p. 610.
104. AVP RF, f. 136, op. 20, p. 167, d. 828, ll. 28–9.
105. AVP RF, f. 05, op. 16, p. 114, d. 1, l. 299.
106. AVP RF, f. 05, op. 16, p. 117, d. 24, l. 106.
107. On Great Britain's policy towards Spain and Eden's positions in the winter 1936–37, see T. Buchanan, *Britain and the Spanish Civil War* (Cambridge: Cambridge University Press, 1997), pp. 54–5.
108. DVP SSSR, XIX, doc. 418, pp. 672–4.
109. AVP RF, f. 05, op. 16, p. 116, d. 22, ll. 38–9.
110. DVP SSSR, XIX, doc. 424, pp. 679–80. DBFP, 2nd series, XVII, doc. 498, pp. 714–15.
111. *Izvestiia*, 11 and 14 December 1936.
112. *Le journal de Moscou*, 15 December 1936.
113. AVP RF, f. 136, op. 20, p. 167, d. 828, l. 34.
114. AVP RF, f. 05, op. 16, p. 114, d. 1, l. 342.
115. DVP SSSR, XIX, doc. 437, pp. 692–3.
116. AVP RF, f. 017a, op. 1, p. 1, d. 4, l. 88.
117. AVP RF, f. 05, op. 17, p. 122, d. 25, l. 9.
118. P. Lapinskii, 'Novaia antanta?', *Izvestiia*, 14 December 1936.
119. P. Lapinskii, 'Angliia i Ispaniia', *Izvestiia*, 5 December 1936.
120. P. Lapinskii, 'Novaia antanta?', *Izvestiia*, 14 December 1936.
121. G. Peri, 'Le problème espagnol et la politique extérieure de la France', *La correspondance internationale*, 12 December 1936.
122. P. Lapinskii, 'Ideologiia i razboi', *Izvestiia*, 1 January 1937.
123. I. Lemin, 'Iaponsko-germanskoe soglashenie', *Mirovoe khoziaistvo i mirovaia politika* 1 (1937), p. 15.
124. N. Maiorskii, 'Ispaniia i vseobshchii mir', *Bol'shevik* 1 (1937), pp. 53, 56.
125. *Le journal de Moscou*, 5 January 1937.
126. *Le journal de Moscou*, 22 December 1936.
127. ASMAE, Affari politici: Urss, 1936, b. 23, fasc. 1. See J. F. Coverdale, *Italian Intervention in the Spanish Civil War* (Princeton: Princeton University Press, 1975), pp. 156 ff.
128. Haslam, *The Soviet Union and the Struggle for Collective Security in Europe*, p. 124.
129. *Izvestiia*, 5 January 1937.
130. See Krivitsky, *J'étais un agent de Staline*, pp. 33–4. See also G. L. Weinberg, *The Foreign Policy of Hitler's Germany: Starting World War II 1937–1939* (New Jersey: Humanities Press, 1994), p. 214.
131. AVP RF, f. 05, op. 17, p. 126, d. 1, l. 17.
132. *Izvestiia TsK KPSS* 3 (1990), pp. 205–13.
133. Ibid., pp. 207–8.
134. Ibid., p. 211.
135. RGASPI, f. 558, op. 11, d. 214, l. 49. Surits submitted Goering's proposal to Litvinov, asking for instructions, in a telegram of 7 December 1936 which is preserved in Stalin's personal papers.
136. DVP SSSR, XX, doc. 17, p. 37.
137. AVP RF, f. 136, op. 21, p. 169, d. 839, l. 2.
138. AVP RF, f. 05, op. 17, p. 126, d. 1, ll. 21–2. Stalin approved Litvinov's proposal; see

'Osobaia missiia Davida Kandelaki', *Voprosy istorii* 4–5 (1991), p. 152.
139. RGASPI, f. 77, op. 1, d. 619, ll. 35–8.
140. *Izvestiia*, 30 November 1936.
141. RGASPI, f. 77, op. 1, d. 626, ll. 66, 73; *Leningradskaia pravda*, 23 November 1936.
142. *Leningradskaia pravda*, 1 December 1936.
143. G. Dimitrov, 'Narodnyi front bor'by protiv fashizma i voiny', *Pravda*, 7 November 1936.
144. *L'Internationale communiste* 10–11 (1936), pp. 1245–61.
145. Ibid., pp. 1251–2.
146. Ibid., p. 1257.
147. RGASPI, f. 495, op. 18, d. 1117, ll. 61–3.
148. Ibid., ll. 6–8.
149. RGASPI, f. 495, op. 73, d. 15a, ll. 2–4.
150. RGASPI, f. 495, op. 12, d. 92, l. 108.
151. See Carr, *The Comintern and the Spanish Civil War*, pp. 86–7.
152. RGASPI, f. 495, op. 18, d. 1132, l. 44.
153. RGASPI, f. 495, op. 2, d. 241, ll. 9–10.
154. Ibid., ll. 36, 40, 46.
155. Ibid., l. 50.
156. Ibid., ll. 69–70.
157. E. Varga, '1936 god: itogi i perspektivy', *Mirovoe khoziaistvo i mirovaia politika* 3 (1937), p. 28.
158. RGASPI, f. 495, op. 12, d. 125, ll. 3–7.
159. Ibid., l. 61.
160. P. Lapinskii, 'Germanskii otvet', *Izvestiia*, 8 January 1937.
161. P. Lapinskii, 'Klub kurilshikov opiuma?', *Izvestiia*, 12 January 1937.
162. P. Lapinskii, 'Velikaia proverka', *Izvestiia*, 21 January 1937. For a similar argument, see G. Peri, 'Le Foreign Office au secours de Franco', *La correspondance internationale*, 20 February 1937.
163. A. Golubev, 'Pered novym etapom grazhdanskoi voiny v Ispanii', *Izvestiia*, 16 December 1936; idem, 'Novyi etap bor'by v Ispanii', *Izvestiia*, 20 January 1937; *Bol'shevik* 1 (1937), pp. 51–2.
164. Thomas, *The Spanish Civil War*, p. 361.

3

The Internal Crisis

TOWARDS THE 'TOTAL SECURITY STATE'

By incessantly stressing the menace of 'capitalist encirclement', the official propaganda machine controlled by the Stalinist leadership connected external threats to the outbreak of the Great Terror. Twenty years after the Revolution, the official diagnosis was that an irreversible capitalist pathology had served as the vector for both the collapse of postwar order and the eruption of war. Only by erasing all demarcation between state and society and by crushing every trace of an internal fifth column – a conspiracy aimed at drawing the country into the catastrophe of war – could the USSR find a way out. This basic outline of the relationship between the external world and the internal regime was to remain the core of Soviet political culture right up to the death of Stalin. But while we find a broadly unified outlook on international politics in the records of the late 1930s, contradictions and hints of divergent perspectives revealed themselves in the twisted manipulations of official vocabulary, whether uttered in public or whispered in private.

In fact, as we look more carefully, a rather complex picture emerges, far more complex than the classic interpretation of the connections between the Great Terror and Stalinist foreign policy. Boris Nikolaevskii and, later, George Kennan suggested that the purges had been aimed at the opponents – both actual and imagined – of an agreement with Hitler.[1] Evgenii Gnedin's memoirs corroborated this view and provided much of the background to the pact with Nazi Germany, beginning with the period following Kirov's assassination.[2] The most sophisticated version of this thesis is that of Robert C. Tucker, who uses evidence drawn from the show trials, especially the last one, to show how a rapprochement with Nazi Germany began.[3] But this classic interpretation presumes a consistent foreign-policy design behind Stalin's moves during the Terror, and such consistency is not borne out by the archival documentation at our disposal. Furthermore this interpretation fails to explain why Stalin chose to concentrate all foreign-policy management and decision-making power in his own hands only in 1939, two years into the mass purges. Teddy J. Uldricks's picture of a 'dysfunctional' Terror still seems to offer the most convincing explanation,[4] even in the field of foreign policy. Although there is evidence of conflict between those charged with shaping Soviet foreign policy, the purges lashed out indiscriminately and lacked a fully defined political aim. However, the impact of the purges on Soviet foreign policy should not be overlooked. As Oleg Khlevniuk has argued, the Terror had a significant foreign-policy aspect, specifically in terms of the relationship between the domestic context and the foreign conduct of Stalinism.[5] In particular, the international tension raised by the Spanish crisis grew simultaneously and interacted with the development of the purges. Jonathan Haslam has highlighted the growing isolationism of Soviet policy in 1937–38.[6] And the main outcome of the purges appears to have been to ensure Stalin and his circle untrammeled discretion over the field of foreign policy.

On 25 September 1936, Stalin and Zhdanov sent a telegram to the other members of the Politburo, recommending the nomination of 'comrade Ezhov' to head the NKVD and noting with grim dissatisfaction that there had been 'a four-year delay' in 'unmasking the Trotskyist–Zinov'evist bloc'.[7] The official announcement of Nikolai Ezhov's appointment appeared one day later.[8] On 29 September a Politburo resolution launched a wave of repression against 'counter-revolutionary elements', initiating a sequence that would climax publicly in the second Moscow trial at the beginning of 1937 and in the February–March plenum.[9] Even before Stalin's and Zhdanov's telegram, Radek and Grigorii Piatakov – the former, as we know, the most authoritative commentator on international affairs in the Soviet press, the latter one of the key figures in forging economic links with Germany – were arrested after having been under observation by Ezhov for some time.[10]

The wave of repression involved also Bukharin.[11] Along with Aleksei Rykov, he had been publicly cleared on 10 September 1936, after Andrei Vyshinskii himself was forced to admit that the 'confessions' extorted from Grigorii Sokol'nikov, their principal accuser, were insufficient grounds for prosecution.[12] But this did not put an end to the persecution of those who had in the past associated with the 'rightist opposition'. When the Politburo issued a set of instructions at the end of September, it specifically included 'previously suspended' cases among those to be considered in the movement aimed at eliminating the Trotskyites, 'the organized and political vanguard of the international bourgeoisie'.[13] By December 1936, when a plenum of the Central Committee was convened, Bukharin was once again in Ezhov's sights.[14]

If Bukharin leapt to defend himself, he never questioned the necessity of the purges. He pointed out that the attempts of fascist spies to infiltrate the state's headquarters had to be forcefully quashed, although he denied that he himself had anything to do with such vile manoeuvres – had he not travelled to Paris as a representative of Soviet foreign policy? He even maintained that, while in 1928 his attitude towards Stalin might have been less than admiring, that had changed as he had become aware of 'where all world events are moving' and of 'the significance of the power and centralization of our dictatorship'.[15]

Bukharin himself connected the Terror with the prospect of war:

> I am happy that all this has been uncovered and that our agencies are in a position to expose so much rottenness before the outbreak of war so that we can emerge victorious, because had we missed it at the outset and caught it only in the midst of the war, this could have led to an extraordinary and terrible defeat for the entire socialist cause.[16]

The paradox here is that Bukharin was handing the masters of Terror an excellent justification for perpetuating their policies. He voiced a rational explanation for the mounting wave of violence now directly menacing the Soviet élites and, at the same time, he helped legitimate the idea that war was inevitable. Quite significantly, Stalin repeated Bukharin's argument shortly thereafter, in a note he wrote in the margin of the text of Molotov's report to the February–March 1937 plenum of the Central Committee. Commenting on Molotov's statement that those who departed from the Soviet party were 'incapable of struggling against the bourgeoisie' and preferred 'to link their fate with that of the bourgeoisie and not of the working class', Stalin wrote: 'That's good. It would be worse if they were to leave during war.'[17]

The second trial held between 23 and 30 January 1937, centred on spying activities said to have been carried out on behalf of the Germans and the Japanese and aimed at unleashing an 'anti-Soviet war' which would involve the USSR in mortal combat with Germany.[18] Stalin's address to the crucial plenum of February–March, delivered on 3 March and published in *Pravda* on 29 March, provided the key to his attitude. In this speech an extreme concept of security was affirmed, one which had emerged in Soviet policy during the previous years. The dictator drew special attention to the activities of 'spies' and 'agents of foreign states' in the USSR, systematically connecting them to the activities of 'Trotskyites', and he solemnly invoked the concept of 'capitalist encirclement'. Just as he had done at the time of the 'Shakhty affair' almost ten years earlier, Stalin declared that this formula was not 'a hollow phrase', but referred to 'a very real and hostile phenomenon': over the Soviet state hung a sword of Damocles, suspended by the thinnest of fraying threads. Only the hopelessly naive could believe in permanent 'good relations', even among 'bourgeois states'. Even as such states roundly declared their undying mutual devotion, it could be demonstrated 'as two plus two make four' that they 'sent their spies behind each other's lines'. Since Napoleon's time this had been the norm in relations among capitalist states. Since such practices were common in states with declared solidarity, it took little imagination to see how much more common it would be when foreign states contended with the USSR.[19]

His indictment of 'Trotskyism' and his commitment to identifying the agents involved in a mortal struggle, taking place behind the scenes, led Stalin to censure Radek and the others whom he accused of encouraging 'the struggle for war against the policy of peace'. He warned Party members that 'economic successes' could not defeat 'capitalist encirclement' and urged them to abandon the illusion that 'class warfare cannot be extended beyond the borders of the USSR'.[20]

Nothing Stalin was saying came as a surprise. Bolsheviks had long since learned to identify 'capitalist encirclement' with the conditions of an uneasy armed truce. Still, the dictator was far more emphatic about this threat than he had ever been in the calculated doses of alarm he had alternated with reassurances over the previous ten years of his sallies into international policy. Although Stalin's continued insistence on the internal troubles faced by the capitalist regimes and on the contradictions inherent to capitalist interstate relations made an impending attack on the socialist state seem unlikely, this time nothing short of a dramatically broadened role for the police and a new wave of political repression could provide security for the USSR. Stalin was obviously exploiting external conditions to break the back of the Soviet bureaucracy and dismantle the old oligarchy; whatever his motives, his words and actions were bound to affect the USSR's relations with the outside world. The fact is that a political culture was cumulatively evolving in the constraints of established doctrinal principles.

Zhdanov took up his master's refrain and repeated much of it verbatim – 'capitalist encirclement' and 'Trotskyism' were the principal elements in a diabolical plan to destroy the Soviet state. Class warfare was growing both within the USSR and in capitalist states: it was this that had 'galvanized' what remained of the 'hostile classes' in the USSR.[21] Molotov argued that the USSR was 'competing with the capitalist system' and that the measures 'which capitalist countries are taking to prepare for the new war' attested to the bitterness of the struggle.[22] It would seem that in Moscow all foreign states were beginning to look the same.

A month after the appearance of Stalin's report the new pressures being exerted from above were expressed in an intervention penned by Manuil'skii. The Comintern official stated that 'the struggle of the world of capitalism against the world of socialism has not ceased and will not cease while these two systems exist'. He warned that the capitalist states were rearming, 'not only to fight each other' but also to overthrow 'the socialist system in the USSR'. The emergence and advancement of fascism proved 'the extreme bitterness of the contradictions between the worlds of capitalism and of socialism'; if none of the fascist regimes had attacked yet, it was only because those regimes were 'not yet ready'.[23]

After presenting an outline of the international picture developed along rigid class lines, Manuil'skii reproached those who imagined that capitalism might be speedily dismantled. Such foolish forecasts underestimated the strength and capability of 'organized capitalism' and social democracy; this was as bad as underestimating the fascist threat and the danger of war. The fantasies of catastrophists were so far from reality that while capitalism was 'a regime historically condemned to extinction' and destined to undergo 'inevitable ruin', nevertheless even as ruin neared 'there have been, there are and there will be temporary improvements'. Indisputably the capitalist states were in the midst of an 'economic revival', even though the basic tendency towards a new economic crisis remained. Dreaming of the downfall of capitalism, as well as imagining that everything would be simplified if the situation in capitalist societies was 'aggravated', was in fact unhealthy if it contributed to war mongering.[24]

This was orthodox Stalinism: Bolshevik doctrine applied to a political realm conceived in the starkest reality. Manuil'skii's assessment of fascist regimes faithfully echoed such guidelines. Resoundingly he attacked any tendency to underestimate fascism's resilience:

> It is said that the heroic struggle of the Spanish people against fascism has had the effect of bringing fascist governments to their senses, that Guadalajara too has cooled the martial ardour of German and Italian interventionists, that in their clashes with the armed Spanish people these last have begun to believe that they have not prepared adequately for a hardfought war and that their own fascist regime may be suffering from internal weakness . . . It is said that discontent is growing on a massive scale not only in Germany and Italy, but among the popular masses in Poland as well . . . It is said that even in Japan the situation is not tranquil . . . There are those who conclude that given such instability behind the lines, fascist governments can neither initiate nor prosecute a war. This is not true: whatever instability fascist governments are struggling with on the domestic front they remain capable of initiating a war. Given the current situation they can initiate and pursue a war even if they can not win it . . . Furthermore, it is said that during the last few months the fascist movements in all

capitalist countries have been in decline, that the victory of the Spanish people will be a severe blow to the prestige of fascism and will contribute to an even more powerful resurgence of the anti-fascist movement. All this is true. But it would be wrong to conclude that the danger of war will therefore subside. For the exploiting classes, war is a means to strengthen reaction and to give a new impetus to the fascist movement.[25]

Manuil'skii would have his comrades awaken to the truth, and he poured cold water on the fires of militant internationalism. However tempting it was to foresee an imminent catastrophe within Hitler's regime, to do so would be a great mistake. This outlook was essentially based on the Soviet need to avoid the entanglements of international relations. On the other hand, Manuil'skii did not dispute the basis of the Soviets' 'catastrophe culture'; fascism was perceived as an epiphenomenon of capitalism, immortal as long as its host still breathed.

At the beginning of June, when a barrage of purges assailed all sectors of the Soviet state, Zhdanov cited the heroic Spanish Republicans as an example worthy of Soviet emulation. If a people without revolutionary experience could successfully resist fascism, the people of the USSR should be all the more tenacious, and might learn a lesson from the compactness exhibited by the Spanish.[26] But Zhdanov did not limit himself to Spain. He took in the entire international situation through the lens of the decline of Western democracy. He saw Britain and France, the guardians of 'what remains of bourgeois democracy', as paralyzed by the thought that at any moment fascism might deliver a death blow:

> I think that the great powers, much as they boast about their greatness, can do nothing useful for the cause of peace. Because their manoeuvres have been so half-hearted the fascists have become less and less interested in peace and more and more inclined to aggression.[27]

As did others among Stalin's supporters, Zhdanov displayed here a tendency to belittle the idea of collective security. This tendency was the expression of an integralist trend that linked doctrinaire ideas, xenophobia and anti-Westernism, and was becoming increasingly central to Stalinism.

THE ATTACK ON TUKHACHEVSKII

At the plenum held in February–March 1937, Molotov vigorously rebutted Voroshilov's suggestions that the military had never been infiltrated by spies and insisted that 'as far as the military institutions are concerned, the question is very large, and though we will not be able to investigate the situation right now, later a thorough review will be necessary'. Subsequent events were to confirm Molotov's words. The turning point came on 21 April 1937 when Ezhov told Stalin, Molotov and Voroshilov that he had heard from 'foreign sources' that a terrorist attack was being prepared against Tukhachevskii. It was to take place the following month while the celebrated military commander was on a visit in London. The following day the Politburo voted to cancel the marshal's trip.[28]

In fact, the process of uprooting and publicly displaying a 'military conspiracy' now began. According to a pre-arranged plan, manipulated confessions were extracted from two military officials previously arrested and then denounced by Radek during the trial of January 1937, V.M. Primakov and V.K. Putna.[29] Both offered carefully rehearsed confessions which cast Tukhachevskii and Trotsky as co-conspirators in a plot to overthrow the Soviet government. The first arrests served to confirm the essentials of this story. Tukhachevskii was relieved of his position as deputy commissar of defence on 10 May and arrested on 22 May. Two days later, after a special Politburo resolution, he was expelled from the Party together with Ian Rudzutak, the vice-president of the Sovnarkom (Soviet Narodnykh Kommisarov, or Council of People's Commissars). On 28 and 29 May commandants Iona Iakir and Ieronym Uborevich, like Tukhachevskii members of the Party Central Committee, were arrested.[30]

Stalin and his supporters used the purge to assert political control over the Red Army. The suicide of Ian Gamarnik, head of the army's political administration, on 31 May made things easier.[31] Of the nine military commanders who served on the Party's Central Committee, only two would survive – Voroshilov and Semen Budennyi. Thirty of the 36 senior commanders elected at the 8th Soviet Congress in December 1936 would disappear from the scene; the same fate would overtake 98 members (out of 108) of the Military Council in the Defence Commissariat. The merciless pursuit of the 'enemies of the people' in the Red Army that took place during the second half of 1937 and the first half of 1938 swept away thousands of military cadres 'from the highest to the lowest rank', to use Voroshilov's words.[32] The damage done to the command structure of the army was incalculable.

Stalin's role was certainly decisive.[33] Archival documentation confirms John Erickson's opinion that the dictator carefully orchestrated a plot to deprive the Russian military of all autonomy.[34] We know that on 1 May 1937 he spoke to Voroshilov of 'enemies' hiding in the military hierarchy. On 13 May, he met the recently cashiered Tukhachevskii; what was said remains unknown, but we can well imagine. During the last ten days of May, Stalin presided over the principal measures taken against the 'military conspiracy', and he supervised the drafting of resolutions ostensibly drawn up by the Politburo.[35] We know that he personally proposed to the Politburo the purges of Tukhachevskii and Rudzutak from the party and authorized the NKVD to handle the entire affair. He received a unanimously favourable response.[36] But it was during the joint session of the Politburo and the military members of the Defence Commissariat of the USSR (at that time already reduced by 20 per cent by the purges), held on 1–4 June 1937, that Stalin really shone.

On that occasion, Voroshilov read a report on the 'counter-revolutionary conspiracy' in the Red Army uncovered by the NKVD. He outlined a hypothesis in which the 'conspirators' had worked closely with the German high command, and noted that, since he had received no warning from the Soviet military command of the existence of 'conspirators' in the armed forces, there had been no 'vigilance' at all. He also spoke of friction between Tukhachevskii and himself which had begun the year before. Apparently at that time Tukhachevskii had accused Voroshilov of seizing and monopolizing authority over all political decisions, only to withdraw the accusation in front of the Politburo. Nevertheless, other prominent military commandants like Iakir and Uborevich, and also the political commissar Ian Gamarnik had apparently been far less accommodating towards the defence commissar.[37] This was one more strand in the complex network of internal tensions within the Soviet oligarchy now being dramatically displayed. These tensions were bound to have repercussions for Soviet foreign policy.

In his intervention of 2 June, Stalin delivered his verdict: 'we are faced with a political and military plot against Soviet power instigated and financed by German fascists'. Along with the well-known military names he accused Trotsky, Bukharin, Rykov, Rudzutak, Avel' Enukidze and Lev Karakhan, the Soviet ambassador to Turkey.[38] No doubt when he fingered a group of leaders already suffering from earlier repressive measures, the dictator intended to deny the existence of any institutional conflict between party leaders and military chiefs. However, while he depicted Tukhachevskii and other military officers as 'German spies . . . marionettes and puppets in the hands of the Reichswehr', Stalin also emphasized the links between the affair and international policy. He declared:

> This plot is therefore not so much internal as external, not so much an indigenously developed tactic as a German Reichswehr policy. They wanted to make the USSR into a second Spain and had found

and employed police spies who were working to that end. That is the situation.[39]

Stalin's condemnation of the attempt by the 'conspirators' to turn the USSR into 'another Spain' is significant from many aspects. It can be viewed as an allusion to an internal 'fifth column', which was being manipulated to sweep away Soviet power. Tukhachevskii was publicly accused, among other things, of trying to become a sort of Soviet Franco.[40] But what were Stalin's real convictions and what did he say just to exploit the international scene for his own purposes? Perhaps he believed in the scenario he presented. Stalin considered the violent repression he was organizing to be the only means to the internal consolidation of his regime in the prospect of war. Though this actually meant a destabilization of national security, apparently he maintained that there was no alternative.

Clearly, the echo of the Spanish events had a major influence on Stalin.[41] Stalin seems to have felt that Spain would serve as a sort of general rehearsal for the expansion of fascism and for future European wars. Though 1914 remained central to his thinking about international conflict, he also had in mind a second model: the Russian civil war and the intervention of Western powers in 1918–19. The internal weaknesses of the regime and of Soviet system rendered such a scenario the most serious possible threat to the USSR, because of the implied unity of the enemy front.

The Red Army's official newspaper ran admonitory editorials on 9 and 10 June 1937. They contained ominous accusations against military commanders who neglected to take appropriate measures to protect military secrets as well as against the army's political administration for its failure to produce a sufficient volume of propaganda on international matters.[42] On 11 June, Tukhachevskii and the other military commanders were accused of high treason.[43] On the same day, they were convicted in a trial held behind close doors. Stalin also signed an edict directed to regional and Republican party committees, calling for meetings of workers and soldiers where the need for repressive measures would be explained.[44] On 12 June the condemned military leaders were executed. Two days later, Voroshilov publicly announced that during the joint civil–military meeting of 1–4 June the 'counter-revolutionary' actions of a 'fascist military organization' had been condemned and that on 11 June the members of this organization, whose names were listed, had been judged spies and traitors by the Supreme Tribunal of the USSR. These criminals had been 'directly linked to fascist bourgeois countries' and would have sabotaged the efforts of the Red Army had war broken out.[45]

The Tukhachevskii affair was surrounded by veiled intrigues and a complex web of misinformation woven by both the German and the Soviet secret services.[46] Among the false leads disseminated by the Germans was a letter signed with the name of the *Pravda* correspondent in Berlin, in which Tukhachevskii was linked to German military officers.[47] We know too that in January and May 1937, President Eduard Beneš of Czechoslovakia communicated to Moscow details of a plot involving Soviet military officers and plans for a coup d'état which was to pave the way for rapprochement with Germany.[48]

The record of a conversation between the Czech president and Sergei Aleksandrovskii, the Soviet ambassador to Prague, on 3 July, sheds further light on these issues. Beneš affirmed that the unmasking of a Soviet military conspiracy had not surprised him – indeed, he had been 'expecting it for some time'. He confided to Aleksandrovskii that, beginning in January, he had received 'indirect signals' regarding a 'strong connection' between the top echelons of the Reichswehr and of the Red Army and he pointed out that he had alluded to this in an earlier conversation with the ambassador; he had surmised a possible rapprochement between the USSR and Germany.[49] Then Beneš indulged in an extended digression. During his conversations with Litvinov, he had become vaguely aware of an ongoing struggle between Soviet 'realists' and 'radicals' – since 1932 the two sides had debated whether the USSR ought to cooperate with European democracies. While he did not believe that foreign spies had penetrated deeply into Russia, he was confident that someone within the regime was involved in an effort to change it. In his opinion, Tukhachevskii was pro-German, and imagined that his country could survive only by fighting alongside Germany against the rest of Europe. Beneš added that when Tukhachevskii visited France he was alleged to have spoken of an alliance between the USSR and Hitler's Germany as a 'new Rapallo'.[50] So Beneš was overjoyed to witness the consolidation of 'Stalin's regime', in his view a fine thing for Europe, and essential to the security of Czechoslovakia.

If President Beneš appears to have naively repeated a whole set of carefully fabricated leaks concerning the military 'plot', he was not the only one. In a conversation with Robert Coulondre on 23 June, Potemkin recalled that some months earlier Edouard Daladier had confidentially informed Moscow that Red Army chiefs enjoyed close relations with certain representatives of the German high command whose aim was 'a fascist coup d'état in the USSR and the formation of an anti-French alliance'.[51] Beneš's belief that Tukhachevskii was oriented towards Germany was shared by many in diplomatic circles at that time. For example, Nicolae Titulescu, the former Rumanian prime minister, had noted the frequent and quite tactless comments Tukhachevskii made about the superiority of Germany's army over France's.[52] The Italian ambassador to Moscow informed Rome of a rumour that Tukhachevskii, Krestinskii and others had petitioned Stalin to limit the power of the police, ameliorate the material well-being of the people and improve relations with Germany.[53] Unfortunately, none of these records left by foreign observers dates from before the 'plot' was publicly exposed – no doubt they were indebted to the orthodox explanation.

Well before the 'conspirators' were condemned there was much speculation about a sudden change in Soviet foreign policy. Beginning early in 1937, British diplomats had begun to anticipate a warming of relations between Germany and the USSR.[54] The German high command was said to have entertained high hopes that the Soviet leaders would initiate a move towards 'nationalism'.[55] According to Italian diplomatic sources, Surits was said to have confided to Attolico that the USSR still hoped for détente with Germany.[56] However, in April, Litvinov asked the Soviet chargé d'affaires in Paris and the Soviet ambassador in Prague to squash rumours of a possible German–Russian rapprochement.[57] In a conversation with Chilston, he denied that these rumours had any basis and insinuated that they had been bred in German diplomatic circles.[58] The loose talk appears to have essentially been a consequence of the suspicions roused in the West by Kandelaki's mission. Hitler's negative attitude ruled out any real basis for a rapprochement between the USSR and Nazi Germany.[59]

Additionally, some reckoned Tukhachevskii to have been pro-French. This view was expressed by Chilston well before the outbreak of the 'affair' and was, above all, espoused by General Köstring, the German military attaché in Moscow.[60] Iakir had also promoted military collaboration with France.[61] But whether the Soviet officers generally favoured Germany or France is not the point. After all, everything we know about Tukhachevskii's public interventions runs contrary to the theory that he smiled upon rapprochement with Germany; in particular, his 1935 article, which as we have seen Stalin felt obliged to redraft. Whatever attention he showed Germany seems to have been inspired in part by the desire to learn from a superior military machine but was largely the result of worrying that Germany might attack the USSR. From this point of view, Beneš's testimony would seem to be relevant. Although his thinking was based on unreliable facts, composed of a combination of dubious information, personal impressions and fantasies born of national interests, it reflected one genuine fact: a conflict had emerged at the top tiers of Soviet foreign policy-making. Such conflict was likewise mentioned in a well-known contemporary document, the 'letter from an old Bolshevik'.[62]

A significant document is Tukhachevskii's 'declaration', held in the

NKVD archives. In this self-indictment we find a detailed explanation of the 'plan for defeat' prepared by the 'plotters'.[63] Since we can neither verify nor refute this document, we can only maintain some reservations about its authenticity. Even if we accept its basic reliability, the document should be read carefully, since it bears the marks of the inquisitors' intervention and was clearly produced under duress. Nevertheless, the wealth of technical details and the accuracy of strategic scenarios make it likely that Tukhachevskii was the principal author.

Tukhachevskii's 'declaration' contains a number of self-exculpatory arguments. Where a traitor might have confessed his attempts to undermine the Red Army's defences, the marshal included reflections calculated to shore up his reputation. In April 1936, immediately subsequent to the Rhineland crisis, Tukhachevskii had collaborated with Iakir and Uborevich to draw up a strategic plan for war with Poland. According to the 'declaration', the military equipment and the disposition of Soviet forces along the Belorussian front, as presented in the April 1936 plan, were inadequate to the challenge of an alliance between Poland and Germany, and would probably have exposed the Soviet armed forces to a deadly blow from eastern Prussia or from the northern parts of Poland. This admission seems to have been the inquisitors' main objective. It transformed the outline of a normal operating plan into an attempt at high treason, a 'plan for defeat'. But Tukhachevskii included the following passage in his declaration:

> I repeat once again that the effective operating plan corresponds to existing forces and pertains only to a war against Poland alone ... It is rather difficult to respond to the question concerning a plan of action against the combination of German and Polish forces. I think this problem needs serious clarification.[64]

In other words, it is not clear whether the plan drawn up in April 1936 had originally involved an alliance between Germany and Poland, and if so, whether the proposed measures represented the definitive view of the high command. To make things more complicated an essential part of the supposed operations had been conceived with the knowledge of the political leaders. The evidence suggests that on 25 February 1935 Tukhachevskii had sent Voroshilov the text of a speech in which he proposed serious modifications to the strategic plans already drafted for war in the West – the principal topic of the talk was the destruction of the Polish state. In his accompanying letter, Tukhachevskii invited Voroshilov to consider the consequences of the current anti-Soviet orientation of German foreign policy, and he maintained that the prospect of a war between the Red Army and the allied forces of

Germany and Poland was quite realistic.[65] The menace represented by an alliance between Germany and Poland remained Tukhachevskii's main concern throughout 1936.[66]

In the 'declaration', three different German gambits were considered: a move against Leningrad, considered militarily significant for Germany but not economically tempting; an attack against Belorussia, conceivable only as part of a master plan aimed at the complete destruction of the USSR, a notion the author himself deemed 'completely imaginary'; and a drive into the Ukraine, considered most likely for economic reasons. Since Tukhachevskii seems to have discarded all but the Belorussian scenario by the time he drew up the plan of April 1936, his confession might have addressed this omission. But the document was somewhat equivocal. Since an attack on the Ukraine would undoubtedly have precipitated a protracted conflict, and since 'a long war with the USSR would undoubtedly draw both France and Britain into war with Germany', as the author of the 'declaration' maintained, the outcome was exceedingly hard to predict.[67] The complications inevitably arising from a German offensive in the Ukraine made it 'very likely' that Germany 'will try to conquer Czechoslovakia and Romania before attacking us' – thereby building a military and economic base from which to launch the far more demanding campaign against the Soviet Union.[68] This complex strategic picture makes the 'plan for defeat' seem far less credible. It is not without significance that an essential component of such strategic complexity was a foreign policy factor – the prospect of an alliance between the USSR and the Western powers against Germany.

NARKOMINDEL PARALYSIS

Following the plenum convened in February–March 1937, Western diplomatic circles began to buzz with speculations about Litvinov's imminent political demise. The most pessimistic forecasts were bolstered by an odd episode. In a letter published in *Izvestiia* on 23 April, 'engineer Khvatkov' reminded his comrades that the crew members of the two ships destroyed by Spanish Nationalists had yet to return home; already several months had elapsed since the sinking of the *Komsomol* and the *Smidovich*, and 'Khvatkov' wanted to know what Litvinov had been doing to expedite the sailors' homecoming.[69] In a response published the following day, the commissar explained that since the Soviet government did not recognize the nationalists as legitimate belligerents the matter was so complicated as to defy speedy resolution.[70]

This comment inspired an immediate diplomatic uproar. The British were confident that Litvinov would soon be cashiered and replaced with

Potemkin, now back in Moscow after his stint in Paris.[71] Potemkin was said to have told Muenzenberg that Litvinov was getting ready to retire.[72] A month before the letter of 'Khvatkov' appeared in *Izvestiia*, Litvinov had spoken to Rosso about the fate of the Soviet naval crews, and by the end of April Rosso was stating that Litvinov had led him to understand 'that the matter is important to him'.[73]

Litvinov also told Rosso that things were degenerating in the Soviet Union, and a general xenophobia took the form of NKVD harassment of foreign citizens.[74] If Litvinov was clearly aware of this, he seemed not overly concerned by the letter of 'Khvatkov' – this is seen from his own letter to Stalin, in which he requested advice on whether to respond.[75] In the spring and summer of 1937 the commissar suffered no direct attacks – the attack moved first against his support in the Narkomindel structure.

In his conclusions at the 1937 February–March plenum, Molotov made no mention of the Narkomindel. But a resolution had been passed calling for an investigation into the 'lessons of sabotage' that involved also the Narkomindel.[76] If the purge of the Narkomindel did not reap as many heads as did the Party and army purges, it was still massive. Between 1937 and 1939, the old generation of diplomats, trained under Chicherin and Litvinov, gave way to a new generation of Stalinists who by the early 1940s had fully consolidated their position – these new men would dominate Soviet foreign policy for a long time.[77] In the spring of 1937 the first group of Narkomindel officials was arrested. The best-known victim was deputy foreign commissar Krestinskii, arrested in June. Meanwhile, a prominent diplomat like Rozenberg had disappeared, after having been recalled to Moscow on 19 February 1937.[78] What befell Rozenberg after his return to Moscow remains unclear.[79] A similar fate befell Antonov-Ovseenko, recalled to Moscow from Barcelona in August 1937.[80]

Though the Tukhachevskii affair did not involve Litvinov personally, it had serious repercussions for the Narkomindel. Beginning in June 1937 the diplomatic ranks suffered mass purges, anti-foreign incidents became routine and the government instituted a series of measures aimed at isolating the Soviet Union from the outside world. Already at the beginning of May, Potemkin had notified Surits of new policies aimed at 'drastically reducing the number of foreign citizens living in the USSR'.[81] In the following months, the number of foreign consulates on Soviet soil was greatly reduced.[82] Such actions made things far more difficult for the Narkomindel by severely restricting its scope of operations. One can speak of a real inertness in Soviet foreign policy during this period.

Over the course of spring 1937, relations between the USSR and Western democracies plunged. In the face of a protracted Spanish crisis political relations had deteriorated and a military collaboration between

Moscow and Paris was beginning to seem unlikely. *Izvestiia* carried articles and letters accusing France of having forged a peace based exclusively on an awareness of its neighbours' arsenals; if the USSR pursued the latest in the 'techniques of modern war', it was really for the sake both of 'defending our borders and of defending peace in general'.[83] If Litvinov's talks with Blum and Yvon Delbos held in Paris in May were lauded by the Soviets as a reaffirmation of 'collective security',[84] regular contacts at the highest level of military leadership were never established. In fact, during the talks Litvinov coldly notified Delbos that such contacts 'can be of no more interest to us than to France'.[85]

Potemkin reckoned Paris's dissatisfaction with the Franco-Soviet pact had risen to unprecedented heights.[86] Certainly, the Tukhachevskii affair had not improved the situation. Potemkin tried to convince Coulondre that by crushing the treasonous 'plot' the Soviet government had demonstrated its commitment to resisting those elements within its own ranks who favoured an alliance with Hitler's Germany. As to the resilience of the Soviet regime, in Potemkin's view it had been proven by identifying, exposing and foiling the 'plot'.[87]

But Soviet diplomats could not always muster the cynicism necessary to parrot this official propaganda. They knew full well that Soviet credibility had suffered. When, on 21 June 1937, Litvinov commented to Surits that he had arrived in France at a 'very unpropitious' moment (Surits had recently moved to Paris from Berlin), he went on to mention both the diplomatic manoeuvres aimed at reviving the 'pact of four' and the Tukhachevskii affair.[88] In one of his first comments on the general state of Franco-Soviet affairs, Surits suggested that the French treated their relations with the USSR only as a device for impeding Soviet rapprochement with Germany and not 'as part of a general strategy for combating the German threat'.[89] At the same time he indirectly admitted the damage the purges had wrought upon the USSR's reputation observing, without further comment, that many viewed the USSR as a country in the grip of a serious internal crisis. All one could do was hope that the impact of the new Soviet constitution on Western public opinion would improve the situation.[90]

The crisis surrounding the pact with France directly affected the east European theatre, mainly the USSR's other ally, Czechoslovakia. We know that on the heels of the Tukhachevskii affair Beneš never missed an opportunity of reassuring Stalin of Czech support. However, on 30 April, even before the Soviet military purges became public knowledge, Aleksandrovskii notified Litvinov that the Czechs had lost 'more than 50 per cent of their earlier confidence' in the effectiveness of mutual aid pacts; should the alliance collapse he reckoned a new agreement between Czechoslovakia and Germany eminently conceivable.[91] What he was hearing from Prague convinced Potemkin that the Czechs were ready 'to capitulate to Berlin', and the French were not far behind.[92] This state of affairs was all the more painful since it had become apparent that Polish foreign policy would not change – the Poles would maintain their relations with Germany, work to undermine France's alliances and above all do everything possible to isolate the USSR from the rest of Europe.[93]

If it seemed obvious that the future of Soviet strategy lay in eastern Europe, events in Spain continued to occupy most of the USSR's diplomatic energies. In an address given in London on 13 March to the Congress of Peace and Friendship with the USSR, Maiskii had drawn connections between the 'iron-fist' philosophy of international relations and the 'impotence of the League of Nations and of the idea of collective security'. But diplomacy need not be of the 'iron-fist' sort, and certainly, said Maiskii, the USSR did not advocate or practice 'a policy of isolation'. Europe was at a 'turning point' and it would soon be necessary to make 'the final choice' between strengthening the League of Nations and limiting the expansion of war. The USSR was waiting to see what path the peaceful countries of Europe would take.[94]

On this occasion, more than at the time of the Rhineland crisis, Maiskii's attempt to deny the existence of an isolationist policy was largely contradicted by events and would be to an even greater degree once Stalin's report to the February–March plenum was made public. Maiskii himself was aware of the conflict between words and deeds and privately communicated his frustration to Eden, who had reproved him for what he saw as excessive pessimism:

> In my opinion, the withdrawal of Western democracies before the fascist aggressors is still taking place. Spain is the best example of this. This withdrawal, this weakness in British and French foreign policy has disillusioned a segment of the Soviet public, and collaboration with Western democracies has become less attractive. Let there be no misunderstandings of any kind: the Soviet government remains committed to its old policy of collective security, to the League of Nations and to supporting the defence of peace by cooperating with all countries that are against war, with France and England at the top of that list. Nothing has changed in Soviet government policy. But some shifts are taking place in certain Soviet circles – these I have just identified.[95]

Lapinskii limited himself to the observation that Germany's attempt to 'atomize' Europe and divide the result into two parts was going ahead without significant resistance.[96] He felt that the February–March plenum had showed everyone that the 'crisis of the old world' involved a much longer and more complex process than had been considered possible in the immediate postwar period. The principal elements were the ruling class' fear of the 'strengthening of democracy' and the rise of fascist 'totalitarianism', which endangered 'the whole of modern civilization'.[97]

Relations between the USSR and Great Britain continued to move pointlessly round and round the ever more inconsistent rhetoric of 'non-intervention'. An agreement to extend the pact to include the problem of the foreign volunteers involved in the Spanish civil war was concluded at the London committee of 16 February and it was expected that the two countries would jointly oversee an evacuation of volunteers set to begin on 6 March. But the conclusion of the agreement did not dissipate Soviet fears that the British government would do all it could to avoid the problems attendant on the war in Spain, and that the British might even stand by while the legitimate government was overturned.[98] It was clear that the Spanish question would continue to be a diplomatic headache for some time yet. Even so, the USSR could not for a moment slacken its commitment to the manoeuvres surrounding the conflict: Litvinov feared that the USSR might be excluded from the negotiations over the containment of the civil war, which would in turn mean the loss of an important tool in future negotiations with Great Britain. This explains his decision to challenge with his British colleague in Geneva the veracity of rumours that the Soviets planned to set up a separate state in Catalonia dominated by the Spanish communists.[99]

Dickering over the volunteers could only be an exercise in negotiations; no one believed that it would have a significant effect on what happened to the volunteers in Spain, but it certainly fueled ongoing polemics regarding British 'neutrality'.[100] Following the German bombardment of Guernica, the Soviets interpreted the British proposals to 'humanize' the war as a further attempt to put both belligerent sides on the same footing.[101] Meanwhile, the crisis in Largo Caballero's government and the formation of Juan Negrin's government in May 1937 appeared to consolidate the links between Republican Spain and the USSR, through the expansion of Communist influence and Soviet control. On 27 May, Moscow sent an official note to London calling for a truce; the note was signed by Potemkin and passed along via Gaikis, the newly appointed Soviet ambassador to Madrid.[102] In the note, Potemkin forcefully rejected the idea of treating the Republican government and the nationalist rebels as 'equals'; he declared that the rebels had to be the first to withdraw from the battlefield.[103]

When he spoke at the Council of the League of Nations in Geneva on 28 May, Litvinov reminded his auditors once again that one group of combatants had been legitimately elected by the people while the other was a handful of rebels. He underscored the importance of the Spanish events 'for European peace and peace in general' and expressed his belief that the civil war could be an important precedent:

> There is no guarantee that the near future will not see a new attempt to raise a rebellion in another country, an attempt to make the leader of the rebels the leader of the government, attempts to send foreign troops and weapons to aid the rebels, which would amount to an act of aggression, the sort of thing that becomes standard policy for an interventionist state. Such states tend to initiate a series of wars, to adopt a policy of aggression and expansionism, all the while employing ideological struggles and political contests as a cover – much like the religious wars of the past. Let us not forget that at the time the rebellion broke out Spain had a government whose policies resembled those of many other countries.[104]

Litvinov did not deny that the Soviet government possessed 'its own ideology' and that it 'would certainly be happy if this ideology spread to other countries'. He reiterated, however, that 'as a state, we are minimally concerned with Spain's current regime'.[105] He concluded with a request that the League of Nations speak out in support of the Spanish people. None of this was detached from the reiteration of positions of principle – clearly the Spanish question was being dragged out interminably. The Soviets were most concerned about the possibility that the military theatre might expand to other countries.

Even the terrible German bombardment of Almeria failed to change the international alignment around Spain, which had become something of a diplomatic quagmire. At the end of June, Maiskii informed Moscow that in his opinion non-intervention could collapse in the near future; a failure to respond swiftly and punitively to fascist maritime incursions would doom the whole enterprise.[106] The Soviet press announced that the policy of 'non-intervention' was in tatters and that the London committee had almost certainly ceased to have any political clout.[107] Nonetheless, the USSR maintained a wary stance. Litvinov instructed Maiskii and Surits to oppose recognition of Franco's troops as legitimate combatants.[108] In a letter to Stalin on 28 July, Litvinov pointed out that only the total evacuation of foreign volunteers would lead to meaningful change.[109]

Soviet diplomats had no faith in Britain's Spanish policy and said so openly. Maiskii believed that their failure to weaken the Rome–Berlin axis by improving relations with Italy had led the British to initiate a rapprochement with Germany. To the extent that Germany would be expected to make concessions in its European activities, Maiskii could not see Hitler favouring such relations – continued Nazi activity in Spain would make it difficult for the British to form any real alliance with Germany.[110] But Soviet leaders still bit their nails as they worried about the prospect of an Anglo-German rapprochement.

News from a variety of sources alternately lifted and let slip Soviet hopes about the relations between the two most powerful western European states. Word in Berlin was that rapprochement was in the air, while the French assured Litvinov that relations between Germany and Britain had cooled.[111] In Geneva on 24 May Litvinov personally warned Eden against 'excessive optimism' in evaluating the international situation.[112] Shortly after Litvinov's talk with Eden, Potemkin notified Maiskii that the information coming from Prague suggested that the British were vigorously pursuing a pro-German and anti-Soviet policy in central and eastern European countries.[113] The prospect of an Anglo-German agreement and the weakening of the pact with France led to deep concerns about eastern European security. Soviet worries regarding Great Britain's policy towards Germany thus merged with the diffidence which the British felt towards the USSR on the eve of the Tukhachevskii affair.

Relations between Germany and the USSR had long been tenuous and chilly when news of the military 'plot' implicated the Nazis in efforts to overthrow the Socialist regime. Serious friction had followed the arrest of German citizens after the trial of January 1937.[114] David Kandelaki was called back to Moscow from Berlin in April,[115] and soon enough he fell victim to the purges. But fitful efforts were still made to improve relations between the two countries. When Surits' successor in Berlin, Konstantin Iurenev, paid a state visit to Hitler, there was an exchange of notes and the suggestion that relations might still be normalized: the Nazi dictator himself mentioned such a possibility.[116] Iurenev came to believe that Germany, because of its economic crisis, was extremely interested in Soviet raw materials and he suggested to Litvinov that he 'follow the previous tactical line'. By this he meant the combination of economic ties with 'an effective normalization of political relations'.[117] We know that Litvinov had not been enthusiastic about this policy in the past, but it was nonetheless pursued.

At the end of July the newly elected British prime minister, Neville Chamberlain, told Maiskii that he thought that 'peace in Europe' could only be achieved by engaging Germany in a dialogue and meaningful negotiations. To Maiskii, the British seemed keener than ever on the idea of a 'pact of four' and on a unilateral 'organization of Western security'.[118] Two days after Chamberlain's comments, Potemkin communicated them to Iurenev, observing that England was playing 'a complex game of international politics which for us involves very great risks'.[119] On 4 August Litvinov informed Surits that, like Maiskii, he saw the British moving towards an alliance that would exclude the USSR: he feared that Chamberlain was contemplating an important agreement with Germany.[120] The commissar's concerns were reinforced, he told Coulondre, by the stalled evacuation of volunteers from Spain and by the suspicion that the British were undertaking separate negotiations with Franco.[121]

Marginalization and inertness had now become the principal characteristics of USSR international policy. So it is no surprise that, faced with the Japanese invasion of China at the beginning of July, Litvinov affirmed the USSR's neutrality.[122] It became harder and harder to pretend that the USSR's policies were anything but isolationist. Terror had been unleashed, and withdrawal from the international scene was a logical corollary. In May, Litvinov had maintained that the Soviets felt they had risked far too much by adhering to a 'collective security' policy; from now on the Soviet Union would avoid taking the initiative on any issue.[123]

How are we then to understand the statement made by Litvinov to the foreign minister of Latvia, on 15 June 1937?

> Unfortunately, people have already begun to forget the number of years that have elapsed since the last world war, and instead are calculating how long it will be until the next war, a war in which all states, both willing and unwilling participants, may, to an unprecedented extent, be stripped of their cultural and material wealth; smaller states are likely to be stripped of their very national existence. Certainly in the present international situation the forces of any two states are still insufficient to guarantee peace. But even while outdated notions of war as an inevitable and salutary event enjoy a localized revitalization, the opinion of large popular masses rejects such thinking. It has become axiomatic that individual states cannot expect an inviolate national security; as a result all states need to consider, in addition to their own borders, how to improve the protections afforded to the borders of other states.[124]

One is led to see in these words, pronounced at the height of the Tukhachevskii affair, a political testament *ante litteram*, an expression of Litvinov's personal thinking still directed towards what he himself continued to define as 'the potential for peace'.[125] But this would be a sort of funeral oration for such hopes. The foreign policy of the Soviet Union would thoroughly turn back to the belief that war could not be avoided.

THE AGONY OF THE COMINTERN

'All of you in the Comintern are working for our enemy.' With these words, spoken to Dimitrov on 11 February 1937, Stalin menacingly expressed the roots of his determination to eradicate 'Trotskyism'.[126] In Spain, where the Comintern had played a crucial role in organizing the international brigades, Stalin's vague threats assumed their most vivid form. There the 'fight against Trotskyism' grew to international proportions, culminating in the communist repression of May 1937 and the assassination of Andrés Nin.[127] The purges taking place in the USSR thus produced immediate and tragic repercussions within the international communist movement and on the anti-fascist front.

Consequently, the appeals for a united action of the international worker's movement, repeated by the leaders of the Comintern throughout the spring and summer of 1937, could not have any serious impact. A suggestion made by Dimitrov in an address to the leaders of the Socialist International prompted a public exchange of letters between the two internationals on how to set up a joint commission.[128] On 4 June, the Comintern secretariat called for a propaganda campaign based on Dimitrov's proposals.[129] When a communist and a socialist delegation met in Annemasse on 21 June the result was a joint request for the removal of the blockade surrounding the Spanish republic. A second meeting on 9 July reaffirmed the need for common action in support of Spain. However, while many had hoped that these meetings would lead to increased international cooperation, this episode was to be the last of its kind.[130]

Nevertheless, in the spring and summer of 1937, Dimitrov did not retreat from the position he had taken up soon after the civil war broke out in Spain. The Comintern secretary continued to insist on mass mobilization as the main bulwark against the threat of war and against fascism as 'the main enemy'. He felt that the early setbacks dealt to those who had elected to intervene in Spanish affairs had exposed 'the inconsistencies and instability of the fascist regime' and had encouraged 'the anti-fascist elements in Italy and Germany'.[131] He also declared that fascists could not stand in the way of a Republican victory – in other words, Franco could be defeated and peace could be maintained.[132]

While Dimitrov joined in Soviet attacks on Western democracies and the League of Nations for having failed to act decisively in the Spanish crisis, his approach still displayed a distinctly political orientation. Not only did he stress 'the obstinate silence' of the League of Nations on the question of sanctions, he vigorously rejected the defence generally offered for such silence – the 'spectre of war'. Dimitrov also protested against the League's 'shameful speculation' about the views of the masses on war and peace, which in his view only obscured fascist activities on the international and domestic scenes.[133] His strongly worded attack appears to be indebted to the conclusions he and Ercoli had come to over a year earlier, in the aftermath of the Rhineland crisis. And he appears also to have targeted the emerging pattern of Soviet disengagement from militant anti-fascism. It should be borne in mind that the Soviet propaganda machine, operating under the cloud of the Tukhachevskii affair, continuously exploited the notion of the 'spectre of war'.

In Dimitrov's eyes, Spain occupied a crucial position along fascism's bellicose trajectory: it was the last barricade and, once flattened, war would roll right over it. The civil war would probably expand to other countries in Europe as a prologue to a more general war. For the fascists, the conquest of Spain was 'one of the main prerequisites for the world war under preparation'. Dimitrov continued:

> The real truth in this matter is that the defeat of the Spanish people would multiply the threat of war a hundred-fold and would greatly assist the fascist aggressors as they prepare for war. If, on the other hand, the Spanish people emerge victorious, a new barrier will have been raised against the outbreak of war. Those who hope to preserve peace must do all in their power to see the fascist invaders expelled from Spain as soon as possible so that the Spanish people can preserve their own liberty and independence.[134]

However, Dimitrov's conviction that a victory over fascism in Spain would guarantee a more general European peace was not shared by all Soviet leaders, even though the struggle in Spain had been rhetorically set at the forefront of a wider 'struggle against war' from the onset of the civil war. When Manuil'skii decried, as we have seen, the tendency to 'exaggerate' the political significance of anti-fascist resistance in Spain, he may have had Dimitrov in mind. Manuil'skii had considerably underestimated the repercussions of a Republican victory in Spain. The way Manuil'skii saw it – taking as axiomatic Stalin's comments about the continuing danger of 'capitalist encirclement' – war was not going to be fended off by any international front or any domestic problems the fascist regimes might be facing; to ensure the security of the Soviet Union, 'inter-imperialistic contradictions' would have to be exploited.[135]

On 1 August 1937 an editorialist announced in *Izvestiia* that 'War is already here'. Little more than a year had been needed for 'real events' to confirm Stalin's hypothesis of March 1936 regarding the 'two focal points of war'. One could now firmly state that 'once again a "great war" is being played out on the battlefield'. Such bold appraisals lent a concrete and highly public form to an idea that had been circulating among Soviet and communist leaders since late 1936. But an essential characterization followed: 'the capitalist world is drifting into war, and fascism is forcing the inconsistencies of imperialism to their limits, with no regard as to whether such behaviour might endanger itself'.[136] In other words, the war which was 'already here' was exclusively a capitalist phenomenon. For the USSR, this suggested that any former compulsion to uphold a general European peace was, under the current conditions, baseless. The consequent priority was simple: avoid entanglement in war. Also in the 1 August issue of *Izvestiia*, the historian Evgenii Tarle noted that the capitalist world was 'morally' better prepared for war than it had been in 1914; one could say that 'total war' already existed, though for the moment it was 'only marking time but at any moment would thrust forward'.[137] *Pravda* proposed a connection between the battles of Guadalajara and of the Marne: had not, in both cases, the attacked taken their revenge against the aggressors? Implicitly, Tarle's judgement was being seconded.[138] The economist Varga drew connections between a predicted short-term economic crisis and the prospect of war. He felt that the financial troubles threatened 'the very existence of the Hitlerite regime', which would look vainly to the war as a possible escape from its economic woes.[139]

Dimitrov held out, maintaining that the defence of peace would mean 'the defeat of fascism' in Spain and in China and that a comparison between 1937 and 1914 was inappropriate – the relations between the 'forces of war and peace' had changed. Working from these principles, he even attempted to justify recent horrors in the USSR: the suppression of 'terrorists', 'Trotskyites' and 'fascist agents' was crucial to the consolidation of Soviet economic, political and military power, which in turn guaranteed both domestic and international peace.[140] However, for the most part the anniversary of the outbreak of World War I was marked by Soviet press commentary that rendered Dimitrov's idea that Spain was 'the last barricade' standing in the way of a new world war seem weak and out of date. More observers seemed convinced that if the Spanish war was the first battlefield in a general war, the USSR had no business getting involved.

On 15 September the Comintern secretariat received a communication from the Spanish communists declaring that pressure from fascist states had pushed the conflict into an 'open war'; Great Britain and France were said to be well disposed towards plans to partition the country into spheres of influence.[141] The Praesidium met on 20 September and Dimitrov presented a request for the organization of a new international aid programme for Spain, a move he said was necessitated by imminent nationalist attacks.[142] The threat of Trotskyism lay heavy over the vulnerable Spanish landscape. Dimitrov had provided a dissertation on Trotskyism in his address to the Praesidium, and Ercoli's early reports from Spain contained anxious essays on the 'opposition bloc' formed by Trotskyists and anarchists as a reaction against the Negrin government.[143] Ercoli's reports were promptly forwarded by Dimitrov to Stalin.[144]

STALIN AND THE INEVITABLE WAR, 1936–1941

At the meeting of the Praesidium, Manuil'skii declared he had come to believe that the Spanish civil war was not to be a brief episode as 'we had earlier believed', and that the role being played by Great Britain and France made a detailed investigation of Trotskyist activities in Spain utterly essential.[145] For the very reason that Spain had 'mounted the barricades at the front line of the battle against fascism',[146] then, if some fighting spirit could be rekindled, the main challenge to be confronted was 'Trotskyism'. According to Manuil'skii, the Spanish anarchists and Largo Caballero had become the USSR's sworn foes. If the Spanish communists were to prevail, they had to study the recent trials held in the USSR.[147] A similar summons addressed to the Spanish party, which had previously been judged the only one with its papers in order in the 'fight against Trotskyism', only added to the paranoia infecting the Comintern.

Manuil'skii refrained from more general evaluations of the international situation. Still, he had presented the Western powers as utterly unreliable and his conviction that the war in Spain would not end soon also fitted with the prevailing view that, from the Soviet perspective, a limited 'war of attrition' in Spain was acceptable, as long as it did not spread to other states. Such a war would tie Hitler up in a strategically peripheral sector.[148] André Marty, one of Spain's Republican military leaders, declared that 'in the past there were two possible international circumstances: war or peace. Now there is a third: undeclared war.'[149] This was clearly an allusion to Stalin's comments to Howard of March 1936. But things had to some extent changed in the 18 months since that interview. No longer was 'undeclared war' a possible scenario: it had become an 'international circumstance', something very different from peace. By describing this new international condition Marty was articulating a widespread belief.

When, on 3 October, the Comintern secretariat passed a resolution concerning 'aid to the Spanish and Chinese people', it emphasized the threat of a war for the USSR.[150] Public declarations were very similar. Manuil'skii stigmatized Japanese aggression, which he saw as a confirmation of Stalin's prophecies.[151] Dimitrov praised the USSR as 'the essential element in the maintenance of world peace' and contended that it provided a basic 'demarcation line': depending on a nation's attitude towards the USSR it belonged either to the forces of fascism and war or to those of democracy and peace.[152] But over the summer Spain had somehow ceased to count, and Soviet military aid to the republic had been severely cut back.[153] The change in policy had become clear even before the Japanese invasion of China. Distrust of potential allies and general apathy were common among European governments facing the Nazi menace. Now Soviet policy showed such an attitude on the surface, but the causes were deeper and mainly endogenous.

During the second half of 1937 the axe fell on the Comintern. There was a general blitz on Europe's communist parties.[154] The first to be decapitated, some time during the spring and summer of 1937, was the German communist party; charges has been brought against its leaders in September 1936. The Polish Communist Party reeled under a harsher blow – its entire political office was arrested in September 1937. Two months later, on 28 November, a Comintern resolution was sent by Dimitrov to Stalin on the dissolution of the Polish Communist Party.[155] When he approved the resolution, Stalin brusquely indicated that already there had been a 'two year delay' in this matter.[156] By the time the leaders of the Comintern finally signed the resolution (August 1938), the Polish party had long since been reorganized. These dramatic actions taken by Comintern leaders left them even more vulnerable to Stalin's despotic power.

A letter Varga sent to Stalin in March 1938 illustrates very eloquently the interaction between internal and external factors during the Great Terror.[157] If Varga cautiously refrained from denying the validity of the purges and even went as far as to claim that it was preferable 'to arrest two innocent people than to let a single spy escape', he did not shrink from describing an atmosphere of oppressive xenophobia and condemned the abuse of power by NKVD officials. The unsubstantiated and secret accusations and subsequent arrests he deplored; they produced uneasiness and misunderstandings, especially among foreign communists, and he requested that the arrests be verified under the supervision of the Comintern leaders. But Varga was most concerned about a political question. Increasingly the Communists at work in fascist states, who should have been leading the way in the prelude to 'the coming war', showed signs of a deep demoralization, as did even 'individual members of the Comintern secretariat'. The consequent 'dangerous atmosphere of panic' was paralyzing those leaders at the very moment they ought to have been preparing for war.[158] Thus Varga reversed the idea of the purges as a necessary preventative measure. But he confirmed that the focus of Soviet policy was the expectation of war.

ISOLATIONISM

Collective security was again on Litvinov's lips at the Nyon conference on 'piracy' in the Mediterranean. On 10 September 1937, while observing that recent international conferences had not led to 'excessive optimism', he insisted that his very presence was proof that the Soviet Union persevered in its commitment to 'preserving peace and international order'.[159] Two days later most of the details of a plan for the monitoring of Mediterranean waters by a combined French and British maritime force had been worked out, and Litvinov embraced the proposal. Compared with other states the Soviet Union stood 'always ready to go further and more rapidly along the road of the defence of peace and to act more decisively'. Because it constituted 'a partial realization of the idea of collective security', the agreement possessed a 'political significance' more sweeping than its 'possible practical results'.[160] Litvinov was doing what he could to turn a scarcely effective affair (neither Germany nor Italy attended the conference) into a public relations coup for the Soviet Union.[161] But when the British insisted on including the Italians in a round of final planning a few weeks later, this spurious climate of optimism melted away like premature snowfall.

Hopes that the United States would abandon its long-term commitment to neutrality in European conflicts were also destined to evaporate. Notwithstanding the renewal of the American Neutrality Act, some imagined that when President Roosevelt spoke out in Chicago in October 1937, denouncing international aggression and pleading for the cause of peace, he had stepped boldly into the international arena. Soviet writers emphasized the affinities between Roosevelt's declarations and Litvinov's statements on policy, and suggested that European democracies might follow the lead of the titans of capitalism and communism.[162] Such extravagant rhetoric did not last and would not recur. The Soviet policy-makers had come to believe that the Western powers would never change their policies in any significant way.

On 21 September Litvinov spoke at the Council of the League of Nations in Geneva. Three days earlier the Republican government had requested a reconsideration of the Spanish question and of 'non-intervention'. Supporting this request, Litvinov angrily declared that there had been times when the League had seemed to be 'collaborating with the aggressors'; no longer would this be thinkable. After the great disappointment of the London committee negotiations, it was no longer possible 'to speak, except ironically, of non-intervention in Spanish affairs'; there could be 'no compromise between aggression and non-aggression, between peace and war'.[163] Litvinov also attacked the three states identified as the bearers of 'an undisguised ideology of armed intervention'. These states had by now revealed their plans for economic expansion and offered 'a quite prosaic explanation' for their anti-communist crusades.[164] It seemed likely, suggested Litvinov, that those who took up anti-communism as their major watchword would come to fear and loathe even democratic states if they saw them as vulnerable to Bolshevik threat or influence. Everyone was at risk: 'Aggression is being built up against the whole of Europe.'

Even as he spoke out, Litvinov could not help joining in the chorus of voices he had long resisted – those who said that a state of war already existed. He noted that 'now is not the time to speak about the threat to peace, because peace has already been violated', and that 'an undeclared war is being conducted on two continents'.[165] Never before had he used such words. While Japanese incursions into China might have affected his thinking, we must also take into consideration the internal evolution of Soviet policy, in the barbarous aftermath of the plenum of February–March 1937. On 28 September, still in Geneva, the commissar stated that non-intervention had failed and that a different policy would have yielded 'better results'.[166] The Spanish republic ought to have been actively supported from the start, and the French and British had shirked this responsibility. There was no follow-up to his address.[167]

Isolationism had come home to roost. In the Soviets' eyes, the participants in the London committee had revived talk of a 'pact of four'.[168] Litvinov told Maiskii to declare that the USSR assumed no responsibility for the Anglo-French proposal of linking recognition of the two belligerent sides in Spain with a 'substantial evacuation' of the volunteers; somewhat paradoxically, the Soviet ambassador to London was instructed to intervene solely on matters that would guarantee 'effective non-intervention'.[169] Litvinov also took Maiskii to task for his public characterization of Soviet policy. Maiskii had erred by stating that far from serving as a mere 'spectator', the USSR hoped to 'participate actively in all matters'. Admittedly Maiskii had found himself in a tight spot, but speaking to Eden as though the 'pact of four' were already a reality had been an error, and in the future he was to avoid displaying 'excessive concern and nervousness about such things as isolation and discussions of the pact'. Litvinov had personally informed Chilston that, in his opinion, non-intervention had failed; and he had also notified him once and for all that isolationism 'does not frighten' the USSR.[170] In other words, Litvinov wanted Maiskii to make it clear that Moscow was seriously contemplating closing itself off from the world outside. Marginalization had to be risked if the alternative was an admission of Soviet weakness. But in a letter to Stalin Litvinov took a different stance. To the extent that Moscow remained a player in world affairs, it should make every attempt to 'obstruct' the alignment of the main European states into a 'pact of four'. Litvinov had not yet given up hope that Moscow could be a player in international affairs.[171]

On 6 November Italy signed the 'anti-Comintern pact', a gesture which failed to strike fear into Litvinov's heart. He observed that if the pact represented 'a diplomatic weapon in the battle of the three aggressors against the ideology of the League of Nations', it was more likely to be aimed at Great Britain than at the USSR.[172] Shtein concurred.[173] Of undeniable significance was instead the meeting between Lord Halifax and Hitler, one of the crucial steps in Chamberlain's policy of appeasement.[174] Among the Soviets, the opinion was now widespread that the British were doing their utmost to turn the Nazi threat towards the USSR. *Le journal de Moscou* limited itself to indicating that the Anglo-German talks were 'in serious contradiction to the interests of peace and collective security'.[175] But the senior Narkomindel official and chief of the press department, Evgenii Gnedin, commenting in *Izvestiia*, saw 'intimations of a clear change in British policy', the groundwork for a European '*pax germanica*'.[176] Gnedin believed that all differences between the three aggressor states had been patched up and that as a bloc they were preparing to launch a war against the USSR – he predicted that this would prove a great threat to those states that had chosen to turn a blind eye to what was going on.[177]

In his speech given in Leningrad on 27 November, Litvinov insisted on the distinction between aggressor and non-aggressor states thereby rejecting such a view of British policy and forecast about Europe's trajectory.[178] Recent international developments occupied him very little; he simply noted the lack of response by the 'so-called "great powers"' to aggression in Spain and China and the great calamities that followed. If he made no explicit mention of Halifax's meeting with Hitler, it was clear enough that he had Great Britain in mind when he deplored the practice of asking aggressor states for 'evidence and explanations' concerning their misconduct. He also suggested that the addition of new signatories to the anti-Comintern pact largely amounted to an effort to 'create confusion'. For the aggressors, having overextended themselves, had seriously weakened their internal resources.

> [They] cannot endure a long and risky war and in the future they will be obliged to look for the path of least resistance. We all know that this path of least resistance will not be found at our borders (applause). They know that the Soviet Union's ability to defend itself depends not on international alliances but on the ever increasing might of the Red Army, the Russian fleet and the Red Air Force. They know that our leader, Comrade Stalin, who cares deeply about the smooth operation of the state machinery in its entirety, devotes the greatest attention to the problem of defending every inch of our land. There is no one who can deprive us of this land.[179]

Soviet policy-makers had retrenched and Litvinov, now a mouthpiece for the most formulaic propaganda, had metamorphosed into a bulwark of state policy. He even mentioned the 'internal work' of NKVD as proof of the USSR's unassailable position. At this time Litvinov had adopted the use of doublespeak: his statements shifted to suit international opinion or internal opinion. Within a month he was telling a correspondent for

Le Temps that the USSR approached foreign policy by waiting and isolating itself from other states.[180] Given his recent policy statements, this hardly amounted to the revelation of a secret.

However, in private, leading Soviet diplomats were more judicious in their analysis. When Maiskii wrote to Litvinov on 22 November, he predicted that soon Chamberlain would recognize German hegemony in central and eastern Europe and abandon Spain to its fate. But he believed that one could not speak about a consistent British foreign policy plan, nor that an agreement between the British and the Germans was likely.[181] Surits saw France as completely subservient to Great Britain. He was quite pessimistic about the direction this pair was headed for but also thought it would have been wrong to suppose that 'the Paris–London axis' would 'surrender its positions to the fascist front without a fight': after all 'any denial of the elementary difference between democratic and fascist countries' was a mistake.[182]

Litvinov wrote to Surits on 3 December to inform him that the Anglo-German talks held in November had not addressed communism or the USSR – he seemed to be discarding the prevailing Soviet belief in a plot intended to open an eastward route for Hitler to approach the USSR. He felt certain that if the British continued to meet with the Germans Chamberlain would be obliged to grapple with 'the complexity of the problems' raised by Germany's 'full programme'.[183] In any case, whether that was good or bad, Britain was far too sympathetic with Germany for a turnabout to happen any time soon. But if Germany and Italy had not budged for another six months, this would in itself have been 'a breakthrough for the cause of peace'. If this happened, 'the most appropriate policy would be to recognize the Italo-German–Japanese coalition and then to oppose it with another union, but not one that involved fixed reciprocal obligations of any kind whatsoever'. Even the Anti-Comintern Pact did not place formal demands upon its members and 'a similar agreement, without precise obligations between the remaining great powers, could easily be contemplated, certainly not in an ideological spirit, but under the banner of the defence of peace'.[184] On 4 December Litvinov communicated these evaluations to Maiskii as well.[185]

All this reveals that even at the end of 1937 Litvinov continued to hope for an agreement with the Western democracies, though he was sceptical about short-term progress. To bring about the realignment, as Litvinov himself acknowledged, a rapprochement between England and the USSR would be essential, and this was not on the cards. He also felt that in the near future there was no possibility of weakening the coalition between the fascist states, even if Italy did not have 'practical material interests binding to the other two partners'.[186] But Litvinov certainly did not consider the evolution of Soviet foreign policy to be irreversible.

Along with his views on future developments, this separated him from other Soviet officials.

Potemkin, for instance, deplored in much harsher tones the direction France and Britain's foreign policies were going. As he noted in a letter written to Surits on 19 December, Chamberlain continued to express hostility towards the Franco-Soviet pact, while the authority of the League of Nations suffered one blow after another thanks to the behaviour of the Western powers. 'In our eyes,' he wrote, 'both England and France are moving away from their previous positions', and in fact, the Western powers were 'unquestionably drifting towards the hostile side of the international field'.[187]

Potemkin outlined an international situation that looked quite different from the pictures offered by Litvinov, Surits and Maiskii. Among his principal concerns was the formation of a compact capitalist bloc of powers opposed to the Soviet Union. He published a pseudonymous article in which he developed an idea long present in his diplomatic correspondence, namely that in both Great Britain and France 'national interests' were systematically subordinated to 'class interests' in foreign policy-making. This meant a policy dedicated both to isolating the USSR and to encouraging anti-Soviet aggression.[188] This article implicitly opposed Maiskii's assertion that the pro-German elements in Great Britain had bungled their attempts to dictate policy and that there would be no 'direct alliance with the aggressor'.[189] Potemkin did not believe that an alliance between the USSR and Western democracies could be forged to counter the fascist bloc, and he rejected all thinking based on the idea of a pair of opposed blocs of major powers. His view of the 'capitalist encirclement' ostracized collective security as an illusion. The radical divergence of Potemkin's views from Litvinov's bespoke grave divisions within the Narkomindel, but USSR foreign policy at the height of the Great Terror consistently reflected Potemkin's views.

Party leaders such as Molotov and Zhdanov also continued to emphasize 'capitalist encirclement'.[190] Zhdanov went further, affirming that all of the capitalist states were to be considered 'the main enemies' of the USSR.[191] Extreme though it was, this view was broadly embraced in Moscow. Only Dimitrov, at the time a candidate for the USSR Supreme Soviet, spoke of Spain and identified the fascist states as the real enemy.[192] But his was an isolated voice.

The Soviet partisans of isolationism began to object to the number of foreign embassies and consulates on Soviet soil. As early as July 1937 the Politburo had directed the Narkomindel to close Polish, Japanese and German consulates in the USSR. By stressing the unprecedented nature of such a move in his reports to Stalin – he noted that the new policy 'has no international precedent and may arouse strong reactions from the states concerned, but I presume that we are aware of all this' – Litvinov rendered his feelings on the subject quite legible.[193] Six months later, on 17 January 1938, Zhdanov publicly attacked Litvinov. Zhdanov complained to the Supreme Soviet that 'in several commissariats there are problems and obscurities' and asked the commissar for foreign affairs some pointed questions regarding his 'practical activity' in this area. Why, he wanted to know, had the state tolerated the establishment of more foreign consulates on its soil than there were Soviet consulates on foreign soil? In his opinion, some of the consulates in Leningrad were involved in 'subversive activities'.[194]

Zhdanov seems to have set out to aggravate existing contradictions by insinuating that the Narkomindel had procrastinated after receiving orders from the Politburo. The concerns Litvinov voiced in the summer of 1937 corresponded to tensions which only increased when the USSR's unilateral decision to close foreign consulates was extended to include Great Britain and Italy. Such decisions had been made without the participation of the Narkomindel. As late as December, Litvinov was complaining to Stalin that he had received no instructions regarding the closure of foreign consulates in Leningrad – he was not even sure which consulates were affected.[195]

Warming to the conflict, Zhdanov also cast doubts on the wisdom of Soviet foreign policy. Did a pact with France 'exist or not? Is it effective or not?' he wondered. It struck him as unwise to maintain close relations with a nation willing to shelter organizations 'that organize and carry out acts of terrorism against the USSR'.[196] (He seems to have had in mind here Trotskyist organizations.) These comments provoked a speedy response from Molotov, who affirmed that 'one cannot but recognize [their] truth'; as to the pact with France, Molotov declared that the Narkomindel should have dealt with the problem.[197] Ultimately, Litvinov would have to explain to the foreign affairs commission of the Supreme Soviet the exact status of the USSR's pacts with foreign states.[198]

The Narkomindel had been struck another severe blow. We know that at the beginning of 1938 Litvinov composed a letter of resignation, addressed to Stalin. Writing on 10 January (that is, before Zhdanov's attack against him) Litvinov announced that he would be leaving the Narkomindel and requested an appointment to the newly formed foreign affairs commission of the Supreme Soviet. Though he probably never sent the letter – as was his recollection years later – he had clearly been overwhelmed by a sense of political impotence. As it turned out, he never needed to send the letter: it fell into Molotov's hands, and Stalin was obviously informed of Litvinov's plan.[199]

It should be noted that around this time Zhdanov's views on foreign policy became increasingly influential, not least because of his election to the presidency of the very foreign affairs commission Litvinov was planning to join.[200] Zhdanov's rise was to continue throughout the years of the Great Terror, and by the end of the 1930s he stood poised to become one of the handful of foreign policy-makers on whom Stalin relied.[201] One means of identifying the members of this clique is simply to look at who received Litvinov's communications: Molotov, Kaganovich, Voroshilov, Ordzhonikidze (until his death in February 1937) and Ezhov (after the February–March 1937 plenum). This was a much tighter nucleus than the Politburo, which had lost much of its role as a decision-making body in the field of foreign policy. The Politburo decline in this area was implicitly acknowledged by the creation in April 1937 of a Politburo commission on foreign policy: its permanent members were Stalin, Molotov, Kaganovich, Voroshilov and Ezhov.[202] Such practice also entailed a decline of the Narkomindel involvement in policy-making, increasing the political and police supervision of the diplomatic administrations, and the purging of many diplomats during 1937 and 1938.[203]

On 14 February 1938, one month after Zhdanov had made his comments to the Supreme Soviet, *Pravda* published Stalin's 'Response to Comrade Ivanov' on the subject of 'socialism in one country'. The article included a reaffirmation of the views on 'capitalist encirclement' Stalin had set forth a year earlier. He explained to the imaginary 'Comrade Ivanov' that, from the point of view of international relations, the victory of socialism could not yet be considered final. Nor could the problem be resolved 'through our country's forces alone': it was necessary to strengthen 'international proletarian links', streamline the Red Army and drum up the 'political support of the working classes in bourgeois countries so that they will oppose an attack against our country'. This emphasis on international solidarity may have been aimed at diluting the blind xenophobia that had emerged during the mass purges – at least this was the reading offered by Varga as part of his protest against indiscriminate arrests.[204] But not all of Stalin's 'Response' inspired hope, for Stalin had proposed a correlation between the Great Terror and the threat of war: one of the state's objectives had to be 'to keep all the people mobilized and prepared in case of an armed attack'.[205] The end of the purges was not yet in sight; Stalin mentioned 'hidden enemies' who would undermine the goal of mobilization by contending that external enemies ('for example, the fascists') would not attack the USSR.[206]

As we have seen, after the plenum held in February–March 1937, Manuil'skii had launched a frontal attack against those who 'overestimated' the weakness of fascist regimes and 'underestimated' the danger of war. Now Stalin was rejecting all arguments that threatened to attenuate the Great Terror. His insistence on the presence of 'internal enemies' only reinforced the Soviet atmosphere of alarm and fear. Quite significantly, the purges targeted not only social and political objectives, but also national and ethnic groups, extending previous ethnic cleansing into a terror campaign begun in the borderlands and soon to involve all the displaced peoples of the Soviet Union.[207] In other words, state orchestrated terror operations were oriented against both socially and nationally defined 'fifth columns'.[208] Internal terror, threat perception, and the 'total security state' revealed their interaction.

The targets of the third trial (held 2–13 March 1938) were depicted as the 'proponents' of a destructive war against the Soviet state. Earlier enemies had included Radek, Piatakov and Tukhachevskii; now it was the turn of Bukharin, Rykov, Krestinskii and Kristian Rakovskii. Like their predecessors, the members of the so-called 'anti-Soviet, Trotskyist, right-wing bloc' were accused of having conspired to drag the USSR into a war and by so doing dismantle Soviet power. The rhetoric and the concerns driving the third trial closely resembled those that had driven the two preceding trials, and the link with the Tukhachevskii affair was especially striking.

At the plenum held in February and March 1937, Ezhov had levelled accusations at Bukharin and Rykov, who had swiftly been expelled from the Party and then investigated by the NKVD. From the moment they were accused they had declared their innocence, bolstering their claims with a series of statements. Bukharin, in particular, vehemently denied having expressed anything but a sanguine view of the USSR's fate should it become involved in a war on two fronts.[209] But their protestations won the two men no clemency, and when Stalin added his weight to the case against them they were certainly doomed.[210] Stalin intervened on 2 July, at the height of the Tukhachevskii affair, and it is curious that he avoided calling the two men Nazi spies: instead he described Bukharin and Rykov as 'certified manipulators of spies', as members of the leadership of the 'political–military plot'.[211] In any case, their fate was sealed.

At the start of the trial, the Soviet press castigated 'the Bukharinist instigators of war' and recalled Bukharin's opposition to Lenin over the signing of the Brest-Litovsk peace treaty in 1918.[212] Stalin himself had referred to the Brest peace during the preliminary investigations of Bukharin, Rykov, Krestinskii and Rakovskii held in late 1936 and early 1937; he had accused Bukharin of 'having created a bloc' with the revolutionary socialists in 1918.[213] The repeated references to Brest provided a core of seeming rationality around which were wound a farrago of grotesque accusations. Brest was an oblique reference to the sort of uncompromising political stance that aimed at a 'preventative war' with Germany, thus threatening Soviet security. In his famously allusive defence strategy, Bukharin implicitly denied having contributed to threatening the security of the state, but he reaffirmed the idea that the USSR was 'a major and potent factor' against Nazism.[214]

The message of the third trial was identical to that of the previous trials: a warning of totalitarian compactness. And like those tried before them the accused were found guilty of taking orders from foreign powers. But this time the foreign powers labouring to subvert the Soviet Union were not all fascist states, for the public prosecutor had spoken of the role played by the British secret service and Bukharin's 'confession' also mentioned the role played by Great Britain.[215] This innovation could not be overlooked: it was to be understood that the capitalist world was universally hostile to the Soviet Union.

In concert with the adoption of the new constitution and with Molotov's speech before the Supreme Soviet, at the beginning of 1938 the party propaganda machine flooded the atmosphere with descriptions of the USSR as a 'great socialist power', incomparably strong and authoritative thanks to the people's 'political and moral unity'.[216] In his contribution to the annual commemoration of Lenin's great achievements, Zhdanov repeated these formulations.[217] The Great Terror had convinced many looking on from abroad that the Soviet regime was in crisis, or even on the brink of collapse; this new wave of propaganda was not likely to change any minds. Nevertheless, great efforts had been initiated to affirm the domestic authority of the state by relaunching the Russian autocratic and imperial principle, now integrated by the modern totalitarian dogma of a unified political and social life. Thus did the regime attempt to reclaim legitimacy at a time when it had ceased to have any commitment to social transformation, nor at this time could stability be achieved. Thus it was that in a speech given at the Kremlin on 7 November 1937, Stalin cast himself as a modern Ivan the Terrible. He exalted the greatness and power of the Russian state created by the tsars and inherited by the Bolsheviks, and he endorsed the physical liquidation of 'internal enemies' and their relatives.[218]

LITVINOV'S LIMITS AND CONTRADICTIONS

Though domestic turbulence and related effects on foreign policy had driven Litvinov to the brink of resignation, when it came to his longstanding policy commitments in the international arena he barely wavered. On 27 January 1938 he declared to the Council of the League of Nations that 'despite the departure of some members from the League' – a reference to Italy's withdrawal in December – 'the Soviet Union continues to believe that the loyalty and goodwill of the many states that remain will ensure that the forces of aggression cannot proceed unchecked'.[219] One could hardly have any other view and continue as a member of the League. Litvinov balanced his statement with a warning: the USSR believed 'that its own forces are more dependable than those of other states, not less dependable'.

Even as he expressed confidence in the League of Nations, Litvinov also suggested that the League would have to change, to adapt to a new international situation, if it was to survive. Since Italy's withdrawal the League of Nations could no longer claim to be 'universal', and the appearance of 'ideological blocs' at the international level changed things. Litvinov called for the recognition of 'a peace bloc which naturally represents the League of Nations'. If the League was to honour its responsibilities, it would have to act as 'an international ideological bloc'. He also noted that this would not represent 'a bloc opposed to the League's non-member States' because 'a major State' existed in the international field which possessed 'the same ideology' as the League of Nations – an apparent reference to the United States. If there were some who found the term 'bloc' unappealing, Litvinov was happy to use the word 'axis' instead – the substance of his proposal remained unchanged. Such remarks had been anticipated in his already quoted letter to Surits of 3 December 1937 – though he had remained basically pessimistic.[220]

Much discussed after the outbreak of the Spanish civil war, international blocs had reappeared as one of Litvinov's pet topics. But his hopes for a 'peace bloc' had not caught on among the key decision-makers – the idea had been put forward only in diplomatic circles. And comments Litvinov had made in Leningrad on 27 November 1937 attest to his profound awareness that the Great Terror and the state's growing isolationism rendered the possibility of building an international alliance for peace small indeed. Subsequently, as we have seen, Litvinov advanced to the brink of resignation and weathered a public attack from Zhdanov. Soberly assessed, his remarks in Geneva on 27 January 1938 appear to have had no solid support inside the USSR.

Even in the years of the Great Terror, Litvinov's views were contradictory and puzzling. To judge from those letters to Stalin in which he was perpetually asking for advice, Litvinov shrank from establishing an independent political personality; yet his political outlook was quite unique. It seems likely that Litvinov's call for maintaining the prospect of an alliance with the Western powers must have had an effect on Stalin himself; perhaps it contributed to the conclusion that by remaining constructively engaged with the League of Nations the USSR could buy some room for manoeuvring – at a time when the Soviet Union was internally weak, and when the international situation was quite unpredictable. On the other hand, however, Stalin's response to 'Comrade Ivanov', published a few days after Litvinov's address in Geneva, embodied a form of political logic largely foreign to Litvinov's thinking on international relations.

STALIN AND THE INEVITABLE WAR, 1936–1941

In February 1938 Constantin von Neurath was discharged from the German foreign ministry and Eden was replaced by Halifax in the British Foreign Office. From Moscow's point of view, these were ominous changes. Maiskii predicted that Chamberlain himself would come to perform the functions of the British foreign secretary, with unfavourable consequences for the USSR. Next would come increasing isolation of the USSR and even an attack by fascist states against the USSR,[221] encouraged by the British, could not be excluded – though Maiskii was confident that Chamberlain had not yet drawn up a concrete policy.[222] The changes in Germany raised questions about the internal evolution of Hitler's regime, and Neurath's dismissal provoked the same reaction from Soviet and Western diplomats alike. This was a day of reckoning, which strengthened both Hitler's personal power and the regime's most radical tendencies.[223] International tensions were likely to rise. The new Soviet ambassador to Berlin, Grigorii Astakhov, described the promotion of Joachim von Ribbentrop as an indubitable sign 'of the Hitlerization of Germany's senior military and diplomatic officers', and likely to end in an attack on Austria,[224] and after Austria, Czechoslovakia. Many other diplomats concurred with Astakhov's assessment.[225] Things had been bad between the USSR and Germany during 1937; now they were worse. Taken together, the traumatic developments in both British and German diplomacy confirmed the most pessimistic forecasts: Britain's appeasing elements and Germany's supporters of a fiercely aggressive foreign policy stance now stood fortified.

Within this context, Maiskii engineered an unusual initiative. On 25 February 1938 he sent a letter directly to Voroshilov in which he demanded substantial military aid for the Spanish republic.[226] Strangely enough, Litvinov did not become involved in this episode. Already in December 1937, he had refused to join Maiskii's efforts to win Stalin's approval of Soviet aid to the Republican fleet. At that time, Litvinov had simply forwarded Maiskii's request to Voroshilov, with the comments that he would not have raised the issue himself and in any case the commissar for defence had already rejected the proposal: Voroshilov saw the matter as one for the Narkomindel alone.[227] Presumably, Litvinov had not budged from the opinion aired late in 1936, when he had sharply disagreed with Maiskii and insisted that Soviet intervention in Spain could only harm diplomatic endeavours. But things had changed in the interim, and the Spanish question was far from a neat resolution. On the other hand, if Litvinov had strongly disagreed with plans to support the Republicans, it would have been difficult for Maiskii to address Voroshilov. It is therefore probable that Litvinov's attitude must be viewed in the light of the serious difficulties which, as we know, he was encountering within the USSR and in his relations with Stalin.

Perhaps he reckoned that support for a stronger military intervention would be construed as a criticism of the role the USSR had been playing in Spain; furthermore, such intervention might not stir the stagnant waters of diplomacy at all, and could even make things worse.

Maiskii himself appears to have felt that he had acted inappropriately, and he apologized to Voroshilov 'for this interference in a sphere which is not entirely within my competence'. Nevertheless, the ambassador strongly defended his request that a supply of aeroplanes and artillery be sent to Spain. From London, he insisted, one could clearly see 'the enormous repercussions any resolution of the Spanish conflict would have on all of Europe': 'a victory for the Spanish Republic would completely change the atmosphere in Great Britain and France and would make such reactionary combinations as a pact of four unthinkable'. With so much at stake, the equivalent of 'two or three days of work by the Red Army in the case of a major war' was not too much to ask. The result, 'at the worst, would be to postpone a major war for a number of years'. 'I feel', Maiskii concluded, 'that the end justifies the means'.[228] Maiskii's arguments were not very different from those he had defended at the end of 1936 in his debate with Litvinov on the war in Spain and its possible international consequences. At that time he had favoured the intervention Stalin had decided on and he had seen in it the possible benefits for Soviet foreign policy – Litvinov had seen only the possible setbacks. But now Soviet engagement in Spain was clearly declining, and Maiskii's appeal seemed futile. As the drive to reinforce the foundations of a 'total security state' in the USSR attained momentum, Spain ceased to be a significant concern in Moscow.

This was implied by Stalin's ambiguous suggestion, made at a meeting with Dimitrov, Manuil'skii, and Molotov on 17 February 1938, that the Spanish communists withdraw from the Republican government. Stalin explained that this move would 'to a certain degree relieve the international situation of the Spanish republic'.[229] Clearly, he had in mind Great Britain's attitude. But Stalin's suggestion was also a step backward from the policy of popular fronts, and contradicted Ercoli's pressure from Spain for increased communist responsibility in the government.[230] Similar hints were sent to the French communists: Stalin made a reference to them during the same February meeting, and later the Comintern secretariat instructed Thorez not to take part in the new Blum government, a position that 'only a state of war against fascist aggression' could change.[231] If the French communists were kept from collaborating with the government, the Spanish communists ultimately remained in the government: but a tense debate revealed the tensions between the interests of Republican Spain and the interests of the USSR.[232] In general, however, Stalin had concluded that the time for anti-fascist alliances in communist policy was over.

STALIN AND THE INEVITABLE WAR, 1936–1941

When Nazi Germany annexed Austria on 12 and 13 March 1938, the Soviets barely blinked. In their eyes, as in the eyes of Western governments, this did not amount to an international crisis; that crisis had yet to come, and it would in Czechoslovakia. Yet on 17 March 1938 Litvinov issued a strongly worded public statement which echoed his address of 27 January. The USSR, he declared, remained committed to the principles that had led it to join the League of Nations – but what of other members? The passivity the League had exhibited in the face of international aggression during the four previous years could not be excused. Litvinov pointed to the Anschluss and stressed that 'this time violence is to be found in the centre of Europe', a threat not only to the states on Germany's borders (he expressed particular concern for Czechoslovakia) but 'to all European and some non-European states'. Litvinov felt that the decisions facing the leading powers obliged them to consider their 'responsibility towards the future of the peoples of Europe and of the world'. The government of the USSR was aware of this problem and stood ready to participate in collective actions aimed at blocking aggression and global conflict: tomorrow might prove too late, but today 'the time to act has not yet expired'.[233]

This dramatic statement was a consequence of Litvinov's pressure on Stalin. In a letter sent to him on 14 March Litvinov argued that remaining 'completely passive' would have a result 'incompatible with our peace policy'.[234] Writing to Aleksandrovskii, Litvinov described his statement as probably 'a final appeal to Europe for a collective effort'; if rebuffed, the USSR would elect to take 'little interest in the future of European affairs'.[235] His comments to Maiskii were even more pessimistic: he did not harbour any illusions regarding the practical results of his statement, that had been meant only to shake up public opinion while dissociating the USSR from any responsibility for 'the final failure of collective security'. The strong pose he had adopted for his public utterance might also help the public image of the USSR at a time when yet another show trial was lending the regime an air of vulnerability.[236]

The government crisis in France did not kindle any special hopes in Litvinov, despite the possibility that Paris might declare non-intervention a failure and reopen the border with Spain.[237] The USSR lacked the concrete political initiative to follow its declarations of intent. Litvinov instructed Surits not to pressure the French for a reply to his statement of 17 March 1838, confiding to his colleague that he had little hope that France would agree to a high-level conference, despite assurances from Blum and Paul-Boncour.[238] If Surits conceded that Litvinov's declaration had left 'a certain impression' on the French, he was unwilling to speculate about practical consequences.[239] In any case, he saw very little support in France for 'preventative wars'.[240] On 24 March, Maiskii reported that the British were uninterested in attending a conference on European problems.[241] When Poland threatened Lithuania at the end of March, Moscow blustered: Litvinov warned Warsaw that his government could not remain indifferent to such unwarranted aggression and he threatened war in eastern Europe if force was used.[242] But despite all of this noise, the Soviet leadership had become too sluggish and pessimistic to act, and when the affair was resolved in Poland's favour there was no outcry in the Soviet Union.[243]

In a letter he wrote to Surits on 4 April 1938, Potemkin ruled out the possibility of an international conference. Even as the European situation noticeably worsened the French seemed incapable of taking a stand.[244] Things looked worse than ever for Czechoslovakia, and Poland appeared to be poised to exploit the situation. Potemkin referred back to the talks between Stalin and Pierre Laval of May 1935 in order to make a strategic forecast: Hitler was counting on Poland succumbing to the USSR in an upcoming conflict; when it did, Germany would quickly snatch the part of Poland unoccupied by the Soviets. Poland as a sovereign state was doomed.[245] The scenario depicted by Potemkin, on the blueprint of a prediction ascribed to Stalin three years earlier, was now considered in Moscow very much real. The moment for averting the impending cataclysm had passed – now was the time to cope. All of this strategic forecasting revealed considerable indifference to Czechoslovakia's fate.

In the wake of the Anschluss, during a discussion with an envoy of the Czech government, Potemkin declared that the USSR would honour its commitments, but also noted that France's attitude would be of 'decisive significance'.[246] Aleksandrovskii reiterated this view to the Czech foreign minister, who demanded that the Soviets take an unequivocal stance.[247] The Soviet ambassador to Prague remarked that his government had received no communications regarding France's intentions and confessed that he had been driven to relying on press reports for information about the international situation.[248] The state of relations between the USSR and France did not create the conditions for a common stance on Czechoslovakia. Moreover, Chamberlain's policy encouraged the most pessimistic expectations.[249]

Soviet relations with Western democracies were beset by obvious problems. On 3 April 1938, Litvinov complained to Surits that the French were once again working against the USSR: they had communicated to Churchill grave doubts about the strength and efficiency of the Red Army.[250] Maiskii wrote to Litvinov, urging him to mention the problem to Stalin; in the ambassador's view 'the myth of the Red Army's weakness' needed to be eradicated.[251] For several months, Soviet diplomats had tirelessly repeated the official version: the purges were proof that the regime remained strong. But few were listening and fewer were convinced of the speakers' sincerity. Maiskii's variation on the credo might have struck some as closer to the truth, but it also revealed embarrassment about the official version: he preferred to suggest that an army commanded by second-rate generals was preferable to one commanded by traitors.[252]

Alas, Hitler's latest show of force had failed to effect an explosion of 'internal contradictions' among the fascist states. Writing to Stein on 21 March, Litvinov hypothesized that Mussolini's former disagreement with Hitler about Austria had abated, which in turn had upset Chamberlain's expectations. Nevertheless, he reckoned that Chamberlain would now try to work out an agreement with Italy; as to France and Italy, no rapprochement was likely as long as the Spanish civil war continued.[253] The commissar's predictions proved to be correct. On 16 April, less than a month later, Great Britain and Italy renewed their 'gentlemen's agreement'. The next day, in a letter to Surits commenting on relations between Italy and Germany, Litvinov observed that Mussolini, along with the Western powers, would probably oppose German expansion towards the Balkans but support Hitler's plans for central Europe and the Ukraine.[254] What the Soviet leaders most feared was improved relations between Great Britain and Germany, and given the renewal of the 'gentlemen's agreement' and the meeting in Rome between Hitler and Mussolini, things looked bad indeed.[255]

By now Litvinov considered Italy a mere pawn in the European game, to be shifted according to Hitler's or Chamberlain's influence. As to the privileged relationship between Great Britain and France, confirmed at the end of April, this seemed to Litvinov irrelevant to the larger European picture – after all, nobody seemed interested in confronting Hitler. But his attitude was representative of a more general problem, a lack of initiative in Soviet foreign policy which amounted almost to immobility. In the two months following Austria's annexation by Germany, European politics presented a very disheartening picture to the Soviets. By 13 June the French border with Spain had been closed again (it had been opened on 17 March), a telling move by the new government led by Daladier, which was following Great Britain's lead quite strictly in matters of foreign policy. In Spain, the republic had been divided in two by the Nationalist offensive and was beginning its final agony, which would be prolonged for about a year. As to eastern Europe, it lacked any collective security measures and seemed destined to serve as the centre of coming international crises.

In the speeches he gave to the Council of the League of Nations in May, Litvinov neglected to mention any number of international developments. He did not even raise the subject of 'blocs'. He restricted himself to bemoaning those past 'errors' which had diminished the 'collective responsibility' of the League of Nations, and declared that over the last two years the League had been subjected to attacks 'from without and within'. Sounding almost threatening, Litvinov announced that were the League abolished, this would harm its other member nations far more than it would the Soviet Union.[256]

The address he gave in Leningrad on 23 June 1938 was much more momentous. Here Litvinov held to the orthodox doctrine of war and shied away from proposals than he had still been pushing a year earlier, at a time when the Great Terror was already raging. His analysis of the international situation amounted to a retraction:

> We are accustomed to distinguishing between a time of war and a time of peace, a habit that contradicts the fact that for as long as the capitalist system exists a long and lasting peace is impossible. What is normally called peacetime should be more correctly considered as a lengthy pause between two wars, in other words, a truce . . . One may justifiably affirm that the world war, which lasted from 1914 to 1918, did not end with Versailles, Saint Germain and the other treaties concluded at that time. The twenty years that have passed since then should only be considered a truce. One could even say that the cannon fire we can now hear in Spain and China sound like the echoes of the last world war.[257]

Litvinov had largely come to side with those who saw the international situation as an armed truce, likely to shift into a state of war. When he cast doubts on the possibility of a lasting peace in the capitalist world, he was reviving old dogmas. Certainly, of all the Soviet leaders, Litvinov had come closest to removing this theory from political and diplomatic activity. More than anyone else, he had championed the idea that the forces of peace could impede the outbreak of a new war. But war was now being presented as an irreversible, albeit barbaric development, one which had gone on nearly uninterrupted for more than 20 years. Inured to the savagery of the last years of Soviet life, and disillusioned by the impact of recent international crises, Litvinov seemed to have grown resigned to the inevitability of war.

Yet he meant to convince his auditors that his political thinking had not changed. According to Litvinov, faced with the dissolution of the postwar order, something had to be done by the USSR. Even if the Soviet Union was not to participate 'in the fight among imperialist interests', it could hardly look idly on as Europe went up in flames. Clearly, German policy had an anti-Soviet thrust and 'no state, no matter how strong or distant [from such aggression] can escape unscathed'. In other words,

Litvinov did not identify himself as an isolationist, though his criticism of the League of Nations and the Versailles System had never been shriller. But what of his hopes for peace?

Litvinov insisted that, gloomy or not, the course he described had to be followed:

> Whether the order established after the world war represented a change for the better or not, we must oppose any change to it, since that would lead to a new and bloody war . . . There is no guarantee that war will yield a better and more just order. One must not forget that the Brest-Litovsk peace . . . was not better than that of Versailles.

Having laid out his premises, Litvinov then defended 'collective security' and bilateral pacts. He observed that the pact with Czechoslovakia, more than any other factor, had served to improve the country's international position. Clearly, alluding to the unfolding crisis, he insisted that the Soviet Union and other nations had to stand firm in their opposition to aggression, that this would not undermine the defence of peace and that he himself had never sided with those who advocated non-intervention in the Spanish conflict as the surest way to preserve peace. As it turned out, then, Litvinov had not given up the substance of his former views.

However, when he made his concluding remarks, the pessimism that had been so evident in his introductory remarks reappeared. Though he had called for collective measures to save mankind from war, he had been heartbroken to see his words go unheeded by the international community. Henceforth the USSR would consider itself 'free from all responsibility for subsequent events'. Two months earlier, *Le journal de Moscou* had already used the same words in a series of comments on the statements made by Litvinov on 17 March 1938.[258] Was this, then, a renunciation? Assuring his audience that the USSR 'asks nothing for itself, and is not imposing itself as a partner and ally' Litvinov insisted that the situation was particularly dangerous for those states who bore responsibility for the postwar order: if the fascist opposition to Western states was as stiff and united as ever, the latter had only Czechoslovakia as support in eastern Europe. There was no need to be concerned about Soviet interests: even if current policies did not save the situation from degenerating, the country could still depend on its stalwart army, newly invigorated after the purging of a fifth column.[259]

All of the advanced views Litvinov had once grouped under what he earlier called a 'potential for peace' he now passed over in silence – this was as true when he addressed a Soviet audience as when he addressed foreigners. Even in past years Litvinov's interventions had not always been consistent with this ideal: from the end of 1936 onwards, he had occasionally mentioned isolationism as a possibility. Now he was less concerned with linking the concept of maintaining a general peace to the task of safeguarding national security.

Above every other concern, Litvinov devoted his energy to countering Hitler's hostility to the USSR by fostering multilateral security arrangements. This distinguished him from Stalin's other advisors, especially Molotov. But he never became a real innovator in foreign policy, and showed no interest in the conceptual correlation between the awareness of the end of the old imperialist order and the new culture of interdependence. Even his conviction that Hitler posed a grave threat to his own country, and Europe as well, amounted to a negative principle. The new approach to Soviet foreign policy was only implicit in such principles as the 'indivisibility of peace' and 'collective security', which Litvinov himself considered his significant contribution 'to the abstract science of peace' (another contribution he considered significant was his definition of 'the aggressor state').[260] But international developments during the second half of the 1930s were essentially seen in the USSR as a combined revival of 1914 (which provided the model for relations between the great powers) and of 1918 (which provided the model for relations between the USSR and the capitalist world). Litvinov never managed to present a forceful alternative to this dogmatic view that dominated Stalinist thinking on foreign policy.

NOTES

1. G. Kennan, *Russia and the West under Lenin and Stalin* (Boston, MA: Little, Brown, 1961), p. 316. Nikolaevskii, *Les dirigeants soviétiques et la lutte pour le pouvoir*.
2. Gnedin, *Iz istorii otnoshenii mezhdu SSSR i fashistskoi Germaniei*.
3. R. C. Tucker, *Stalin in Power: The Revolution from Above, 1928–1941* (New York: Norton, 1990), p. 4.
4. T. J. Uldricks, 'The Impact of the Great Purges on the People's Commissariat of Foreign Affairs', *Slavic Review* 36 (June 1977), pp. 187–203.
5. O. Khlevniuk, 'The Reasons for the Great Terror: The Foreign Political Aspect', in Pons and Romano (eds), *Russia in the Age of Wars*, pp. 159–69.
6. Haslam, *The Soviet Union and the Struggle for Collective Security in Europe*, pp. 156–7.
7. N. S. Khrushchev, *Khrushchev Remembers* (London: Little, Brown, 1971), p. 93.
8. *Pravda*, 26 September 1936.
9. *Izvestiia Tsk KPSS* 9 (1989), p. 39.
10. 'O tak nazyvaemom "parallel'nom antisovetskom trotskistskom tsentre"', *Izvestiia Tsk KPSS* 9 (1989), p. 37.
11. 'O tak nazyvaemom "antisovetskom pravotrotskistskom bloke"', *Izvestiia Tsk KPSS* 1 (1989), p. 130. 'O partiinosti lits, prokhodivshikh po delu tak nazyvaemogo "antisovetskogo pravotrotskistskogo bloka"', *Izvestiia Tsk KPSS* 5 (1989), p. 70.
12. *Pravda*, 10 September 1936.
13. *Izvestiia Tsk KPSS* 5 (1989), p. 72.
14. RGASPI, f. 17, op. 2, d. 575, l. 57.
15. Ibid., ll. 77, 91.
16. Ibid., l. 69.

17. See Khlevniuk, 'The Reasons for the Great Terror', in Pons and Romano (eds), *Russia in the Age of Wars*, p. 165.
18. *Pravda*, 1 February 1937. Molotov returned to the same concept at the plenum of February–March 1937; see 'Materialy fevral'sko-martovskogo plenuma TsK VKP(b) 1937 goda', *Voprosy istorii* 8–9 (1992), pp. 19–29; 'Materialy fevral'sko-martovskogo plenuma TsK VKP(b) 1937 goda', *Voprosy istorii* 8 (1993), pp. 24–6; 'Materialy fevral'sko-martovskogo plenuma TsK VKP(b) 1937 goda', *Voprosy istorii* 8 (1994), pp. 27–8; *Pravda*, 21 April 1937.
19. 'Materialy fevral'sko-martovskogo plenuma', *Voprosy istorii* 3 (1995), pp. 5–6. Stalin, *Works* 1, pp. 194–7.
20. 'Materialy fevral'sko-martovskogo plenuma', *Voprosy istorii* 3 (1995), pp. 7, 10. Stalin, *Works* 1, pp. 210, 214.
21. 'Materialy fevral'sko-martovskogo plenuma', *Voprosy istorii* 5 (1993), pp. 4–5. *Pravda*, 21 March 1937.
22. 'Materialy fevral'sko-martovskogo plenuma', *Voprosy istorii* 8 (1993), p. 25. *Pravda*, 21 April 1937.
23. D. Manuil'skii, 'O kapitalisticheskom okruzhenii SSSR', *Bol'shevik* 9 (1937), pp. 25–7.
24. Ibid., p. 28.
25. Ibid., pp. 29–30.
26. RGASPI, f. 77, op. 1, d. 659, ll. 64–5 (10 June 1937).
27. Ibid., l. 64.
28. 'Delo o tak nazyvaemoi "antisovetskoi trotskistskoi voennoi organizatsii" v Krasnoi Armii', *Izvestiia Tsk KPSS* 4 (1989), pp. 42–62.
29. See Krivitsky, *J'étais un agent de Staline*, p. 211.
30. 'Delo o tak nazyvaemoi "antisovetskoi trotskistskoi voennoi organizatsii" v Krasnoi Armii', *Izvestiia Tsk KPSS* 4 (1989), p. 49.
31. Iu. Petrov, *Partiinoe stroitelstvo v sovetskoi armii i flote*, pp. 284–9.
32. *Izvestiia Tsk KPSS* 4 (1989), pp. 58–9.
33. D. Volkogonov, *Triumf i tragediia*, vol. 1, pp. 267 ff.
34. Erickson, *The Soviet High Command*, p. 465.
35. 'Delo o tak nazyvaemoi "antisovetskoi trotskistskoi voennoi organizatsii" v Krasnoi Armii', *Izvestiia Tsk KPSS* 4 (1989), pp. 49–52.
36. Volkogonov, *Triumf i tragediia*, vol. 1, p. 259.
37. 'Delo o tak nazyvaemoi "antisovetskoi trotskistskoi voennoi organizatsii" v Krasnoi Armii', *Izvestiia Tsk KPSS* 4 (1989), p. 53.
38. Ibid.; RGASPI, f. 558, op. 11, d. 1120.
39. *Izvestiia Tsk KPSS* 4 (1989), p.54; RGASPI,f. 558, op. 11, d. 1120, ll. 43–4.
40. Volkogonov, *Triumf i tragediia*, vol. 1, p. 268.
41. On the influence of the Spanish civil war on Stalin's decision for a policy of repression, see remarks by Khlevniuk, 'The Reasons for the Great Terror', in Pons and Romano (eds), *Russia in the Age of Wars*, p. 163.
42. *Krasnaia zvezda*, 9 and 10 June 1937.
43. *Pravda*, 11 June 1937.
44. 'Delo o tak nazyvaemoi "antisovetskoi trotskistskoi voennoi organizatsii" v Krasnoi Armii', *Izvestiia Tsk KPSS* 4 (1989), p. 57.
45. *Krasnaia zvezda*, 14 June 1937.
46. For an assessment of Western diplomatic sources relevant to the 'Tukhachevskii affair', see D. C. Watt, 'Who Plotted Against Whom? Stalin's Purge of the Soviet High Command Revisited', *Journal of Soviet Military Studies* (March 1990).
47. 'Delo o tak nazyvaemoi "antisovetskoi trotskistskoi voennoi organizatsii" v Krasnoi Armii', *Izvestiia Tsk KPSS* 4 (1989), p. 61.
48. See R. Conquest, *The Great Terror: A Reassessment* (London: Hutchinson, 1990) pp. 198–9.
49. *Vestnik MIDa* 8 (1989), pp. 44–7.
50. Ibid.
51. AVP RF, f. 136, op. 21, p. 169, d. 837, l. 6.
52. AVP RF, f. 136, op. 21, p. 170, d. 843, l. 88 (28 September 1937).

53. ASMAE, Affari politici: Urss, 1937, b. 23, fasc. 2.
54. PRO FO 371/21094, N546/45/38.
55. PRO FO 371/21095, N1694/46/38 (25 March 1937).
56. ASMAE, Affari politici: Urss, 1937, b. 25, fasc. 10.
57. DVP SSSR, XX, doc. 110, pp. 174–5.
58. PRO FO 371/21095, N2231/46/38 (23 April 1937).
59. See Weinberg, *The Foreign Policy of Hitler's Germany*, p. 214.
60. PRO FO 371/20347, N5715/187/88 (16 November 1936). See also Erickson, *The Soviet High Command*, pp. 394–5.
61. B. M. Orlov, 'V poiskakh soiuznikov: komandovanie Krasnoi Armii i problemy vneshnei politiki SSSR v 30-kh godakh', *Voprosy Istorii* 4 (1990), pp. 40–53.
62. On the foreign policy implications of the 'Tukhachevskii affair', see remarks by Carr, *The Comintern and the Spanish Civil War*, p. 51.
63. *Voenno-istoricheskii zhurnal* 8 (1991), pp. 45–53; *Voenno-istoricheskii zhurnal* 9 (1991), pp. 55–63.
64. Ibid., p. 61.
65. Rossiiskii Gosudarstvennii Voennii Arkhiv, *Marshal M.N. Tukhachevskii (1893–1937gg.). Komplekt dokumentov iz fondov RGVA* (Moscow: 1994). See L. Samuelson, 'Tukhachevsky and the Military–Industrial Complex, 1925–37', in Pons and Romano (eds), *Russia in the Age of Wars*, p. 207.
66. See V. Pozniakov, 'The Enemy at the Gates: Soviet Military Intelligence in the Inter-War Period and its Forecasts of Future War, 1921–41', in Pons and Romano (eds), *Russia in the Age of Wars*, p. 223.
67. *Voenno-istoricheskii zhurnal* 8 (1991), p. 47.
68. Ibid.
69. *Izvestiia*, 23 April 1937.
70. *Izvestiia*, 24 April 1937.
71. PRO FO 371/21353, W8415/23/41; PRO FO 371/21353, W8499/23/41.
72. See Haslam, *The Soviet Union and the Struggle for Collective Security in Europe*, p. 132.
73. A record of the March conversation between Litvinov and Rosso is in ASMAE, Affari politici: Urss, 1937, b. 25, fasc. 2. The attempt to contact the Italian government had been suggested to Stalin by Litvinov: AVP RF, f. 05, op. 17, p. 126, d. 1, l. 111. A record of the April conversation between Litvinov and Rosso is in ASMAE, Affari politici: Urss, 1937, b. 25, fasc. 2.
74. ASMAE, Affari politici: Urss, 1937, b. 24, fasc. 7. The Soviet record of the conversation contains only Litvinov's statement that it was impossible for the Narkomindel to exercise influence on the NKVD: AVP RF, f. 05, op. 17, p. 126, d. 4, l. 34.
75. AVP RF, f. 05, op. 17, p. 126, d. 1, ll. 178–9.
76. RGASPI, f. 17, op. 2, d. 612, l. 98.
77. See Uldricks, 'The Impact of the Great Purges', p. 194.
78. Three months before Rozenberg's return to Moscow, Stalin, Molotov and Voroshilov had signed a letter to Largo Caballero in which they offered to find a replacement for Rozenberg if the Spanish government so desired. See Carr, *The Comintern and the Spanish Civil War*, pp. 86–8.
79. On 4 August 1937, Litvinov told Surits to inform the French that the rumours about Rozenberg's arrest were without foundation; AVP RF, f. 136, op. 21, p. 169, d. 837, l. 8.
80. See Conquest, *The Great Terror*, pp. 209, 424–5.
81. AVP RF, f. 136, op. 21, p. 169, d. 839, l. 20.
82. ASMAE, Affari politici: Urss, 1937, b. 24, fasc. 2.
83. A. Noritskii, 'Uroki dvukh let', *Izvestiia*, 5 May 1937.
84. *Izvestiia*, 20 May 1937.
85. DVP SSSR, XX, doc. 142, p. 234.
86. AVP RF, f. 136, op. 21, p. 169, d. 839, l. 27.
87. AVP RF, f. 136, op. 21, p. 169, d. 837, ll. 5–6.
88. AVP RF, f. 136, op. 21, p. 169, d. 839, l. 32.
89. AVP RF, f. 136, op. 21, p. 169, d. 840, l. 84.

STALIN AND THE INEVITABLE WAR, 1936–1941

90. Ibid., ll. 80–1.
91. AVP RF, f. 136, op. 21, p. 170, d. 843, ll. 52–3.
92. DVP SSSR, XX, doc. 149, p. 241.
93. Ibid., doc. 124, pp. 193–7; doc. 234, pp. 365–9.
94. *Izvestiia*, 15 March 1937. PRO FO 371/21103, N1479/272/38.
95. DVP SSSR, XX, doc. 69, p. 129.
96. P. Lapinskii, 'Dazhe ne shirma', *Izvestiia*, 26 March 1937.
97. P. Lapinskii, 'Ot gigantskogo tolchka do gigantskikh pobed', *Izvestiia*, 18 March 1937.
98. DVP SSSR, XX, doc. 48, p. 86.
99. Ibid., doc. 29, pp. 60–1.
100. *Izvestiia*, 14 April 1937.
101. DVP SSSR, XX, p. 722; doc. 170, pp. 264–5.
102. Ibid., doc. 177, p. 271.
103. *Izvestiia*, 29 May 1937.
104. M. Litvinov, *V bor'be za mir* (Moscow: Politizdat, 1938), p. 152.
105. Ibid., p. 153.
106. DVP SSSR, XX, doc. 217, p. 337.
107. *Izvestiia*, 5 July 1937. *Le journal de Moscou*, 6 July 1937.
108. DVP SSSR, XX, doc. 224, p. 350; doc. 225, p. 351.
109. AVP RF, f. 05, op. 17, p. 126, d. 1, l. 293.
110. DVP SSSR, XX, doc. 212, pp. 331–2.
111. Ibid., doc. 164, p. 256 and doc. 166, pp. 258–9.
112. Ibid., doc. 172, p. 266.
113. Ibid., doc. 230, p. 363.
114. AVP RF, f. 05, op. 17, p. 126, d. 4, ll. 17–18.
115. Ibid., l. 20.
116. *Izvestiia*, 23 July 1937.
117. DVP SSSR, XX, doc. 276, p. 434.
118. Ibid., doc. 269, pp. 414–18.
119. Ibid., doc. 275, p. 431.
120. AVP RF, f. 136, op. 21, p. 169, d. 837, l. 9.
121. Ibid., ll. 11–13.
122. DVP SSSR, XX, doc. 245, p. 384.
123. PRO FO 371/21102, N2608/255/38.
124. Litvinov, *V bor'be za mir*, p. 156.
125. *Le journal de Moscou*, 13 July 1937.
126. Dimitrov, *Dnevnik*, p. 123.
127. On the anti-Trotskyite persecutions in Spain, see A. Elorza and M. Bizcarrondo, *Queridos camaradas: La Internacional Comunista i Espana, 1919–1939* (Barcelona: Planeta, 1999), pp. 362 ff.
128. *La correspondance internationale*, 12 June 1937, p. 595.
129. RGASPI, f. 495, op. 18, d. 1202, l. 8.
130. See Carr, *The Comintern and the Spanish Civil War*, pp. 48 ff.
131. G. Dimitrov, 'L'unité de la classe ouvrière supreme exigence de l'heure actuelle', *La correspondance internationale*, 8 May 1937, pp. 493–4.
132. G. Dimitrov, 'Les leçons d'Almeria', *La correspondance internationale*, 12 June 1937, pp. 593–4.
133. G. Dimitrov, 'God geroicheskoi bor'by ispanskogo naroda', *Pravda*, 18 July 1937. *La correspondance internationale*, 24 July 1937, p. 726.
134. Ibid.
135. D. Manuil'skii, 'O kapitalisticheskom okruzhenii SSSR', *Bol'shevik* 9 (1937).
136. *Izvestiia*, 1 August 1937.
137. E. Tarle, 'Rozhdenie voiny', *Izvestiia*, 1 August 1937.
138. *Pravda*, 1 August 1937.
139. E. Varga, 'Kapitalisticheskoe khoziaistvo v pervoi polovine 1937g.', *Mirovoe khoziaistvo i mirovaia politika* 8 (1937), p. 58.
140. G. Dimitrov, 'Fashizm, eto voina', *Pravda*, 1 August 1937. *La correspondance*

internationale, 7 August 1937, pp. 773–5.
141. RGASPI, f. 495, op. 18, d. 1224, ll. 83–93.
142. RGASPI, f. 495, op. 2, d. 256, l. 80.
143. Togliatti, *Opere*, IV, 1, p. 261.
144. Dallin and Firsov (eds), *Dimitrov and Stalin 1934–1943: Letters from the Soviet Archives*, p. 60.
145. RGASPI, f. 495, op. 2, d. 256, l. 127.
146. RGASPI, f. 495, op. 2, d. 257, l. 1.
147. RGASPI, f. 495, op. 2, d. 257, ll. 3–4.
148. See Thomas, *The Spanish Civil War*, pp. 746–7.
149. RGASPI, f. 495, op. 2, d. 257, l. 20.
150. RGASPI, f. 495, op. 18, d. 1225.
151. *La correspondance internationale*, 11 December 1937, pp. 1245–7.
152. G. Dimitrov, 'Sovetskii Soiuz i rabochii klass kapitalisticheskikh stran', *Pravda*, 7 November 1937. *La correspondance internationale*, 13 November 1937.
153. See Thomas, *The Spanish Civil War*, pp. 702 ff.
154. See Conquest, *The Great Terror*, pp. 399 ff.
155. Dallin and Firsov (eds), *Dimitrov and Stalin 1934–1943. Letters from the Soviet Archives*, pp. 28–31.
156. F. Firsov, 'Stalin i Komintern', *Voprosy Istorii* 9 (1989), p. 16.
157. RGASPI, f. 495, op. 73, d. 48.
158. RGASPI, f. 495, op. 73, d. 48, ll. 100–1.
159. *Izvestiia*, 12 September 1937.
160. *Izvestiia*, 15 September 1937.
161. *Le journal de Moscou*, 21 September 1937.
162. *Le journal de Moscou*, 12 October 1937; *Izvestiia*, 8 October 1937. But also, earlier, P. Lapinskii, 'Amerika i problemy voiny i mira', *Izvestiia*, 8 April 1937.
163. Litvinov, *V bor'be za mir*, pp.174–5.
164. Ibid., p. 176.
165. Ibid., p. 179.
166. *Izvestiia*, 30 September 1937.
167. The USSR still demanded that recognition of the warring sides take second place to evacuation of the volunteers: DVP SSSR, XX, doc. 374, p. 560; doc. 377, p. 562.
168. Ibid., doc. 380, p. 564; doc. 381, p. 566.
169. Ibid., doc. 386, p. 574.
170. Ibid., doc. 390, pp. 578–9.
171. AVP RF, f. 05, op. 17, p. 126, d. 1, l. 348.
172. DVP SSSR, XX, p. 764.
173. Ibid., doc. 422, pp. 623–30.
174. See R. A. C. Parker, *Chamberlain and Appeasement. British Policy and the Coming of the Second World War* (London: Macmillan, 1993), pp. 99–100. See also Weinberg, *The Foreign Policy of Hitler's Germany*, pp. 119–20.
175. *Le journal de Moscou*, 1 December 1937.
176. E. Aleksandrov, 'Anglo-germanskie peregovory i delo mira', *Izvestiia*, 27 November 1937. The use of the pseudonym 'E. Aleksandrov' when commenting on international policy has been revealed in the memoirs of the same Gnedin; see Gnedin, *Iz istorii otnoshenii mezhdu SSSR i fashistskoi Germanei*.
177. E. Aleksandrov, 'Blok trekh agressorov', *Bol'shevik* 22 (1937), pp. 83–4.
178. Litvinov, *V bor'be za mir*, p. 188.
179. Ibid., p. 192.
180. Haslam, *The Soviet Union and the Struggle for Collective Security in Europe*, pp. 153–4. Litvinov would have recognized that rapprochement between the USSR and Germany was possible. This assertion lends itself, however, to various interpretations, depending on whether it refers simply to a search for a *modus vivendi*, or instead to the search for a more meaningful understanding, à la Kandelaki.
181. AVP RF, f. 05, op. 17, p. 122, d. 25, ll. 230–2.
182. DVP SSSR, XX, doc. 423, pp. 632–3.

183. AVP RF, f. 136, op. 21, p. 169, d. 839, l. 49.
184. Ibid., l. 48.
185. AVP RF, f. 05, op. 17, p. 128, d. 24, ll. 70–1.
186. AVP RF, f. 136, op. 21, p. 169, d. 839, l. 47.
187. DVP SSSR, XX, doc. 446, pp. 671–3. AVP RF, f. 136, op. 21, p. 169, d. 839, ll. 61–3 (10 December 1937).
188. V. Galianov, 'Fashistskie agressory i ikh posobniki', *Bol'shevik* 1 (1938), pp. 58–69.
189. DVP SSSR, XX, doc. 427, p. 637. On 14 December, Maiskii proposed to the Narkomindel that the USSR declare its willingness to join Great Britain in a 'joint struggle' against the aggression in the Far East, on the condition that a similar struggle be waged in Europe too, under the aegis of the League of Nations; Litvinov agreed to this proposal: DVP SSSR, XX, doc. 440, pp. 657, 768.
190. *Pravda*, 10 November 1937.
191. *Leningradskaia pravda*, 10–11 December 1937.
192. *La correspondance internationale*, 25 December 1937, pp. 1312–14.
193. AVP RF, f. 05, op. 17, p. 126, d. 1, l. 296.
194. GARF, f. 7523, op. 3, d. 14, ll. 141–5; *Pravda*; 18 January 1938.
195. AVP RF, f. 05, op. 17, p. 126, d. 1, l. 430.
196. GARF, f. 7523, op. 3, d. 14, l. 144; *Pravda*, 18 January 1938.
197. *Pravda*, 20 January 1938.
198. RGASPI, f. 77, op. 3, d. 18.
199. RGASPI, f. 82, op. 2. In a private conversation of February 1948 (as recorded in these same Molotov papers), Litvinov said that more than a year before his dismissal he had written a letter to Stalin, asking to be released from the Narkomindel. As he recalled it, his main point was that he lacked direct contact with Stalin, and that a member of the Politburo should therefore be appointed as people's commissar; but he had decided not to send the letter, worrying that it could be interpreted as a request to become a member of the Politburo. He himself, however, believed that someone had given the letter to Stalin. Litvinov's letter to Stalin of 10 January 1938, quoted above, did not contain any mention of the Politburo nor complaints about his scant communication with Stalin – although the latter argument might have been implicit.
200. Zhdanov had been proposed by Beriia: see GARF, f. 7523, op. 3, d. 12, ll. 57–8.
201. See O. Khlevniuk, *Politburo. Mekhanizmy politicheskoi vlasti v 1930-e gody* (Moscow: Rossiiskaia politicheskaia entsiklopediia, 1996), pp. 246–7.
202. RGASPI, f. 17, op. 3, d. 986.
203. S. Dullin, 'Litvinov and the People's Commissariat of Foreign Affairs: The Fate of an Administration under Stalin', in Pons, Romano (eds), *Russia in the Age of Wars*, pp. 136 ff.
204. RGASPI, f. 495, op. 73, d. 48, l. 100.
205. Stalin, *Works*, vol. 1, pp. 271–2.
206. Ibid., pp. 269–70.
207. See T. Martin, 'The Origins of Soviet Ethnic Cleansing', *Journal of Modern History* 4 (1998), pp. 852–8.
208. Khlevniuk, 'The Reasons for the Great Terror', in Pons, Romano (eds), *Russia in the Age of Wars*, p. 162. See also O. Khlevniuk, 'The Objectives of the Great Terror', in J. Cooper, M. Perrie, E. A. Rees (eds), *Soviet History, 1917–1953. Essays in Honour of R. W. Davies*, (London: Macmillan, 1993).
209. 'Materialy fevral'sko-martovskogo plenuma', *Voprosy istorii* 2–3 (1992), p. 11. Bukharin maintained that even on the front regarded as the 'most difficult', namely the German front, one could count on the Polish masses allying themselves with the USSR. He also considered it safe to assume that Germany's independent economic basis would prove inadequate. At the same time, he declared that 'the cowardice of Great Britain and France is enormous, and we have to be able to rely on our own resources'.
210. *Izvestiia Tsk KPSS* 5 (1989), pp. 77 ff.
211. *Izvestiia Tsk KPSS* 4 (1989), p. 54.

THE INTERNAL CRISIS

212. *Pravda*, 10 March 1938.
213. *Izvestiia Tsk KPSS*, 5 (1989), p. 76.
214. On the defence strategy of Bukharin, see Cohen, *Bukharin and the Bolshevik Revolution*, chap. 10.
215. *Pravda*, 12 March 1938.
216. *Pravda*, 15 January 1938.
217. *Pravda*, 21 January 1938.
218. Dimitrov, *Dnevnik*, pp. 128–9.
219. *Le journal de Moscou*, 21 and 28 December 1937. *Izvestiia*, 28 January 1938.
220. AVP RF, f. 136, op. 21, p. 169, d. 839, l. 48.
221. DVP SSSR, XX, doc. 52, p. 85. See remarks by Parker, *Chamberlain and Appeasement*, p. 122.
222. AVP RF, f. 05, op. 18, p. 140, d. 27, l. 71.
223. Weinberg, *The Foreign Policy of Hitler's Germany*, p. 51.
224. DVP SSSR, XX, doc. 46, pp. 79–81. A similar argument was made by Surits in a letter to Litvinov of 11 February 1938: AVP RF, f. 136, op. 22, p. 172, d. 865, ll. 186–8.
225. DVP SSSR, XX, doc. 54, pp. 89–93.
226. AVP RF, f. 05, op. 18, p. 140, d. 27, ll. 39–43.
227. AVP RF, f. 05, op. 17, p. 122, d. 25, l. 258.
228. AVP RF, f. 05, op. 18, p. 140, d. 27, l. 43.
229. Dimitrov, *Dnevnik*, p. 132.
230. Dallin and Firsov (eds), *Dimitrov and Stalin 1934–1943*, p. 72.
231. Ibid., pp. 36–7.
232. See Elorza and Bizcarrondo, *Queridos camaradas*, pp. 410–17.
233. *Izvestiia*, 18 March 1938.
234. AVP RF, f. 05, op. 18, p. 137, d.1, l. 118.
235. AVP RF, f. 05, op. 18, p. 149, d. 166, l. 5.
236. AVP RF, f. 05, op. 18, p. 140, d. 26, l. 16.
237. Thomas, *The Spanish Civil War*, pp. 804 ff.
238. DVP SSSR, XX, doc. 94, p. 138.
239. Ibid., doc. 97, p. 142.
240. AVP RF, f. 136, op. 22, p. 172, d. 865, l. 175.
241. DVP SSSR, XXI, doc. 102, pp. 149–51.
242. Ibid., doc. 83, p. 129; see also ibid., p. 144.
243. Haslam, *The Soviet Union and the Struggle for Collective Security in Europe*, p. 164.
244. AVP RF, f. 136, op. 22, p. 172, d. 865, l. 66.
245. Ibid., l. 71. Potemkin asserted that Hitler hoped to push Poland into war with the USSR also in an article written under a pseudonym: V. Galianov, 'Kuda idet Pol'sha', *Bol'shevik* 8 (1938). According to the French summary of talks held in Moscow in May 1935, the Soviet leaders displayed particular concern about the Polish question and were sceptical about Warsaw's real intention of collaborating in European security: *Documents Diplomatiques Français* (hereafter: DDF), première série, X, doc. 388, p. 575.
246. DVP SSSR, XXI, doc. 79, pp. 125–6.
247. Ibid., doc. 98, p. 145.
248. Ibid., doc. 110, p. 162.
249. E. Aleksandrov in *Izvestiia*, 26 March 1938.
250. AVP RF, f. 136, op. 22, p. 172, d. 865, l. 79.
251. AVP RF, f. 05, op. 18, p. 140, d. 27, ll. 109–10.
252. PRO FO 371/21102, N6317/250/38.
253. DVP SSSR, XXI, doc. 96, p. 141.
254. AVP RF, f. 136, op. 22, p. 172, d. 865, l. 63.
255. DVP SSSR, XXI, doc. 183, p. 264.
256. *Izvestiia*, 14 and 16 May 1938.
257. *Leningradskaia pravda*, 24 June 1938.
258. *Le journal de Moscou*, 22 March 1938.
259. *Leningradskaia pravda*, 24 June 1938.
260. B. D. Wolfe, *Strange Communists I Have Known* (New York: Stein & Day, 1965), p. 211.

4

The Eastern Crises: Czechoslovakia

THE PROBLEM OF 'PREVENTATIVE WAR'

The Western powers cannot be held exclusively responsible for the withdrawal and inaction of the USSR in the face of an increasingly tense European atmosphere. More and more, Soviet foreign policy was one of watchfulness rather than involvement; this was due, to a large extent, to internal political trends and deliberate strategic choice. Consequently, the Soviet advocacy of firmness in the defence of general peace turned out to be rather less binding than Litvinov's exhortations to the League of Nations had suggested. This passive posture became all the more evident as the European crises expanded eastward. The Czech crisis soon proved that the Soviet Union lacked the will and the means to play a significant role in European affairs: Moscow retreated still further from the international stage.

On 18 May 1938, Beneš sent an appeal to Stalin, Molotov, Voroshilov and Litvinov declaring he was determined to defend the frontiers and sovereignty of the state 'with all the means at his disposal', thereby announcing the mobilization undertaken a few days later.[1] On 23 May the Prague government reacted to German pressure at its frontiers by calling for a partial military mobilization. London and Paris approved the Czech move, and though Hitler did not give up his plan of eventually invading, he did postpone the attack on Czechoslovakia.[2] The Soviet response to the Czech mobilization was positive, and the press showered praise on the Czech leadership for standing up to the Nazi aggressors: this was a fine example of defending peace and preventing international catastrophe.[3] The Soviets remained aware, however, that this was no final solution, and that this first skirmish presaged more serious developments.[4] Things had not really changed much since the *Anschluss*. Dispatches arriving in Moscow from Berlin spoke of imminent danger. Since the end of April, Astakhov had repeatedly opined that German designs on Czechoslovakia could be thwarted only if widespread military retaliation seemed inevitable.[5] But the British were not prepared to level such a threat, and Soviet diplomats in Great Britain made this clear to their superiors in Moscow. During a conversation with Wilson, Maiskii learned that Chamberlain did not consider the USSR a fit wartime ally.[6] For the Soviets this was not an unexpected discovery, but it was now aggravated by the knowledge that the French shared Chamberlain's view and that the appeasement favoured by Britain was going to prevail. Surits informed the Narkomindel that Chamberlain had mounted a campaign to convince Daladier to avoid any actions that could be interpreted as the prologue to a 'preventative war'.[7] As mutual mistrust between the French and the Soviets became more visible, Czech leaders grew alarmed.

However, in spite of their public praise, the Soviets were reluctant to lend unilateral assistance in support of the Czechs without assurance of French intervention. On 19 May 1938, Litvinov informed Aleksandrovskii about conversations he had held with Halifax and with the new French foreign minister, Georges Bonnet. When Bonnet had asked how the USSR would behave in the event of a crisis between Prague and Berlin, followed by a French mobilization, Litvinov had spoken of the need to negotiate with the states that stood between the USSR and Czechoslovakia (the Baltic countries, Poland, Romania). He insisted that at every step there would have to be careful discussions between the general staffs of the Soviets, the French and the Czechs.[8] Though it had never quite shaken the Western democracies out of their torpor, Litvinov proposed to continue the policy pursued since the *Anschluss*. As to the specifics of the Czech case, he was handing over responsibility to the French: did not the mechanics of the Czech–Soviet pact depend wholly on the implementation of the Franco-Czech pact? And how could the German menace be halted in Central Europe if the Spanish question risked provoking a split between the USSR and Europe's western democracies? When Litvinov pointed out this problem to Coulondre he was reviving old Soviet threats to withdraw from the London committee.[9]

This mode of conduct, aimed simply at reaffirming well-known positions, had up to now produced mixed results. It had effectively alerted European countries to the German danger, but had also revealed the absence of a fully developed Soviet policy. This problem had been exposed most starkly in the speech Litvinov had given in Leningrad in late June. Despite his insistence that the USSR would not stand idly by as events took their course and that the case of Czechoslovakia demonstrated the special role of the USSR in relieving international tensions, the impasse was evident.[10]

But the point was not just Narkomindel impotence. In May and June 1938 Zhdanov addressed foreign-policy questions in two speeches given in Leningrad, effectively outlining the position of Litvinov's opponents among Soviet leaders. In his opinion, the wave of 'imperialist wars' already crashing over Spain and China was about to overrun Czechoslovakia and so threaten the USSR. This meant that it was time to prepare for the 'final victory over capitalism', which would be guaranteed by the support 'of the proletariat of all countries'.[11] Zhdanov believed that 'there exist democracies that can strike at fascism': these were not the familiar Western democracies but another growing sort of state, the 'workers' democracy'. The opposition in both Spain and China to fascism and capitalism belonged to a truly global phenomenon, and the Czechs too belonged to the international workers' democracy.[12] Zhdanov recalled that in the struggle against fascism, 'arms play a part in determining the outcome, but so does the spirit of the fighting man'. Should the USSR become the target of aggression, it would have to rely on 'moral and political factors' and on the people's 'moral and idealistic commitments'; it would also have to renew its commitment to 'encouraging revolution in all countries'.[13]

This could still be distinguished from Dimitrov's idea that the anti-fascist struggle in Spain 'has delayed and continues to delay the outbreak of a new world war'.[14] The secretary of the Comintern clung obstinately to the conviction that the wagers had not yet been placed, adducing three reasons: the struggle in Spain was not yet definitely compromised; the Czech people would offer resistance much as the Spanish had; and popular discontent was undermining the apparent stability of the fascist regimes.[15] Though he distinguished himself from Zhdanov's fanaticism, Dimitrov exhibited a reliance on propaganda and wishful thinking to a far greater extent than did the Narkomindel. He trusted in a mass response, though in the most important European countries this was rather unlikely. As for Spain, the ephemeral successes on the Ebro in July 1938 convinced no one that defeat could be long postponed. This comfortless perception had the opposite effect to that hoped for by Dimitrov. With the advance of the Czech crisis, anti-fascists fighting in Spain came to believe that a general war would soon break out in Europe and that only such an event would put an end to the isolation of the Spanish republic.[16] In other words, the pressure to establish a link between the war in Spain and universal war was not diminishing; thanks to desperation it was growing. Actually, many in the Soviet Union approved of such a link, but it rendered the Spanish question less urgent. There is no evidence that Ercoli's repeated appeals for more effective assistance to Republican Spain which were forwarded by Dimitrov to Stalin found an echo in Moscow.[17] At the end of August, Stalin approved the decision to dismantle the International Brigades.[18]

Soviet commentators compared 1938 with 1914. 'Only a blind person', declared a writer, could fail to see that 'the present situation, much more so than that of 1914, bears the unmistakable signs of the beginning of a world war'. This was almost exactly what Radek had said two years earlier. The writer hastened to remark, however, that even if 'the contradiction between the two systems, socialist and capitalist, appears to be the fundamental one of our age' this did not diminish the potential for conflict between the imperialist states. In fact, the 'contradictions' between Great Britain and Germany, the greatest powers in a declining capitalist world, could not be alleviated by diplomacy, and had to be considered the most significant factor in the current conflict.[19] Acknowledgement that the war was taking its course and concentration on the internal divisions in the capitalist world: these were the watchwords of the day in Moscow.

All of this justified passivity. Pessimism prevailed among the leading Soviet diplomats. At the end of July, in a long letter to Litvinov, Surits provided compelling arguments for giving up hope on a French initiative independent of Great Britain. For the French, it was Czechoslovakia rather than Spain that constituted 'an inseparable part of the general European problem'. The reason was simple: with the conquest of Czechoslovakia, Germany would gain a tremendous strategic advantage in a future war. Though this might have been expected to prod Paris to concern and compromise, the French showed no interest in an alliance with the USSR.[20] Moreover, it looked to Surits as though the British meant to convince the Czech leaders through peaceful means to yield what Hitler seemed poised to take by force; he suggested the possibility that Britain would soon open 'broad negotiations' aimed at reviving the 'pact of four'.[21] By this point, even those diplomats least susceptible to Party ideology had concluded that a European settling of accounts was in the offing, and that probably war was bound to follow.

During the next two months, the gap dividing the USSR from the Western powers widened. On 11 August 1938 Litvinov reminded Aleksandrovskii that the liquidation of the 1918–19 treaties had a special resonance for the West: certainly the USSR was interested in ensuring Czech independence, 'but without the Western powers, we would have difficulty undertaking anything substantial'.[22] Maiskii reported to Moscow that, in accordance with the Narkomindel's instructions, he had declared to Halifax that the USSR considered both the British and the French policies 'weak and short-sighted'; the Western countries would have to 'bear the responsibility for the approach and outbreak of a new world war'.[23] A few days later, in a letter to Litvinov, Maiskii maintained that Chamberlain's authority was declining, both domestically and internationally.[24] Meanwhile, Astakhov reported from Berlin that German preparations were intensifying; he predicted that by mid-September decisive steps would be taken.[25]

The most convulsive and decisive phase of the crisis had begun. On 22 August 1938 Litvinov communicated with Aleksandrovskii and Aleksei Merekalov, the new Soviet representative to Berlin: he had expressed to Schulenburg the firm conviction that 'the united Czech people will fight for their independence to the last man; in the event of an attack on Czechoslovakia,[26] France will intervene against Germany; regardless of Chamberlain's desires, Great Britain will not be able to leave France unaided; the USSR will honour its commitments to Czechoslovakia'. He was the only one of the European foreign ministers to use such direct and unequivocal language, but Schulenburg and his superiors would have seen little reason to take the statements of the Soviet commissar for foreign affairs at face value, since the USSR clearly was not the dynamic diplomatic player Litvinov made it out to be.

On 29 August 1938 Sir Robert Vansittart approached Maiskii and demanded to know why the USSR had yet to take a stand on the situation in central Europe. The ambassador's reply suggested resentment and was certainly evasive: he could not say what 'specific steps' the USSR would take in the event of war. Certainly the USSR would respect 'the commitments it had made', but really the matter hinged on France and Great Britain. 'London and Paris are in no rush to inform us of their plans and activities in central Europe, so why should we behave differently?'[27]

As in the past, Maiskii had been meeting regularly with Churchill. Since the end of March, Churchill had been pressing the Soviet ambassador for a 'firm declaration' on Czechoslovakia. He no longer aired his doubts about the reliability of the Red Army, and went so far as to declare that the USSR was an essential component in the military alliance that would ensure European peace.[28] On 31 August Churchill once again appealed to Maiskii, noting that war could break out within weeks. Maiskii was not moved; he would only repeat Litvinov's declaration of 17 March.[29]

At almost the same time, Litvinov was responding to a similar enquiry from the French. The French ambassador in Moscow, Jean Payart, wanted to know what the Soviet Union would do for Czechoslovakia. Litvinov responded that in any case France was obliged 'to help Czechoslovakia, independently of our help, since our potential assistance depends on that of France'. He declared that Moscow would honour its commitments, provided that Paris did likewise. But first a meeting of all three nations 'interested in the maintenance of peace' was in order.[30] Once Litvinov had checked with Stalin, he reaffirmed his position, and his stance remained consistent during subsequent meetings with Bonnet, Paul-Boncour and Edouard Herriot in Geneva.[31]

Most diplomats, from both democratic and fascist states, now assumed that the USSR would remain aloof from any conflict in Czechoslovakia. Even German military experts, who rated Soviet military strength very high even after the purges, adopted this opinion.[32] Others simply continued to think of Soviet policy as isolationist; they reckoned that Moscow would do all it could to avoid becoming embroiled in a European war.[33] These opinions were right on target. The Soviet policy-makers were unwilling to assume a risk any greater than that assumed by the Western democracies, and they were not inclined to repeat their experience in Spain – though the Soviet media continued to underline the analogies between the two crises and suggested that France and Britain were responsible in both cases. The Soviet rulers were no more likely to rush into a 'preventative war' than their Western counterparts.

On 15 September 1938 Chamberlain met with Hitler for the first time at Berchtesgarden, and the two men drew up the Sudetenland compromise, a move that both confirmed fears long held by Prague and pushed Moscow further from diplomatic centre stage.[34] The Soviet response was immediate: *Le journal de Moscou* printed a denunciation of this 'attempt to dismember Czechoslovakia' and a repudiation of British surrender to what amounted to a 'bluff' by Hitler.[35] But still there had been no official Soviet declaration on German aggression towards Czechoslovakia. The Soviet stance was eventually defined by a decision made by the Politburo and communicated to Aleksandrovskii – it served as a reply to Beneš. As long as France remained faithful to its commitments the pact between the two states would be honoured; and if Germany attacked Czechoslovakia the Soviet Union would, 'as a member of the League of Nations', support a Czech appeal to that body.[36]

The hollowness of this pledge had already become all the more apparent when Potemkin flatly declared, in the presence of the Czech representative Zdenek Fierlinger, that nothing said during Litvinov's recent meetings in Geneva had tempted the Soviets to consider aid to the Czechs.[37] In fact, it is now clear that the Soviets had never seriously entertained such a step, and Potemkin had now rejected the possibility of a future unilateral Soviet initiative. In a conversation with the Italian ambassador, Potemkin had some very harsh things to say about France, and declared the outcome of the crisis preordained to satisfy Hitler's demands. Potemkin went on to wonder who Germany's 'next victim' would be, repeating the prophetic remark he had made some six months earlier about 'the fourth division of Poland'.[38]

Then on 21 September 1938 Litvinov broke the USSR's official silence at Geneva.[39] Bitterly and loudly he complained that one more state, Czechoslovakia, 'has had its internal affairs disrupted by a neighbouring state'. Why was this issue not on the agenda? He then revived the question of sanctions, remarking that the League of Nations was 'still sufficiently strong to prevent or end aggression through collective action'. As to the criticism of sanctions offered in the past, Litvinov rebutted them one by one. He saw within the League of Nations 'two tendencies, two conceptions' feuding over the maintenance of peace: to date the feebler and less resolute tendency had always prevailed, though the aggressors had been, and still were, 'weaker than the peace-loving states would be if they united'.

But just when it looked as if Litvinov would spell out the requirements for establishing 'collective security', he ducked. Perhaps he simply despaired of seeing his hopes materialize. On Soviet policy, Litvinov said nothing more than 'the Soviet government bears no responsibility whatsoever for what is now happening, or for the fatal things yet to come'. This amounted to a reiteration of the Soviet declaration made in the wake of the *Anschluss*. According to Litvinov, the Soviet Union fully intended to stand by its pact with Czechoslovakia and would, together with France, and by 'exploiting the means available to us', provide what help the beleaguered state might need. Soviet military chiefs stood prepared to meet with their French and Czech counterparts so that they all might work out how this help could be provided. Litvinov concluded with a severe warning, which was to prove a tragic and lucid prophecy: should the capitulation which seemed daily more likely occur, it would have 'catastrophic consequences'; it was quite possible that the decision to 'avoid a doubtful war today' would lead to 'a real and universal war tomorrow'.[40]

Two days later, while addressing the League of Nations' political commission, Litvinov insisted on the importance of sanctions in discouraging aggression and cited Article 16 of the League's statute. Had not the negotiations between the USSR, France and Czechoslovakia been conceived as preliminary steps towards what was to be a single, unified regional pact including Poland and Germany? And had not the failure to achieve this regional agreement been the direct cause of the pair of bilateral pacts, and the cause of the subordination of Soviet to French aid? Nevertheless, even after London and Paris had presented their ultimatum to Prague insisting on a modification of Czechoslovakia's frontiers, Moscow declared itself determined to uphold its pact with the Czechs.[41] The question was much more political than moral. France had actually reneged on its vows and abandoned an ally to its grim fate. But Litvinov did not use this argument, which would only have weakened his stance. As it was, he came across as steadfast and appeared to be abandoning the detached pose maintained up to that point by the USSR.

Litvinov's speech took place on the same day a new event exacerbated the international crisis, drawing the USSR into the turmoil. In response to Prague's announcement of general mobilization, Moscow alerted the Polish government that an incursion of Polish troops into Czech territory (rather likely at the time) would effectively abrogate the non-aggression pact the USSR and Poland had signed in 1932.[42] The Narkomindel explained that it was both warning off potential aggression and exposing the egregious mendacity of those who accused the Soviet Union of seeking pretexts for shirking its duties to Czechoslovakia.[43] At the same time, Litvinov sent a confidential telegram to Stalin, begging him to orchestrate 'more convincing displays' of firmness, the sort of words and deeds that would impress Hitler more deeply than any summit meeting or declaration by the powers:

> I believe that a European war is against our interests, since we will be drawn into it. In fact, it is incumbent upon us to do all we can to prevent such a war. Shouldn't we call for a mobilization, or a partial mobilization, and mount a press campaign so as to persuade Hitler and Beck that a major war is in the offing, one in which we will play a part . . . ? It may be that France will join us in declaring a partial mobilization. We must act swiftly.[44]

Three aspects of the telegram deserve particular attention. Above all, Litvinov presented the threat of 'preventative war' as an effective means of deterring Hitler. Clearly, he meant to relaunch a policy of firm resistance, thereby implicitly acknowledging that the USSR had not convincingly opposed the approach Chamberlain had adopted towards Hitler. Second, this was to be an autonomous and unilateral move: possibly France would follow suit, but in either case it was crucial to move forward. Third, Litvinov had not yet abandoned all hope in collective security; the policy he advocated was still intended to avoid a European war – matters had not progressed beyond the point of no return. And as Litvinov said, the war in Europe ran contrary to the interests of the USSR – even, evidently, if it broke out among the capitalist powers.

If accepted, Litvinov's proposal implied that the USSR would soon abandon the passivity with which it had met foreign events since the *Anschluss*. As Litvinov pointed out in a second dispatch, also sent on 23 September, with Chamberlain and Hitler's negotiations stalemated France and Great Britain were bound to see 'the necessity of serious measures'. Litvinov pleaded to know how to act.[45] Two days later, taking his cue from Litvinov, Potemkin suggested to Stalin that the Western powers might consider the old Soviet proposal for an international conference; if they did, it would be enough to demand that representatives of the USSR be present at all of the meetings, without exception, and that they be fully informed about negotiations.[46]

STALIN AND THE INEVITABLE WAR, 1936–1941

We know nothing about Stalin's reaction to Litvinov's suggestions. But clearly he did not approve them, since no diplomatic confrontation took place and no measure aimed at dissuading Hitler was taken. The Soviet Union remained silently seated in its old place, far from the action. A warning had been delivered to Poland, and once more the Soviets waited, hoping rather gloomily that there would be a change of heart in Paris.[47] Moscow's wait-and-see attitude had been re-affirmed. The French continued with their passive stance.[48] The diplomatic initiative was in the hands of Chamberlain, who continued to meet Hitler during the days leading up to the Munich conference.[49]

Soviet predictions on the final outcome wavered. In the diary he kept during his time in Geneva, Maiskii recorded his growing fear that the world could soon 'slip uncontrollably into a new world war'.[50] Though he undercut his grim exercise in pragmatic forecasting with the comment that 'life is not always logical', Maiskii could not resist anticipating the war he thought 'inevitable', one bound to involve both France and the USSR.[51] Maiskii reported that Litvinov clung to the opposite view, expecting the Western powers to yield and the anticipated war to evaporate.[52]

Outside the diplomatic sphere, the terms significantly changed. When the Muscovite press weighed in, it was to predict a war between Germany and Czechoslovakia as protracted as the recent war in Spain.[53] Manuil'skii offered the same forecast in a pair of speeches he gave on 11 and 16 September 1938.[54] Dimitrov too had been maintaining, since mid-September, that it would be necessary 'to face up to war soon'.[55] Among the Comintern leaders, the Spanish civil war was projected as a model of the new crisis, but the expectation was that no 'localization' of the conflict could now be achieved. Dimitrov clearly expected popular resistance in Czechoslovakia: in his opinion, there was nothing 'worse than giving up without a fight', and only Czech resistance would lead the British and the French to change their attitude.[56] To this end, he repeated his call for an international workers' conference, which would serve as a means for mass mobilization against Chamberlain and Daladier.[57] Dimitrov's tense correspondence with Manuil'skii, Moskvin and Kuusinen during the second half of September scarcely deviated from these issues.[58] But all of these forebodings precipitated no concrete action at all; in fact, Stalin seems to have been resisting any sort of move. As late as 29 September, on the immediate eve of the conference at Munich, Dimitrov wrote to Manuil'skii and Moskvin:

> Have you received any advice, directives, or remarks from Comr. St[alin] or from our comrades in the Politburo regarding our current work ? I hope you have informed St[alin] about the main initiatives we have taken.[59]

CZECHOSLOVAKIA

The variety of opinion that continues to surround discussions of the purposes and the scale of Red Army mobilization in September 1938 need not be resolved in the current study.[60] The different conclusions pointed to by materials kept in the archives of Russia, on the one hand, and those of Czechoslovakia, on the other, are sufficient to suggest the difficulty of such an endeavour.[61] But whatever its scale, Soviet military mobilization was not accompanied by clear warnings from Moscow meant to deter German aggression, despite Litvinov's requests. And concerns about Poland were motivating the mobilization.[62] The conclusion to be based on all of the relevant documents at our disposal is that the prevailing Soviet attitude was aimed at avoiding any unilateral assistance to Czechoslovakia against Nazi Germany.[63]

On 29 September 1938, in a public speech in Geneva, Litvinov returned to the question of evacuating foreign combatants from Spain. But so interwoven were the Spanish question and the Czech that when he stated that 'every war or threat of war is the business of the whole League of Nations', Litvinov may have had eastern Europe in mind rather than western.[64] On that same day, the likelihood of war receded, without bringing the USSR back into play either politically or diplomatically. In informing Maiskii of the agenda for the meeting Great Britain, France, Germany and Italy would attend in Munich, Halifax explicitly denied that there was a plan afoot to resuscitate the 'pact of four'.[65] But what the British foreign minister had to say was scarcely suitable for the circumstances. To the Soviets, the consensus beginning to take shape among the four powers looked less like a peaceful way out of a predicament than a disastrous capitulation of the Western powers to Hitler. Churchill's similarly gloomy outlook reinforced this assessment.[66] Soviet worries did not decrease when Britain proposed that the USSR play a part in the emerging territorial compromise by serving as a guarantor of Czech borders once they had been redrawn without the Sudetenland. By 30 September Maiskii had informed the Narkomindel that the USSR was not even mentioned in the Munich agreement.[67]

Great Britain and France had abandoned Czechoslovakia. For a moment, Beneš hoped that the USSR might still come to his aid, and he sent a desperate message to Moscow. No reply was forthcoming; a few hours later a defeated Beneš withdrew his question.[68] All faith in the Czech–Soviet pact had evaporated in Prague, Aleksandrovskii reported, and there were many who speculated that the Franco-Soviet pact would be the next casualty in Munich.[69] As all hope of popular Czech resistance faded, it became evident to all that the Soviet Union had been effectively exiled from international politics. In Paris, Litvinov opened a tense conversation with Bonnet by declaring that Hitler had been presented with territorial gifts at the very moment he might have retreated: 'in all likelihood, he was even more afraid of war than Chamberlain'.[70] But whereas this had long been Litvinov's view, it remained unclear whether Stalin fully agreed. Though Litvinov insisted that Hitler had to be confronted, no European power was likely to do so any time soon – even Litvinov began to allude to a 'fourth division of Poland'.[71]

WAITING FOR WAR

What had the manoeuvers at Munich done to limit Germany's ambitions? Nothing, replied the Soviets, and meanwhile war had drawn nearer. Was the Munich accord the victory for the forces of peace Chamberlain and Daladier had called it? No, roared *Izvestiia* on 4 October 1938.[72] *Le journal de Moscou* focused its polemical attack on France: long before international public opinion had begun to doubt 'the pledges made to Russia and the value of the Franco-Soviet pact', the French government had adopted policies that had left France strategically isolated in the face of Hitler. Tacitly suggesting an imminent abrogation of the treaty with France, the editorialist boldly stated that 'because it has capitulated in the face of aggression, France must be prepared to pay by losing its allies and retreating into isolation'.[73]

The Soviet leaders had seriously discussed dissolving the pact – Litvinov told Surits so on 17 October 1938 – but eventually decided to await more decisive events before making such a move.[74] By early November Moscow had backed away from that step, opting to exploit the period following the Munich conference to observe and evaluate its repercussions.[75] This was, if we credit the gossip then current in Western diplomatic circles, a period of great difficulty for Litvinov, who spent many hours in tense conversation with Stalin and Molotov.[76] As late as 22 October, Maiskii would inform the Chinese consul in London that 'the Soviet government is studying the conditions created in Munich and is not rushing to any conclusions'.[77]

In Moscow there was great concern that some might try to involve the Soviet Union in responsibility for the outcome of the Munich conference. Potemkin viewed the British, in particular, with deep suspicion, and had sharply warned Maiskii on 3 October 1938 to avoid all personal intercourse with British diplomats.[78] The prestige of the USSR was at stake, and Potemkin issued precise instructions to the diplomatic corps.[79] The French too were under suspicion, and Litvinov advised Surits not to attach too much importance to Bonnet's reassurances about Franco-Soviet relations.[80]

Hitler would not threaten the Soviet Union, Litvinov told Coulondre – that was simply too risky. He was far more likely to exploit the atmosphere of appeasement by supplanting the British and grabbing the reins of their empire.[81] Likewise, Maiskii told Halifax that, in his opinion, Germany would certainly turn its attention westwards, having subdued central Europe and the Balkans.[82] And Potemkin told the Turkish ambassador that he believed the German expansion towards eastern and south-eastern Europe would threaten British and Italian interests above all.[83]

These arguments were hardly devoid of realism. But their ambiguity remained unchanged: were they warnings of common peril or justifications for self-isolation? Were they spoken out of deep conviction or did they amount to a purely instrumental argument? Whatever the motives for this now revived view, one cannot fail to overlook its connection with the sharpening Soviet perception that in post-Munich Europe the Western powers were likely to launch a policy aimed at diverting the Nazi menace eastward. A series of confidential reports circulating in the Narkomindel and the secret services lent credence to the possibility that a grand anti-Soviet coalition was forming.[84]

This thinking was not articulated in public forums. The Soviet press put forward the theory that German aggression would be intimidated by Soviet strength and so turn elsewhere.[85] However, no one was writing about 'inter-imperialist contradictions', which was a likely indication of lingering uncertainties. Gnedin declared that it was 'impossible to isolate the USSR from Europe'.[86] But there hung over all such statements an air of anxiety: was the Soviet Union fated to meet a coalition of European powers in a great confrontation?

Soviet denunciation of the failure of the Munich agreement to guarantee European peace got right to the point: Hitler would be encouraged, rather then restrained, in his plans for conquest. But what of the Soviet view that the war in Europe had already started? Outlined long before September 1938, this idea belonged to the period of the purges and the return to isolationism. Well before Munich, when the *Short Course* of party history was announced, arguably the most important domestic political step taken after the Great Terror, this idea of an extant European war was explicitly sanctioned.

On 19 September 1938 the twelfth chapter of the *Short Course* appeared in *Pravda*. It read, in part:

> The second imperialist war has already started . . . This war is against the interests of Great Britain, France and the USA, since it is meant to divide the world and the spheres of influence in favour of the aggressive states, and at the expense of the so-called democratic states. The characteristic trait of the second imperialist war is that it is carried on and widened by the aggressive powers, while the other powers, the 'democratic' ones, against whom the war is being waged, pretend that the war does not concern them.[87]

The outcome of the Munich conference was seen as the full confirmation of this postulate. On 29 October, Zhdanov, who had a hand in the wording of this text, gave it public endorsement.[88] During the celebration of the anniversary of the revolution, Molotov gave it official blessing by using the passage to underscore his remarks. Molotov drew from the *Short Course* the theory that the key to understanding Western treatment of aggressor states lay in the belief that fascism might be the best weapon against social revolution. He held that one could talk of two 'victories' in the Czech crisis: the victory of 'Europe's four most powerful imperialist states over little Czechoslovakia', and the victory of Great Britain and Germany over France, which had been forced to renege on its obligations to its ally, the Soviet Union. The 'understanding arrived at by the imperialists' left no room for the Soviet Union, which had nonetheless remained absolutely true to its commitments. According to Molotov, this was of 'enormous international significance', in view of 'the coming international struggle against fascism'. Events in east Asia had shown that a steadfast USSR could successfully resist 'the spread of the second imperialist war'. His forecast, however, was distinctly pessimistic: the present war would not end soon and would not be easily circumscribed; Molotov asserted that 'it is evident that new areas of conflict are likely to flare up and the war is bound to extend' beyond its current boundaries.[89]

Clearly, Molotov had in mind a widening of the war within the capitalist world. But, like others who had addressed the subject, he cautiously avoided mentioning 'contradictions' between capitalist states, nor did he mention the strategic direction of Nazism. In other words, Molotov did not palliate the danger the USSR was now facing. Nevertheless, he did not acknowledge Munich as a fundamental turning point. Rather, in his view, it offered the opportunity to express views long held. There could be no more 'struggle for peace' – war was at hand. The phrase could only be used, and rather awkwardly at that, to refer to the Soviet Union's efforts to avoid being caught up in an imperialist war. This necessitated a self-representation as a neutral state, extraneous to the basic nature of the conflict, relevant only as a point of reference for those peoples involved in the war.

For many months Stalin resisted making any public comment on the policy his subordinates were outlining. However, in a series of remarks given during a top level meeting on the *Short Course* held on 1 October 1938, Stalin stressed the perilousness of the international situation and the importance of following an extremely pragmatic path: any alliance of the capitalist states against the Soviet state had to be avoided at all cost.[90] This had always been a fixed element in Soviet foreign policy and in the strategy of 'socialism in one country'. After the appeasement at

Munich this had become, far and away, the major priority in the eyes of the Soviet leaders, even more so since the true weakness of the international communist and pacifist movements had been revealed.

The Stalinist leaders had always been largely distrustful and pessimistic about those movements, but even they had not foreseen the direness of late 1938. Manuil'skii appears in Ernst Fischer's memoirs as the man who most manifestly depicted the widespread pessimism among the Soviet leaders, declaring that: 'I would be ready to sign a pact with the devil in order to drive away this war, but even the devil is on their side.' Aggrieved by the failure of Europe's masses to respond to the Nazi threat, he felt that soon the USSR would stand alone against Hitler.[91] The 'popular democracies' extolled by Zhdanov a few short months earlier appeared to be in their death throes and utterly insignificant. In spite of Dimitrov's hopes, no 'spirit of resistance' infused the Czech masses and no 'Spanish scenario' moved anti-fascist movements and European governments to confront Hitler – and all the while the Republican struggle in Spain shuffled towards its tragic conclusion.

On 7 October 1938 Dimitrov wrote in his diary that an alliance was being formed between the fascist states and the 'imperialist reaction of England and France'.[92] He prophesied the formation of an 'antidemocratic, counter-revolutionary bloc', linking the fascist states to the Western powers.[93] In a letter to Manuil'skii written on 11 October, he bitterly remarked that 'once more the working class (and this means also the communist party) of the capitalistic countries has not passed the test'.[94] This was not just the view from Moscow. After participating at a conference of the communist parties in Paris, Ercoli wrote to Dimitrov that 'there is no clear understanding of the main reason why the Czech people failed to resist'; he said that he perceived among the pacifists and intellectuals of France and Spain 'a sense of impotence, which may turn into hostility towards our popular front policy'.[95]

On 23 October 1938 Manuil'skii sent a letter to Dimitrov on the perspectives of the communist parties. He admitted that a feeling of disappointment was widespread and recommended revising the popular front policy. According to Manuil'skii, the communists should not speak 'in the name of the popular front, as in the name of the whole nation', particularly in central–eastern Europe. But this could be done only by abandoning their 'pacifist illusions' and by fighting against the governments of their own countries. Though Manuil'skii proclaimed himself convinced that this stance would provide 'a new anti-fascist wave', he was clearly proposing to give up the anti-fascist policy of making alliances with democratic and socialist forces, which he accused of speaking 'the language of fascists'.[96] We do not know Dimitrov's reaction to such ambiguous 'national-fundamentalist' perspective. But on

25 October he explained to Moskvin that the Czech Communist Party should make every effort to preserve its connections with the socialist and democratic forces.[97] Publicly Dimitrov simply insisted that 'the people have yet to utter their last word', and maintained that German aggression would stalk central and western Europe first, though the USSR would certainly be next – the attack was scheduled, he asserted, for the fall of 1941.[98]

Speaking to a commission of the Comintern Praesidium on 16 January 1939, Dimitrov expatiated on the Czech question and, more generally, the international dilemmas facing the Soviet Union.[99] We may think of these as the concluding remarks to a debate begun in the wake of Munich. Certainly, declared Dimitrov, the Czech situation differed from that of Spain – this had been proved by the feeble response with which the popular masses had met the news of appeasement. But if he agreed with Manuil'skii on that point, he forcefully rejected his colleague's suggestion that 'Czech capitulation was inevitable, because of the international situation of the time'.[100] Did not such a fatalistic view suggest that 'the struggle is hopeless'? In his view, the Czech masses were prepared to fight – it was only a question of figuring out what was holding them back. As for the Czech Communist Party, he recalled that in the past there had been resistance to the united front policy: the negative consequences of such a stance had naturally followed.[101] Beneš should never have been trusted to stand firm, and a timely military mobilization would have thrown political force behind Czechoslovakia's position.[102]

The critical tenor of Dimitrov's comments cannot be missed. Manuil'skii's pessimism had clearly reflected the stubborn unwillingness of the Soviet leadership to contemplate lending military assistance to the Czechs. Dimitrov spoke up now against resignation. He believed that the situation in Czechoslovakia was 'very unstable', and that 'the question is not yet closed'; he advocated 'a coherent struggle' against a fascist takeover of the Czech republic and called for 'the defence of the people', while it was still possible.[103] For him the 'lesson' of Munich coincided with the mobilization strategies already outlined. The working class would have to put itself forward, actively, as the defender of the 'national interests of the people' – if national foreign and military policies generally remained 'terra incognita' for the workers' movement, that was lamentable, and had to change.[104]

But this was wishful thinking. Even Dimitrov now believed that the struggle to prevent the outbreak of war had been lost. The visible disintegration of the postwar era's international system amounted to proof, in Soviet political culture, that the very structure of capitalism inevitably provoked catastrophes. After Munich, the expectation that the masses would steal a march on the cynically manoeuvring European statesmen no longer played a significant role in Soviet policy-making. Now it would all be about the actions of states.

THE 'LESSONS' OF MUNICH

Throughout the winter of 1938–39, as the European situation stagnated, Soviet diplomacy remained inert. How long could the 'pause for reflection' after Munich be extended? And how could the USSR now play a role in European affairs, especially those of eastern Europe? According to Litvinov, many in Soviet political circles believed that Czechoslovakia could still play a part in international policy, in spite of everything; but he was not convinced.[105] Soviet foreign policy was oriented towards Poland. At the end of November, the six-year-old non-aggression pact between Poland and the USSR was extended.[106] In theory, this was a significant event, inasmuch as the USSR thereby achieved a *modus vivendi* with the country that had blocked efforts to form an 'Eastern pact'. Additionally, the Soviet Union suddenly seemed far less isolated and the move certainly accelerated the deterioration of German–Polish relations that had begun after the conference at Munich. But Soviet leaders remained distrustful of Beck and never did make much of the normalization of relations.[107] Zhdanov greeted the accord lukewarmly, describing it as a Polish initiative dictated by a sudden awakening of the 'survival instinct'.[108]

Warsaw had, in fact, initiated the talks, and the following months showed clearly that the accord was not the consequence of a recovering initiative in Soviet foreign policy. Diplomatically speaking, the Polish problem remained closely linked to Soviet relations with the Western democracies until the summer of 1939. The Soviet leaders were ready to tackle the problem from a different perspective, however, freed from 'collective security' considerations and focused on relations of strength among the powers, an outgrowth of their conviction that the European war would inevitably spread. An outspoken isolationist from the moment of his return to the USSR, Potemkin had acknowledged the crucial importance of the Polish question after the *Anschluss*, since it directly affected the Soviet borders. In this light, the reason why the Polish Communist Party was so ferociously purged becomes more apparent; in the Soviet leaders' eyes, the advancing dangerous scenarios of international policy required a tight control of the communists' conduct in that country.

Afflicted by lack of initiative, leading Soviet diplomats debated the outcome of Western appeasement after Munich. At the end of October 1938, Maiskii told Litvinov that he reckoned Chamberlain would continue his craven 'retreat'.[109] A few days later, in a letter to Surits,

Litvinov confidently asserted that the British leader would go to 'the very end of the road', and that France would do likewise, offering no resistance.[110] Surits was unconvinced. After all, except for its own territory, what did France have left to offer to Hitler? The way of *Drang nach Osten* remained open, but even though the Western democracies might well have idly looked on while Hitler launched his attack on the USSR, the prospect was clearly unattractive to Germany.[111] Surely, France itself would soon be threatened by Nazi expansionism. This meant that there could be no basis for a lasting Franco-German accord; this lesson could be applied to Franco-Italian relations as well.[112] Surits believed that European diplomacy might be entering a new era. But even if Litvinov shared Surits's opinion on Hitler's reluctance to confront the USSR, he believed that appeasement would continue for some time to come.[113] Maiskii, for his part, predicted that Chamberlain would continue his policy, in spite of the impression made on the British public by the anti-Jewish pogroms in Germany.[114]

Suddenly, at the end of 1938, rumours began flying that Hitler was preparing to launch an attack on the Ukraine. In October, Maiskii heard from the British journalist Stidd that Hitler had decided to crush the USSR and dismember it.[115] Subsequently, a great deal of more or less confidential information on the subject was exchanged, all of which seemed to confirm the worst.[116] The rumours bounced around in the Western press, and were picked up even in Berlin.[117] Though the Soviets scoffed at the loose talk, they saw in it confirmation of a plot to push German aggression eastward – in their view, the British and the Poles were colluding in this scheme.[118] The Germans themselves made no secret of their hopes of reclaiming Memel, Danzig and what remained of Czechoslovakia. Whether or not Hitler feared the might of the Red Army, whether or not Britain invited him to pillage eastern Europe, he might have moved that way. And even the presumed disincentives, such as the prospect of a mass upwelling of support for the Soviet Union, could not guarantee that he would stay away.

On 4 December Litvinov sent two letters, one to Maiskii and one to Surits. To Maiskii he pointed out that only France could oppose Chamberlain's policy, but counting on this would be 'too optimistic'.[119] To Surits he maintained that, after Munich, the French had been doing all they could to disentangle themselves from their commitments to the USSR and Poland: they were possibly expecting Hitler to attack the Ukraine. If France opposed a rapprochement between Poland and the USSR it was because of the fear that such a move might discourage Hitler from looking eastward. But such fears were baseless, given the precariousness of the relations between Moscow and Warsaw.[120] Litvinov felt that France was now as deeply committed to the policy of appeasement as Great Britain; whether or not the Soviet Union remained an ally was a matter of indifference to the French who, along with the British, wanted above all to push Hitler east. The joint declaration made after the talks held by Ribbentrop and Bonnet in Paris at the beginning of December even suggested to Litvinov the possibility of a secret political and economic agreement between France and Germany.[121] In any case, France seemed to him to be washing its hands of any responsibility for European security.[122]

In his reply, Surits agreed that France was distancing itself from central European questions, but he would not admit of any telling evidence that Hitler had been given a free hand in eastern Europe and the Ukraine. Possibly an attempt was underway to separate European from colonial problems, but in the ambassador's opinion this could not succeed.[123] Litvinov offered reassurances to Surits in a letter of 31 December: according to information in Astakhov's possession, Hitler did not expect to resolve the 'Ukrainian problem' for five or six years – even then, it was to be resolved peacefully. Certainly this did not appear to be a pressing matter to the Nazis.[124]

The discussion continued into the new year, with Maiskii opining that Chamberlain was, as Litvinov had said, encouraging Hitler to look to the east, and that, nevertheless, the Ukraine was not immediately imperiled. He also suggested that British opinion might shift as it became clear that the concessions made at Munich had not assuaged Hitler's appetite. But a 'change of direction in British foreign policy' was unimaginable, because that would have meant the removal of Chamberlain; for the moment, anyway, that was out of the question.[125]

A month later, however, Maiskii changed his opinion. 'Although', he wrote to Litvinov, 'you regard the possibility of a war between the "Axis" powers and the "Western democracies" with great scepticism, I would maintain that such a prospect cannot be completely ruled out, especially in 1939.'[126] Hitler and Mussolini seemed sure to act, but not (according to the confidential Narkomindel materials Maiskii cited) by launching campaigns against Poland or the USSR in the near future, or against Romania or the smaller targets mentioned up until then. The British would soon find themselves directly threatened by the Nazis, with scarcely a bone to throw them.

Surits's old argument about France was being revived, only now it was Great Britain rather than France that would be pushed into a corner. Appeasement had exhausted its possibilities; it would have to be cast aside and a new political phase would arise in Europe. However, this might lead to war, since Hitler was keenly aware that just at that moment his military and political strength were peerless. The split between Great Britain and France, on one side, and the USSR, on the other side, sketched a scenario propitious to a German military advance. Maiskii did not speculate about the fate of Chamberlain, whom he continued to consider an 'extremely important ally' of the fascist states, but he was quite certain that the next six months would prove to be 'an extremely dangerous period in European politics'; preparations should be made for every eventuality.[127]

Though from our perspective it seems clear that Maiskii failed to perceive the gravity of the Polish situation, his grasp of the European political scene seems otherwise quite astute.[128] This is especially so since his evaluations were based squarely on political considerations and were remarkably free of ideological cant; he neither crowed about Soviet isolation nor did he cite 'inter-imperialist contradictions' in explaining the likely sources of conflict. Rather, the war might arise out of basic, unresolved political differences between the Western powers and the USSR.

Though Litvinov would not have agreed with the paean to isolationism sung by Potemkin in an article published in *Bolshevik*,[129] he wrote to Maiskii to inform him that 'your letter has failed to convince me that Hitler and Mussolini will succeed in pushing Chamberlain into war this year'. Litvinov remained convinced that the Western powers would continue to avoid war 'at all costs', and he denied that they had nothing left to surrender to Hitler. He instanced both the colonies and eastern Europe: Britain and France could still guarantee Hitler not only a partial neutrality, but 'active help' in the event of conflict in the east, and Poland could not be counted on to resist.[130]

At the beginning of March 1939 Maiskii met with Chamberlain, and though the British prime minister declared that fascism would have no further easy victories, the Soviets were given no reason to hope for any substantial political transformation.[131] And on 4 March Litvinov was again telling Maiskii that he could not conceive of Chamberlain opting to collaborate with the USSR.[132] Underlining his comment, the Soviet delegation chose that day to withdraw from the London committee. Though the move was in a practical sense insignificant, symbolically it resonated. *Le journal de Moscou* prudently spoke of the British public as 'inclining to resist the aggressors' and noted that sooner or later its leaders would have to bow to that inclination.[133]

On 10 March 1939 Stalin presented his report to the 18th Party Congress. Confirming the evaluation of the international situation offered by Molotov five months earlier and adding little to it, Stalin lowered the curtain on 'the system of so-called postwar pacifism' and announced that a 'new imperialist war' was in full swing. Since the capitalist world generated a constant state of war, Stalin could not give a chronology for the onset of hostilities; instead he divided the economic depression of the last decade into two stages. The first had produced conflict between the great powers and provoked serious international crises; the second, characterized from 1937 onwards by a generalized rearmament and an insufficiency of the resources necessary for economic recovery, had led inevitably 'to a further intensification of the imperialist struggle'. As conflict drove states to form alliances according to a 'new division of the world', a succession of crises, culminating with the Czech crisis, had generated the 'new imperialist war'.[134] No 'world war' had yet erupted, but Stalin gave no reason to hope that things would not get worse.

The 'lessons' of Munich and the ideology of 'inter-imperialist contradictions' were converging.[135] Stalin rejected the notion that the weakness of the Western powers lay at the root of their decision to yield before fascist aggression. He blamed instead their fear of the revolutions that would follow a universal war, and their cynical attempt to take shelter under the banner of neutrality, while pushing the Nazis eastward. These theories were not new, but the latter now had Stalin's public blessing. Furthermore, he established a precise order of importance. In his mind, the hope that Hitler might be pushed towards the Soviet Union had played a greater part in shaping Western policy than had fear of revolution.[136] The implicit assumption was that the USSR would no longer rely on the internationalist appeal or on war's social effects; rather, strategic planning and power rivalries among states would be the focus of Soviet efforts. On this point, Stalin declared himself a fervent supporter of the distinction between moral and political considerations. But he warned the countries which had, in his opinion, removed themselves from a 'collective security' alliance, that 'the great and perilous game, begun by the defenders of the policy of non-intervention, could end in a serious failure'. Hence the injunction he then addressed to his foreign audience: the Soviet Union would resist 'being dragged into conflicts by those who provoke war, those who are accustomed to getting others to pull their hot chestnuts from the fire'.[137]

Compared with the interventions he had made over the previous three years, this bespoke a significant shift in Stalin's thinking on international policy. Stalin had shifted from the civil war model which had been so important, as we know, in 1937, and put forward a picture of the world drawn in the manner of World War I. In the aftermath of the Great Terror, the lethal danger of a new Russian civil war fomented or encouraged by foreign powers had been averted – at least in Stalin's phantoms. And after the disappointment of the Czech crisis, international conflicts could hardly be expected to inspire popular uprisings.

As was his wont, Stalin had strewn his speech with palpable gaps and deliberate ambiguities. He maintained a distinction between aggressor and non-aggressor states, but attacked only the second group, as far as the Western powers were concerned. This permitted him to present the USSR as a third pole in the international political scene. At the same time, Stalin did not explicitly mention the possibility of directing the German threat westwards, but his meaning was clear. What interest he had once had in general European security had been erased and his guiding principle appeared to have become the complete strategic autonomy of the Soviet Union during the massive conflict bound to sweep over Europe.

When he addressed the Congress as the 'CPSU's representative' in the Comintern, Manuil'skii presumed to fill in one of the palpable gaps in Stalin's speech. Assessing the chances of stemming the spread of war and of defeating the fascists, he concluded that it was 'possible, but more difficult than before'.[138] But it was clear that with the official Stalinist reading of the 'lessons of Munich' in place, the communist movement was not bound to fight against the outbreak of a world war.[139]

Stalin's famous lauding of the state in his speech of March 1939 came as no novelty to his close comrades. It emerged from the familiar discourse of 'capitalist encirclement' on the same pattern of the plenum of February–March 1937. It had already been established on three occasions which were not made public: as we have seen, in his speech at the Kremlin on 7 November 1937, Stalin had celebrated the power of the Russian state; in his speech of 1 October 1938 he had declared that the state would not extinguish itself, contrary to Marxist predictions; and on 7 November 1938, again at the Kremlin, he emphasized his excommunication of all those who allegedly tried to undermine the power of the Soviet state, 'dismember the USSR', and even transform it into 'a protectorate' of the major powers.[140] As a consequence of the Great Terror, the building of a 'total security state' had been outlined, in Stalin's eyes a state more powerful regardless of any enfeeblement provoked by purging the dominant élites. Originally aimed at extirpating 'class enemies' and their 'fifth column', now it provided the rulers with tremendous executive control over the mobilization of the country's resources and over the future war effort. The destruction of the old ruling class and the installation of autocratic power had produced a political monolith more concentrated than any other European state, including the most powerful of totalitarian states, Nazi Germany.

NOTES

1. DVP SSSR, XXI, doc. 191, p. 276.
2. Weinberg, *The Foreign Policy of Hitler's Germany*, pp. 366 ff.
3. E. Aleksandrov, 'Chekhoslovatskaia respublika, bastion mira', *Izvestiia*, 26 May 1936.
4. *Le Journal de Moscou*, 24 May 1938.

CZECHOSLOVAKIA

5. DVP SSSR, XXI, doc. 151, p. 221.
6. Ibid., doc. 172, p. 247.
7. Ibid., doc. 161, p. 228.
8. Ibid., doc. 197, pp. 284–6.
9. Ibid., doc. 209, p. 304.
10. *Leningradskaia pravda*, 24 June 1938.
11. RGASPI, f. 77, op. 1, d. 684, l. 10 (28 May 1938).
12. RGASPI, f. 77, op. 1, d. 692, ll. 191–4 (9 June 1938).
13. Ibid., l. 195.
14. G. Dimitrov, 'Deux années de lutte héroique du peuple espagnol', *La correspondance internationale*, 23 July 1938.
15. See, for example, G. Dimitrov, 'Le gage de la victoire', *La correspondance internationale*, 7 May 1938.
16. Thomas, *The Spanish Civil War*, pp. 686–7.
17. *Dimitrov and Stalin 1934–1943: Letters from the Soviet Archives*, pp. 73–8.
18. Dimitrov, *Dnevnik*, p. 133.
19. P. Lisovskii, '1914–1938', *Mirovoe khoziaistvo i mirovaia politika* 7–8 (1938), pp. 3–14.
20. DVP SSSR, XXI, doc. 275, p. 396. *Le journal de Moscou*, 30 August 1938.
21. DVP SSSR, XXI, p. 401.
22. AVP RF, f. 05, op. 18, p. 149, d. 166, l. 24.
23. DVP SSSR, XXI, doc. 300, p. 436.
24. AVP RF, f. 05, op. 18, p. 140, d. 27, ll. 144–52.
25. DVP SSSR, XXI, doc. 301, pp. 438–9.
26. Ibid., doc. 305, p. 447.
27. Ibid., doc. 318, pp. 458–9.
28. Ibid., doc. 103, p. 152; doc. 176, pp. 253–4.
29. Ibid., doc. 321, pp. 464–5.
30. Ibid., doc. 324, pp. 470–1. DDF, 2e série, XI, doc. 29.
31. AVP RF, f. 05, op. 18, p. 137, d. 1, l. 138. DVP SSSR, XXI, doc. 343, pp. 487–8 and doc. 348, pp. 493–4.
32. ASMAE, Affari politici: Urss, 1938, b. 28, fasc. 3.
33. The opinion of Rosso, shared by other foreign diplomats in Moscow, was that the USSR looked with favour on a European war and in fact was working to encourage it, while keeping outside it. In any case, the Italian ambassador reported that Litvinov himself had confessed to regarding war in Europe as inevitable. See ASMAE, Affari politici: Urss, 1938, b. 28, fasc. 1.
34. See Parker, *Chamberlain and Appeasement*, pp. 162–3.
35. *Le journal de Moscou*, 20 September 1938.
36. RGASPI, f. 17, op. 162, d. 24, l. 5. The Politburo decision was connected to a question posed by Aleksandrovskii, which had been transmitted by Potemkin to Stalin on 20 September 1938; AVP RF, f. 05, op. 18, p. 138, d. 3, l. 219.
37. DVP SSSR, XXI, doc. 349, p. 495.
38. ASMAE, Affari politici: Urss, 1938, b. 30, fasc. 7.
39. *Izvestiia*, 22 September 1938.
40. Ibid.
41. *Izvestiia*, 24 September 1938.
42. *Izvestiia*, 26 September 1938.
43. *Le journal de Moscou*, 27 September 1938.
44. DVP SSSR, XXI, doc. 369, p. 520.
45. Ibid., doc. 370, pp. 520–2.
46. AVP RF, f. 05, op. 18, p. 138, d. 3, l. 232.
47. DVP SSSR, XXI, doc. 376, p. 528.
48. See Jordan, *The Popular Front and Central Europe*, pp. 287–8.
49. See Parker, *Chamberlain and Appeasement*, pp. 167 ff.
50. AVP RF, f. 017a, op. 1, p. 1, d. 5, l. 129.
51. Ibid., l. 148.
52. Ibid., l. 154.

53. *Krasnaia zvezda*, 11 September 1938. *Pravda*, 29 September 1938.
54. RGASPI, f. 523, op. 1, d. 90.
55. RGASPI, f. 495, op. 73, d. 61a, l. 1.
56. Ibid., l. 13.
57. Ibid., ll. 6–8, 17–18.
58. Dimitrov, *Dnevnik*, pp. 136 ff.
59. Ibid., p. 141.
60. See J. Hochman, *The Soviet Union and the Failure of Collective Security, 1934–1938* (Ithaca, NY: Cornell University Press, 1984). See also G. Jukes, 'The Red Army and the Munich Crisis', *Journal of Contemporary History* 26 (1991), pp. 195–214.
61. See I. Lukes, 'Stalin and Beneš at the End of September 1938: New Evidence from the Prague Archives', *Slavic Review* 1 (1993), pp. 28–48; and H. Ragsdale, 'Soviet Military Preparations and Policy in the Munich Crisis: New Evidence', *Jahrbücher für Geschichte Osteuropas* 47 (1999), pp. 210–26.
62. DVP SSSR, XXI, p. 738.
63. See Z. Steiner, 'The Soviet Commissariat of Foreign Affairs and the Czechoslovakian Crisis in 1938: New Material from the Soviet Archives', *The Historical Journal* 42 (1999), pp. 751–79.
64. *Izvestiia*, 30 September 1938.
65. DVP SSSR, XXI, doc. 390, pp. 541–3.
66. Ibid., doc. 391, p. 543.
67. Ibid., doc. 396, p. 550.
68. Ibid., doc. 393, pp. 548–9; ibid., doc. 394, p. 549.
69. Ibid., doc. 400, p. 554.
70. Ibid., doc. 402, p. 556.
71. See R. Coulondre, *De Moscou à Berlin* (Paris: 1959), p. 165.
72. *Izvestiia*, 4 October 1938.
73. *Le journal de Moscou*, 4 October 1938.
74. AVP RF, f. 136, op. 22, p. 172, d. 865, l. 30.
75. DVP SSSR, XXI, doc. 446, p. 619.
76. DBFP, 3rd series, III, doc. 217, pp. 192–4.
77. DVP SSSR, XXI, doc. 435, p. 603.
78. Ibid., doc. 406, p. 560.
79. Ibid., doc. 408, p. 561.
80. Ibid., doc. 428, p. 594.
81. Ibid., doc. 423, p. 590.
82. Ibid., doc. 414, p. 573.
83. Ibid., doc. 431, p. 597.
84. Erickson, 'Threat Identification and Strategic Appraisal', in E. R. May (ed.), *Knowing One's Enemies: Intelligence Assessments Before the Two World Wars* (Princeton, NJ: Princeton University Press, 1984), p. 404.
85. E. Aleksandrov, 'Miunkhenskii balans', *Izvestiia*, 23 October 1938. I. Lemin, 'Miunkhenskii sgovor fashistskikh agressorov i ikh posobnikov', *Mirovoe khoziaistvo i mirovaia politika* 10 (1938), pp. 11–26.
86. E. Aleksandrov, 'Fashistskaia reaktsiia i sily mira', *Izvestiia*, 7 November 1938.
87. *Pravda*, 19 September 1938.
88. *Pravda*, 4 November 1938.
89. *Izvestiia*, 10 November 1938.
90. *Istoricheskii Arkhiv* 5 (1994), p. 13. RGASPI, f. 558, op. 11, d. 1122, ll. 54 ff.
91. E. Fischer, *Erinnerungen und Reflexionen*; Italian trans. *Ricordi e riflessioni* (Rome: Editori Riuniti, 1973), pp. 485–6.
92. Dimitrov, *Dnevnik*, p. 146.
93. RGASPI, f. 495, op. 73, d. 61a, ll. 41–2, 48.
94. Dimitrov, *Dnevnik*, p. 149.
95. Ibid., p. 152.
96. Ibid., pp. 155–6.
97. Ibid., pp. 156–7.

98. G. Dimitrov, 'Edinyi front protiv fashizma', *Pravda*, 7 November 1938. See *La correspondance internationale*, 12 November 1938.
 99. RGASPI, f. 495, op. 2, d. 265a, ll.1–22. Dimitrov, *Dnevnik*, p. 164.
100. RGASPI, f. 495, op. 2, d. 265a, l. 11.
101. Ibid., ll. 16–17.
102. Ibid., ll. 13–15.
103. Ibid., ll. 19, 21–2.
104. Ibid., l. 4.
105. AVP RF, f. 05, op. 18, p. 149, d. 166, l. 35.
106. *Izvestiia*, 27 November 1938.
107. DVP SSSR, XXI, doc. 432, p. 600, doc. 484, p. 666.
108. RGASPI, f. 77, op. 1, d. 871, l. 120.
109. *God krizisa 1938–1939. Dokumenty i materialy*, 2 vols. (Moscow: Politizdat, 1990), vol. 1, doc. 42, p. 84.
110. DVP SSSR, XXI, p. 618.
111. *God krizisa*, vol. 1, doc. 49, p. 96 (11 November 1938).
112. Ibid., p. 98.
113. AVP RF, f. 136, op. 22, p. 172, d. 865, l. 22.
114. *God krizisa*, vol. 1, doc. 60, p. 114 (25 November 1938).
115. DVP SSSR, XXI, doc. 437, pp. 604–5.
116. Ibid., doc. 474, p. 658; doc. 479, pp. 661–2; doc. 481, p. 664. *God krizisa*, vol. 1, doc. 65, p. 120.
117. Ibid., doc. 84, p. 144.
118. DVP SSSR, XXI, p. 658.
119. *God krizisa*, 1, doc. 71, p. 127.
120. Ibid., doc. 72, pp. 127–9.
121. DVP SSSR, XXI, doc. 484, pp. 666–7. On the German–French talks of December 1938, see Weinberg, *The Foreign Policy of Hitler's Germany*, pp. 507–8.
122. *God krizisa*, 1, doc. 90, pp. 154–5 (19 December 1938).
123. Ibid., doc. 95, p. 161.
124. Ibid., doc. 98, pp. 164–5.
125. Ibid., doc. 107, pp. 179–82.
126. Ibid., doc. 150, p. 223.
127. Ibid., p. 225.
128. AVP RF, f. 017a, op. 1, p. 1, d. 5, l. 218.
129. V. Galianov, 'Mezhdunarodnaia obstanovka vtoroi imperialisticheskoi voiny', *Bol'shevik* 4 (1939), pp. 49–65.
130. *God krizisa*, vol. 1, doc. 156, pp. 231–3.
131. Ibid., doc. 168, pp. 246–8.
132. Ibid., doc. 170, pp. 248–50.
133. *Le journal de Moscou*, 3 March 1939.
134. Stalin, *Works* 1, pp. 328–35.
135. I. Lemin, 'Svoeobraznoe razvertivanie voiny. Rasstanovka sil i osnovnye uzly protivorechii', *Mirovoe khoziaistvo i mirovaia politika* 3 (1939), pp. 87–104.
136. Stalin, *Works* 1, pp. 338–9.
137. Ibid., p. 341.
138. *Pravda*, 12 March 1939.
139. D. Manuil'skii, 'Stalin i mirovoe kommunisticheskoe dvizhenie', *Pravda*, 20 April 1939.
140. RGASPI, f. 558, op. 11, d. 1122, ll. 80, 160. See *Istoricheskii arkhiv* 5 (1994), p. 20.

5

The Eastern Crises: Poland

THE FALL OF LITVINOV

On 15 March 1939, Nazi Germany occupied Czechoslovakia. The fragile European truce, which had lasted since the time of the Munich conference, collapsed. One week later, the Memel dispute was settled by force. In the meantime, the Spanish republic was in the final stage of its death throes. Since the advance of the European conflict now directly threatened Poland, the Soviet rulers had to grapple with the scenario they had feared more than any other. From Moscow's perspective, this was a continuation of the permanent crisis theorized by Stalin at the 18th Party Congress. While blaming the West for giving up on the idea of deterring Hitler through a programme of general security, Stalin had said nothing about peacemaking in Europe – instead he had dwelt on the importance of keeping the USSR out of the conflict. This stance was destined to exert a decisive conditioning on Soviet foreign policy during the Polish crisis and the first stage of World War II.

On 18 March the USSR proposed a meeting of Soviet, British and French representatives, with the participation of the Poles and Rumanians.[1] The following day, Litvinov repeated however to Maiskii his belief that Chamberlain and Daladier would speak out 'in defence of the Munich line' and that no Western rapprochement with the USSR could reasonably be expected. In any event, it was advisable to 'leave the initiative' to the British and the French.[2] In short, Litvinov viewed the international conference as futile, at least for the moment, and did not abandon the wait-and-see attitude he had struck in the aftermath of the Munich conference, even though Hitler was on the move.

The upcoming English trade mission to Moscow was hardly calculated to overcome such an attitude. It was unclear to the Soviet leaders what sort of mandate had been given to the delegation headed by Robert Hudson, though Halifax had assured Maiskii that problems of a political nature would be discussed.[3] In the meantime Maiskii limited himself to reporting to Moscow on the British political situation. In his judgement, the policy of concessions had become unpopular and the British public was growing increasingly determined to resist aggression, which meant that new negotiations between London and Berlin would be impossible for the foreseeable future. This made it seem likely that the British would make overtures to the USSR. Still, one massive impediment remained: as long as Chamberlain presided over the government, no change in Great Britain's foreign policy could be expected.[4]

In a message to Stalin, dated 20 March 1939, Litvinov stressed that Germany's recent activities were fully consistent 'with the presumed implications of Hitler's eastward expansion, on which the Munich agreement was based'. However, the commissar warned against giving Chamberlain any pretext 'to speak of our "self-imposed isolation"'. Instead of a set of proposals to be tendered, Litvinov submitted to Stalin the draft of a declaration to be made to Hudson. In addition to noting the recent occasions on which the USSR had issued statements on the threat posed by Nazi Germany and to condemning the 'capitulation at Munich', the document stated that 'even now' the USSR 'will not forswear cooperation with other countries', as long as there was to be 'a common resistance to the aggressors'. Stalin approved the document.[5]

The British proposal that Britain, France, Poland and the USSR sign a joint declaration was received without enthusiasm in Moscow. Litvinov told the new British ambassador, Sir William Seeds, that the Soviet government would sign the declaration as soon as France and Poland had done so; at the same time, he informed Maiskii and Surits that the USSR would not sign without Poland.[6] On 23 March, during his first conversation with Hudson, Litvinov insisted that 'after five years of initiatives, of every type of proposal on our part, and of unsuccessful efforts to win international cooperation, we have the right to assume a waiting stance, watchful for the initiatives and proposals of others'.[7] Though Litvinov did leave an opening, declaring that he was interested in 'what is going on in the heads of the British', his caution was extreme. His words on any given subject varied little, whether he was reporting in confidence to Stalin, to his own diplomats, or informing a foreign diplomat of the USSR's position.

During this period a persistent difference of opinion between Litvinov and Potemkin arose. At a meeting with the Italian ambassador to Moscow, Litvinov expressed the opinion that a conference between the powers favouring peace was inevitable, that Germany would not be satisfied with Czechoslovakia, and that as a result many countries, including Italy, should be worried.[8] Meeting with Rosso only two days earlier, Potemkin had made no mention of a conference, preferring to stress the 'shared interests' of Italy and the USSR in the face of German *Drang nach Osten*. This old theme had never been completely abandoned by the Soviets, but it was definitely not in harmony with Litvinov's acceptance of the bloc of fascist states as a *fait accompli*.⁹ Even after Munich, Litvinov had not rethought his basic position concerning 'collective security' – although his evaluation of British policy had become more pessimistic than ever, significantly bleaker than the outlook of the diplomats close to him.

On 24 March 1939 Maiskii again distanced himself from Litvinov in his assessment of British policy. Replying to Litvinov's letter of 19 March, Maiskii admitted that Chamberlain and Daladier would continue, as far as possible, the policy of appeasement. He maintained, nonetheless, that their difficulties would greatly increase because the Western public was now firmly convinced that any compromise with fascist dictators was impossible and that the only way forward lay through a defensive grand alliance, 'effectively a return to the principle of collective security'. But Maiskii had not exhausted his views. He returned to the speculations he had advanced in February, before Stalin's speech at the party congress, emphasizing that even if the appeasers tried to push the aggressor eastward, Hitler probably understood 'the great danger of attacking the USSR . . . [and] would think ten times before risking a similar adventure'. In Maiskii's opinion, it was much more likely that Hitler would turn westward instead. This forecast was not shaken by Hitler's recent moves in eastern and central Europe: according to Maiskii, these moves were part of Hitler's attempt to create a *Mitteleuropa*, an 'economic colony' that could guarantee Germany the resources needed to inflict a 'great blow' on the West.¹⁰

All this was but confirmation of opinions Maiskii had previously expressed. However, on one crucial point he did modify his view. Maiskii had always firmly rejected the possibility that Chamberlain could deviate from the behaviour he had exhibited in the past. This time he did not repeat such a judgement. He maintained, rather, that 'in a not-too-distant future' the new mass consciousness could induce even the British leader to consider a 'grand alliance'. If indeed Chamberlain was swayed, Moscow too would have to consider joining such an alliance, to consider whether it would make sense to guarantee, along with England and France, the borders of Poland, Romania, the Netherlands and of other European countries. Maiskii took this question very seriously, and asked Litvinov for information, stressing 'the exceptional importance' of the matter. He pointed out that up until then the USSR had evaluated those international agreements that had been concluded in terms of their 'pre-war significance'. But now that the whole of Europe found itself under the threat of a 'second imperialistic war', the duties involved in mutual assistance pacts took on a new meaning. This led to a second question, strictly related to the first: how to respond should the British propose a pact of reciprocal aid.¹¹

Two days later, Surits echoed Maiskii's appeal for reappraisals, though in a more cautious key. He drew attention to the evident change in French public opinion towards Germany: it was even possible to say that anti-German sentiment in France had risen to its highest point since World War I. One need not look far for an explanation – the dreams of peace prompted by the 1938 Munich conference had been destroyed by Hitler's recent moves. Even those who had envisioned a German attack on Romania, followed by an attack on the USSR, backed away from their earlier predictions. That sort of war would be a great risk to Hitler; he was far more likely to take on France. In Surits's opinion, the *miunkhentsy*, or 'supporters of Munich', had not yet given up their hopes: but they might accept the help of the USSR.[12]

Maiskii and Surits intently collected reliable news on the international political situation and on the attitudes of Western leaders. In particular, the speeches Chamberlain gave on 17 and 23 March 1939 left a deep impression on Maiskii. It was then that Chamberlain, for the first time, left open the possibility of a military response to aggression. Suddenly it seemed possible that the British might assume responsibilities in eastern Europe.[13] At the same time, Maiskii believed that the British were coming around to the view that an alliance with the USSR could make sense. The truth is that at this precise time Britain's rulers confirmed their judgement that Russia was politically and militarily untrustworthy.[14] Neither side had any 'grand alliance' on its agenda: that was only so much wishful thinking on Maiskii's part.

But Maiskii's approach to the 'second imperialistic war' thesis deserves comment. He referred to it not to justify isolationism, but rather to stress the need to face new duties and responsibilities. The possibility of war in the West, in his eyes, forced everyone to think about collective security, not neutrality. His understanding of the international situation led Maiskii, together with Surits, to grant much more credit to Western democracies than would Litvinov. This divergence illustrates the apathy of the political élites in Moscow facing the question of collective security.

On 25 March 1939 Litvinov made clear to Seeds and Hudson that without Poland the USSR would not support any declaration: 'if Poland is not with us, it is against us'. His impression, fairly close to the truth as it turned out, was that Hudson's mission looked like a simple probe, designed to explore the USSR's willingness to defend Poland and Romania and possibly to join an alliance with the Western states. But, at the same time, the British representative had come without the authority and intent to conclude such an agreement.[15] Two days later, Hudson spoke with Potemkin on the subject of military cooperation: their conversation ended in deadlock. Potemkin pointed out that a meeting between the major states would only be possible given prior agreement 'on the necessity and the possibility of joint military action against a general danger', but added that the current climate would not permit mutual trust between the representatives of the two armies.[16] In other words, the USSR was not prepared to open military negotiations unless they were preceded by a political agreement. It was clear that the Soviets felt that Hudson's mission did not even constitute a first step in this direction. Litvinov's comments to Maiskii were completely negative, a condition aggravated by Halifax's clumsy attempt to suppress all references to political talks in the official communiqué.[17]

Though it was founded on indisputable facts, this negative assessment prevented Litvinov from grasping the changes taking place in British policy. On 29 March he advised Surits to think of the proposed conference and joint declaration as 'devoid of importance'. The effects of Hitler's most recent acts of force were waning and the supporters of Munich were gaining ground, taking advantage of Polish hostility towards the USSR. At this stage, the question was whether Britain would guarantee assistance to Poland without the participation of the USSR – France's position was seen as scarcely relevant. To Litvinov, the answer was clearly negative.[18] On that same day, Maiskii informed Moscow that Chamberlain had publicly confirmed British commitments in eastern Europe and that Lord Cadogan had declared Britain ready to go to war in the event of a German attack on Poland, as long as France agreed.[19] Two days later, Chamberlain announced that the British were guaranteeing Poland's security – Paris had approved the plan. In Halifax's presence, Maiskii could only complain that his government had not been consulted and declare that the USSR would be a 'careful observer' of ensuing events; he refrained from any evaluation of Great Britain's decision. He did point out, however, that there were 'no grounds for discussing any sort of Soviet support for Poland'.[20]

The British government had taken a step only Maiskii had judged possible; Litvinov had ruled out the possibility of such a move. Appeasement underwent a significant modification, though not a reversal.[21] This was in line with the scenario sketched in advance by Moscow's ambassadors in London and Paris, but Moscow seemed to remain deaf and indifferent. Litvinov's first reaction was to deny that a change of any significance had taken place and to read Chamberlain's move as the umpteenth attempt to marginalize the USSR. Affecting coolness, he said to Seeds that the meaning of Chamberlain's declaration was not 'completely comprehensible' to him: was Britain determined to enter the lists against the aggressors or was it simply aiming for a vague agreement with France, Poland and Romania? In any event, said Litvinov, the Soviets considered themselves 'free from any obligation' and were exclusively oriented towards protecting their own interests.[22]

POLAND

This was why he would not be accepting the invitation, sent by Halifax through Maiskii on 6 April, to consider Chamberlain's declaration and subsequent Anglo-Polish negotiations as a first step towards the formation of a 'grand coalition'. Litvinov's distrust at this juncture may have been increased by Halifax's vague reply to Maiskii, when the Soviet ambassador asked him whether Britain would intervene in the case of a German attack on Lithuania involving Poland in a war.[23]

If Litvinov was not hastening to commit the USSR to an alliance with Great Britain, it was not solely because of personal distrust. Stalin had long decreed that in diplomatic issues the initiative should be left to others while the USSR retained full freedom of action. Such an approach weighed on Litvinov, especially after Munich. Experience had taught the Soviets to cast a wary eye on British declarations, and though Chamberlain's recent announcements heralded change, an overwary Moscow failed to appreciate this. On 4 April 1939 Litvinov told Maiskii that he remained sceptical of Britain's intentions and maintained that it was impossible to predict whether Chamberlain would really be willing to go to war with Germany. In accordance with Stalin's instructions, he stated that it was preferable for the USSR 'not to tie its hands'. Autonomy would be especially important if it turned out that Chamberlain's declaration strengthened Poland in its negotiations with Germany: if Hitler chose to guarantee Polish neutrality, he could turn 'his own forces elsewhere', in other words, towards the Soviet Union.[24]

Quite significantly, at the beginning of April two prominent Soviet leaders reaffirmed Stalin's instructions. On 4 April in Kiev, Lev Mekhlis, the man who had presided over the restoration of political controls in the army during the two previous years, declared that the USSR did not need allies and he predicted that the attempts to provoke a war between the USSR and Germany were destined to fail.[25] On 10 April in Vladivostok, Zhdanov gave a speech not published by the central press in which he vented his own anti-Westernism. He felt that the analysis Stalin had offered of the international situation a month earlier had been completely confirmed. The German invasion of Czechoslovakia, the end of the Spanish republic, Italian aggression against Albania – all these events showed not only that the 'second imperialistic war' was in progress, but also that British and French policies were expanding the geographic scope of the conflict. Poland and Romania were the most recent locus of the attempt to direct aggression against the USSR, and Chamberlain's hollow words in no way guaranteed that he would challenge Hitler. In short, far better that the Soviets count exclusively on their own forces.[26] Zhdanov also praised the totalitarian state as the only bastion of national security in a time of 'capitalist encirclement'. And he quoted a formulation of Stalin's from the 1920s: 'we should not forget our historical mission, which consists in preparing ourselves, day in and day out, for the moment when communist encirclement will replace capitalistic encirclement'.[27] Though this was by no means a realistic perspective, such words provided the basis for an undifferentiated ideological view of the outside world.

On 9 April 1939 Litvinov recommended to Stalin that the Soviet government communicate to Paris a willingness to examine 'any concrete proposal' – while considering itself free of obligations to Poland and Romania.[28] In a letter to Surits written two days later, Litvinov advised against making any statements that could be manipulated to justify further 'capitulations'; but he also made clear that no 'concrete proposals' were to be put forward. In a response to Bonnet's proposal that the USSR forge an agreement with Poland and Romania,[29] Litvinov wondered why the USSR should assume the sort of 'unilateral obligations' demanded by the Western powers. But the main point was something else. Litvinov had concluded that 'Britain's pact with Poland is in fact also against us'; any sort of coalition between the Western powers, Poland, and Romania would also be an anti-Soviet move.[30] Two days later, Litvinov sent Maiskii a telegram approved by Stalin warning him not to repeat declarations like the one he had just made to Halifax: there was to be no more criticism of 'separate agreements' and no more insistence on 'a single general agreement and on specific forms of collective security'.[31]

Litvinov found Britain's recent policy shift an unreliable move by an unreliable government and he maintained that the positions adopted by Moscow after Munich would not change. He did not believe that the British guarantee would effect a definite break between Warsaw and Berlin; instead he saw it as a prelude to pushing German aggression eastwards. This interpretation was widely shared in Soviet political circles, and Litvinov came to it rather late. His views were definitely influenced by the ambiguity in Chamberlain's declaration: the British leader had spoken only of Poland's 'independence' and not of its territorial integrity. In Moscow, Chamberlain's choice of words could hardly be seen as unintentional: it looked as though Poland was destined to the same fate Czechoslovakia had suffered at Munich.[32]

Then things started to happen. Soon after Great Britain announced its decision to extend to Romania and Greece the guarantee it had offered Poland, France extended an invitation to the Soviet Union to join it in offering assistance to eastern Europe.[33] On 15 April Litvinov presented Stalin with the draft of an interview in which he would offer an official reply to the Western declarations, as well as a preliminary proposal for a four-point agreement between the USSR, France and Great Britain. In the interview was the declaration that during the past five years the USSR had played a leading role in militating for peace, 'even though we were convinced that aggression would be directed in the first instance against those who had participated in peace treaties at Versailles and Saint Germain, as well as other peace treaties with which the USSR had not been involved'. Litvinov made clear that a unilateral commitment towards Poland and Romania was not in Soviet interests. Those interests could not be guaranteed if the other countries were free 'of any commitment to the USSR'. Nevertheless, he stated, the USSR 'has not renounced and will not renounce cooperation for collective resistance against aggression'; such an objective could be achieved 'not only with a general agreement but also with bilateral, trilateral and other types of agreements'.[34]

As they prepared the draft for an agreement with Great Britain and France, Litvinov again urged Stalin to adopt a foreign-policy initiative. Clearly giving up the position taken by the Soviets in recent months, Litvinov suggested that 'we too must make our wishes known to some extent' since 'it is not advisable to wait for the other side to offer us what we want'. The proposal's key point was a commitment by the signatories to mutual assistance should one of the three suffer aggression because of assistance given to a country in eastern Europe (to be precise, Litvinov wrote: 'to one of the USSR's European neighbours'). Litvinov pointed out that such a stipulation differed from the British proposals because it made no mention of unilateral declarations: it also differed from the French proposals because it included the Baltic states and Finland among the possible victims of aggression.[35] He also insisted that Maiskii, who had been summoned to Moscow, should remain for the moment in London, since it was 'extremely dangerous and unfavourable for us to conduct negotiations through foreign diplomatic representatives'.[36]

Though the draft interview he had shown to Stalin never saw the light of day, Litvinov's design for a trilateral pact became the basis for the proposal officially put forward by the USSR. On 17 April 1939 Litvinov presented to the other potential signatories an eight-point plan for an agreement between the USSR, France and Great Britain. The Soviet proposal envisaged a five- or ten-year mutual assistance pact with military provisions. The signatories would guarantee their assistance to all the countries of eastern Europe included in the territorial belt from the Baltic Sea to the Black Sea; would discuss and establish the form to be taken by their military assistance in the shortest possible time; would commit themselves not to engage in separate wartime agreements with the aggressors; and would initiate negotiations with Turkey. It was further envisaged that Britain would declare its guarantee to Poland contingent only upon German aggression; that the treaty between Poland and Romania would be assumed to be unrelated to those nations' relations with the USSR; that the pact would be signed at the same time as the military convention.[37]

A significant difference in approach had emerged when Litvinov discussed the final draft of the plan with Stalin and Molotov. The Soviet leaders were concerned with the inclusion of Lithuania, fearing German aggression in the Baltic area. For a long time the possibility of a German attack via the Baltic region had preoccupied Soviet strategists.[38] After the cold reception accorded by Latvia and Estonia to the USSR's unilateral guarantee after the German occupation of Memel, the Baltic countries had been considered unreliable by Moscow. In the wording of the plan, Litvinov was pushing for the 'territorial belt' language, rather than list the states of eastern Europe one by one. He pointed out that there was little to be gained by mentioning the countries by name in negotiations with France and Great Britain since, in his judgement, this would 'inevitably be seen as a proposal to Germany to conquer Lithuania', and the Western powers would have no reason to exclude a country whose defence was important to Poland.[39] But, despite Litvinov's plea for vagueness, the tenor of the final Soviet proposal ended up being quite firm, even confrontational; this was particularly so with regard to Poland and Romania, which Litvinov had not mentioned in his earlier communication to Stalin.

In any case, the eight-point plan seemed to mark a diplomatic turning point. This was the first concrete proposal put forward by the Soviets in a long time, and it was also the first time that a diplomatic attempt at an alliance between the USSR and the Western powers had been essayed without any apparent plan to include Germany. After a long period of official passivity, the Soviets appeared to be willing to take the initiative, and they showed a new openness towards the formation of a bloc opposed to the fascist powers. Given the limits of our present knowledge, this change remains quite difficult to explain. During the days leading up to 15 April 1939, Litvinov had not shown any sign of modifying the position he had embraced after Munich – watchful waiting. But he had noticed the movement taking place along the entire diplomatic front, which by this point included Roosevelt's warning to Hitler and Mussolini (14 April). After all, Litvinov had long hoped for a 'grand alliance' between the USSR and the Western powers. At the beginning of 1938, though his relations with Stalin had already soured, he had spoken hopefully about the formation of a bloc of peace-loving powers. Though he had retreated from such a prospect after Munich, his thinking had not substantially shifted. We can assume that even in April 1939 Stalin would not have initiated a rapprochement with the Western democracies without strong pressure from Litvinov: there had been nothing to indicate that Stalin was considering such a project in his speech of 10 March at the 18th Party Congress. On the other hand, Stalin's decision to accept Litvinov's design for a trilateral pact did not necessarily entail a reversal of the policy then proclaimed of keeping Soviet hands free.

We may gain insight into Stalin's limited faith in a revitalized 'collective security' approach from a simple episode. A request from the French communists led Dimitrov and Manuil'skii to write to Stalin on 20 April; they needed to know whether 'the party, given the present international situation, should serve as leader on behalf of collective security [and] a strengthening of the Franco-Soviet pact, or would it be better if the party did not place itself in the vanguard on these issues'. Primary among the responsibilities of the French Communist Party, according to the Comintern leaders, were 'tirelessly criticiz[ing] the duality of the "new" foreign-policy course of Chamberlain–Daladier–Bonnet', and showing how 'the policy of collective security and the Franco-Soviet pact serve above all the interests of France'. But they were waiting, as usual, for Stalin's opinion.[40] On 26 April Stalin gave his laconic response to Dimitrov, revealing his scant consideration of the question: 'We are very occupied now. Decide these questions by yourselves.'[41]

The British and French governments reacted to the Soviet eight-point plan of 17 April 1939 without any zeal. Rather, the Western governments proved themselves once again deeply insensitive to Soviet policy-making, confirming Litvinov's suspicion that the legacy of Munich still haunted Europe.[42] Ten days after the Soviet proposal had been transmitted he was still complaining that he had not received any signal from Seeds.[43] In the meantime, Surits had received a counter-proposal from Bonnet, who wanted a Soviet commitment to assist the Western powers should the USSR become involved in a war against Germany in central and eastern Europe; in exchange, the Western side would provide military assistance if Moscow's entry into such a conflict made it the target of Nazi aggression. On 28 April, in a message to Stalin, Litvinov called Bonnet's counter-proposal 'almost a mockery' since it flouted any reciprocity between French and Soviet commitments. Nevertheless, he conceded that the French had referred to the whole of central and eastern Europe, not only to Poland and Rumania – this was clearly positive.[44]

However, even after the prompt revision of their formula by the French, there was no agreement on the definition of central and eastern Europe. Within the USSR, a rigid position on the Baltic states was emerging. This was quite different from the position on Lithuania that Litvinov had suggested to Stalin and Molotov when the proposal of 17 April 1939 was being formulated.[45] The British government continued to lie low. On 29 April Maiskii returned to London after several days of briefings in Moscow and promptly met with Halifax, only to be informed that if he wanted the British response to the Soviet proposal he would have to wait.⁴⁶ On 3 May Seeds urged Litvinov to be patient for a little longer.⁴⁷ On the same day, Litvinov assured Stalin that in his discussions with the French he would insist on the inclusion of the Baltic states among the countries to be guaranteed protection. He would assert the concept of an 'uniform defence' on Europe's eastern front; thus far the Western powers had offered guarantees only to Poland and Romania.⁴⁸

Litvinov thus found himself in a vice, squeezed on one side by the attitude of the British government and on the other by the limits that Stalin had clearly imposed. After Munich Litvinov's fate had been far from secure, and now he was in a dramatic situation. Should the proposal offered on 17 April fail to draw takers, his role would be over; and it had received an extremely cool response. Chamberlain's foreign-policy shift did not dictate a unique Soviet response. As they decided to take Great Britain's guarantee to Poland seriously, Soviet policy-makers felt that the moment for extending negotiations with the West on the whole east European theatre had perhaps come. In their view, improved security was less a matter of accepting Western proposals, and confrontation with Germany, than of exploiting the German threat to Britain and France to promote a definition of Soviet interests in eastern Europe. And if Hitler's explicitly anti-Polish and anti-British orientation raised the value of Soviet participation in a mutual assistance pact with the Western powers, it might also open the way for an agreement between Germany and the USSR, negotiated according to the blueprint of 'parallel diplomacy' as performed in 1936–37. Should things move in that direction, Litvinov would no longer be indispensable to Stalin.

On 3 May 1939, the Politburo removed Litvinov from his position as commissar for foreign affairs, ostensibly at his own request; Molotov was nominated to succeed him.⁴⁹ On the same day, a telegram personally signed by Stalin informed Soviet diplomats that Litvinov had been dismissed due to a 'serious conflict' with Molotov which had arisen from Litvinov's 'disloyal attitude'. The telegram went on to say that he had asked to be relieved of his duties, and that Molotov would take over the direction of Soviet foreign policy, while retaining his post as leader of Sovnarkom.⁵⁰ On 4 May, the Soviet press briefly reported this event without making any reference to 'conflict'.⁵¹

THE ROAD TO 'RELATIVE SECURITY'

Immediately after the fall of Litvinov, top Soviet authorities insisted that there be no change in their foreign policy. This was the main topic of Molotov's meeting with Seeds on 8 May, when the ambassador handed over his government's tardy reply to the Soviet proposal of 17 April. The reply simply reiterated previous British positions. During the meeting, the new commissar stressed that the Soviet position remain unchanged 'as long as there are no changes in the international situation and in the position of the other powers'.[52] Molotov also met with Payart, to whom he casually remarked that ministerial changes often took place in the French and British governments without giving rise to 'complications'.[53]

Loud as these protestations of continuity rang, brutal changes immediately affected the Narkomindel. Not only had Litvinov been removed, many in the upper ranks of the Narkomindel followed as all trace of the former commissar for foreign affairs and his influence were purged.[54] A Politburo decision of 3 May established a commission headed by Lavrentii Beriia and charged it with cleaning up the Narkomindel and with reporting the results directly to Stalin and Molotov.[55] As Gnedin points out in his memoirs, 1939's purge of the top ranks of the Narkomindel completed the work begun in 1937: many who had survived the two previous years thanks to Litvinov's protection now tumbled. Litvinov himself was accused by the NKVD of inciting war against the USSR – a typical indictment used during the Great Terror.[56]

As men were promoted to fill the vacated positions, the Narkomindel assumed a different aspect: Soviet foreign policy would now be formulated and implemented by Stalin and Molotov. This did not escape the notice of European diplomats.[57] Ten years later, Molotov himself noted that a desire for tighter control of foreign policy had figured prominently in the decision to dismiss Litvinov. He asserted that:

> The decision of the CC of the VKP(b) was taken in May 1939 in response to the necessity of bringing the Ministry of Foreign Affairs closer to the CC and of making it into a more directly controlled organ of the CC; it was also taken to put an end to the period in which the Ministry for Foreign Affairs was a refuge for the opposition and for every type of dubious element.[58]

But such goals also implied a strategic reorientation of USSR foreign policy, one Stalin only now judged possible. Litvinov's resistance to such a reorientation had become painfully apparent during a debate with Molotov in the final days of April, quite probably during a foreign-policy meeting attended by top Soviet diplomats, Maiskii and Merekalov among them.[59] Maiskii remembers a very sharp exchange between Litvinov and Molotov on 27 April over the negotiations with the Western powers:

> For the first time I saw how relations stood between Litvinov, Stalin and Molotov. The atmosphere at the meeting was extremely explosive. Even though Stalin seemed relaxed and smoked his pipe throughout, one felt that he was extremely hostile towards Litvinov.

STALIN AND THE INEVITABLE WAR, 1936–1941

Molotov incessantly raged and inveighed against Litvinov, accusing him of every cardinal sin.[60]

We know that the conflict between Litvinov and Molotov had not suddenly arisen; it dated back at least to 1936, when Molotov had publicly adopted a pro-German orientation. In the aftermath of the Rhineland crisis such a posture could not be reconciled with the 'collective security' approach. Even during the Great Terror the two men had been at odds, and Zhdanov sided with Molotov against Litvinov, increasingly losing Stalin's confidence. But it was not until May 1939 that the underlying conflict between the two competing strategies rose to the surface of Soviet politics; Stalin definitively made his choice at that time. Many years later, Molotov himself remembered Litvinov as the proponent of an alliance with the Western powers, a man who could not be fully trusted.[61] According to Manuil'skii's report to Dimitrov of 28 May 1939, the accusations leveled against Litvinov immediately after his dismissal concentrated on his willingness to accept the French and British proposals without reservation. This is how Manuil'skii described the May plenum of the Central Committee:

> Viacheslav Mikhailovich Molotov has contributed a report on the international situation [i.e., on negotiations with Britain and France]. The British have proposed that the Soviet Union guarantee Poland, Romania and other states against aggression, without assuming any responsibilities towards the Soviet Union. Litvinov has proposed that we accept this. We have refused . . . We declare that we favour a peaceful alliance of all the peaceful states to oppose aggression. We are ready to conclude all related pacts on a reciprocal basis, but we will maintain our autonomy . . . Litvinov submitted his explanations, but Iosif Vissarionovich [Stalin] maintained that they were unsuitable. He scorned Litvinov as a 'specialist' in international affairs who would assail the Politburo's ineptitude in international affairs.[62]

Molotov's words, as reported by Manuil'skii to Dimitrov, were obviously not entirely accurate, though they are sufficiently clear. Willing to go beyond a simple endorsement of British and French proposals, Litvinov had showed his readiness to find a compromise formula in his draft presented to Stalin on 15 April 1939. Moreover, Molotov's attack to Litvinov reveals the decision to launch a 'twin-track' policy. Stalin had decided to negotiate with the Western powers along a challenging and uncompromising approach while all the time keeping open the possibility of a *revirement* towards Nazi Germany.[63]

Intimations of coming change had been visible since May: a

perceptible change in tone and further stiffening and raising of the stakes vis-à-vis the West.[64] On 11 May 1939 an editorial on the international situation published in *Izvestiia* focused on negotiations with the Western powers.[65] According to the author (probably Molotov),[66] the British reply had in no way shifted the terms of the problem, which were still anchored to the proposal for a unilateral declaration: in order to 'create a barrier against aggression in Europe' it was necessary that Great Britain, France, the USSR and Poland form a united front – or, if not all of them, at least the first three. The editorial demanded that the Western counter-proposals respect the principle of reciprocity and denied that the defence of Poland and Romania would of itself automatically constitute a defence of the USSR's western front. The editorial also noted that recent developments represented a 'turn for the worse'. These included a speech of Hitler's in which he announced the end of both Germany's maritime agreement with Britain and the pact with Poland at the same time that he mentioned the new pact between Germany and Italy.

None of the editorial's affirmations was new, nor did they contrast with positions so far taken by Soviet diplomats. On 14 May 1939 the Soviets rejected the British proposal made on 8 May citing its lack of reciprocity; once again the Soviets repeated their demand for a global agreement, to include not only a mutual assistance pact between the three powers and a guarantee to the countries of eastern Europe but also 'a concrete pact', that is, a separate military agreement. They insisted now that Finland be included in the negotiating package along with the Baltic republics. These provisions amounted to guarantees against a (hardly likely) massive German attack from western Prussia while also providing for the comprehensive defence of the USSR's western and northern borders.[67] At the same time, the Soviet leadership made no comment at all about the French proposals and seemed utterly unconcerned about the 1935 pact with France. In the *Izvestiia* editorial of 11 May the very existence of the Franco-Soviet pact had been ignored.[68] In his first meeting with Paul Emile Naggiar, the new French ambassador to Moscow, which took place on 31 May, Molotov maintained that negotiations for a trilateral agreement had indeed put a damper on the Franco-Soviet pact.[69]

However, Soviet diplomacy in the post-Litvinov era devoted its greatest efforts to a re-launching of the old attempt to link economic negotiations to the search for a political understanding with Germany. Since the early days of 1939 Moscow had moved to accommodate the unexpected signals that emerged from Berlin after Hitler secretly decided to direct his war plans against the Western powers. Among Stalin's personal papers from this period, a number attest to the importance he assigned to economic relations between Germany and the USSR.[70] In early January 1939 Anastas Mikoian had announced the Soviet government's willingness to conclude a new credit agreement along the lines proposed by Germany; this would follow the trade agreement the two countries had reached in December 1938.[71] Over the following days a visit to Moscow was arranged for the German emissary, Julius Schnurre, in order to open negotiations. Writing under a pseudonym, Potemkin stated that the treaty of Rapallo was still in force and that Schnurre, 'Hitler's right-hand man', would be conducting 'important negotiations' in Moscow.[72]

In diplomatic circles, there were renewed rumours of a shift in the Narkomindel line. British reports indicated that Moscow would avoid making a choice between the two blocs of capitalist powers and might well be receptive to overtures from Nazi Germany.[73] But on 28 January 1939 Merekalov announced that because of the excessive concern generated by talk of a German–Soviet rapprochement Schnurre's visit had been cancelled.[74] Though this last-minute loss of nerve did not bode well for relations between Germany and the USSR, both sides remained interested in talks and in February, Schulenburg and Mikoian met to outline a trade and credit agreement. It became clear that the Soviet side wanted a broader agreement than Germany was willing to consider and soon negotiations were at a stalemate.[75] Things were not improved by the note Litvinov handed Schulenburg strongly protesting against the German invasion of Czechoslovakia.[76] Nevertheless, talks were resumed later.

On 17 April 1939, the same day the Soviet proposal was offered to the Western powers, Ribbentrop's deputy, Ernst von Weizsäcker, met with Merekalov. According to the Soviet record of the meeting the German diplomat raised subjects of a 'general political nature', while the Soviet representative questioned his interlocutor on the 'outlook for relations between the USSR and Germany': Weizsaecker suggested that 'ideological contradictions' could be overcome to bring about improvements in the two nations' economic relations.[77] These newly available Soviet documents neither confirm nor contradict the German documents on which historians have long relied: the latter show Merekalov manoeuvring towards rapprochement, using the promise of Soviet neutrality as bait, stating that Moscow was 'interested in removing the threat of war' and in 'resolving the situation that has arisen'.[78] Merekalov's conclusions were not encouraging. On 18 April, before returning to Moscow for consultations, Merekalov reported to the Narkomindel that on the previous day Weizsäcker had spoken of 'political divergences of principle' between their two countries, even as he had insisted on Berlin's commitment to expanding economic relations.[79]

It was only after the fall of Litvinov that the frequency and fruitfulness of Soviet contacts with Germany perceptibly increased. The key man was Grigorii Astakhov, who replaced Merekalov as plenipotentiary in Berlin after his predecessor had announced to the Politburo that he felt certain a war would soon break out between Germany and the Soviet Union.[80] According to Gnedin, Astakhov had been especially instructed to establish new relations with the Germans.[81] Nevertheless, Astakhov was very cautious as he moved around this post-Litvinov arena, and he limited himself to noting that, for the moment, the only new element he perceived was the newly favourable tone with which the German press treated the USSR.[82] On 15 May he declared to Schnurre that Moscow was open to an improvement in relations but that it all depended on Berlin.[83]

A notable initiative, however, came from the newly staffed Narkomindel. On 20 May 1939, Molotov told Schulenburg he regretted that the economic talks were going nowhere and declared that the USSR would not tolerate any kind of 'game'. This was a raising of the stakes. According to Molotov, the Soviet government had concluded that 'for economic negotiations to succeed, a corresponding political base must be created'. When Schnurre asked him to say more, he became guarded and stated that 'both we and the German government must reflect on this'. However, the German proposal to dispatch Schnurre immediately to Moscow could not be entertained, because political understanding had to precede economic negotiations.[84] In the record he kept of the meetings, Molotov wrote that he had intentionally avoided lending too much specificity to this formula. Whatever Molotov's trepidation, he had declared the USSR willing to enter into an agreement with Germany that would go further than any other pre-1933 approach and would serve as the basis for future relations between the two countries. Such move was the outcome of a 'parallel diplomacy' cast in bright sunshine after much time in the shade. But the present did differ from the past: the rulers of the Soviet Union had engaged openly in diplomatic manoeuvres with the Germans. Significantly, a record of the conversation between Molotov and Schulenburg lay on Stalin's desk on the day the two representatives met.[85]

In his speech to the Supreme Soviet on 31 May 1939, Molotov demonstrated that the new Narkomindel had taken to heart the directives issued by Stalin at the 18th Party Congress. The Soviet Union, he announced, had managed to position itself midway between the 'aggressive states' and the 'democratic states'.[86] Following up his detailed summary of the topics listed in *Izvestiia* on 11 May, Molotov admitted that the democratic states had inched closer to taking a stand against aggression. However, he remained sceptical: 'We shall see how serious these changes are.' Though Western public opinion favoured abandoning the orientation adopted at Munich, this was not enough.

STALIN AND THE INEVITABLE WAR, 1936–1941

The Soviet Union thus moved very cautiously towards negotiations with the Western powers. Molotov described as a novelty the Western attempt to include the USSR in a cooperative effort, in this case the creation of 'an effective defensive front' among non-aggressive countries. To do this, a minimum of three conditions had to be met: a pact of mutual assistance between the three powers had to be drawn up; guarantees had to be offered by the three allies to the states of central and eastern Europe, including every state bordering on the USSR; a 'concrete agreement' between the three powers would be necessary, one which defined the form defensive mutual assistance would take (and since it was to be exclusively defensive, the agreement would be quite different from the pact concluded between Germany and Italy on 22 May 1939). What was lacking, according to Molotov, even in the most recent Anglo-French proposals, was a proper application of the principle of 'reciprocity'. This sort of respect, he insisted, was indispensable and would form the basis for such an agreement: not only would reciprocity have to be written into the chosen formulas, it would also be a crucial standard in identifying which countries' borders were to be guaranteed.

None of Molotov's suggestions was a surprise or a novelty. But now he stated that 'even as we conduct negotiations with Britain and France, we do not consider it at all necessary to refrain from business relations with countries such as Germany and Italy'. Why give up the economic negotiations with Germany which had been underway since the beginning of the year? This announcement, made in exquisite bureaucratese, constituted in fact the first positive public signal sent by Moscow to Berlin since Molotov's interview of March 1936. Things had changed since Litvinov was in charge of foreign policy, and Molotov did not settle for the Anglo-French proposal offered on 27 May, which only accepted the principle of a political–military alliance. Until he could expect to see a plan for mutual defence on the table, there would be no negotiations; this had been Molotov's position in his meeting with Seeds and Payart on 31 May.[87] The negotiations between the USSR and the Western powers stalled.

In an interview with Halifax in Geneva, Maiskii suggested that the USSR had two choices. One was a policy of isolation: the Soviets would keep their hands free while enjoying 'relative security'. The other was the formation of a 'peaceful bloc' with Western powers: the USSR would enjoy less freedom of action but the outbreak of a world war might be avoided, and the security of the country would be enhanced. Maiskii believed that the Soviet leadership was unlikely to choose the second option if no concrete gains were forthcoming.[88]

Maiskii did not prefer 'relative security'. In a letter to Molotov he wrote on 10 May, the ambassador reiterated his conviction that 'the logic of things' would oblige Great Britain to stand up resolutely to German aggression – this was, after all, the prevailing orientation of British public opinion.[89] Maiskii also thought that the guarantees Great Britain had given to Poland, Romania and Greece rendered 'a rapid understanding with the USSR necessary' – otherwise Britain would be incapable of delivering on its promises.[90] Writing to Potemkin on 26 May, Surits reiterated the assertion that a 'decisive turn' had taken place in British and French foreign policy after Hitler's seizure of Prague. He underlined the shift in western European public opinion towards firmness and towards cooperation with Moscow, and acknowledged that in the past he had underestimated these sentiments.[91] However, the views of the two diplomats who had been closest to Litvinov were not likely to gain a sympathetic hearing from Molotov.

For over a month the two scenarios that had been set out for Soviet foreign policy at the end of May remained the top choices. On 2 June 1939 the Soviet government presented the Western powers with a counterproposal that envisaged a mutual assistance agreement outside the procedures of the League of Nations and included Estonia, Latvia and Finland among the European countries to be placed under guarantee.[92] After Germany, on 7 June, concluded two non-aggression pacts with Latvia and Estonia, Moscow pushed for a response from Paris and London. On 10 June Molotov stated to Maiskii that, in the absence of a satisfactory solution to the Baltic problem, 'it will not be possible to conclude the negotiations'.[93] On 13 June this concept was publicly repeated in *Pravda*, along with the assertion that 'the problem of maintaining the neutrality of the three Baltic countries represents a vital interest from the point of view of Soviet security'.[94] The matter was not resolved by later exchanges of proposals and notes. Molotov continued to express to Maiskii and to Surits his view that the Western side showed no sign of wanting to reach an agreement corresponding 'to the principle of reciprocity and of equality of obligations'.[95] The change that had taken place in Soviet post-Litvinov foreign policy was reflected even in Maiskii's conduct, when he agreed to preach to Halifax 'a sort of Monroe Doctrine in eastern Europe' for the USSR.[96] In the meantime, the Soviets were unhappy with the talks conducted in Moscow by William Strang, a second-rank Foreign Office official, and they let their feelings be known.[97]

In an unpublished speech he gave in mid-June Manuil'skii explicitly declared that the USSR should aim at remaining outside of the catastrophe soon to engulf Europe. If it failed to follow its own path the capitalist states would see all the more cause to seek the destruction of the Soviet regime.[98] This anticipated a major pronouncement by one of the chief authority figures in Stalin's entourage. On 29 June a signed article by Zhdanov appeared in *Pravda* with the bald heading 'The

British and French Governments Do Not Want a Pact on Equal Terms with the USSR'.[99]

This was, to say the least, an unusual event in Soviet diplomacy. Even more unusual was the way in which the article was presented. The author began by noting that the negotiations had entered 'a blind alley'. He purported to wonder about the causes of this state of affairs, and made bold to set forth his own 'personal opinion' although, he declared, 'my friends do not agree with it'. It is not clear where Zhdanov's artificially casual manner ended. In the past Zhdanov had aggressively opposed Litvinov. Now, in the aftermath of Litvinov's fall, his influence seemed to be growing. Zhdanov outlined his opinions in strokes impossible to misconstrue: 'I believe and I shall try to demonstrate with facts that the British and French governments do not want a pact with the USSR on an equal basis.' The 'facts' adduced by the author were largely related to the slow pace of negotiations. He considered 'clearly unfounded' the Western objections that the Baltic states had refused to receive the guarantees the USSR viewed as fundamental to any three-way agreement and voiced his suspicion that the Western powers were conducting negotiations 'with other objectives' in mind. In his conclusion, he wrote that the USSR would no longer tolerate Western conduct which tended to open the way 'to a compromise with the aggressors'. Zhdanov's *Pravda* piece was a heavy-handed announcement that the Soviet leadership was ready to embrace the option Maiskii had defined as leading to 'relative security'. No one who read his article could misunderstand it and no one could doubt its seriousness.

THE PACT

Though in the first half of July a new Anglo-French proposal overcame the obstacle of guarantees – they were to be dealt with in a secret protocol – the negotiations did not mark a decisive step. There had not yet been any movement on the question of 'indirect aggression'. By this, the Soviets meant not only the actions by force that had happened in Austria and Czechoslovakia, but also a possible fascist coup d'état in neighbouring countries. This point was linked with a precise interpretation of the expansion of war which went back to the Spanish experience.[100] It revealed that a boundless concept of national security was interlaced with Moscow's obstinate request for a comprehensive defence of the USSR's western and northern borders – which had also included a specific insistence on the demilitarization of the Aaland Islands.[101] Soviet apprehension was much more justified on the eastern borders. After the conflict with Japan during the summer of 1938,

Manchuria looked like a far greater danger than the Baltic states or Finland. Around mid-June 1939 the USSR and Japan were involved again in a serious incident, which added a threat of war to the hostility lingering from the previous year.[102] The dreadful scenario of an international situation menacing both the USSR's western and eastern borders quite probably increased the Soviets' acute sense of insecurity. In any event, for Moscow the Japanese question remained connected to the German question. This in turn had already become part of a diplomatic double game played both by the Soviets and by the British.[103]

On 23 July the Western powers announced that they had accepted the substance of Soviet requests for a meaningful military agreement and opened the way to military negotiations, to be pursued jointly with political negotiations. This removed the negative precedent represented by the Franco-Soviet pact that had continued to weigh heavily on Moscow's views. But there was no jubilation in the Soviet camp: reserve prevailed and it was agreed that the negotiations had yet to show real progress. Moscow was now more tied than ever to its old philosophy of maintaining freedom of action and of assuming binding undertakings only when conditions were extremely favourable. The USSR had not committed itself unreservedly to the conclusion of a trilateral agreement. Otherwise why would Molotov have resisted signing a joint political communiqué announcing the opening of military negotiations?[104]

The main lines of the negotiations between the Western powers and the USSR which began in Moscow in August 1939 are sufficiently well known. While the commissar for defence, Voroshilov, was the leader of the Soviet delegation, the British and French had made up their delegations from second-rank officials. This was a rather unmistakable indication that they were less committed to the negotiations than the Soviets. Such a delegation, as Maiskii promptly remarked, would never be endowed with full decision-making powers. His dissatisfaction was certainly shared by Molotov and Stalin.[105] But they probably would not have shared the opinion expressed in Maiskii's diary, that 'the bloc is gradually being formed'.[106] When, after many delays, the Western delegations reached Moscow, Soviet irritation increased: was the whole affair a sham, never meant to serve any purpose pressuring Germany? From Stalin's viewpoint, if the French and British were playing at phantom negotiations, all for the benefit of a player not seated at the bargaining table, it was a game dangerously similar to the one being played by the Soviets.

The negotiations did not begin until 12 August. It then became evident that the Western side did not have a mandate to conclude a military agreement. Two days later, negotiations foundered on the first issue of any substance: safe passage of Soviet troops through Polish and

Romanian territory in the event of war with Germany. The Soviet delegation had been instructed to state that 'without this condition, no treaty is possible'.[107] Though talks continued, they were meaningless from that point forward. On 17 August the Soviets suspended talks for the first time. Four days later, they decided to interrupt the negotiations indefinitely, effectively conceding a failure which had been evident from the start.[108] Maiskii noted in his diary that 'there had already been a strong inclination in Moscow to liquidate them [i.e., the talks] in July'.[109]

Even before the Soviet and Anglo-French military delegations met, relations between the USSR and Germany had entered a new phase. This is now documented not only in German sources, but in newly available Soviet sources as well. Communication with Germany had not progressed along the lines Molotov had envisioned the end of May. According to German information relying on a Bulgarian source, around mid-June the Soviet leadership stood undecided before three possible courses of action: forming a pact with the West, gaining time by drawing out negotiations, or effecting a rapprochement with Germany. Stalin was said to prefer the third option but to consider the second more realistic.[110] Evidence from Soviet documents only refers to comments that Peter Draganov, the Bulgarian ambassador to Berlin, made to Astakhov: he felt that Germany would immediately go to war if the USSR, Britain and France concluded an alliance.[111] In a letter to Molotov, Astakhov dwelt on this information.[112] Draganov was also said to have suggested that negotiations with the West be drawn out, hypothesizing that an agreement between the Soviets and the Germans might be possible on the basis of a configuration of their spheres of influence. In German documents these positions were attributed by Draganov to Astakhov (with the omission of the reference to spheres of influence).

In any event, no significant progress was made in the meeting between Astakhov and Schulenburg on 17 June. The Soviet representative confirmed that Moscow hoped to improve relations, but a German initiative would be required.[113] On 28 June Molotov expressed pleasure when Schulenburg declared Germany's desire 'not only to normalize but also to improve' relations with the USSR. But the Soviet commissar for foreign affairs made it clear that this was still not enough.[114] Two days earlier, Moscow had been informed of a 'Schulenburg plan' aimed at a rapprochement between Germany and the USSR. The news was the result of an indiscretion by Italy's foreign minister, Galeazzo Ciano, in conversation with L. B. Gel'fand (Helfand), then Soviet ambassador to Rome; the Narkomindel had received word from Gel'fand on 26 June. According to what Gel'fand passed on of his talks with Ciano, the 'Schulenburg plan' had foreseen a German assistance in eliminating friction between Japan and the USSR, a broad commercial agreement, and either a 'non-aggression pact' or a guarantee given jointly to the Baltic countries.[115] Over the ensuing weeks the Soviets watched carefully for the sorts of signs that would either confirm or contradict the rumour.

When Astakhov and Schnurre met on 24 July, following the official reopening of economic negotiations, the two countries took a significant step towards normalizing relations. Even though each diplomat was clearly waiting for the other to make the first move, when Schnurre said Germany intended to respect Soviet interests in the Baltic region he sounded forthcoming to the Soviets.[116] Two days later Schnurre told Astakhov that Hitler now saw Great Britain as his 'main enemy'. Also, since there was no possibility that German–Polish relations could be restored, a further deterioration in German–Russian relations was unthinkable; it was quite conceivable that even USSR–Japanese relations could improve.[117] When Schnurre made a reference to the 'Rapallo period', his suggestions seemed more credible. Astakhov, however, remained reserved.

Molotov approved of his subordinate's demeanour and decided that the Soviet position should remain unchanged: Moscow stood willing to improve relations, but the matter depended entirely on the Germans, who would have to be solely responsible for designing the political content of an eventual rapprochement.[118] In the meantime, Astakhov reported to Potemkin that 'the German attempt to improve relations with us is sufficiently insistent and has been confirmed by the complete cessation of their press campaign as well as other actions against us'. In his opinion, it was now possible to 'involve the Germans in far-reaching negotiations'; he recommended 'keeping them on the boil for a while' so as to secure 'a card which can be played if necessary'.[119] By the end of July the USSR's position both at the negotiating table and in the wider political double game being conducted by all the European powers, had grown considerably stronger.

In the first days of August 1939, while tensions over Danzig were increasing, German–Soviet contacts became more frequent and prolonged. On 2 August, in a meeting with Astakhov, Ribbentrop stated that the conclusion of economic negotiations could form a basis for improved political relations; he saw no contradictions between the two countries 'from the Black Sea to the Baltic'. Astakhov immediately wanted to determine which 'concrete proposals' might be put forward.[120] At the same time, Molotov held a long meeting with Schulenburg during which he repeated yet again that the Soviets hoped to conclude a commercial and credit agreement, that they had always 'favoured normalization and improvement of relations' and that everything depended on the Germans. As to Schulenburg's unhappiness over the Soviet Union's plans to negotiate a treaty with

France and Great Britain, Molotov pointed out that this might only be 'a defensive agreement against aggression'.[121] On 4 August Molotov informed Astakhov of the USSR's readiness to 'continue the exchange of views on improving relations'.[122] But he did not care to include a statement to that effect in the German–Soviet economic agreement being drawn up even as the Western delegation was arriving in Moscow to discuss military cooperation.[123]

In a letter to Molotov written on 8 August 1939, Astakhov offered some predictions about issues that would have to be discussed with Germany. He suggested that a range of existing pacts, including the Rapallo Treaty, might be combined into 'a new pact' or 'under the guise of a mention in a protocol'. Then Astakhov notified Molotov that the moment was ripe for broadly-based political negotiations. Ribbentrop's words about the absence of contradictions between Germany and Russia 'from the Black Sea to the Baltic' provided the grounds for a possible understanding based on spheres of influence. In Astakhov's judgement, a German declaration of no interest in the Baltic region, Bessarabia and 'Russian Poland', together with a renunciation of all aspirations towards the Ukraine, could be balanced by an analogous Soviet declaration on Danzig, 'German Poland' and Galicia. He observed that such an agreement could exist only in the absence of a political and military understanding between the USSR, Britain and France.[124] On 11 August, before the start of negotiations with the Western delegation, Molotov notified Astakhov of his interest and proposed that talks take place in Moscow.[125] On 13 August Astakhov reported that the Germans had agreed. He stressed the speed at which events were developing and the growing German interest in an understanding 'on political and territorial themes' which would allow Hitler freedom of action in the event of conflict with Poland.[126] The road to parallel negotiations was opening up, just as negotiations with the Western delegation were breaking down. This helps to explain the deliberate Soviet decision to end negotiations with the West without further ado.

Between 15 and 19 August 1939 three decisive meetings between Molotov and Schulenburg took place. In their first meeting, Schulenburg submitted a six-point document, confirming German hopes for a political agreement. There were to be no contradictions between the two countries from, once again, 'the Black Sea to the Baltic' and there would have to be some 'clarification' in view of the worsening relations between Germany and Poland. Though he had avoided doing it up to then, Molotov thought that the time had come to take a position. He repeated what Gel'fand had reported about his conversation with Ciano of the end of June and asked Schulenburg flatly whether there was a 'Schulenburg plan'. According to Schulenburg's flustered response, the indiscretion had in fact been Rosso's: Schulenburg had talked with the Italian ambassador to Moscow about a possible improvement in German–Soviet relations, though only in quite general terms. But Molotov kept up the pressure, declaring that the information from the Italian source contained 'nothing improbable' and had effectively been confirmed by the conclusion of a German–Soviet credit agreement. Schulenburg then admitted that the subject of his meeting with Rosso had 'reflected' instructions received from Berlin. A satisfied Molotov hastened to explain that he had raised the issue of this so-called 'Schulenburg plan' precisely because of his impression that the German ambassador had not simply been reporting personal views to the Italians. He did not, however, accept the German ambassador's invitation to take the 'plan' as a basis for discussion and instead proposed that the meeting proceed according to 'more concrete terms'. He mentioned the need to conclude the economic negotiations rapidly and the pressing question of Soviet–Japanese relations.[127] As the meeting drew to a close, Molotov maintained the initiative as he drove towards the most pressing issue: had the German government formed 'a definite opinion on the problem of concluding a non-aggression pact with the USSR'? Molotov urged Schulenburg to clarify this with Ribbentrop; if the German side were well disposed a pact might be drawn up without delay.[128]

The compressed series of diplomatic gambits and follow-ups carefully calculated by Stalin's new foreign-policy commissar provoked Schulenburg's presentation of the German proposal in mid-August, one of the most significant milestones on the road to the pact. On 17 August Schulenburg informed Molotov that Berlin was ready to open negotiations as indicated by the Soviets; a meeting should be held as soon as possible. Molotov gave Schulenburg a letter approved by Stalin applauding the new 'development' in German policy and which mentioned the principle of 'peaceful coexistence' as a basis for mutual understanding. The Soviets requested that all economic negotiations be concluded before beginning the political negotiations; they also wanted a decision on whether to confirm the agreement of 1926 or to conclude a new non-aggression pact. Molotov especially insisted on discussing an additional protocol on foreign-policy problems, the contents of which would be the subject of discussion between the two sides.[129] By 19 August the economic agreement had been wrapped up and Schulenburg was pressing for a rapid resolution of all outstanding issues; both the questions of Germany's benign intervention for improving relations between Japan and the USSR, and of reciprocal guarantees to the Baltic countries had been resolved. But Molotov continued to insist on the additional protocol and indicated that this was the only remaining problem before proceeding to arrange the meeting with Ribbentrop.[130]

Another diplomatic milestone was the exchange of letters between Hitler and Stalin on 21 August. Hitler welcomed the conclusion of the economic agreement, proposed a new 'non-aggression pact', accepted the inclusion of an additional protocol and hinted at an imminent conflict with Poland. He suggested that Ribbentrop visit Moscow no later than 23 August. The Soviet dictator was more concise: he hoped the pact would mark a step forward in political relations between the two countries and accepted the date Hitler had proposed.[131] On 22 August the Soviet press announced that since the two countries had concluded an economic agreement, consideration was being given to 'improving political relations between Germany and the USSR' through a 'non-aggression pact', and that Ribbentrop would arrive in Moscow on the following day.[132] The pact was rapidly concluded on the first day of talks between Ribbentrop, Molotov and Stalin. The Politburo ratified the agreement on 27 August.[133]

Exchanging toasts with Ribbentrop, Stalin eloquently opined that Britain would fight with tenacity.[134] It is unclear how genuine this conviction was, given the Soviets' nagging suspicion that the Munich game could be set in motion all over again.[135] In any case, Stalin probably believed that this time things could go very differently than they had one year earlier and that the USSR would be kept out of the imminent pan-European conflict.

The official Soviet position was set out by Molotov to the Supreme Soviet on 31 August, after Voroshilov had publicly stated that the USSR had been led to conclude the pact with Germany after negotiations with the Western military delegation had broken down.[136] Molotov began by vaunting the pact's importance in an 'increasingly tense' international situation. He underlined the Soviet Union's neutral position and declared that the USSR would go to war neither 'on the side of Britain against Germany, nor on the side of Germany against Britain'. He even pretended that the pact had been drawn up 'out of a general interest in peace', arguing that the scope for military operations would now be considerably restricted. The truth is that the Soviet side knew that Hitler would move rapidly against Poland: this was implicitly confirmed by the published text of the pact, which omitted any clause annulling the pact in the event of an attack by either signatory on a third country. But for Molotov the main point of the pact with Germany was not only the achievement of neutrality. His pleasure at seeing the USSR acknowledged as a great European power was thinly disguised. Great Britain had never adequately conceded this status, Molotov asserted. If the pact was to be seen as 'a turning point in the development of Europe', it was because it constituted proof of the USSR's 'growth in influence'.[137]

Once he had explained the achievement represented by the pact, Molotov went on to describe the agreement's gestation and in so doing offered a view of the contemporaneous orientation of the Soviet leadership. He repeated the words he had used during the 23 August 1939 meeting with Ribbentrop and maintained that the turning point had been Stalin's report to the 18th Party Congress.[138] Above all, Stalin's statement had opened the way for a clear foreign-policy line, implicitly linked to Molotov's own interview of March 1936, in which he had revealed the existence of two incompatible orientations among Soviet leaders. At the time he had described the pro-Germans as the majority; now he proclaimed them the victors:

> As you can see, Comrade Stalin has scored, unmasking the intrigues of those Western European politicians who tried to throw Germany and the Soviet Union into conflict with each other. It has to be admitted that even in our own country some have been short-sighted, so excited by simplistic anti-fascist agitation that they forgot that our enemies were trying to provoke us. Comrade Stalin kept the circumstances in mind and even then asked whether the relations between Germany and the USSR could be friendly, those of good neighbours in effect. Now it is clear that in Germany these declarations by Comrade Stalin were correctly understood on the whole and it is clear, too, that practical lessons were drawn from them. The conclusion of the German–Soviet non-aggression pact attests to the brilliant realization of Comrade Stalin's historical forecast.[139]

The speaker explained that states ruled by regimes with different social and political philosophies could enjoy a 'peaceful coexistence'. He also offered a generalization in the most classic Stalinist style: in the field of international relations, political science was not a matter of 'increasing the number of one's enemies', but was rather a matter of 'diminishing the number of such enemies'. But Molotov went further and, in an implicit reference to the Rapallo precedent and to the need for special relations between Germany and the USSR, noted that these were the two countries that had suffered most from World War I: hostility between them was harmful to the interests of their respective peoples. In other words, he identified Soviet interests with a longstanding rejection of the Versailles system, thus hinting at a tradition considerably more deep-seated in Soviet political culture than 'collective security' had ever been. The ultimate justification of all this was the pact's secret protocol, which envisaged the reorganization of central and eastern Europe according to German and Russian 'spheres of influence'. In the eyes of the Stalinist rulers, inclusion of the protocol demonstrated the USSR's role as a great

European power and made of the pact a central element in the security policy which they had now outlined.

From September on, events unfolded largely according to the Stalinist rulers' expectations. They looked on as the Germans attacked Poland, provoking the reciprocal declarations of war of the principal European powers, which signaled the beginning of the great conflict. The course of the war, however, took an unexpected turn. Western passivity and the sudden collapse of Poland, which neither the Soviets nor the West had foreseen, created a very different scenario from that drawn up some weeks earlier, at the time of the signing of the pact. Though the partition of Poland had been envisioned in the secret protocol, how and when had been left undetermined.

Acting rather quickly, given the speed of the German advance, Moscow decided on 9 September 1939 to invade Poland from the east.[140] But the Soviet commanders were unable to commence operations until 17 September.[141] On that day, Molotov shamelessly announced in a radio broadcast that the pact between the USSR and Poland was invalidated, that the new situation constituted a threat to the security of the USSR and that Soviet armies were moving to protect the western 'brother nations' of Ukraine and Belorussia from the collapse of the Polish state. He justified Soviet 'neutrality' and made no reference to Germany.[142] This thesis, according to which an 'internal inconsistency' had doomed the Polish state, had been formulated by Zhdanov in an article published without signature in *Pravda* on 14 September.[143]

No longer was Poland a buffer between Germany and the USSR. Some might think that this was hardly an ideal option for the Soviet Union. Indeed, in a confidential conversation held on 20 September 1939, Maiskii asserted that Poland should survive as a 'cushion state', inasmuch as the Soviets did not want Germany at its own borders.[144] But soon enough all such muttering had ceased.[145] Though they had been taken by surprise, the Soviet leaders came to see the partition of Poland as an event bound to increase the role of Soviet power in eastern Europe and sure to strengthen USSR security by means of territorial expansion. After all, a state long considered hostile in Moscow had been erased from the map of Europe. It seemed to the Soviet leaders that the advancing of the USSR's borders balanced German penetration in eastern Europe, and both respected the parameters laid down in the pact.

However, the stalemate of the war in Europe prompted concern and brought back the spectre of a 'second Munich'.[146] This may well have been a key factor in convincing the Soviets to seek another rapprochement with Germany, an option their own strategic and political choices were pushing them towards. As early as August a new political logic had thoroughly taken shape in Moscow, and it was visible in the proposal

Molotov made to Schulenburg on 19 September to clarify spheres of influence.[147] On 25 September Stalin presented the Soviet proposals to Schulenburg himself: since there was to be no autonomous Polish state, Germany should absorb the territory of Lublin and part of Warsaw province into its sphere of influence, leaving Lithuania to the USSR.[148]

On 27–28 September Molotov and Stalin met in Moscow with Ribbentrop and Schulenburg.[149] Stalin expressed agreement with Ribbentrop's thesis that Great Britain did not want a long war. As for Schulenburg's proposal of a joint declaration to confirm German–Soviet cooperation (without any suggestion that the USSR would provide war assistance to Germany), Stalin did not fail to mention the Rapallo Treaty, which in his view provided the basis for an extension of reciprocal relations. He declared that the Soviet government had always wanted to maintain good relations with the German government; Great Britain, on the contrary, it had never cared for. The cooperation now established between the two countries, said Stalin, 'represents in itself such a force that all other combinations must give way before it'. This assertion led to the core of Stalin's intervention, and he spoke of the political significance that the new talks presented for the USSR. Certainly, observed Stalin, Ribbentrop had 'spoken well' in insisting that Germany would never involve the USSR in the war because Germany needed no help and would need no help. Then Stalin declared:

> If, in spite of its forecasts, Germany should find itself in a difficult situation, then it can be sure that the Soviet people will come to Germany's assistance and will not allow it to be strangled. The Soviet Union is interested in a strong Germany and will not allow it to be knocked to the ground.[150]

Stalin showed himself poised to appeal for a true alliance between the USSR and Germany. However, it is probable that the aims of his rhetoric were more limited. Perhaps behind his bold declaration lay nothing but the expectation that a European war could well drag on for a spell and that the USSR might become a crucial third player. If the report recorded his words faithfully, they may have been inspired by the desire to derive maximum advantage from the 'inter-imperialistic contradictions' that had escalated into armed conflict, confirming in his eyes their successful exploitation by the USSR.

As to redefining respective spheres of influence, Stalin remained committed to his own proposals even as he laboured to reduce any friction with Germany. The initial Soviet plan had involved maintaining an 'independent but reduced Poland', though the Soviets had been at pains to allow that this would probably guarantee 'a constant hotbed of trouble in Europe'. Since that plan had to be shelved, there remained two variant options: either a division of Poland along the lines described in the secret protocol of 23 August, which would have meant imposing two different political and social systems on the Polish population; or a partition along ethnic lines, which would have left the entire Polish population in the hands of the Germans, while transferring Lithuania to the Soviet sphere of influence. Arguing in favour of the second solution, in spite of Ribbentrop's reservations, Stalin explained that it would help avoid future complications in German–Soviet relations.[151]

On 28 September 1939 Ribbentrop announced Hitler's consent to the Soviet requests, thus removing all obstacles to the conclusion of a new treaty. The revision of the August territorial agreements to compensate for the events of the previous month was achieved without difficulty. And Stalin's declaration of solidarity between the German and Soviet peoples had not gone unheard: while Ribbentrop repeated that Germany did not need military aid, he underlined the strategic importance to Germany of the economic support being provided by the USSR. An understanding was thus secured for subsequent intensive economic cooperation between the two countries.

There was only one snag, quickly resolved thanks to a telephone call to Hitler. This was Stalin's reluctance to include in the joint communiqué a reference to the 'imperialistic objectives' of the Western powers: he had his way and the idea was expressed 'in a more veiled form'. On the other hand, Stalin did assure Ribbentrop that the USSR would not establish formal ties to the Western powers. Finally, Ribbentrop raised the possibility of a meeting between Hitler and Stalin. Rather cryptically, Stalin replied that 'if we should be alive' such a meeting would be 'desirable and possible'.[152] As with the August pact, the new treaty was accompanied by a secret protocol recording the agreed changes to the spheres of influence. The joint declaration proclaimed the inauguration of a 'lasting peace' in eastern Europe and demanded 'an end to the present war'. Otherwise France and Britain would have to assume responsibility for the conflict.[153]

At this point, the Soviet position on the European war was less that of a neutral actor than that of 'non-belligerent': from this perspective the USSR looked much like Italy.[154] In a meeting with the Turkish foreign minister on 1 October 1939 Stalin interpreted the Soviet position:

> Events have their own logic: we say one thing, but the events go in another direction. We have divided Poland with Germany. Britain and France did not declare war on us, but this may happen. We have a mutual assistance pact with the Germans, but if the British and the French declare war on us, we will have to fight them.[155]

Such words, however, overlooked the fact that the Soviets bore responsibility for the outbreak of World War II, having decisively contributed to the conditions for Hitler's invasion of Poland. From this historical perspective, the non-aggression pact of August 1939 and the friendship treaty of September 1939 can be seen as a single development, which formed a turning point in Soviet foreign policy. The new entente with Germany that was being forged during wartime appeared to be much more substantial than the alliance with France of four years earlier. The sensibilities of the Soviet policy-makers were far more susceptible to appeals based on pro-Rapallo and anti-Versailles sentiments than they were based on anti-fascism.

Viewed in this light, the Soviet rapprochement with Nazi Germany demands a series of revisions in earlier interpretations. There is no choice but to reject the old standby of Russian historians of the Soviet period who alleged that the decision to enter into a pact with Germany was the only route open to a country otherwise exposed to unacceptable levels of danger.[156] And it no longer makes sense to see the Soviet policy change of August–September 1939 as an improvised reaction to the events of the preceding months, above all to the failure of negotiations with the Western powers.[157] Naturally, Stalin's decision for a pact with Hitler grew in 1939 from specific circumstances, including the new British firmness and Hitler's determination to make war on the Western powers. However, the 'collective security' option had been perceptibly undermined after 1936 by clinging to isolationism and to a policy of untrammeled autonomy in international affairs. Other interpretations hardly fare better, especially the contention that Stalin had a consistent plan from the time of Hitler's rise to power.[158] The evidence surveyed over the preceding pages suggests instead that Soviet foreign policy in the second half of the 1930s resulted mainly from conflict among various strategic orientations formulated as responses to the European crises. The real element of continuity was the permanent conditioning exercised by the isolationist concept of security, which came to be the pivot of Stalin's policy.

The background to Stalin's pact with Hitler was a combination of inner conditions, perceptions of international crises, and traditional axioms applied to the outside world. Thanks to the growth in the ideological influence of 'capitalist encirclement' during the Great Terror, a passive attitude sprang up in international crisis management, merged with an approach aimed at avoiding involvement in an increasingly tense European theatre.

This was the basic mechanism undermining the Soviet 'collective security' response to Hitler's rise, which would instead require political initiative and participation in international affairs. Consequently, the stage was set for foreign-policy conflict up to the decisive phase of the spring of 1939. Such conflict may be understood as reflecting the same dilemma faced by Western leaders: would firmness against Hitler really prevent war, or rather hasten its outbreak? Eventually Stalin's choice was for Litvinov's removal and for Soviet appeasement.[159] However, this was not simply a reverse image and a reaction to Western appeasement. Soviet appeasement as it emerged in the aftermath of the European crises was basically linked to the longstanding tradition of isolationism, an autonomous source conditioning all USSR policy-makers and diplomats. Munich only reinforced an already existing notion among the Soviet political élites – the capitalist world was a powder keg ready to explode at any minute. Given such a premise, it should not be startling that many in the Soviet Union came to believe that the principal strategic goal of the Western powers was unleashing the Nazi threat eastwards. Firmness against Hitler came increasingly to be seen as hardly offering the most secure option. The real test of security came to be how Soviet zones of interest might be guaranteed.

This orientation also presupposed a limited understanding of Hitler's strategy. The Great Terror had removed from office with remarkable thoroughness all of those who had persistently drawn attention to the radical character of Nazi ideology as the determining factor in German foreign policy. The view of Hitler most widespread in Soviet circles stressed the continuity between his strategic thinking and the traditional guiding principles of German imperialism and nationalism – an interpretation oblivious to the evolution of Nazi foreign policy. Such an emphasis on continuity blinded Soviet policy-makers to the increasing influence of anti-Bolshevik ideological principles emerging with the Spanish crisis and the radical course taken by Hitler in winter 1937–38, despite the impact of the Nazi threat on the insecurity of the Soviets. Stalin and Molotov favoured this inclination, which clearly was not shared by Litvinov. They continued to see contemporary events as a repetition of the days leading up to the Great War, and believed that a temporary understanding could be reached with Nazi Germany as long as central Europe was acknowledged as a German region; eastern Europe could be divided.

On the other hand, it is improbable that the Stalinist rulers intended to achieve an organic alliance based on an affinity between the two totalitarian regimes and on their mutual aversion to the West.[160] The political understanding reached by the two totalitarian states could hardly have had a truly strategic character on either side. After all, the compass by which Stalin navigated was always the tension between the capitalist and socialist systems, though his policy had been oriented to exploiting 'contradictions' between capitalist powers. This made it all the

POLAND

more likely that sooner or later the USSR would be drawn into the conflict, even against Germany. Soviet security and power would be guaranteed by a new 'inter-imperialistic conflict' inflicting deep wounds on the West and Germany. From August–September 1939 on, Stalin's strategic thinking was dominated by this idea.

Adam Ulam maintains that when Stalin offered Germany support in September 1939 he departed from Lenin's conduct towards the capitalist world and the legacy of that conduct.[161] The Soviet rulers saw two great benefits in the new arrangement: the USSR would avoid immediate involvement in the pan-European war and at the same time it could embark on a search for security through spheres of influence in eastern Europe. Over the course of negotiations with the Nazis, the Soviet rulers outlined their own sphere of influence and how it should be formed, both through territorial annexation, as had happened in Poland, and also through a *cordon sanitaire* turned against the threat of the capitalist world. This was implicit in references to Poland as a 'buffer state' and to a limited sovereignty for the Baltic states. Combined with this concept was to be the procedure of exporting the Soviet political and social system, 'sovietizing' foreign territories or entire countries. The Leninist vision of separation from the rest of the world remained dominant, but after the political turning point of August–September 1939 it underwent a correction and an adjustment: a new expansionist tendency appeared, based much more on a territorial conception of Soviet security than on the idea of revolution in Europe.

NOTES

1. *God krizisa*, 1, doc. 198, p. 294.
2. Ibid., doc. 204, p. 298.
3. Ibid., doc. 196, pp. 292–3.
4. Ibid., doc. 207, pp. 306–7.
5. *Dokumenty vneshnei politiki* (hereafter: DVP), XXII, 1, doc. 157, pp. 209–11.
6. *God krizisa*, 1, doc. 215, p. 314.
7. Ibid., doc. 220, p. 318.
8. ASMAE, Affari politici: Urss, 1939, b. 32, fasc. 3 (20 March 1939).
9. Ibid. (18 March 1939).
10. *God krizisa*, 1, doc. 224, pp. 322–3.
11. Ibid.
12. Ibid., doc. 228, pp. 329–34.
13. AVP RF, f. 017a, op. 1, p. 1, d. 6, l. 76.
14. See D. C. Watt, *How War Came: The Immediate Origins of the Second World War 1938–1939* (New York: Pantheon Books, 1989), p. 180.
15. *God krizisa*, 1, doc. 225, pp. 324–6.
16. Ibid., doc. 230, pp. 335–7.
17. Ibid., doc. 234, pp. 340–1. See Watt, *How War Came*, p. 220.
18. *God krizisa*, 1, doc. 236, pp. 342–3.
19. Ibid., doc. 239, pp. 345–6; doc. 240, pp. 246–7.
20. Ibid., doc. 246, pp. 351–3.

21. See comments by Parker, *Chamberlain and Appeasement*, pp. 204–5, 216.
22. *God krizisa*, doc. 248, pp. 354–5. Litvinov himself recorded having received the British ambassador 'very coldly'. Shortly afterwards, he warned the Polish ambassador that his country was exposing itself to danger at a moment when Anglo-German relations were undergoing much tension, and that it would perhaps turn to the USSR 'when it will be already too late'; ibid., doc. 251, p. 359.
23. Ibid., doc. 255, pp. 361–3.
24. AVP RF, f. 06, op. 1, p. 5, d. 34, ll. 48–9.
25. *Krasnaia zvezda*, 6 April 1939.
26. RGASPI, f. 77, op. 1, d. 880, ll. 5–6.
27. Ibid., l. 23.
28. DVP, XXII, 1, doc. 206, p. 262.
29. *God krizisa*, 1, doc. 260, p. 367.
30. Ibid., doc. 262, pp. 370–2. In a postscript, Litvinov insisted that 'it is now necessary to be precise and brief in the talks about our position with regard to today's problems'.
31. DVP, XXII, 1, doc. 216, p. 270; doc. 217, pp. 270–1.
32. E. Radetskii, 'Sobytiia v iugo-vostochnoi Evrope i Polsha', *Mirovoe khoziaistvo i mirovaia politika* 4 (1939), p. 101.
33. *God krizisa*, 1, doc. 269, pp. 380–1.
34. DVP, XXII, 1, doc. 223, pp. 275–7.
35. Ibid., doc. 224, pp. 277–8.
36. Ibid., p. 278.
37. *God krizisa*, 1, doc. 276, pp. 386–7. Concerning the last point, Litvinov explained to Seeds that the lack of precise indications of the military obligations in the mutual help pacts between the USSR, France and Czechoslovakia had had a 'negative role' in the fortunes of this last country; ibid., doc. 275, p. 385.
38. G. Gribov, 'Podryvnaia deiatelnost' germanskogo fashizma v Pribaltike', *Leningradskaia pravda*, 3 April 1938.
39. DVP, XXII, 1, doc. 228, p. 283.
40. Dullin and Firsov (eds), *Dimitrov and Stalin 1934–1943*, pp. 40–3.
41. Dimitrov, *Dnevnik*, p. 172.
42. *God krizisa*, 1, doc. 290, p. 397.
43. Ibid., doc. 300, p. 408.
44. DVP, XXII, 1, doc. 259, pp. 315–16.
45. *God krizisa*, 1, doc. 296, p. 403.
46. Ibid., doc. 303, pp. 410–12.
47. Ibid., doc. 312, p. 423.
48. DVP, XXII, 1, doc. 267, p. 325.
49. RGASPI, f. 17, op. 3, d. 1009. On Molotov's rise in the field of foreign policy after 1936, see D. Watson, 'Molotov, Foreign Policy, and the Politburo 1926–1939', paper presented to the conference 'Stalin's Politburo 1928–1953', European University Institute, Florence, 30–31 March 2000.
50. DVP SSSR, XXII, 1, doc. 269, p. 327.
51. *Izvestiia*, 4 May 1939.
52. *God Krizisa*, 1, doc. 325, pp. 435–6.
53. Ibid., doc. 337, p. 450.
54. See Uldricks, 'The Impact of the Great Purges', p. 191.
55. RGASPI, f. 17, op. 162, d. 25, l. 28.
56. E. Gnedin, *Katastrofa i vtoroe rozhdenie* (Amsterdam: Herzen Foundation, 1977).
57. ASMAE, Affari politici: Urss, 1939, b. 32, fasc. 3. DDF, 2e série, XVI, doc. 45, pp. 107–8.
58. This statement was made by Molotov in a speech of 6 January 1949, at a conference held by the USSR Foreign Ministry; see V. Sokolov, 'Narkomindel Maksim Litvinov', *Mezhdunarodnaia zhizn'* 4 (1991), p. 120.
59. I.M. Maiskii, *Vospominaniia sovetskogo diplomata 1925–1945 gg.* (Moscow: Mezhdunarodnie otnosheniia, 1987), p. 394.

POLAND

60. See Sheinis, *Maksim Maksimovich Litvinov*, p. 362.
61. *Sto sorok besed s Molotovym. Iz dnevnika F.Chueva* (Moscow: Terra, 1991), p. 95.
62. Dimitrov, *Dnevnik*, pp. 175–6.
63. In the light of these considerations, the paradoxical 'revisionist' proposition, according to which the fall of Litvinov was brought about by his resistance to negotiate a triple alliance and not by his willingness to conclude an agreement with the Western powers seems devoid of foundation; cf. G. Roberts, 'The Fall of Litvinov: A Revisionist View', *Journal of Contemporary History* XXVII (1992), pp. 639–57. For a criticism of such a 'revisionist' view and a nuanced approach to the 'collective security' content of Litvinov's fall, see A. Resis, 'The Fall of Litvinov: Harbinger of the German–Soviet Non-aggression Pact', *Europe-Asia Studies* 52 (2000), pp. 33–56.
64. See remarks by M. J. Carley, *1939: The Alliance that Never Was and the Coming of World War II* (Chicago, Il: Ivan R. Dee, 1999), pp. 153–4.
65. *Izvestiia*, 11 May 1939.
66. According to Roshchin's memoirs, the author of the editorial was indeed Molotov; see A. Roshchin, 'V dovoennom Narkomindele', *Mezhdunarodnaia zhizn'* 11 (1991), p. 122.
67. *God krizisa*, 1, doc. 342, pp. 458–9.
68. Ibid., doc. 337, pp. 450–1.
69. DDF, 2e série, XVI, doc. 322, p. 623. When Payart pointed out to Molotov that the editorial of *Izvestiia* of 11 May contained the clamorous assertion that the USSR had no pact of reciprocal help 'with either Great Britain and France, or with Poland', Molotov recognized the 'formal' imprecision of the sentence, but also maintained that 'the effective character of a pact is more important than its formal existence'; ibid., doc. 337, pp. 450–1.
70. See L. A. Bezymenskii, 'Sovetsko-germanskie dogovory 1939g.: Novye dokumenty i starye problemy', *Novaia i noveishaia istoriia* 3 (1998), pp. 3–26.
71. *God krizisa*, 1, doc. 104, pp. 167–8.
72. V. Galianov, 'Mezhdunarodnaia obstanovka vtoroi imperialisticheskoi voiny', *Bol'shevik* 4 (1939), p. 64.
73. PRO FO 371/23677, N1029/57/38.
74. *God krizisa*, 1, doc. 126, pp. 200–1.
75. *God krizisa*, 1, doc. 155, p. 231.
76. *Izvestiia*, 20 March 1939.
77. DVP, XXII, 1, doc. 236, pp. 291–3.
78. Ibid., p. 292. See Watt, *How War Came*, p. 230.
79. *God krizisa*, 1, doc. 279, p. 389.
80. Bezymenskii, 'Sovetsko-germanskie dogovory 1939g.', pp. 13–4.
81. Astakhov revealed to Gnedin, whom he met in a concentration camp at the end of 1941, that he had been entrusted with establishing relations with the Germans immediately after the fall of Litvinov. See Gnedin, *Iz istorii otnoshenii mezhdu SSSR i fashistskoi Germaniei*.
82. DVP, XXII, 1, doc. 282, p. 339. *God krizisa*, 1, doc. 341, p. 457.
83. Ibid., doc. 349, p. 465.
84. Ibid., doc. 362, pp. 482–3. For the German record, see *Documents on German Foreign Policy* (hereafter: DGFP), D, VI, doc. 424, pp. 558–60.
85. Bezymenskii, 'Sovetsko-germanskie dogovory 1939g.', p. 17.
86. *Pravda*, 1 June 1939.
87. *God krizisa*, 1, doc. 379, pp. 508–11.
88. AVP RF, f. 017a, op. 1, p. 1, d. 6, ll. 134–5.
89. AVP RF, f. 06, op. 1, p. 5, d. 35, l. 9.
90. DVP, XXII, 1, doc. 320, p. 382.
91. *God krizisa*, 1, doc. 377, pp. 501–7.
92. *God krizisa*, 2, doc. 387, pp. 5–6.
93. Ibid., doc. 396, p. 17.
94. *Pravda*, 13 June 1939.
95. *God krizisa*, 2, doc. 408, p. 35; doc. 426, p. 51.

96. DBFP, 3rd series, VI, doc. 135, p. 152.
97. *Izvestiia*, 16 June 1939.
98. RGASPI, f. 523, op. 1, d. 92.
99. *Pravda*, 29 June 1939.
100. *God krizisa*, 2, doc. 459, p. 82; doc. 467, p. 90.
101. *God krizisa*, 1, doc. 356, p. 477, doc. 361, pp. 481–2 e doc. 369, pp. 490–2; *God krizisa*, 2, doc. 399, pp. 19–20, doc. 433, pp. 57–8 e doc. 447, pp. 69–70.
102. See J. Haslam, *The Soviet Union and the Threat from the East, 1933–41: Moscow, Tokyo and the Prelude to the Pacific War* (London: Macmillan, 1992), pp. 130–1.
103. See Carley, *1939*, pp. 175–82.
104. DBFP, 3rd series, VI, doc. 414, pp. 456–60; doc. 473, p. 523.
105. G. Roberts, *The Unholy Alliance: Stalin's Pact with Hitler* (Bloomington, IN: Indiana University Press, 1989), pp. 140–1.
106. DVP SSSR, XXII, 1, doc. 452, p. 583.
107. Ibid., doc. 453, p. 584.
108. See Carley, 1939, pp. 195 ff. And also M. J. Carley, 'End of the "Low, Dishonest Decade": Failure of the Anglo-Franco-Soviet Alliance in 1939', *Europe-Asia Studies* 2 (1993), pp. 303–41.
109. AVP RF, f. 017a, op. 1, p. 1, d. 6, l. 214.
110. DGFP, D, VI, doc. 529, pp. 728–9.
111. *God krizisa*, 2, doc. 403, pp. 29–30.
112. DVP, XXII, 1, doc. 370, p. 466.
113. Ibid., doc. 378, pp. 483–6.
114. *God krizisa*, 2, doc. 442, pp. 65–7. For the German record, cf. DGFP, D, VI, doc. 579, pp. 805–7; doc. 607, pp. 834–6.
115. *God krizisa*, 2, doc. 437, pp. 61–2.
116. Ibid., doc. 494, pp. 120–1.
117. Ibid., doc. 503, pp. 136–9.
118. Ibid., doc. 510 e doc. 511, p. 145.
119. Ibid., doc. 504, p. 139.
120. DVP, XXII, 1, doc. 445, pp. 566–9. *God krizisa*, 2, doc. 523, pp. 157–8.
121. Ibid., doc. 525, pp. 159–63. For the German record, cf. DGFP, D, VI, doc. 766, pp. 1059–62.
122. *God krizisa*, 2, doc. 528, p. 175.
123. Ibid., doc. 532, p. 177.
124. Ibid., doc. 534, pp. 178–80.
125. Ibid., doc. 540, p. 184.
126. Ibid., doc. 541, pp. 185–6; doc. 542, pp. 186–8; doc. 549, p. 209.
127. Ibid., doc. 556, pp. 229–31.
128. Ibid., p. 231. For the German record, cf. DGFP, D, VII, doc. 79, pp. 87–90.
129. *God krizisa*, 2, doc. 570, pp. 269–73. Cf. DGFP, D, VII, doc. 105, pp. 114–6.
130. *God krizisa*, 2, doc. 572, pp. 274–6. Cf. DGFP, D, VII, doc. 132, pp. 149–50.
131. *God krizisa*, 2, doc. 582, p. 302 e doc. 583, p. 303.
132. *Izvestiia*, 22 August 1939.
133. RGASPI, f. 17, op. 3, d. 1013.
134. DGFP, D, VII, doc. 213, p. 227.
135. DVP, XXII, 1, doc. 493, p. 644; doc. 502, p. 659; doc. 516 and doc. 517, p. 682.
136. *Pravda*, 27 August 1939.
137. *Izvestiia*, 1 September 1939.
138. DGFP, D, VII, doc. 213, p. 228.
139. *Izvestiia*, 1 September 1939.
140. DGFP, D, VIII, doc. 37, p. 35.
141. Erickson, *The Soviet High Command*, p. 539.
142. *Pravda*, 18 September 1939.
143. RGASPI, f. 77, op. 1, d. 886, ll. 18–22. *Pravda*, 14 September 1939.
144. PRO FO 371/23103, C14877/13953/18.
145. DVP SSSR, XXII, 2, doc. 636, p. 131.

146. DVP, XXII, 2, doc. 621, p. 118.
147. DGFP, D, VIII, doc. 104, p. 105.
148. DGFP, D, VIII, doc. 131, p. 130.
149. *Mezhdunarodnaia zhizn'* 7 (1991), pp. 126–38.
150. Ibid., p. 132.
151. Ibid., p. 133.
152. Ibid., p. 138.
153. *Pravda*, 29 September 1939.
154. Roberts, *The Unholy Alliance*, p. 179.
155. DVP, XXII, 2, doc. 654, p. 149.
156. The traditional Soviet interpretation has been re-affirmed by V. Ia. Sipols, *Tainy diplomaticheskie. Kanun Velikoi Otechestvennoi Voiny, 1939–1941* (Moscow: Novina, 1997). For a different position of a Russian author, see M. I. Semiriaga, *Tainy Stalinskoi diplomatii 1939–1941* (Moscow: Vysshaia Shkola, 1992). For criticism of Sipols from a Russian author, see Bezymenskii, 'Sovetsko-germanskie dogovory 1939g.'
157. See G. Roberts, 'The Soviet Decision for a Pact with Nazi Germany', *Soviet Studies*, XLIV (1992) 57–78; and Roberts, *The Soviet Union and the Origins of the Second World War*. See also I. Fleischauer, *Der Pakt. Hitler, Stalin und die Initiative der Deutschen Diplomatie 1938–1939* (Berlin: Ullstein, 1990).
158. See Tucker, *Stalin in Power*. See also R. C. Tucker, 'The Emergence of Stalin's Foreign Policy', *Slavic Review*, XXXVI (1977) 563–89. For a criticism of this view and a more balanced evaluation of the 'collective security' line, see T. Uldricks, 'Soviet Security Policy in the 1930s', in Gorodetsky (ed.), *Soviet Foreign Policy*.
159. For a historical view substantially assimilating Soviet and Western policies of appeasement towards Hitler, see Carley, *1939*.
160. Gnedin, *Iz istorii otnoshenii mezhdu SSSR i fashistskoi Germaniei*.
161. A. Ulam, *Expansion and Coexistence: Soviet Foreign Policy, 1917–1973* (New York: Praeger, 1974), p. 286.

6

The War Crisis

'WAR OF ATTRITION'

Very early in the European war, Stalin began to present his vision of the conflict, which involved great strategic emphasis on 'inter-imperialistic contradictions'. On 7 September 1939, during a conversation with Dimitrov, Molotov and Zhdanov, Stalin declared that two equally matched groups of capitalist countries were fighting for world domination. Though he said he would have preferred an agreement with the British and the French to that made with the Germans, he was hopeful about the inevitable 'war of attrition'. Stalin felt certain that the opposing sides would 'weaken one another' and that 'Hitler, all unawares and certainly against his wishes, is shaking and undermining the capitalist system'. In his view, the USSR possessed ample room for manoeuvre, room to 'push one side against the other', and the pact with Germany was a part of that sort of strategy. Accordingly, the pre-war distinction between democracies and fascist regimes was fading, having lost 'its previous meaning'. In the same conversation, the dictator made it clear that the elimination of Poland would permit the extension of the 'socialist system to new territories and populations'.[1] In other words, Stalin had concluded that the violent collapse of the Versailles system and the escalation of a European war between the two blocs of 'capitalist powers' were in the interest of the USSR. The unfolding of this idea formed the basis for strategic thinking in Soviet foreign policy. As we have seen, Stalin's strategy was promptly made flesh in the German–Soviet friendship treaty of the end of September.

As Stalin began to exercise more visible influence over foreign policy than ever before, previous wavering and conflict were swept away and Soviet policy came to appear fairly consistent. After all, a definite choice had been made between different options and the aim to keep the USSR safe from war had been attained. Furthermore, the 'war of attrition' strategy looked to be consistent with longstanding doctrinaire assumptions. However, incongruous elements and underlying contradictions were gradually to arise.

THE WAR CRISIS

Basically, the Soviets could not be anything but ambivalent about Germany. The pivot of the Soviet 'security system', as conceived by Stalin and Molotov, now lay in the acquisition of further territory and the division of eastern Europe into spheres of influence in partnership with Nazi Germany. In other words, Soviet security had been chained to the prospect of consensual partition of interests with a regime that had never concealed its expansionist ambitions in eastern Europe, with a country that continued to be seen as a serious threat in Moscow. And it was difficult to treat the Soviet sphere of influence in eastern Europe, worked out in September 1939, as a given, or as a lasting guarantee against involvement in a pan-European war. Faith in a prolonged 'war of attrition' between capitalist states, that would leave the USSR intact and presumably more powerful than any other European country in warfare capacities, was far from certain.

In any event, the new Soviet strategy was established after Stalin's directives of 7 September 1939. This transition occasioned trouble in the circles that had been more committed to anti-fascist policies, including the Comintern. On 22 August the Comintern secretariat had decided to recommend that its membership oppose the 'anti-Soviet campaign' ignited by the negotiations between the USSR and Germany. It would be necessary to insist that the conclusion of a pact of non-aggression between the USSR and Germany would not exclude 'the possibility and necessity' of an agreement between Great Britain, France and the USSR; that the USSR was fighting the aggressors and driving a wedge between them, while preparing to confront Japan; that any attempt to direct fascist aggression towards the USSR was being blocked. The secretariat recalled the need to 'renew our commitment to the struggle against the aggressors, particularly against German fascism'.[2]

Over the following fortnight, the Comintern modified its objective, but it did not cease to urge the communist parties to join the struggle against fascism. Still, on 2 September, in a draft project prepared by Manuil'skii, the war was declared imperialistic on both sides, and, at the same time, the defeat of Nazism was identified as the main aim of the communist movement.[3] So confused were the Comintern leaders as they tried to chart a course for the future that on 5 September Dimitrov wrote an urgent letter to Zhdanov, requesting a meeting with Stalin to resolve the 'exceptional difficulties' he was facing.[4]

Full conversion took place once Stalin had issued his new strategic plan on 7 September. The next day, the Comintern secretariat officially defined the war as a struggle between two groups of imperialist states battling for 'world domination', and declared that the distinction between democratic and fascist countries had lost all significance.[5] Yet the conversion was not instantly and universally accomplished. Only 20 days after Stalin's dictum, at the end of September, a draft of the Executive Committee, drawn up by Dimitrov, was presented to Stalin, Molotov and Zhdanov.[6] The document substantially modified the stand the Comintern had originally taken: the appeals to combat fascism were removed, the suggestion that the current war was anti-fascist was denied, and the Western democracies were assailed for displaying aggression towards the Soviet Union that went beyond the aggression of the fascist states. But no elaboration of these declarations was offered for some time. Meanwhile, the perplexity raised among the Comintern leaders by the abandonment of the anti-fascist orientation began to assume dramatic proportions for several communist parties; this was particularly true of the French.[7] A rift was opening up in the Communist movement between those committed to opposing fascism and those committed to defying imperialism.[8]

However, the purely executive role played by the Comintern and the communists' rigid adherence to Soviet foreign policy were no longer being discussed. On 19 and 20 October 1939 the Praesidium of the Executive Committee drew up a set of procedures for addressing 'errors' committed by the Communist parties during wartime; among the stipulations was one that all 'elements inclined to surrender', even the leading circles, were to be liquidated.[9] The new direction in communist policy manifested itself clearly in a document signed on 22 November by the leaders of the communist parties of Germany, Austria and Czechoslovakia: it stressed the imperialistic nature of the war and the collapse of all 'pacifist illusions'.[10] An article that was to mark Dimitrov's public conversion was also drawn up. In a meeting with Dimitrov on 25 October, with Zhdanov present, Stalin carefully revised the draft text. He toned down the revolutionary appeals, remarking that one should not demand the overthrow of governments that called for peace: in other words, there were to be no more calls for the overthrow of Hitler and his regime.[11] On 29 October Dimitrov sent Zhdanov the revised text of his article, which was eventually published on 7 November.[12]

When Dimitrov managed to bring about the Comintern's public conversion to the 'turn' in Soviet foreign policy, the radical policy change had taken about two months to be implemented, and had required Stalin's personal intervention. Citing the interview Stalin had given Howard in 1936, the secretary of the Comintern recalled that the 'second imperialist war' had begun with attacks 'on the peoples of Abyssinia, Spain and China', and was now showing its true nature as a continuation of the struggle that had broken out between the 'capitalist powers' in 1914. Previously European states could be classified as either aggressive or non-aggressive, but that classification scheme 'no longer' corresponded to reality; there was reason to believe that 'the British and

French imperialists' were now 'the most diligent partisans fighting for the continuation and intensification of the war'. According to Dimitrov, France and Britain had done all in their power to turn the war eastwards, but at the critical moment Germany had rebelled against this plan, both on account of the economic and military strength of the USSR and because the 'majority of the German people' would not have accepted it. Now all of the 'fundamental contradictions' of the capitalist world would be aggravated. The workers' movement would have to struggle against the 'imperialist war' and against those responsible for it, acting 'first of all in their own country' by rejecting the 'legend' of the war's anti-fascist nature promulgated by the social democrats.[13] Thus fell the last of Dimitrov's previous positions, his insistence on the difference between the international situation in the second half of the 1930s and that of 1914.

The influence exercised by Zhdanov in reshaping Soviet positions can be deduced from an article he wrote shortly after the speech of 6 October in which Hitler launched his 'peace campaign'. Zhdanov thought that the 'break-up' of Poland had also removed the 'causes for the continuation of the war in Western Europe' and that there was no point in championing the re-establishment of Poland, as the British and the French had begun to do. Zhdanov hurled himself into an attack on what he considered the 'ideological' struggle of the Western powers against Hitler, which he called a screen concealing Western imperialist objectives; he went as far as to compare the Western struggle against Nazi Germany to the persecution of heresies, adding that 'none of the world's ideologies and ideas can be eliminated with the sword and with fire'.[14]

Not only did Zhdanov's argument conform to the decision to abandon all attacks on fascism, it also lent tangible support to Hitler's 'peace campaign', taking to its extreme logic the anti-imperialist outlook now triumphant in Moscow. The blind dedication to an undifferentiated vision of the outside world would even legitimate Nazi ideology. Though the Soviet leadership never adopted such arguments into its political propaganda, Zhdanov's words were revealing of an ambiguous ideological conditioning interlaced with Stalin's *Realpolitik*.

Stalin set the example for both. In a conversation with Dimitrov, held after the parade of 7 November, Stalin declared that 'the petit bourgeois nationalists' in Germany were not bound 'to capitalist traditions' and speculated that they might engage in sudden turnabouts.[15] This was more than a functional justification of the pact with Germany: Stalin appears to have been hinting that, given a sufficiency of anti-Western propaganda and a long enough war with Britain and France, relevant sectors of Hitler's support would rise up en masse. Though the purges of 1937–38 had been partly motivated by the decision to banish speculation about Nazism's imminent collapse and a possible revolutionary war, Stalin wavered between a realistic acceptance of the stability of Hitler's regime and belief in his future overthrow – a belief sounding much like Radek had before he disappeared in the purges.[16] Now that war had begun, the same Nazi ideology and mass organizations that had brought Hitler to power might be seen as preconditions for popular upheaval. Stalin seemed to consider the possibility that the war in the West might not simply weaken the German war machine, but would actually topple Nazism, providing a chance to strengthen Soviet power in central–eastern Europe and even plant communist influence in Germany. However, in the same conversation with Dimitrov, Stalin also declared that the Bolshevik slogan of transforming the imperialist war into civil war had been suited only to Russia, and was not applicable to the more developed European countries. No doubt Stalin was cautioning his lieutenant, warning him to refrain from adopting a simplistic revolutionary perspective.[17]

On 30 November 1939 a statement from Stalin appeared in *Pravda* in response to recently published and embarrassing reports in the French newspaper, *Le Temps*. According to the reports, Stalin had maintained, in a 19 August meeting of the Politburo, that a European war that did not involve the USSR was in the interests of the state: it could facilitate territorial expansion and the creation of a Soviet sphere of influence in eastern Europe. He had also been quoted as saying that the USSR would not benefit from a rapid Western victory, and that it would therefore offer financial support to Germany. Finally, Stalin was said to have declared that a German victory would not pose an immediate danger to the USSR, since Germany would inevitably emerge exhausted from the war effort.[18]

There can be little doubt as to the accuracy of the French reports. They reflected to a reasonably faithful extent the contemporaneous Stalinist outlook on the 'war of attrition', as recorded by Dimitrov. Unfortunately, the text of Stalin's statement that has been found in the archives is not the original, but a French translation possibly circulating in Comintern circles.[19] The dubious provenance of this text makes it difficult to determine its authenticity. Moreover, it has proved impossible to ascertain whether or not a meeting of the Politburo was actually held on the eve of the pact.[20] According to the text, Stalin said that the pact with Germany would be concluded because the expectation that a 'war of attrition' between the two opposing blocks of capitalist powers would weaken both sides; even if it had postponed the outbreak of war, an agreement with the Western powers would have facilitated the consolidation of a capitalist anti-Soviet front. A pact with Germany had the advantages of granting the USSR a free hand in the Baltic countries and of forming a Soviet zone of influence in Eastern Europe which would include not only Bulgaria, but also Romania and Hungary. As for prognostications about different possible outcomes of the conflict, both a German victory (not considered likely) and a German defeat were pondered.

Up to this point, the text contains no surprises. But then doubts and reservations arise. Proposed scenarios for a 'sovietization' of Germany or France that appear in the text have little to do with what we know about Stalin's thinking at the time, even given his vague wishful thinking about changes in Germany. Detailed speculation about the various possible outcomes of the war, and the corresponding role granted to national communist parties, particularly the French Communist Party, further strain credibility. We should assume that the document was partly manipulated and possibly even backdated. Nevertheless, its main features reflect Stalin's post-pact strategy in convincing terms and overlap with Dimitrov's diary notes of 7 September; we may even suppose that the text of Stalin's 'speech' was another version of those notes.

'SPHERES OF INFLUENCE'

The guidelines for Soviet foreign policy after the friendship treaty with Germany were illustrated by Molotov in a speech to the Supreme Soviet given on 31 October 1939.[21] Molotov did not simply underline Soviet neutrality, as he had done on 31 August: he publicly admitted the shift in USSR foreign policy, emphasizing that the 'decisive change of direction' in the relations between 'the two most powerful states in Europe' would affect 'the whole international situation'. Conditions were bound to change profoundly on account of the war, stated Molotov, although he maintained that the war was only 'in its first round', and withheld his opinion on the possible outcome of the conflict. But he did not conceal that the leadership was reconsidering the position it had maintained over the previous years and had reiterated at the 18th Party Congress of March 1939:

> In connection with these important changes in the international situation, several old formulas, which we used until a short time ago, and which many were very accustomed to, are clearly out of date and no longer applicable. If we are to avoid making serious mistakes in assessing Europe's nascent political situation, we must acknowledge this. It is known, for example, that, in the last few months, such concepts as 'aggression' and 'aggressor' have acquired new, concrete

implications and have taken on a new meaning. If I may mention the great European powers, Germany finds itself in the position of aspiring to the most rapid conclusion of the war, and to peace; while Great Britain and France, which yesterday declared themselves opposed to aggression, are all for continuing the war and against concluding a peace. The roles, as you see, have been reversed.

Molotov was referring to the 'peace campaign' initiated by Hitler immediately after the conclusion of the friendship treaty with the USSR. He scoffed at the Anglo-French declarations that the war under way represented a conflict between democracy and Nazism and that the aims of the West were simply 'the liquidation of Hitlerism'. For him, this was a lame attempt to conceal behind the smokescreen of an 'ideological war' the real causes of the conflict, which, in his opinion, involved 'material interests' and the struggle for world domination; everything said by the French and British only revealed the fundamentally 'imperialistic nature' of the pan-European war. As for the USSR's position, Molotov reaffirmed its neutrality, maintaining that German–Soviet relations were based 'on a lasting foundation of reciprocal interests'; he claimed that this was proven by the agreement on the new boundaries defined by the division of Poland. Both Germany and the USSR, he said, stood outside of the Versailles system. The Stalinist leadership had laid out the basis that Soviet foreign policy would maintain until the very eve of the German invasion.

Then there was the dramatic expansion of the Soviet sphere of influence into eastern Europe to be explained away. For the USSR had occupied both western Ukraine and Belorussia, and had imposed the signing of 'pacts of reciprocal assistance' on Lithuania, Latvia and Estonia – the pacts sharply limited the sovereignty of the three Baltic states. And Molotov tossed Finland into the pile of countries forcefully grouping under the aegis of the USSR. He also noted serious tensions, deriving, he said, from the interference of 'third party powers' in negotiations about borders and the security of Leningrad. Ultimately, declared Molotov with a measure of satisfaction, the Soviet position on the international scene had been noticeably strengthened.

A few days later, in a speech commemorating the Revolution, Molotov underlined the part played by the 'contradictions of capitalism' in the European war, the outbreak of which he backdated to well before September 1939. Though 'schemes' designed to involve the USSR in the war had failed, there was still every reason to imagine that the present conflict might turn into a true world war. In other words, the defence of the USSR against the threat of war remained the principal password of Soviet foreign policy. In the past, noted Molotov, 'the threat posed to the

USSR by capitalist encirclement had been underestimated'. In a manner rather less triumphant than usual, he described Soviet policy as one centred 'on the security of our state', which though it had cost 'many material losses', had prevented the involvement of the USSR in war.[22] This interpretation sounded much like the thesis of the outbreak of the 'second imperialist war', as put forward a year earlier in the *Short Course*. Apparently the Soviet point of view was not undergoing substantial alterations. There was one important modification, however: the image of the Nazis as aggressors and warmongers had disappeared completely, just as Stalin had commanded.

In his 30 November statement in *Pravda*, Stalin reiterated the emerging Soviet position on Hitler's 'peace campaign'. He confirmed that the USSR supported the peace proposals put forward by Germany; since the Western powers had rejected such proposals they were responsible for the prolongation of the war.[23] Stalin's statement appeared on the same day that the Soviets initiated their campaign against Finland. The previous day Moscow had announced the rupture of diplomatic relations with Helsinki. In a radio speech Molotov had declared the need to guarantee 'the security of the Soviet Union, and, above all, of Leningrad', and had referred pointedly to the Finnish government's 'anti-Soviet links with the imperialists'.[24] The state of war in Europe, Stalin was suggesting, required full freedom of manoeuvre on both sides; the 'responsibilities' which, he maintained, Great Britain and France had assumed in this matter indirectly justified the Soviet Union's aggressive actions.

During the negotiations with the Finns, which were suspended at the beginning of November, the Soviets repeated their concerns about the security of Leningrad, a theme they had been sounding since spring 1939. The Finns were prepared to make limited territorial concessions, but Stalin and Molotov were not satisfied – they clung to the demands they had voiced at the outset and refused to negotiate. Clearly, Stalin wanted to impose on Finland a treaty similar to those already imposed on the Baltic states; in order to draw Finland into the Soviet sphere of influence, the Soviet leaders wished to limit the state's sovereignty. Eventually, the scope for diplomatic action was drastically reduced and Moscow came to rely first on pressure, then on the threat of military action, and finally on real military force. When Moscow attempted to present the armed conflict as the result of Finnish obstinacy, none could see this as anything but clumsy and unconvincing. Subduing Finland was part of the effort to neutralize all perceived threats and to distance the USSR from the West, in spite of the vague efforts made over the previous three months to maintain a dialogue.

This ill-fated job had been entrusted to Maiskii. From September 1939 onwards, he had tried to convince his British contacts of Moscow's distance from the two warring parties and of its intention to maintain relations with London. On 20 September, in a conversation with Lord Strabolgi, he repeated that the USSR had only decided to enter into an agreement with Germany after talks with the West had broken down. He compared the Soviet isolationist policy with that of the Americans, and declared that the USSR desired neither a German victory, nor a German presence on the Black Sea.[25] On 27 September, as the new German–Soviet talks began, Maiskii was much more circumspect, stating to Collier that in Poland the Soviets were restricting themselves to taking back what had been lost in the war of 1920.[26] While the signing of the friendship treaty between the USSR and Germany provoked much distress, Maiskii continued to meet with British diplomats and government figures. At the end of September, Maiskii met Halifax to lay the groundwork for a commercial agreement with Britain, an endeavour approved by Molotov.[27] In October and November he had talks with various British political figures, beginning with Churchill, and met again with Halifax.[28]

During this period, Maiskii began to exhibit signs of recovering some independence of thought. On 20 November, for example, in a meeting with W. Elliott, he presented a rather unorthodox thesis: peace seemed likely because Hitler was in no condition to move either westwards or eastwards. Implicitly, he made Hitler the aggressor, which was quite different from what Molotov had said a few days earlier. Furthermore, Maiskii rejected the objection that peace could not be achieved in a time as confused and violent as the present, and he expressed the opinion that if the war continued the situation would be still worse. Elliott decided that Maiskii was anti-German.[29] Maiskii, for his part, wrote a long letter to Molotov three days later, informing him that the British appeared to be willing to conclude a peace treaty.[30] But the Soviets placed the security of Leningrad foremost, intent as they were on consolidating a 'security system' even if it meant a break with London, and possibly other governments. The belief that the Western powers still very much intended to push Hitler eastwards, as Maiskii himself feared, reinforced this attitude.[31]

As an effort to extend the Soviet sphere of security, as had recently been done in Poland, the 'winter war' against Finland exposed the weakness of the Red Army in the aftermath of the purges.[32] There would be no blitzkrieg. The grave difficulties encountered by the Red Army further compromised its international prestige, provoking considerable alarm among the Soviet leadership. At a plenum of the Central Committee in March 1940 attended by Stalin, Voroshilov acknowledged that the Red Army had been largely unprepared.[33] Voroshilov was promptly dismissed, and reforms to Soviet military policy and doctrine were undertaken.[34]

On the political and diplomatic front, the consequences were no less grave. Soon after Kuusinen was installed as the puppet leader of a 'popular government of Finland' it became apparent that such a manoeuvre was in fact counterproductive. On 2 December the Soviet press published an official declaration from the Kuusinen government, supporting the actions of the Red Army, and advocating the establishment not of a Soviet-style state but of a 'democratic republic' capable of forming a mutual assistance pact with the USSR.[35] Molotov had revised Kuusinen's original outline for the declaration, which had not included any mention of the establishment of a democratic republic.[36] However, even such a moderate formula convinced no one of the legitimacy of the 'popular government', and soon the Soviets were obliged to withdraw their own claim that the Kuusinen government serve as the sole representative of the Finns in negotiations with the USSR. Accused of international aggression, the USSR found itself expelled from the League of Nations. The League had by that point lost much of its authority and Stalin had no doubt rated the cost of expulsion rather low while planning the Finnish war. The crisis in relations with Great Britain and France, however, became very acute. As the Western powers contemplated intervening, the Soviets had to consider the possibility that they would become embroiled in a larger Scandinavian war.

At the end of 1939 Maiskii suggested that members of the British government were hoping that the USSR would side with Germany in a coming war; the British would then form an agreement with Germany that would oblige the USSR to face the combined might of all of the capitalist states.[37] The instructions Maiskii received from Molotov show the rigidity of the Soviet position. Molotov wanted three specific points underlined: every rumour about a military agreement between the USSR and Germany was unfounded; the central question was the security of the USSR; should some foolhardy nation decide to engage the USSR in war, 'our country has taken all necessary precautions'.[38] On 26 January, in a letter to Molotov, Maiskii returned to the risk of the war spreading and the USSR's possible involvement, suggesting that similar ideas could have prevailed in Britain.[39] Again, in February 1940, Maiskii noted that it was urgent that the Finnish question be settled promptly, because otherwise 'we might easily become involved in a great war'.[40] The peace treaty was concluded on 12 March 1940: though the territorial agreement differed little from the original Soviet demands, it certainly did not justify the military expense paid by the USSR.

The decision to wage war against Finland emanated from the Stalinist concept of security. The pact with Germany had outlined how a Soviet sphere of influence might be established in eastern Europe by means of force. The first step in this direction had been the military invasion and violent 'sovietization' of western Ukraine and Belorussia; deportations became standard policy.[41] Such grim measures expressed the aggressive features undergirding the security regime of the USSR as the theatre of the European war visibly grew. The atrocities culminated in the monstrous massacre carried out by the Soviets at Katyn in April 1940.[42]

The Soviet leaders appeared to be satisfied that they had achieved their security objectives. On 29 March 1940 Molotov addressed the Supreme Soviet to laud the successes gained on the security front after closing the chapter of the 'winter war'. His arguments cleaved to an ideological outlook and articulated a remarkably contorted security concept. Again he blamed the Western powers for inciting the war and for having planned to use Finland as the base for a campaign against the USSR. He went so far as to claim that the Red Army had faced not only Finnish troops, but also 'the united troops of a series of imperialist countries, including Britain, France and others'.[43] But the territories coveted by Moscow had been conquered. And relations with Germany were intact: Hitler had maintained that Soviet aggression towards Finland was quite understandable and the USSR's German policy need only be a matter of respecting the divisions between spheres of influence. Although the original plan to expand the Soviet 'security system' by a limited war effort had been thwarted, Moscow reckoned that the game had been worth the candle. On 17 April Stalin presented once again the argument that the security of Leningrad had to be guaranteed while war was being carried on in western Europe.[44]

Since his position as political head of Leningrad had placed him in a special position throughout the 'winter war', Zhdanov was particularly well grounded in the official perspective. In a speech given in Leningrad on 13 April, he repeated the familiar 'imperialist war' thesis, assigning Great Britain and France principal responsibility. He maintained that the Western powers were plotting to take vengeance upon the USSR because it had once refused to enter 'the orbit of imperialist policy', and he revealed that Molotov now defined relations between the USSR and the West as 'hostile'. The Finnish war had ensured the security of Leningrad, a city which had always been an objective in the 'imperialist game', since it was seen as 'the key to Moscow'. For Zhdanov, as for Molotov, the war had not been a simple clash between the Finnish and Soviet armies; it had been a historic confrontation between the Red Army and 'the united forces of the imperialists'. In his view, the international imperialist force had nearly repeated the sort of Western intervention carried out in the midst of the Russian civil war.[45] Now the conclusion of the Finnish war and the launching of Hitler's campaign in

Denmark and Norway provided a chance for further consolidation of Soviet strategy vis-à-vis Germany. Better that north-western Europe should be occupied by Germany than by the Anglo-French bloc, since the latter stood ready to attack the USSR. Had not the German attack 'kept the war from approaching our frontiers'?[46]

The basic orientation underlying Molotov's and Zhdanov's foreign-policy declarations was not likely to bring equilibrium to Moscow's international position, and the international consequences of the 'winter war' only reinforced this orientation. The USSR remained committed to Nazi Germany's 'peace campaign', as Molotov repeatedly confirmed to Schulenburg, and to strengthening relations with Berlin.[47] Quite significantly, even before the end of 1939 Stalin decided to approve a series of trade agreements with Germany. His meeting with Schnurre on the last night of 1939 set in motion the negotiations – all of which took place at meetings attended personally by Stalin – for a binding economic pact, signed on 11 February 1940.[48] The agreement was destined to take trade between the two countries to unprecedented levels, supporting the German war effort, and giving substance to the policy of détente towards Hitler.[49]

In the spring of 1940 Beneš was informed that the Stalinist leadership had split into two groups over the European war. One group advocated supporting Germany to the bitter end, without endorsing massive military support, in the expectation that Hitler's eventual defeat would open the way for a German revolution. This group, said to be led by Zhdanov, maintained that in the future the Western democracies would be the greatest enemies of the USSR. The second group supposedly reflected, via Voroshilov, the opinion of the military: best that the USSR remain somewhat aloof from Germany, which might well be defeated, a scenario particularly probable in the event of the United States entering the war. It appeared that early support from Stalin had given Zhdanov's group the upper hand, but more recently the dictator was said to be vacillating, while Molotov had not taken sides.[50] Beneš's information has not yet been confirmed by Russian archival documentation, and it seems largely hypothetical. Nevertheless, it does present concisely two logical options for Soviet policy, connected to two different concepts of neutrality: the first, hinging on the prospects of the 'war of attrition' and on the relationship with Germany; the second, implying a shift in Soviet strategy, aimed at finding a position closer to the centre point between the two sides involved in the hostilities.

In fact, the scenario of German defeat and collapse of the Nazi regime had been considered, as we know, by Stalin. But the idea that Hitler's regime suffered from fragility generated dilemmas. Some might see this as a chance for expanding Soviet influence in central and eastern

Europe, but the prospect that Nazi Germany might soon fall also worried the Soviets. The bitter military experience of the Finnish war may have generated perplexity in Moscow about Soviet strategic commitment to Germany, as the weaker belligerent. The Soviets were aware that, compared with Germany, the West maintained significant industrial superiority – this superiority would be preponderant if the United States added its productive might to that of France and Great Britain. If the war in western Europe were stemmed, the divided poles between which the capitalist powers had stretched their potential front would have the chance to reunite. Manuil'skii thought that the defeat of Germany would encourage a war against the USSR and that for this reason a revolutionary policy aimed at stirring up 'civil war' in Germany would have been inappropriate, as Stalin had indirectly suggested in his 7 November conversation with Dimitrov.[51]

It seems likely that the image of a German war machine driven towards Soviet soil by the Western powers continued to occupy Soviet policy-makers. During the negotiations with the Finns, Stalin admitted that Soviet insistence on the security of Leningrad was not only connected to the possibility of British and French attacks, but also to a possible threat from Germany.[52]

At the beginning of 1940 Dimitrov and Manuil'skii sent a letter to Stalin, in which they maintained that the German Communist Party should not be restricted to strengthening friendship with the USSR and demanding the end of the 'imperialist war'. The two Comintern leaders thought that a 'second front' could be formed, consisting of the bourgeois, pro-Western forces and opposed to the Nazi regime, 'which, though it has signed a friendship pact with the Soviet Union, will not necessarily continue to pursue a policy of friendship'. As the war became more of an ordeal, the Germans might contravene their agreement and consider 'a war against the USSR'. It was therefore necessary to struggle 'on these two fronts', to create a 'third front', 'a completely popular front', to prepare 'for the moment when...the present regime finds itself in crisis'.[53]

In any event, the essential point here is that the main scenarios imagined by the Soviet leadership were completely displaced by the developments of the European war. As they assessed Germany's first military move after the invasion of Poland, the Stalinist leaders were clearly pleased. The Nazi choice of the northwest suggested that a clash between Germany and Great Britain lay in the offing; Moscow hoped that the Danish and Norwegian offensive would prove the first real skirmish in the 'war of attrition'. At the beginning of the German offensive in Holland and Belgium, the Soviets openly predicted a long war in the West.[54]

THE WAR CRISIS

Then came the abrupt military collapse of France in June 1940. This was the true beginning of a new phase in the war and a complete surprise to Moscow. As in a few days the Nazi forces swept into Paris, suddenly the likelihood of a 'war of attrition' between the capitalist powers seemed remote. Contrary to all of the Soviet forecasts, Germany emerged more powerful than ever from the first major clash of the European war. With western continental Europe under Hitler's thumb, the USSR became much more vulnerable. The strategy Stalin had been formulating since August–September 1939 was given a violent shake. Khrushchev records in his memoirs the disappointment with which Stalin received the news of the French collapse.[55]

The Soviets' greatest fear was that Germany and Great Britain would sign a peace treaty. Manuil'skii had already confessed his fear of such an event in a letter to Dimitrov on 19 June.[56] At the end of June, Varga admitted publicly that the French defeat had been completely unexpected, and, at the same time, he articulated the concern that would preoccupy the Soviet leadership for many months: 'How long will Britain be able to sustain this war?' Viewed economically and militarily, the question was debatable. But according to Varga, the primary consideration was political: it was quite possible that the British leadership might yield to the temptation of signing a peace treaty with Hitler, in the hope of directing the German armies against the USSR.[57] Before it could adopt a firm position, the Soviet Union would have to evaluate the will and capacity of the British to resist Germany, and the attitude of the United States as well.

In July 1940 a plenum of the Central Committee was convened, and Molotov gave a report on foreign policy which went unrecorded in the minutes.[58] We do know, however, that a dramatic exchange took place between Molotov and Litvinov, still a member of the Central Committee. In response to Molotov's reiterated attacks against the pro-Western line maintained by Litvinov until May 1939, the former commissar for foreign affairs stated that the collapse of France raised the likelihood of war between Germany and the USSR significantly – an argument hard to refute, that came across as a criticism of Stalin's and Molotov's choice for appeasement.[59] Anxiety about the consequences of German victory in the West also thrived within the Comintern: Ercoli, in particular, felt that the pact with Germany could not last.[60] But the Stalinist leadership did not draw the conclusion that the time had come for a fundamental shift in Soviet strategy.

Molotov publicly presented the official position of the USSR at a meeting of the Supreme Soviet held on 1 August 1940.[61] He pointed out that the Germans had not attained their principal objective, 'the conclusion of the war on the conditions they had hoped for'. This meant that, as the first year of open hostilities drew to an end, 'the conclusion of this war is not yet in sight'. Rather than peace, Europe was facing 'the beginning of a new stage in the intensification of war between, on one side, Germany and Italy, and, on the other, Britain, helped by the United States'. In other words, Italy's entry into the war in June 1940 had done more to encourage the war in the West than France's surrender had done to discourage it. This was a weak argument. But the Soviet leaders had decided to trust the British government's declared intent to continue the war – or had concluded they had no other chance but to do so, given their foreign-policy orientation. Molotov proclaimed that nothing had altered Soviet foreign policy 'at all', and he took care to specify that 'not only have the recent events in Europe failed to weaken the German–Soviet pact of non-aggression, they have actually emphasized its importance and the need to develop it further'. He explained that this was so because the pact was founded not 'on casual and coincidental considerations', but 'on basic state interests'.[62] France's failure to appreciate 'the role and significance of the USSR in European affairs' was indicated as one of the causes of its defeat.

Following up these declarations with a broadly reassuring picture of the international situation, Molotov dwelt at length on relations with Japan, which he said had now begun to 'normalize'. The only sour note seemed to be relations with the United States. Molotov also described the USSR's recent territorial acquisitions, which he presented as further consolidating Soviet security. In particular, there was the conquest of Bessarabia and northern Bukovina, carried out at the end of June with Germany's acquiescence and with the forced consent of Romania. The populations of these regions, to quote the words of Stalin's commissar, had joined 'the ranks of Soviet citizens with great joy'. Most important, according to Molotov, was the absorption of the three Baltic states, brought about by imposing on them governments well disposed towards the USSR. This had transpired in the face of a brutal threat of military intervention, and had been formalized at the same session of the Supreme Soviet at which Molotov spoke.

Assessing in retrospect the pacts of mutual assistance with Lithuania, Latvia and Estonia he himself had praised some four months earlier, Molotov placidly observed that 'they did not yield the desired results'. In fact, earlier diplomatic correspondence between Moscow and the Soviet ambassadors to the three Baltic states shows that the Soviet leaders had contributed to the deterioration of relations. On 14 June 1940 Molotov himself had openly accused the three governments of 'hostile activity' towards the USSR.[63] After that, the situation rapidly degenerated, thanks to the work of Vladimir Dekanozov in Lithuania and the Soviet plenipotentiaries in the other two Baltic republics: Vyshinskii in Latvia and

Zhdanov in Estonia.[64] Nevertheless Molotov hailed the formation of the three 'Soviet socialist republics' as an event which strengthened 'the power of the great Soviet Union'.[65]

Moscow's principal aim was now the reinforcement of the Soviet 'security system' following the pattern of territorial annexation. At the time of his meeting with Ribbentrop in September 1939, Stalin made no effort to conceal the possibility of introducing the Soviet system into Latvia and Estonia, though he said he had no plans to do so immediately.[66] On 25 October 1939, he told Dimitrov that the sovietization of the Baltic states was not on the agenda.[67] Indeed, the Soviets had initially reckoned it shrewder to limit themselves to drawing the Baltic states into the Soviet sphere of influence. The events of May–June 1940 amounted to the belated application of an option in Stalin's security thinking.[68] The consolidation of the Soviet sphere of influence would take place in parallel with outright territorial expansion – the Polish and Finnish wars provided the blueprint. This was how Soviet policy-makers reacted to Germany's dramatic triumph over France.

OPPOSING THE 'OLD ORDER' IN EUROPE

Continuity in Soviet foreign policy had already emerged in June 1940, during negotiations with Italy. Having overcome the interruption in diplomatic relations between the USSR and Italy caused by the Finnish war, the Soviets set out to achieve an understanding with the Italians about the Balkans. They hoped both to involve Germany in an agreement and to avoid exclusion from an area fundamental to USSR interests, especially during a period when military scenarios seemed to change nightly. In a conversation with Schulenburg, Molotov referred to the words of the German ambassador in Rome, Hans von Mackensen, who had told Gel'fand, his Soviet counterpart, that the Balkan problem could be settled 'without a war', through an agreement between Germany, Italy and the Soviet Union.[69] Mackensen's statement was undoubtedly encouraging for Moscow, though Schulenburg failed to confirm it.

On 13 June, in his first meeting with Rosso, Molotov made it clear that he wanted more than a formal re-establishment of diplomatic relations; he stated that while Great Britain and France were clearly in decline 'the voices of Germany and Italy, and also of the Soviet Union, will be even stronger than they were one year ago'.[70] During the second meeting on 20 June Molotov proposed a practical discussion on spheres of influence, and expressed particular interest in the Black Sea, Turkey and the Danube area.[71] For Moscow this was the real point of the negotiations. Meanwhile, Molotov received confirmation from Schulenburg that Mackensen's words did in fact express the point of view of his government.[72] On 25 June he delivered to Rosso a memorandum that stressed Soviet interests in Bulgaria, Romania and the Black Sea, presented the USSR as the 'main power' of the region and suggested a trilateral agreement over Turkey.[73] The memorandum included the speculation that the war would continue until the beginning of the following winter, 'if indeed it should finish before the end of the year'.[74] While Molotov made Soviet geopolitical interests clear, he seemed to suggest that the assessment of war targets was not a short-term task.

When Moscow opted for continuity in its wartime strategies, it opted for a limited amount of expansion – through the annexation of Bessarabia, northern Bukovina, and the Baltic states – and against any political steps that could be interpreted as abandoning a pro-German position. The decision to negotiate with Italy soon after Mussolini had entered the war on Hitler's side was probably aimed at demonstrating the USSR's commitment to Germany even after the collapse of France. The Balkan arena was now the geopolitical centre of Soviet strategy based both on territorial security and appeasement. In his conversations with Molotov, Rosso perceived quite clearly that the Soviets had no intention of changing their foreign policy, though the unexpected success of German military operations and the preponderance of German power in Europe had left them unsettled.[75] According to the Soviet record, Molotov emphasized at the time that the USSR was not interested in defending Great Britain's power in Europe.[76] The same concept was more frankly expressed in the Italian record: 'European stability was never an obsession for Russia, which has no intention of defending the present equilibrium.'[77] Rosso believed that the Soviet leaders understood that breaking off relations with Germany would be very risky and so were simply seeking a path for coming to an understanding on the Balkans.[78]

Continuity in Soviet foreign policy was also confirmed by a very clear negative attitude to relations with Great Britain. In his speech of 1 August, Molotov affirmed that he foresaw no 'major changes' in Anglo-Soviet relations and that any change would be difficult, despite the recent appointment of Stafford Cripps as ambassador to Moscow.[79] The new British ambassador had arrived in Moscow in the middle of June, though he had made an earlier trip, in February of that year, in an unofficial capacity. Cripps was preceded by his reputation: a socialist and a critic of appeasement, he was known to be open to dialogue with the USSR and was on close terms with Maiskii. Though his February encounter with Molotov had not gone well – only icy relations could be expected between the two countries in the immediate wake of the Soviet–German pact and the Finnish war – Cripps had remarkable credentials.[80] Not least, he had been nominated after Winston Churchill – the best-known adversary of appeasement – had become leader of the British government in the aftermath of German advance into Holland and Belgium. His mission presented the Soviets with an opportunity to restart a delicate dialogue with the British after the fall of France.[81]

Over the course of Cripps's posting to Moscow, Stalin articulated his strategic thinking and his unwillingness to step outside of very strictly defined boundaries. On 1 July 1940 Cripps delivered a message from Churchill to Stalin, proposing a discussion on the threat of German domination of Europe. Stalin's reply was most eloquent, and neatly summarized his foreign-policy ideas.[82] Particularly, he explained his plan to alter 'the old European balance of power, which has been unfavourable to the USSR'. Stalin pointed out to Cripps that the starting point for the discussions that had culminated in the Soviet–German pact had been a shared determination to overthrow that balance; if Churchill wished to restore it, the Soviets would not be able to reach an agreement with him. A few days earlier, Molotov had made a similar comment to the Italian ambassador. At the same time, Stalin opined that Germany lacked the strength necessary for dominating the whole of Europe, and suggested that Hitler's true intentions were something quite different, though this contradicted Hitler's own statements. As for the aims of Soviet foreign policy, Stalin maintained that they did not include control of the Balkans and that excessive exposure in that region could prove dangerous. He led Cripps to understand, however, that the USSR took very seriously the question of the Turkish Straits.

Stalin's statements threw a retrospective light on the pact with Hitler and brought into the open an aversion to the Versailles system shared by Germany and the USSR. He believed that at that moment Soviet interests coincided much more closely with German interests than with British. The end of Versailles and the collapse of the old balance of power would redound to the interests of the USSR – a view quite the reverse of that which Litvinov had enunciated before 1939 with Stalin's approval. Two simple conclusions may be drawn from Stalin's statements to Cripps: the USSR continued to consider relations with Germany the principal axis for Soviet foreign policy, a great point scored by Soviet power in the European theatre; and the 'war of attrition' was still seen as the most likely scenario for the European conflict, since German power was not considered in Moscow as mighty as it appeared.

At the beginning of August 1940 Molotov confirmed to Cripps that he saw the pact with Germany as the best guarantee of Soviet interests. He recognized that a neutral Soviet Union would never be seen as politically equidistant from Great Britain and Germany, and he acknowledged that one could not 'close one's eyes' to the evident disparity between Moscow–London relations and Moscow–Berlin relations.[83] At the same time, Molotov was keeping Schulenburg informed. The notes the latter received about the talks between Stalin and Cripps were generally an accurate synopsis, including, for example, Stalin's polemic about the 'old order'; on the other hand, these notes did not mention Stalin's negative assessment of Germany's military strength.[84]

Between August and September 1940, Varga had written something in much the same vein. He declared that the outcome of the pan-European war was still uncertain and that Germany did not seem to be in a position to deliver a 'decisive blow' against Great Britain. In his view, this meant that the 'inter-imperialist contradictions' remained at centre stage. For the moment, the contradiction between the two European powers dominated all strategic planning.[85] Although the very failure of the German offensive against Great Britain suggested that the USSR could be in danger, Varga explicitly equated the Anglo-German war with the Western front of World War I. Furthermore, his identification of the United States as a sort of 'second factor' due to come into play perpetuated the image of a capitalist world riddled with internal 'contradictions'.[86] During his meeting with Cripps, Stalin too had mentioned the United States as a factor destined to oppose German supremacy in the West.[87] And on 12 September 1940 Stalin wrote a letter to Varga, agreeing with his main theses. In particular, Stalin believed that the question of 'capitalist contradictions' had 'radically changed' after the fall of France, since the old 'contradiction' between Great Britain and the United States – a traditional Bolshevik leitmotif – had now disappeared, and instead a bloc comprising these two Western powers opposed the bloc grouped around Germany.[88]

However, if the thought of conflict between the capitalist powers may have reassured Soviet policy-makers in late summer 1940, the same was hardly true of the situation in the Balkans, the main geopolitical testing ground for Soviet–German relations. Attempts made at the end of June to sound out the Italian ambassador to Moscow regarding Italian and German intentions in south-eastern Europe had produced no results. Then, at the end of August, the Italo-German guarantee of Romanian territorial security set the relations between the fascist powers and the Soviet Union under strain. The Soviets began their remonstrations on 31 August, arguing that the principle of reciprocal consultation described in the non-aggression pact had been violated.[89] Molotov even resorted to Mackensen's declaration, dating from June, concerning the collaboration between the USSR, Germany and Italy in south-eastern Europe; this had no concrete effect.[90] On 21 September Molotov delivered to Schulenburg the text of the declaration the USSR had made to Italy on 25 June 1940.

At the same time, the Soviet government sent to Berlin a statement which, while complaining at Germany's unilateral conduct, left room for negotiations.[91]

The mounting tensions between Moscow and Berlin were apparently relieved by a confidential communication made to Molotov by the German diplomat Werner von Tippelskirch, on 26 September: he spoke of the imminent signing of a new military alliance between Germany, Italy and Japan.[92] Two days later the Soviet representative in Germany, Aleksandr Shkvartsev, passed on to Molotov a copy of a declaration made by Ribbentrop, to the effect that the new triple alliance would not compromise Soviet–German relations in any way.[93] The Soviets saw an opportunity to insist on the importance of Soviet–German relations and to consolidate the strategic stance constructed in the aftermath of the fall of France. An editorial written by Molotov in *Pravda* called the alliance of the fascist states evidence that the war had entered a 'broader phase'. Molotov expressed grave misgivings about the 'spheres of influence' planned by the three partners. But since the three new partners denied that their alliance contradicted or compromised the relations each maintained with the USSR, this was seen as a 'confirmation of the strength and the importance' of the pact between the USSR and Germany. Molotov also noted that Moscow did not find the triple alliance unexpected, since the Soviet government had been warned in advance by the Germans.[94] He told Cripps that the alliance merely formalized a pre-existing situation, and denied that it was a danger to the USSR.[95]

Things looked better still when, at a meeting between Ribbentrop and Shkvartsev on 9 October 1940, the German foreign minister announced that Stalin would soon receive a letter from his government inviting Molotov to Berlin.[96] Sent 13 October, the letter declared that the Germans had by now won the war and formally proposed that the USSR enter into the alliance with the three fascist states so as to establish 'the limits of respective interests', as part of a 'long-term policy'.[97] On 19 October Molotov alerted Schulenburg that Stalin would accept the proposal.[98] Two days later, Stalin sent his reply, expressing a desire to improve relations between Germany and the USSR, working from the 'solid basis of a long-term definition of their respective interests'.[99] The exchange of messages opened the way for Molotov's mission to Berlin, which took place between 12 and 14 November 1940. The proposal to examine one another's 'respective interests' was the prelude to a discussion of spheres of influence: for the Soviets this meant reviving and widening the agreement of a year before. But the discussions to come on how to divide up Soviet and German interests in eastern and southern Europe could not be separated from Hitler's war plans. Exactly what would be involved in the 'new order' Nazi Germany planned to found?

In the aftermath of the purges, the Soviet secret services had to be largely rebuilt from scratch since longstanding information networks had disappeared. By 1939 and early 1940 the re-establishment of foreign intelligence was still under way, particularly in Germany.[100] Nevertheless, during the summer and fall of 1940 Moscow was able to collect a great deal of confidential information about Hitler's war plans in the east, which he finalized after the fall of France.[101] Richard Sorge had passed along to Moscow a remarkable collection of leaks from official sources.[102]

Although the Soviets continued to count on the 'contradictions' between the capitalist powers, they had not ceased to calculate their prospects in a war with Germany. The effective war plan prepared by the new defence commissar, Marshal Semën Timoshenko, and personally approved by Stalin in September 1940, still identified Germany as the Soviet Union's most dangerous enemy, and described a scenario in which it would be necessary to fight a war on two fronts, against Germany and Japan.[103] This was how things had looked before the pact of 1939 had been signed.[104] A memorandum on the Nazi 'new order' prepared in October 1940 by Molotov's secretariat in the Narkomindel pointed out that should Great Britain fall, Germany's relations with the USSR could 'change very rapidly for the worse', as political, strategic and class motives pushed the German war machine eastward. Tempted by the energy resources possessed by the Soviet Union, the Nazis might well attack the widest convenient frontier, upsetting the leading role the USSR had held among the Slavs and with the same blow effectively eradicating the political alternative to Nazism represented by Soviet socialism. The memorandum cited nothing to deter such a plan besides the popularity the USSR enjoyed among the European popular masses – a popularity that much greater since Germany had terminated its anti-Soviet propaganda.[105]

Despite all of this, Molotov headed to Berlin with a set of plans strictly faithful to the guidelines designed in August–September 1939. The instructions agreed on by Molotov and Stalin on the eve of the journey, as well as the Soviet record of the meetings and the correspondence between Molotov and Stalin over the course of the negotiations, show that the Soviets aimed at consolidating their own sphere of influence in eastern Europe, and that they gave this objective priority over everything else. The policy of détente towards Germany was seen as a vital necessity. No political and diplomatic alternative had been considered, and no answer had been given to Cripps's overtures.[106]

The notes Molotov made on 9 November 1940 after discussions with Stalin recorded the principal points the Soviets hoped to raise with the Nazis.[107] Moscow wanted to know the significance of the tripartite pact, and whether acceptable spheres of influence could be drawn up – for

THE WAR CRISIS

surely the agreements of 1939 could not be more than a stopgap measure. From the Soviet leaders' point of view, the military agreement signed by the Germans and the Finns had to be clarified; an explanation had been requested as far back as September, in vain.[108] Mostly, though, they imagined that this meeting would present an opportunity to extend the pact in a geopolitical sense. They saw both the Danubian and Balkan regions as crucial strategic areas of interest, especially after the Italo-German guarantee to Romania and the Italian attack on Greece at the end of October. For Stalin and Molotov, the 'main problem' was Bulgaria, which was to be included in the Soviet zone according to the same formula used by Germany and Italy for Romania. Special emphasis was reserved for Soviet interests vis-à-vis Turkey.

In his first conversation with Ribbentrop, held on 12 November, Molotov laconically played the part Stalin had scripted for him. He listened as the German foreign minister spoke at length about the imminent fall of the British empire, about the USSR's future involvement in the alliance between Germany, Italy and Japan, and about the division of spheres of interest among the four powers. According to the Nazis, this last arrangement needed to be given a global dimension to guarantee Soviet interests on the Black Sea and direct them southward, in particular towards the Persian Gulf. When his turn to speak came, Molotov was much more concrete. He requested clarification about Germany's proposal for the boundaries of the spheres of influence and wanted to know the meaning of the formula 'great east Asian space' in the Nazi political vocabulary. 'Some precise explanations' of the subdivision of the spheres of interest would be required in the long term, and he asked Ribbentrop to be more specific. After all, the agreements reached about territory and influence during the previous year had long since been put behind them, 'with the exception of the Finnish question'.

From his first words, Molotov was insisting on discussing in detail the spheres of influence in Europe. And he insisted on dealing with the delicate question of how German troops could be stationed in a country like Finland, assigned to the USSR in the arrangement agreed upon the previous year.[109] Upon receiving Molotov's cabled account of this first meeting, Stalin had a single if substantial piece of advice: Molotov was to keep in mind that the pact with Germany was settled and clear; it was only the secret protocol attached to it that had to be revised.[110]

When Hitler met with Molotov it became clear that the terms of the talks would not change. The scenario presented by Hitler mirrored that already traced by Ribbentrop: once the war with Great Britain had been victoriously concluded and the British Empire had been disintegrated, spheres of influence would be shared out among the allies; conflicts between Germany and its partners were to be avoided at all costs. In other words, despite Molotov's injunction to Ribbentrop, Hitler would say nothing concrete, and only provided a vague sketch of how colonies and sea routes would be divided among Germany, Italy and the USSR – though he did concede the importance of Russian interests in the Balkans and the Black Sea. In his turn, Molotov repeated to Hitler what he had explained to Ribbentrop: the Soviets felt that Germany had honoured the terms of its pact with the USSR, with one exception, that of Finland. He also wanted to know more about the tripartite alliance, and suggested, in connection with all this, a discussion of the particulars of control over the Black Sea and the Balkans. But he got little satisfaction. Hitler proposed that the USSR map out its own interest zones, and renewed the invitation to join in the alliance, whose key was anti-Americanism. Molotov insisted on the need for clarification, stating that the USSR could participate 'only as a partner, and not as an object'.[111]

It must be surprising that in his report to Stalin, Molotov described his meeting with Hitler in quite optimistic terms. He said that 'Hitler is evidently very interested in reaching an agreement with Russia and in strengthening friendly relations with the USSR about the spheres of influence', though there was much that remained to be discussed. Clearly Turkey would be discussed, whereas, when the issue of Finland was raised, Molotov explained, 'they do not reply, but I shall compel them to talk'.[112] Stalin urged his representative to ensure that the talks produce an agreement 'of principle' concerning eventual declarations and he wanted something done about 'security' on the Black Sea. In other areas, Stalin recommended the use of pointed questions; he suggested that a second round of negotiations be carried on in Moscow. Future negotiations were to involve Turkey, the Persian Gulf and China, but the first above all, since the Straits were the most pressing problem for the USSR. Stalin advised Molotov to accept a peaceful solution to the Turkey question involving a Soviet 'guarantee' to Bulgaria – only if the Germans proposed the division of Turkey would Moscow 'show its cards'.[113]

When he did meet with Hitler again, Molotov began with the topic Stalin had emphasized: he stated that while the German–Soviet pact was settled and beyond discussion, the secret protocol was a separate issue. On the question of Finland, Molotov displayed his considerable obstinacy, recalling that it was 'not without the influence of the pact with the USSR' that Germany had enjoyed such stunning military victories – 'disagreements on matters of secondary importance', such as the Finnish problem, should be avoided. In response, Hitler only repeated that Finland was indeed within the Soviet sphere of influence. But he sidestepped Molotov's follow-up question, refusing to say whether his statement meant that Finland's position was like that of Estonia and of

THE WAR CRISIS

Bessarabia. Molotov, for his part, declined Hitler's repeated invitations to discuss the interests of the two powers in global or planetary terms – a thinly veiled attempt to avoid making precise commitments. Again following Stalin's instructions, Molotov insisted on the question of Turkey and the question of Bulgaria. He maintained that the guarantee given to Romania by both Germany and Italy clearly violated Soviet interests, unless Moscow could effect a balance in the region by offering a guarantee to Bulgaria, thereby shoring up Soviet security concerns in the Black Sea. These questions were, however, postponed for discussion at a future meeting in Moscow, after Italy had been consulted.[114]

The last meeting between Molotov and Ribbentrop closely resembled a conversation between two deaf people. The German foreign minister proposed that the USSR align itself with the 'peaceful' intentions of the tripartite alliance, guarantee economic support and agree not to engage in other alliance arrangements. Molotov replied by acknowledging the need for a real rapprochement between the USSR and Japan, then promptly returned to the question of the Balkans. He spoke again about the possibility of a Soviet guarantee to Bulgaria: the security of the USSR could not be guaranteed by a simple accord with Turkey. He mentioned one last time Moscow's concerns about security on the Black Sea, adding that the USSR had very real practical interests 'in the destiny of Hungary and Romania', both of which bordered the USSR, and that he hoped to know the plans of Germany and Italy vis-à-vis Yugoslavia and Greece. Molotov even asked whether the agreements the USSR and Germany had reached on the 'destiny of Poland' were still valid.[115] But he was destined to see his questions evaded. In taking his leave, Molotov told Hitler that the USSR was determined to take part in deciding the 'great questions in Europe and Asia'.[116] But his last step was to bid Ribbentrop farewell, commenting that he would consult Stalin on the German proposals, and insinuating very obliquely that the war with Great Britain would not be won as easily as his hosts pretended.[117]

In a report he sent to Stalin, Molotov now acknowledged with some frustration that the conversations with Hitler and Ribbentrop had not had 'the desired results' and that there was nothing 'to be complacent about'. No concrete plans for sending Ribbentrop to Moscow had been made, and the gains made in the talks amounted to little beyond an impression of 'Hitler's present mood, which must be borne in mind'.[118] Decades later, when Molotov wrote his memoirs, he concluded that Hitler had been far more intent on involving the Soviet Union in an 'adventure' than in concluding a real agreement.[119] If we compare the notes Molotov took on 9 November 1940 as he planned his visit with the actual results of his trip to Berlin, we must conclude that the talks ended in complete failure for the Soviets. The fact is that Hitler had not recognized the

STALIN AND THE INEVITABLE WAR, 1936–1941

Soviet Union as a European power – though the Soviet leaders had always claimed that their pact with Nazi Germany had proven just the opposite. And none of the Soviet security objectives in south-eastern Europe had been seriously considered. It seems likely that had there been a frank discussion on this topic the underlying tensions between Berlin and Moscow would have been terribly exacerbated.

A significant difference between the rulers of the two totalitarian states had emerged during the Berlin talks. The Soviet rulers had scarcely shown any inclination to discuss global strategies. Effectively, Stalin and Molotov had returned to the traditional objectives of imperial Russian foreign policy.[120] The territorial security objectives outlined from August–September 1939 onwards had consistently served as the basis for Molotov's efforts in Berlin. The Soviets were girding themselves for a prolonged conflict, one which might well expand to involve the USSR. Their commitment to a territorial 'security system' led them to play Hitler's game, even if they did not believe in a strategic alliance any more than Hitler himself did – after all, the role he assigned to Russia in his global strategy had nothing to do with partnership. Here one can see the basis for the enduring conviction of the Soviet leaders that their deep-seated hostility towards 'the old order' in Europe could still serve to guarantee an understanding with Nazi Germany.

The communiqué that appeared in the Soviet press described the Berlin talks as an 'exchange of opinions'.[121] Naturally, no one failed to see that the talks had ended without significant progress.[122] Nevertheless, though no new phase in the relations between Moscow and Berlin had opened, Moscow maintained that a foundation had been laid. That was the idea expressed in a letter Molotov sent to Maiskii on 17 November: in Berlin there had been no breakthrough on how to 'delimit spheres of interest' or on 'the part the USSR would play in the pact of the three powers', but the 'exchange of opinions' had opened the road to diplomatic negotiation.[123]

Stalin's prompt response to Ribbentrop's proposals illustrated how deep were his illusions about future talks. The request for the tabling of further negotiations that Molotov submitted to Schulenburg on 25 November 1940 contained four counter-proposals: withdrawal of German troops from Finnish territory; a mutual aid pact between the USSR and Bulgaria; recognition of Soviet rights to the area south of Batum and Baku; and renunciation by Japan of its claims for economic concessions in the Sakhalin region.[124] Erickson has observed that Stalin's conditions for joining the alliance amounted to a test of Hitler's grand plan: would he be willing to trade further freedom of action to the West for measures that would make any plan to take on the Soviet Union, particularly areas in the Balkans and around Leningrad, that much more difficult?[125] But while Moscow readied for negotiations, Hitler responded not at all: he was no longer interested in relations with Stalin, and already he was planning the invasion of Russia.[126]

Meantime, Moscow provoked Hitler by unilaterally offering Bulgaria a reciprocal aid pact. This was the most significant diplomatic enterprise in the wake of the Berlin talks and it was doomed. Furthermore, it did not amount to a genuine change in Soviet foreign policy. While a pact with Bulgaria was being discussed, Dimitrov received Molotov's consent to resume the Comintern's activities against the Nazi occupying forces in Europe.[127] But on 25 November, still before Sofia's negative response, Stalin confided to Dimitrov that although he saw the Bulgarian venture as a defence of Soviet interests, it was destined to be part of a renewed understanding with Germany. Stalin had hopes that once an agreement with Bulgaria had been reached both Bulgaria and the USSR could join the tripartite pact. He also believed that, despite close ties with the Italians, the Germans could not fail to acknowledge that Soviet interests in the Straits had to take precedence.[128] In other words, a change in Soviet behaviour was not on the agenda even in the Balkans.

Between the end of 1940 and the first months of 1941, the USSR did not substantially modify its foreign conduct. Despite mounting evidence of Hitler's true purposes, a firm line was not taken with Germany. Soviet foreign policy had found itself in a cul-de-sac, though diplomatic games and intelligence operations would unfold on a three-dimensional chessboard between Moscow, Berlin and London until June 1941.[129] In vain, the Soviets laboured to reconcile a defence of their security in eastern Europe with détente towards Nazi Germany. Soviet strategy towards Nazi Germany was more obstinate than consistent. For an unreasonably long time, the Soviet leaders tried to safeguard Soviet power interests as they were conceived in the aftermath of the pact with Hitler. Their conduct grew out of the priority of dividing spheres of influence between the USSR and Germany. No room was left for converting Soviet appeasement into an adequate strategy of deterrence against Hitler's expansion, though many in Moscow considered war with Germany a distinct possibility. The apparent emerging incompatibility between Soviet security objectives and détente towards Hitler was completely overlooked. Stalin's decision, made in August–September 1939, to build a 'security system' by appeasing Nazi Germany proved contradictory, ineffective and, finally, disastrous.

NOTES

1. Dimitrov, *Dnevnik*, pp. 181–2.
2. See M. M. Narinskii and M. S. Lebedeva, *Komintern i vtoraia mirovaia voina. Chast' 1: 1939–1941 gg.* (Moscow: Pamiatniki istoricheskoi mysli, 1994), pp. 69–70.

3. *Izvestiia Tsk KPSS* 12 (1989), p. 206.
4. *Komintern i vtoraia mirovaia voina*, 1, p. 88.
5. Ibid., pp. 88–9.
6. Ibid., pp. 108–20.
7. See M. Narinsky, 'Le Komintern et le Parti Communiste Français (1939–1941)', *Communisme* 32–4 (1993). See also P. Spriano, *I comunisti europei e Stalin* (Turin: Einaudi, 1983), ch. 10.
8. See K. McDermott and J. Agnew, *The Comintern: A History of International Communism from Lenin to Stalin* (London: Macmillan, 1996), p. 198. Conversely, a number of different pieces of evidence indicate that anti-fascist propaganda affected Soviet opinion, particularly that of military cadres; see Tucker, *Stalin in Power*, p. 599.
9. *Komintern i vtoraia mirovaia voina*, 1, pp. 141–3.
10. RGASPI, f. 495, op. 18, d. 1296, ll. 133–43.
11. *Izvestiia Tsk KPSS* 12 (1989), p. 210.
12. *Komintern i vtoraia mirovaia voina*, 1, p. 171. See G. Dimitrov, 'Voina i rabochii klass kapitalisticheskikh stran', *Bol'shevik* 20 (1939), pp. 23–33.
13. Dimitrov, 'Voina i rabochii klass kapitalisticheskikh stran', *Bol'shevik* 20 (1939).
14. RGASPI, f. 77, op. 1, d. 886, ll. 28–33.
15. Dimitrov, *Dnevnik*, p. 185.
16. An influential figure like Varga routinely suggested up to the summer of 1939 that Germany might soon totter and did not shy away from talk of wartime class struggle. E. Varga, 'Kapitalizm nakanune pervoi i vtoroi imperialisticheskikh voin', *Bol'shevik* 13 (1939).
17. Dimitrov, *Dnevnik*, p. 185.
18. DVP, XXII, 2, doc. 813, p. 343.
19. *Novyi mir* 12 (1994), pp. 232–3. See also Iu. N. Afanas'ev (ed.), *Drugaia voina, 1939–1945* (Moscow: Rossiiskii gosudarstvennii gumanitarnii universitet, 1996), pp. 61–3.
20. See Bezymenskii, 'Sovetsko-germanskie dogovory 1939 g.', pp. 3–4.
21. *Pravda*, 1 November 1939.
22. *Pravda*, 7 November 1939.
23. *Pravda*, 30 November 1939.
24. Ibid.
25. PRO FO 371/23103, C14877/13953/18.
26. AVP RF, f. 017a, op. 1, p. 1, d. 6, ll. 261–64. PRO FO 371/23697, N4803/1459/38.
27. DVP, XXII, 2, doc. 627, p. 124 and doc. 634, p. 130.
28. Ibid., doc. 667, pp. 167–9; doc. 682, pp. 183–4; doc. 689, pp. 190–1; doc. 695, pp. 196–7; doc. 811, pp. 340–2.
29. PRO FO 371/23678, N6574/57/38.
30. DVP, XXII, 2, doc. 806, pp. 330–4.
31. Ibid., doc. 806, p. 334.
32. See C. Van Dyke, *The Soviet Invasion of Finland, 1939-40* (London: Frank Cass, 1997).
33. Dimitrov, *Dnevnik*, p. 191.
34. Van Dyke, *The Soviet Invasion of Finland*, pp. 189 ff.
35. *Pravda*, 2 December 1939.
36. *Vestnik MIDa* 22 (1989), pp. 74–9.
37. AVP RF, f. 017a, op. 1, p. 1, d. 6, ll. 365–6.
38. DVP, XXII, 2, doc. 888, p. 446.
39. DVP, XXIII, 1, doc. 27, pp. 53–6.
40. AVP RF, f. 017a, op. 1, p. 1, d. 7, l. 55.
41. See J. T. Gross, *Revolution from Abroad: The Soviet Conquest of Poland's Western Ukraine and Western Belorussia* (Princeton, NJ: Princeton University Press, 1988). DVP, XXII, 2, doc. 536, pp. 19–22.
42. See *Katyn. Plenniki neob'iavlennoi voiny* (Moscow: ROSSPEN, 1997).
43. GARF, f. 7523, op. 3, d. 236, ll. 3–25; *Pravda*, 30 March 1940. Before Molotov's

speech of 29 March, a plenum of the Central Committee was held, during which Molotov presented a report. No record of this report was included in the minutes of the plenum; RGASPI, f. 17, op. 2, d. 656.
44. *Zimniaia voina 1939–1940*, 2 (Moscow: ROSSPEN, 1998), pp. 272–3.
45. RGASPI, f. 77, op. 1, d. 745, ll. 4–9 and 27.
46. Ibid., ll. 33–5.
47. DVP, XXII, 2, doc. 699, pp. 200–1; doc. 773, pp. 285–7.
48. DVP, XXIII, 1, doc. 1, pp. 7–11; doc. 29, pp. 57–61; doc. 38, pp. 77–8; doc. 41, pp. 80–5.
49. See M. Zeidler, 'German–Soviet Economic Relations during the Hitler–Stalin Pact', in *From Peace to War. Germany, Soviet Russia and the World, 1939-1941*, edited by B. Wegner (Oxford: Berghahn Books, 1997), pp. 95–111. See also the documentation presented in V. Ia. Sipols, 'Torgovo-ekonomicheskie otnosheniia mezhdu SSSR i Germaniei v 1939–1941 gg. v svete novykh arkhivnykh dokumentov', *Novaia i noveishaia istoriia* 2 (1997), pp. 29–41.
50. PRO FO 371/24844, N5517/30/38.
51. RGASPI, f. 523, op. 1, d. 33.
52. PRO FO 371/24843, N504/30/38.
53. RGASPI, f. 495, op. 74, d. 155, ll. 1–3.
54. I. Lemin, 'Novyi etap voiny v Evrope', *Mirovoe khoziaistvo i mirovaia politika* 4–5 (1940), p. 28.
55. N. Khrushchev, *Khrushchev Remembers*, p. 134.
56. *Komintern i vtoraia mirovaia voina*, 1, p. 370.
57. E. Varga, 'Mezhdunarodnoe polozhenie (na konets iiunia)', *Mirovoe khoziaistvo i mirovaia politika* 6 (1940), pp. 15–16.
58. RGASPI, f. 17, op. 2, d. 676.
59. See Gnedin, *Katastrofa i vtoroe rozhdenie*. See Tucker, *Stalin in Power*, pp. 595, 614.
60. Fischer, *Ricordi e riflessioni*, pp. 510–11. See also *Komintern i vtoraia mirovaia voina*, 1, p. 26.
61. *Bol'shevik* 14 (1940), pp. 10–16. The text of Molotov's speech of 1 August 1940 was not included in the record of the session of the Supreme Soviet: GARF, f. 7523, op. 3, d. 273, l. 5; f. 7523, op. 9, d. 269, l. 6.
62. *Bol'shevik* 14 (1940), p. 11.
63. See *Polpredy soobshchaiut ... Sbornik dokumentov ob otnosheniiakh SSSR s Latviei, Litvoi i Estoniei, avgust 1939g.– avgust 1940g.* (Moscow: Mezhdunarodnie otnosheniia, 1990), doc. 238, pp. 370–1.
64. Ibid., docs. 261, 262, 271, 273. Semiriaga, *Tainy stalinskoi diplomatii*, p. 238.
65. *Bol'shevik* 14 (1940), p. 13.
66. *Mezhdunarodnaia zhizn'* 7 (1991), pp. 133, 135.
67. Dimitrov, *Dnevnik*, pp. 184–85.
68. A specific emphasis on the new departure in Soviet conduct of May–June 1940 can be found in Roberts, *The Soviet Union and the Origins of the Second World War*, pp. 111–12. See also G. Roberts, 'Soviet Policy and the Baltic States, 1939–1940: A Reappraisal', *Diplomacy & Statecraft* 3 (1995), pp. 672–700.
69. DVP, XXIII, 1, doc. 178, p. 312.
70. Ibid., doc. 200, p. 342.
71. Ibid., doc. 210, pp. 357–8. AVP RF, f. 06, op. 2, p. 15, d. 155, l. 211. DDI, IX series: 1939–1943, V, doc. 73, pp. 57–9; doc. 81, pp. 63–8.
72. DVP, XXIII, 1, doc. 217, p. 365.
73. Ibid., doc. 224, pp. 372–4. DDI, series IX, V, doc. 104, pp. 88–90.
74. DVP, XXIII, 1, doc. 224, p. 373.
75. DDI, series IX, V, doc. 90, pp. 72–4.
76. DVP, XXIII, 1, doc. 210, p. 357.
77. DDI, series IX, V, doc. 73, p. 59.
78. Ibid., doc. 90, p. 73.
79. *Bol'shevik* 14 (1940), p. 11.
80. DVP, XXIII, 1, doc. 45, pp. 91–4.

STALIN AND THE INEVITABLE WAR, 1936-1941

81. See G. Gorodetsky, *Stafford Cripps' Mission to Moscow, 1940-42* (Cambridge: Cambridge University Press, 1984).
82. DVP, XXIII, 1, doc. 240, pp. 394-9. PRO FO 371/24844, N5937/30/38 and N5621/30/38; PRO FO 371/24845, N6526/30/38.
83. DVP, XXIII, 1, doc. 311, pp. 485-88. PRO FO 371/24845, N6105/40/38.
84. DVP, XXIII, 1, doc. 264, pp. 434-5. A copy of the text given by Molotov to Schulenburg was in Maiskii's possession: AVP RF, f. 017a, op. 1, p. 1, d. 7, l. 220.
85. E. Varga, 'Obzor mezhdunarodnogo polozheniia (na konets avgusta 1940 g.)', *Mirovoe khoziaistvo i mirovaia politika* 8 (1940).
86. E. Varga, 'Obzor mezhdunarodnogo polozheniia (sentiabr' 1940 g.)', *Mirovoe khoziaistvo i mirovaia politika* 9 (1940).
87. DVP, XXIII, 1, doc. 240, p. 396.
88. RGASPI, f. 558, op. 11, d. 1124, l. 146.
89. DVP, XXIII, 1, doc. 348, pp. 546-7.
90. Ibid., doc. 367, pp. 583-84.
91. Ibid., doc. 394, pp. 615-21.
92. Ibid., doc. 402, pp. 627-30.
93. Ibid., doc. 408, pp. 635-6.
94. *Pravda*, 30 September 1940. See L. Bezymenskii, 'Vizit V.M. Molotova v Berlin v noiabre 1940g. v svete novykh dokumentov', *Novaia i noveishaia istoriia* 6 (1995), p. 126.
95. AVP RF, f. 017a, op. 1, p. 1, d. 7, ll. 319-20.
96. DVP, XXIII, 1, doc. 425, p. 658.
97. DGFP, D, XI, doc. 176, pp. 291-7.
98. DVP, XXIII, 1, doc. 456, pp. 695-6.
99. Ibid., doc. 458, p. 699.
100. Erickson, 'Threat Identification and Strategic Appraisal', pp. 403, 408.
101. Pozniakov, 'The Enemy at the Gates', pp. 230-1.
102. *Izvestiia Tsk KPSS* 4 (1990), pp. 202-3.
103. *Voenno-istoricheskii zhurnal* 1 (1992), pp. 24-9.
104. Bezymenskii, 'Vizit V.M. Molotova v Berlin v noiabre 1940g.', p. 126.
105. AVP RF, f. 06, op. 2, p. 16, d. 165, ll. 31-4.
106. Maiskii, *Vospominaniia sovetskogo diplomata*, p. 557.
107. See 'Direktivy I.V. Stalina V.M. Molotovu pered poezdkoi v Berlin v noiabre 1940 g.', *Novaia i noveishaia istoriia* 4 (1995). DVP, XXIII, 2, doc. 491, pp. 30-32.
108. DVP, XXIII, 1, doc. 402, p. 628.
109. 'Poezdka V.M. Molotova v Berlin v noiabre 1940 g.', *Novaia i noveishaia istoriia* 5 (1993), pp. 69-73. DVP, XXIII, 2, doc. 497, pp. 36-41. According to the German record, Molotov insisted that a new understanding between the USSR and Germany was the preliminary condition for the USSR joining the alliance between the three fascist states: DGFP, D, XI, doc. 325, pp. 533-41. The Russian version shows only that Molotov insisted on explanations about the nature and significance of the alliance between Germany, Italy and Japan.
110. *Mezhdunarodnaia zhizn'* 6 (1991), p. 126. DVP, XXIII, 2, doc. 501, p. 48.
111. *Novaia i noveishaia istoriia* 5 (1993), pp. 74-78. DVP, XXIII, 2, doc. 498, pp. 41-7. Cf. DGFP, D, XI, doc. 326, pp. 541-9.
112. *Mezhdunarodnaia zhizn'* 6 (1991), p. 132. DVP, XXIII, 2, doc. 502, pp. 49-51.
113. *Mezhdunarodnaia zhizn'* 8 (1991), pp. 104-5. DVP, XXIII, 2, doc. 508, pp. 60-1.
114. *Novaia i noveishaia istoriia* 5 (1993), pp. 80-88. DVP, XXIII, 2, doc. 511, pp. 63-71. Cf. DGFP, D, XI, doc. 328, pp. 550-62.
115. *Novaia i noveishaia istoriia* 5 (1993), pp. 88-94. DVP, XXIII, 2, doc. 512, pp. 72-9.
116. *Novaia i noveishaia istoriia* 5 (1993), p. 87. DVP, XXIII, 2, doc. 511. Cf. DGFP, D, XI, doc. 328, p. 562.
117. *Novaia i noveishaia istoriia* 5 (1993), p. 93. DVP, XXIII, 2, doc. 512. Cf. DGFP, D, XI, doc. 329, p. 563. See V. Berezhkov, *At Stalin's Side: His Interpreter's Memoirs from the October Revolution to the Fall of the Dictator's Empire* (Secaucus, NJ: Carol Publishing Group, 1994); Italian version: *Interprete di Stalin* (Rome: Editori Riuniti, 1973), p. 47.

118. *Mezhdunarodnaia zhizn'* 8 (1991), p. 117. DVP, XXIII, 2, doc. 515, pp. 80–1.
119. *Sto sorok besed s Molotovym*, pp. 23 ff.
120. V. Mastny, *Russia's Road to the Cold War. Diplomacy, Warfare, and the Politics of Communism, 1941–1945* (New York: Columbia University Press, 1979), p. 31. See also G. Gorodetsky, 'Geopolitical Factors in Stalin's Strategy and Politics in the Wake of the Outbreak of World War II', pp. 235–50.
121. *Pravda*, 15 November 1940.
122. S. M. Miner, *Between Churchill and Stalin. The Soviet Union, Great Britain, and the Origins of the Grand Alliance* (Chapel Hill, NC: University of North Carolina Press, 1988), p. 103.
123. *Mezhdunarodnaia zhizn'* 8 (1991), p. 119. DVP, XXIII, 2, doc. 526, p. 92.
124. DVP, XXIII, 2, doc. 548, pp. 135–7. DGFP, D, XI, doc. 404, pp. 714–5.
125. Erickson, 'Threat Identification and Strategic Appraisal', p. 414.
126. See G. L. Weinberg, *A World at Arms: A Global History of World War II* (Cambridge: Cambridge University Press, 1994), p. 202.
127. *Komintern i vtoraia mirovaia voina*, 1, pp. 40, 454–5.
128. Dimitrov, *Dnevnik*, pp. 202–3. See Bezymenskii, 'Vizit V. M. Molotova v Berlin v noyabre 1940 g.', p. 142.
129. For a detailed analysis of diplomatic, geopolitical and strategic dilemmas of Stalin's foreign policy from the second half of 1940 to June 1941, see Gorodetsky, *Grand Delusion*.

Epilogue: Stalin and the War

In November 1940 Stalin met with A. Ierusalimskii, a Soviet historian preparing a Russian edition of Bismarck's memoirs, and made a request. He would take it as a personal favour if Ierusalimskii's introduction to the volume did not harp on the German statesman's fearful respect for Russian military power. Apparently, Stalin could see no reason for sending Hitler a warning, however oblique and obscure.[1] The historian understood: when he published an article later that year devoted to outlining the 'aims of the second imperialist war', he never mentioned Nazi Germany's war objectives.[2]

As is well known, despite the cacophony of alarm signals warning him of Hitler's preparations for war in the east, Stalin resolutely, blindly, obstinately maintained his stance. The detailed information the Soviet secret services gathered on Hitler's 'Operation Barbarossa' from the end of 1940 onwards never convinced Stalin of the imminence of the threat, although a German attack was at the centre of Soviet strategic thought. As for warnings from London, Stalin cynically viewed them as new moves in an interminable game of chance. Up to the eve of the invasion, Stalin's startling behaviour was not noticeably affected by the ever more precise confidential information about German war preparations. Confronted with this seemingly irrational conduct, the historian must look beyond purely psychological aetiology and also interrogate the interaction of political, diplomatic and strategic concerns.[3]

Stalin simply could not believe that Hitler would attempt to wage war on two fronts. Now that continental Europe had been conquered by the Germans, Stalin anticipated that Great Britain's resistance would prolong the war in the West or even that the USSR would play a major role in a European peace agreement. Such thinking led him to cleave as firmly as possible to the pact with Germany and to do what he could to combat any scenario of a united capitalist front. Molotov's memoirs lay great emphasis on the Soviet leaders's hopes of 'putting off war'.[4]

In a public speech given in January 1941, Varga provided clues to

EPILOGUE

Soviet strategic thinking and to the framework that surrounded it. In his opinion, the struggle between the 'two systems' was enjoying a momentary lull; no one ought to delude himself with the fantasy that the war would spare the USSR. Besides, the Marxists did not think that peace was always better than war – were there not 'progressive and revolutionary wars'? Varga felt that the war in the West would last a long time yet and would finish by shaking the capitalist world to its foundations.[5] The Soviets continued to focus on the idea of a 'war of attrition'.

Accordingly, the most prominent feature of Soviet policy between the end of 1940 and the first half of 1941 was détente towards Germany. Hoping to end the silence with which Hitler had met Stalin's proposals of 25 November, Moscow moved to open talks with both Germany and Italy. On 21 December Molotov assured Schulenburg that despite problems between their two countries Moscow hoped to open the road 'for the further development of relations between the Soviet Union and Germany'.[6] In negotiations over a new economic agreement between Germany and the USSR, Germany won many concessions from the Soviets, who had palliated their demands as early as November – the accord was signed on 10 January 1941.[7] But the old strategy did not work. Though they had made economic concessions, the Soviet leaders soon found that they had reaped no political reward. On 17 January Molotov found himself pressing Schulenburg for an explanation of the silence Germany had maintained since Soviet proposals were made on 25 November – in vain.[8]

Nor did the resumption of talks with Italy – clearly a sop to Berlin – ease Soviet anxieties. On 30 December Molotov submitted to Rosso the same points he had stressed during the Berlin talks and he even mentioned the memorandum he had given Rosso in June. In keeping with the points made in the earlier memorandum, he reaffirmed Soviet interests and security needs in the Turkish straits, pointed out that with the annexation of Bessarabia the Danube had gained a new importance to the USSR and criticized once more the Italo-German security arrangements for Romania.[9] On 27 January 1941 Molotov claimed that the Soviet Union would not be satisfied with a 'merely theoretical' consideration of the problem of the straits, since the likely involvement of Turkey in the conflict rendered Moscow's security concerns more pressing.[10] Nothing came of the new talks with Italy. At the end of February, on the eve of the entry of German troops into Bulgaria, Molotov called the Italian position on Turkey 'unclear' and abandoned the negotiations.[11] The Bulgarian debacle had exposed as a pipe dream the hope that Soviet security objectives in eastern Europe could be maintained without confrontation with Germany.

At the same time, the Soviets had failed to cultivate an alternative policy. Though Eden had returned to prominence in Great Britain, no serious attempt was made to achieve some sort of rapprochement. As always, the first move had to be made by the British.¹² Only Maiskii, as far as we know, had grave misgivings about the appeasement of Germany. When Germany trampled on the non-aggression pact signed by the USSR and Yugoslavia by invading the latter in April 1941, Maiskii noted that Soviet foreign policy had by now exhausted the 'German card' and proposed that the 'time for looking for other cards' was fast approaching.¹³ But such statements were isolated and had no effect on Soviet policy-makers.

None of the Soviet leaders appears to have been broadening his outlook on foreign policy at this time. The decision to sign a treaty with Yugoslavia on the eve of that country's invasion by Germany and Italy did not mark a reversal of Soviet policy. Rather than make any attempt to confront Germany, the Soviets played a diplomatic game, always hoping that negotiations would continue.¹⁴ When he sent a message to Yugoslavian communists through the Comintern, Molotov urged caution in dealing with the fascist expansion.¹⁵ Even after the 'Balkan events', Zhdanov stated that there would be no change in the Soviet position on the 'imperialist war' or on 'the opposing capitalist groups'. In other words, the USSR would not break its pact with Germany, would not go back to embrace anti-fascism and would not welcome rapprochement with Great Britain.¹⁶

The main achievement of Soviet foreign policy was the neutrality pact concluded with Japan on 13 April 1941. But if originally Moscow had hoped to improve relations with Tokyo by forming an alliance with Berlin, the pact ended up being signed because of growing tensions with Berlin.¹⁷ The Soviet Union had failed to move any closer to the political objectives Stalin had envisioned at the time of the Berlin talks. In his meeting with the Japanese minister of foreign affairs, Stalin remarked that the time for the USSR to ally itself with the three fascist powers had 'not yet come'.¹⁸ Nevertheless, as late as May the Soviet leadership had not lost hope that Germany would prove willing to settle the issues Molotov had raised in Berlin. That was when Dekanozov once again broached the subject of the Balkans with Schulenburg, hoping for a clarification of the underlying tensions between Germany and the USSR.¹⁹ So intent were the Soviet leaders on a rapprochement that they blundered. On 12 May Dekanozov responded to a proposal of Schulenburg's meant to 'put an end to the rumours that relations between Germany and the Soviet Union have soured'. Stalin and Molotov stood ready to participate in an exchange of letters with Nazi leaders; Molotov would be in charge of negotiating the content of the

EPILOGUE

letters on the Soviet side. Caught off guard, the German ambassador could only stammer that he had expressed a personal suggestion; his government had never mentioned such a plan.[20] The episode says much about Moscow's diplomatic conduct. Stalin's blind devotion to appeasing Hitler was unshakable up to the very eve of the German attack.

On 5 May 1941 Stalin delivered a speech to graduates of the Soviet military academies. The text of this speech, which had never been published, has only recently been unearthed in the Russian archives.[21] There are, in fact, various distinct documents involved. The first of these is a résumé of the speech, according to which Stalin restricted himself to stressing the lessons of the French defeat and the necessity for both military and political preparations for war. By 'political preparation' he meant the formation of international alliances, the sort of enterprise in which Germany, so he calculated, had succeeded, while France and Great Britain had not. He was thus referring to the Molotov–Ribbentrop pact. Only in the last of three toasts he gave at a reception following his speech (a transcript was saved of the toasts) did Stalin declare that the moment had come to proceed 'from defence to attack' in military strategy – the goal of propaganda would henceforth be the inciting of 'offensive spirit'.[22]

The content of these documents should be compared with the testimony witnesses gave about Stalin's comments on the international situation.[23] According to Alexander Werth, Stalin declared that war with Germany could still be put off for several months, that it would become inevitable in 1942 and that the USSR, given a favourable international situation, could take the initiative and attack first, striking a blow against German domination in Europe.[24] According to Hilger, Stalin maintained that the time for thinking about defence was over: the time had come for offensive action designed to expand socialism in Europe.[25] Other witnesses claimed that Stalin had quite openly declared that armed conflict with Germany could not be avoided.[26] In his diary entry for 5 May 1941 Dimitrov recorded the slogan about 'offensive spirit' and stressed the necessity of 'preparing for war'.[27]

The historical debate around Stalin's speech of 5 May has been focused on trying to determine whether it revealed Soviet preparations for an imminent preventative attack on Germany.[28] Evidence about Soviet diplomatic and political strategies hardly confirms that such preparations were being made in the short run. In particular, it is unlikely that Stalin had unexpectedly converted to the pure and simple idea of revolutionary war. On this point he had always maintained an ambiguous stance. In his speech of October 1938, he had remarked that the Bolsheviks were not necessarily 'against all wars ... the fact that we never go beyond kicking up a fuss about defence is a veil – a veil. All states adopt masks: if you live among wolves, you must behave like a wolf'.[29] And in his November 1939 conversation with Dimitrov, as we have seen, he hinted at possible radical developments in Germany. But in both cases he refrained from any forecast about the role that the Soviets would be likely to play.

Furthermore, we know that on 20 April 1941, a fortnight prior to his speech to the military academies' graduates, Stalin had spoken to Dimitrov and some members of the Politburo about liquidating the Comintern. Stalin felt that the Comintern had outlived its usefulness, and that the development of the communist parties required more independence than a centralized organization would grant. Soon after he had made his feelings known, Dimitrov met with Ercoli and Thorez to discuss the formation of a new organization charged with the task of mediating communication between the various Communist parties.[30] On 12 May Dimitrov met with Zhdanov, who provided details about Stalin's thoughts on the communist movement: most important, 'national feelings' were to take precedence over 'cosmopolitanism'.[31] This new direction had far more to do with foreign policy – specifically, Soviet relations with Germany – than it did with the internal evolution of the Comintern. Two years later, when the Comintern was finally dissolved, Stalin still based his thinking primarily on diplomatic concerns, though by then his foil was the Western powers. On the other hand, the switch to an emphasis on the 'nationalization' of the communist parties seemed geared to an impending war against Germany and its domination of Europe, not to revolutionary war.

We cannot exclude the possibility that Stalin was envisaging a blow against Hitler.[32] After all, such a scenario was implicit in the 'war of attrition' strategy: but this strategy implied that the Soviet Union would have entered the war only when the vitality and effectiveness of Nazi Germany's warfare capacities were seriously weakened. In May–June 1941 this was hardly an immediate prospect, though it was not dismissed in Soviet thinking. Molotov's memoirs are not entirely accurate in denying that a plan for a preventative attack was ever fully articulated, and asserting that before the war broke out the only question in the air was whether to retreat 'as far as Smolensk or as far as Moscow'.[33] In fact, a strategic plan drawn up by Georgii Zhukov and Timoshenko ten days after Stalin's speech mentioned the possibility of preemptive offensive action. But the plan does not appear ever to have been approved by the policy-makers. On the contrary, it seems that Stalin disapproved of the strategic proposal.[34]

We have more consistent evidence about the direction propaganda was meant to take. In two speeches Shcherbakov gave on 8 and 9 May, and one Zhdanov gave on 15 May, clear reference was made to Stalin's words in an effort to re-launch the propaganda work as the shadow of war advanced. The following month Zhdanov, Aleksandr Shcherbakov and Georgii Malenkov began the work of drafting new political propaganda for the army and for society as a whole. Among the measures decided on, Varga would be urged to reverse his depiction of Germany in the journal he edited: previously Germany's economic and military potential had been 'overvalued'.[35] But no full-blown anti-German campaign was actually promoted.

All of this tells us little about the strategic decisions of the Soviet leaders; it has much more relevance for an understanding of their political thinking. Most importantly, neither the archival documentation nor the anecdotes handed down in memoirs really contradict those aspects of Stalin's thought this study has dwelt on: he was waiting for war; he remained convinced that he still had some time and space for manoeuvre; he expected Germany to be hit hard by the 'war of attrition'. The concern driving Soviet propaganda in May and June 1941 appears to have been the prospect of war with Germany, which was on the horizon – but who knew when? Only in May–June 1941 can we see the first signs of Moscow's decision that war with Germany was in the offing. Stalin's 5 May speech was therefore probably intended to mark the opening of a new phase, not a reversal, in the 'war of attrition' strategy.

While the speech of 5 May was not published, an article by Stalin was published that month in the theoretical journal *Bol'shevik*. This was a set of notes Stalin had sent to the Politburo seven years earlier, on 19 July 1934, commenting on Engels's theses on Russian foreign policy. Criticizing Engels's willingness to distinguish Tsarist Russia from bourgeois Germany, Stalin insisted on the imperialist origins of World War I.[36] But he did not limit himself to Lenin's theory of imperialism. Stalin also championed a policy of non-involvement in 'the second imperialist war' and obliquely suggested that Russian power would soon rise again.[37] Why had Stalin chosen to publish these notes in May 1941? Perhaps to demonstrate the consistency of his outlook, as if to say he had long foretold the fall of the 'old European order'.

The evidence marshalled in the previous pages and chapters runs contrary to Andreas Hillgruber's thesis, that Stalin relied on a consistent 'war programme' from the first days of German aggression.[38] Instead, the brunt of the facts suggests that before June 1941 Stalin trusted in a 'war of attrition' to protect the Soviet Union and to strengthen its power in Europe. This does not exclude the ambition Hillgruber assigned to Stalin, that of expanding the Soviet sphere of influence in central–eastern Europe. The Soviet strategy designed to forge a privileged relationship with Germany from August–September 1939 onwards did not envision a stable division of power in Europe. Stalin hoped, rather, to consolidate the USSR's strategic positions and to foment the war between the capitalist powers. Though a temporary agreement with Nazi Germany, drawn up on the basis of their respective geopolitical interests, was possible, it was but one fragile haven in the midst of a relentlessly hostile and antagonistic world.

This thinking was consistent with the traditional Soviet doctrine on war, and every event of the last years struck the Stalinist leaders as confirming that doctrine. For them, it was not Nazi ideology as such, but Germany's capitalist and imperialist social order that determined the strategic direction of Hitler's foreign policy. There was no reason to expend effort in testing Nazi ideology, whether seen as a radical threat to peace and socialism, or as a reply to bourgeois 'degeneration', albeit ineffective and skimpy. Ultimately, the Soviet perspective conceded that Nazi Germany was utterly incompatible with the Soviet Union: but the fundamental antagonism between the two states arose from those features that made Nazi Germany more like than unlike the Western powers, a harbinger of the irreversible decline of capitalism and democracy. Tragically, Hitler's doctrines and ambitions had been largely overlooked in this analysis. The Soviet doctrine of the inevitability of war and the political culture of permanent conflict embedded in the psychosis of encirclement were hardly a congruous platform from which foreign policy could be formulated.

The axioms underlying Stalin's strategic thinking had a long history, though they were formulated as an integral foreign policy only in the summer of 1939. Stalin's axioms included the conviction, first, that traditional power policy remained the axis of interstate relations, as in the classic age of empires before World War I; second, that it was possible to establish a temporary peaceful international order by carefully regulating a balance of power, but that this order was doomed to break down thanks to the emergence of irreconcilable 'systems' on the world scene; third, that nothing but a combination of territorial strength with isolation and a divisive diplomacy would protect the security interests of the socialist state from its hostile capitalist environment, thus preserving its power intact for future conflict. This strategic thinking was based on a notion of the requirements of Soviet security that combined systemic confrontation and power policy, ideology and 'old diplomacy', isolationism and expansion. In this light, the analogies between Stalin's foreign policy and the foreign policy of the Russian empire were overshadowed by the new inter-dependence between the internal regime, the perception of the outside world and the conception of state security. At the same time, the ideological factors playing a crucial role in Stalin's foreign policy were no longer simply identified with revolutionary motivations, nor were they an organic

EPILOGUE

doctrinaire body on which policy-making was integrally based; they were rather archetypes in the vision of international politics, which exercised persistent influence on Soviet political culture.

By the end of the 1930s it had become clear that Stalin's policies were increasingly guided by his determination to revise the Versailles order. If Versailles had seemed for a time to protect a status quo against Hitler's aggressive policies and had represented a lesser evil for the Soviet Union, this changed between 1938 and 1939. It was not by chance that Litvinov raised his voice to maintain, as late as 1938, that the Brest peace 'was no better' than that of Versailles. By that time, Stalin had already ceased to believe that there was any hope of preventing war, and had switched focus into the 'Brest paradigm', which might serve to legitimate a unilateral withdrawal from the European war. Stalin looked at two overlapping scenarios for how war could develop, the '1914 model' and the '1918 model', which between them accounted for the contemporaneous explosive mixture of civil wars and war between great powers. In the aftermath of the European crises, he built his foreign policy in accordance with the belief that a united capitalist bloc was the Soviet Union's main enemy, that every effort should be made to avoid entanglement in a collapsing 'old order' and that a great trench dug across eastern Europe was the best possible protection. He definitely came to see the USSR as embroiled in an unrelenting 'war of position' with the capitalist world. The longstanding cultural implant of this thinking helps us understand why the security concept forged by Stalin on the eve of World War II would survive the failure of Soviet foreign policy in face of the Nazi threat.

NOTES

1. M. Ia. Gefter, *Iz tekh i etikh let* (Moscow: Progress, 1991), pp. 261–2.
2. A. Ierusalimskii, 'O tseliakh vtoroi imperialisticheskoi voiny', *Bol'shevik* 10 (1940).
3. On this question, see Gorodetsky, *Grand Delusion*.
4. *Sto sorok besed s Molotovym*, pp. 32–3.
5. E. Varga, 'O mezhdunarodnom polozhenii', *Mirovoe khoziaistvo i mirovaia politika* 3 (1941).
6. AVP RF, f. 06, op. 2, p. 15, d. 57, l. 50.
7. Zeidler, 'German–Soviet Economic Relations', in Wegner (ed.), *From Peace to War*, p. 108.
8. DVP, XXIII, 2, doc. 654, pp. 343–4.
9. Ibid., doc. 625, pp. 263–6. DDI, series IX, VI, doc. 375, pp. 361–4; doc. 382, pp. 370–7.
10. DVP, XXIII, 2, doc. 665, pp. 363–7. DDI, series IX, VI, doc. 502, pp. 508–10; doc. 506, pp. 512–17.
11. DVP, XXIII, 2, doc. 689, pp. 417–18. DDI, series IX, VI, doc. 634, pp. 628–31.
12. DVP, XXIII, 2, docs. 670, 731.
13. AVP RF, f. 017a, op. 1, p. 1, d. 8, l. 79.
14. See Gorodetsky, *Grand Delusion*, pp. 147 ff.
15. *Komintern i vtoraia mirovaia voina* 1, pp. 519–20.

16. Dimitrov, *Dnevnik*, p. 225.
17. Haslam, *The Soviet Union and the Threat from the East*, pp. 149–50.
18. DVP, XXIII, 2, doc. 772, p. 562.
19. Ibid., docs. 814, 823.
20. Ibid., doc. 828, p. 675.
21. *Istoricheskii Arkhiv*, 2 (1995), pp. 23–31. DVP, XXIII, 2, doc. 812, pp. 648–51. See Volkogonov, *Triumf i tragediia*, II, 1, pp. 55–7; L. Bezymenski, 'Die rede Stalins am 5 Mai 1941 dokumentiert und interpretiert', *Osteuropa* 3 (1992), pp. 242–64; O. V. Vishlev, 'Rech' I. V. Stalina 5-ogo maia 1941 g. Rossiiskie dokumenty', *Novaia i noveishaia istoriia* 4 (1998), pp. 77–89.
22. *Istoricheskii Arkhiv* 2 (1995), pp. 28, 30.
23. *Voenno-istoricheskii zhurnal* 2 (1995), p. 23.
24. A. Werth, *Russia at War, 1941–1945* (New York: Carroll & Graf, 1984), pp. 122–3.
25. Hilger, *The Incompatible Allies*, p. 330.
26. *Voenno-istoricheskii zhurnal* 2 (1995), p. 23.
27. Dimitrov, *Dnevnik*, pp. 230–31.
28. The 'preventative war' thesis has been argued by V. Suvorov, *Icebreaker: Who Started the Second World War?* (London: Hamish Hamilton, 1990). For a well-grounded criticism of Suvorov's theses, see G. Gorodetsky, *Mif 'Ledokola'. Nakanune voiny* (Moscow: Progress-Akademiia, 1995); and Gorodetsky, *Grand Delusion*. For an accurate review of the debate, see T. J. Uldricks, 'The Icebreaker Controversy: Did Stalin Plan to Attack Hitler?', *Slavic Review* 3 (1999), pp. 626–43.
29. *Istoricheskii Arkhiv* 5 (1994), p. 13. RGASPI, f. 558, op. 11, d. 1122, l. 55.
30. Dimitrov, *Dnevnik*, pp. 227–8.
31. Ibid., p. 233.
32. A strong emphasis on this point, though in the context of criticism towards Suvorov, can be found in M. Meltiukhov, *Upushchennyi shans Stalina. Sovetskii Soiuz i bor'ba za Evropu: 1939–1941* (Moscow: Veche, 2000).
33. *Sto sorok besed s Molotovym*, pp. 31, 45. The same view has been affirmed by Kaganovich in his memoirs: see G. A. Kumanev, 'Dve besedy s L. M. Kaganovichem', *Novaia i noveishaia istoriia* 2 (1999), p. 109.
34. G. K. Zhukov, *Vospominaniia i razmyshleniia* (Moscow: Novosti, 1992), p. 367. Cf. *Voenno-istoricheskii zhurnal* 3 (1995), pp. 40–46.
35. V. A. Nevezhin, *Sindrom nastupatel'noi voiny. Sovetskaia propaganda v preddverii 'sviashchennykh boev' 1939–1941 gg.* (Moscow: AIRO-XX, 1997), pp. 188–95, 246–7.
36. Stalin, *Works*, 1, pp. 2–10.
37. Tucker, *Stalin in Power*, p. 342.
38. A. Hillgruber, *Die Zerstörung Europas. Beiträge zur Weltkriegsepoche 1914 bis 1945*; Italian edn: *La distruzione dell'Europa. La Germania e l'epoca delle guerre mondiali, 1914–1945* (Bologna: Il Mulino, 1991), p. 271. See also A. Hillgruber, *Der Zweite Weltkrieg 1939–1945: Kriegsziele und Strategie der grossen Mächte* (Stuttgart: Kohlhammer, 1982).

Bibliography

ARCHIVES

Archive of the Foreign Policy of the Russian Federation, Moscow (Arkhiv vneshnei politiki Rossiiskoi Federatsii – AVP RF)
Historical Archive of the Ministry for Foreign Affairs, Rome (Archivio storico del Ministero degli Affari Esteri – ASMAE)
Public Record Office, Archives of the Foreign Office, London (PRO FO)
Russian State Archive for Social and Political History, Moscow (Rossiiskii Gosudarstvennyi Arkhiv sotsialno-politicheskoi istorii – RGASPI)
State Archive of the Russian Federation, Moscow (Gosudarstvennyi arkhiv Rossiiskoi Federatsii – GARF)

OFFICIAL PUBLISHED DOCUMENTS

Documents on British Foreign Policy (DBFP), 2nd series (London: 1947–1984); 3rd series (London: 1949–1957).
Documents Diplomatiques Français (DDF), 1ère série (Paris: 1964–1984); 2e série (Paris: 1963–).
Documenti Diplomatici Italiani (DDI), VIII serie (Rome: 1952–); IX serie (Rome: 1954–1990).
Documents on German Foreign Policy (DGFP), series D (Washington: 1949–1956).
Dokumenty vneshnei politiki SSSR, 23 vols. (Moscow: 1958–1978).
Dokumenty vneshnei politiki, XXII–XXIII (Moscow: 1992–1998).
God krizisa. Dokumenty i materialy, 2 vols. (Moscow: 1990).
Polpredy soobshchaiut ... Sbornik dokumentov ob otnosheniiakh Sssr s Latviei, Litvoi i Estoniei, avgust 1939g.– avgust 1940g. (Moscow: 1990).

BOOKS AND ARTICLES

Afanas'ev, Iu. N. (ed.), *Drugaia voina 1939–1945* (Moscow: Rossiiskii gosudarstvennii gumanitarnyi universitet, 1996).

STALIN AND THE INEVITABLE WAR, 1936–1941

Agosti, A., *La Terza Internazionale. Storia documentaria*, III, 2 (Rome: Editori Riuniti; 1979).

Ahmann, R., 'Soviet Foreign Policy and the Molotov–Ribbentrop Pact of 1939: An Enigma Reassessed', *Storia delle Relazioni Internazionali* 2 (1989).

Barros, J. and Gregor, R., *Double Deception. Stalin, Hitler, and the Invasion of Russia* (DeKalb, IL: Northern Illinois University Press, F. Agneli, 1995).

Bauer, O., *Tra due guerre mondiali? La crisi dell'economia mondiale, della democrazia e del socialismo* (Turin: Einaudi, 1979).

Benvenuti, F. and Pons, S., *Il sistema di potere dello Stalinismo. Partito e Stato in Urss 1933–1953* (Milan: Angeli 1988).

Berezhkov, V., *At Stalin's Side: His Interpreter's Memoirs from the October Revolution to the Fall of the Dictator's Empire* (Secaucus, NJ: Carol Publishing Group, 1994).

Besymenski [Bezymensky], L. A., 'Die Rede Stalins am 5 Mai 1941 Dokumentiert und Interpretiert', *Osteuropa* 3 (1992).

Bezymenskii [Bezymensky], L. A., 'Sovetsko-Germanskie dogovory 1939g.: Novye dokumenty i starye problemy', *Novaia i noveishaia istoriia* 3 (1998).

Bezymensky, L. A., 'The Secret Protocols of 1939 as a Problem of Soviet Historiography', G. Gorodetsky (ed.), in *Soviet Foreign Policy, 1917–1991*, (London: Frank Cass, 1994).

Bezymensky, L. A., 'Vizit V. M. Molotova v Berlin v noiabre 1940g. v svete novykh dokumentov', *Novaia i noveishaia istoriia* 6 (1995).

Buchanan, T., *Britain and the Spanish Civil War* (Cambridge: Cambridge University Press, 1997).

Carley, M. J., 'End of the "Low, Dishonest Decade": Failure of the Anglo–Franco-Soviet Alliance in 1939', *Europe-Asia Studies* 2 (1993).

Carley, M. J., *1939. The Alliance that Never Was and the Coming of World War II* (Chicago, IL: Ivan R. Dee, 1999).

Carr, E. H., *A History of Soviet Russia: Foundations of a Planned Economy 1926–1929*, III, 1 (London: Macmillan, 1976).

Carr, E. H., *The Twilight of Comintern 1930–1935* (London: Macmillan, 1982).

Carr, E. H., *The Comintern and the Spanish Civil War* (London: Macmillan, 1984).

Cattell, D., *Soviet Diplomacy and the Spanish Civil War* (Berkeley and Los Angeles, CA: University of California Press, 1957).

Chubaryan, A. O. and Gorodetsky, G. (eds), *Voina i politika 1939–1941* (Moscow: Nauka, 1999).

Chuev, F., *Sto Sorok Besed s Molotovym* (Moscow: Terra, 1989).

BIBLIOGRAPHY

Cohen, S., *Bukharin and the Bolshevik Revolution: A Political Biography, 1888–1938* (New York: Knopf, 1973).
Conquest, R., *The Great Terror. A Reassessment* (London: Hutchinson, 1990).
Cooper, J., Perrie, M., Rees, E.A. (eds), *Soviet History, 1917–1953. Essays in Honour of R.W. Davies* (London: Macmillan, 1993).
Coulondre, R., *De Moscou à Berlin* (Paris: 1959).
Coverdale, J. F., *Italian Intervention in the Spanish Civil War* (Princeton, NJ: Princeton University Press, 1975).
Dallin, A. and Firsov, F. I. (eds), *Dimitrov and Stalin 1934–1943: Letters from the Soviet Archives* (New Haven, CT: Yale University Press, 2000).
Dallin, D. J., *Soviet Russia's Foreign Policy 1939–1942* (New Haven, CT: Yale University Press, 1942).
Dimitrov, G., *Dnevnik 9 mart 1933–6 februari 1949* (Sofia: Universitetsko izdatelstvo 'Sv. Kliment Okhridski', 1997).
Di Biagio, A., *Le origini dell'isolazionismo sovietico. L'Unione sovietica e l'Europa dal 1918 al 1928* (Milan: Angeli, 1990).
'Direktivy I. V. Stalina V. M. Molotovu pered poezdkoi v Berlin v noiabre 1940 g.', *Novaia i noveishaia istoriia* 4 (1995).
Dullin, S., 'Litvinov and the People's Commissariat of Foreign Affairs: The Fate of an Administration under Stalin', in S. Pons and A. Romano *Russia in the Age of Wars 1914–1945* (Milan: Annali Feltrinelli, 2000).
Elorza, A., Bizcarrondo, M., *Queridos camaradas. La Internacional Comunista i Espana, 1919–1939* (Barcelona: Planeta, 1999).
Erickson, J., *The Soviet High Command: A Military–Political History 1918–1941* (London: Macmillan, 1962).
Erickson, J., 'Threat Identification and Strategic Appraisal by the Soviet Union, 1930–1941', in E. R. May (ed.), *Knowing One's Enemies* (Princeton, NJ: Princeton University Press, 1984).
Erickson, J. and Dilks, D. (eds), *Barbarossa: The Axis and the Allies* (Edinburgh: Edinburgh University Press, 1994).
Firsov, F., 'Stalin i Komintern', *Voprosy istorii* 9 (1989).
Fischer, E. *Erinnerungen und Reflexionen*; Italian version *Ricordi e riflessioni* (Rome: Editori Riuniti 1973).
Fleischauer, I., *Der Pakt. Hitler, Stalin und die Initiative der Deutschen Diplomatie 1938–1939* (Berlin: Ullstein, 1990).
Gefter, M. Ia., *Iz tekh i etikh let* (Moscow: Progress, 1991).
Gleason, A., *Totalitarianism. The Inner History of the Cold War* (Oxford: Oxford University Press, 1995).
Gnedin, E., *Katastrofa i vtoroe rozhdenie* (Amsterdam: 1977).
Gnedin, E., *Iz istorii otnoshenii mezhdu SSSR i fashistskoi Germaniei*

(New York: Khronike, 1977).
Gorlov, S. A., 'Sovetsko-Germanskii dialog nakanune pakta Molotova–Ribbentropa 1939g', *Novaia i noveishaia istoriia* 4 (1993).
Gorodetsky, G., *Stafford Cripps' Mission to Moscow, 1940–42* (Cambridge: Cambridge University Press, 1984).
Gorodetsky, G., 'The Impact of the Ribbentrop Pact on the Course of Soviet Foreign Policy', *Cahiers du Monde Russe et Soviétique* (January–March 1990).
Gorodetsky, G., (ed.), *Soviet Foreign Policy, 1917–1991* (London: Frank Cass, 1994).
Gorodetsky, G., *Mif 'Ledokola'. Nakanune voiny* (Moscow: Progress-Akademiia, 1995).
Gorodetsky, G., *Grand Delusion. Stalin and the German Invasion of Russia* (New Haven, CT and London: Yale University Press, 1999).
Gorodetsky, G., 'Geopolitical Factors in Stalin's Strategy and Politics in the Wake of the Outbreak of World War II', in S. Pons and A. Romano (eds) *Russia in the Age of Wars 1914–1945* (Milan: Annali Feltrinelli, 2000).
Gross, J. T., *Revolution From Abroad: The Soviet Conquest of Poland's Western Ukraine and Western Belorussia* (Princeton, NJ: Princeton University Press, 1988).
Haslam, J., *The Soviet Union and the Struggle for Collective Security in Europe, 1933–1939* (London: Macmillan, 1984).
Haslam, J., 'Soviet Foreign Policy 1939–1941', *Soviet Union/Union Soviétique* 1–3 (1991).
Haslam, J., *The Soviet Union and the Threat from the East, 1933–41: Moscow, Tokyo and the Prelude to the Pacific War* (London: Macmillan, 1992).
Haslam, J., 'Litvinov, Stalin, and the Road Not Taken', in G. Gorodetsky (ed.), *Soviet Foreign Policy 1917–1991* (London: Frank Cass, 1994).
Haslam, J., 'Soviet–German Relations and the Origins of the Second World War: The Jury Is Still Out', *Journal of Modern History* 4 (1997).
Hilger, G., Meyer, A. G., *The Incompatible Allies: A Memoir History Of German–Soviet Relations 1918–1941* (New York: Macmillan, 1953).
Hillgruber, A., *Der Zweite Weltkrieg 1939-1945: Kriegsziele und Strategie der grossen Mächte* (Stuttgart: Kohlhammer, 1982).
Hillgruber, A., *Die Zerstoerung Europas. Beitraege zur Weltkriegsepoche 1914 bis 1945* (Berlin: 1988).
Hochman, J., *The Soviet Union and the Failure of Collective Security, 1934–1938* (Ithaca, NY: Cornell University Press, 1984).
Jacobson, J., *When the Soviet Union Entered World Politics* (Berkeley, CA: University of California Press, 1994).

BIBLIOGRAPHY

Jordan, N., *The Popular Front and Central Europe: The Dilemmas of French Impotence, 1918–1940* (Cambridge: Cambridge University Press, 1992).
Jukes, G., 'The Red Army and the Munich Crisis' *Journal of Contemporary History* (April 1991).
Kennan, G., *Russia and the West under Lenin and Stalin* (Boston, MA: Little Brown, 1961).
Khlevniuk, O., 'The Objectives of the Great Terror', in J. Cooper, M. Perrie, E. A. Rees (eds), *Soviet History, 1917–1953: Essays in Honour of R. W. Davies* (London: Macmillan, 1993).
Khlevniuk, O., *Politburo. Mekhanizmy politicheskoi vlasti v 1930-e gody* (Moscow: ROSSPEN, 1996).
Khlevniuk, O., 'The Reasons for the Great Terror: The Foreign–Political Aspect', in S. Pons and A. Romano (eds) *Russia in the Age of Wars 1914–1945* (Milan: Annali Feltrinelli, 2000).
Khrushchev, N. S., *Khrushchev Remembers* (Boston, MA: Little Brown, 1970).
Krivitsky, W. G., *J'étais un agent de Staline* (Paris: Champ Libre, 1979).
Kumanev, G. A., 'Dve besedy s L. M. Kaganovichem', *Novaia i noveishaia istoriia* 2 (1999).
Larina, A., *This I Cannot Forget: The Memoirs of Nikolai Bukharin's Widow* (New York: Norton, 1993).
Lerner, W., *Karl Radek. The Last Internationalist* (Stanford, CA: Stanford University Press, 1970).
Litvinov, M., *V bor'be za mir* (Moscow: Politizdat, 1938).
Lukes, I., 'Stalin and Beneš at the End of September 1938: New Evidence from Prague Archives', *Slavic Review* 1 (1993).
Maiskii, I. M., *Vospominaniia sovetskogo diplomata 1925–1945 gg.* (Moscow: Mezhdunarodnie otnosheniia, 1987).
Martin, T., 'The Origins of Soviet Ethnic Cleansing', *Journal of Modern History* 4 (1998).
Mastny, V., *Russia's Road to the Cold War. Diplomacy, Warfare, and the Politics of Communism, 1941–1945* (New York: Columbia University Press, 1979).
May, E. R. (ed.) *Knowing One's Enemies: Intelligence Assessments Before the Two World Wars* (Princeton, NJ: Princeton University Press, 1984).
McDermott, K., Agnew, J., *The Comintern: A History of International Communism from Lenin to Stalin* (London: Macmillan, 1996).
Meltiukhov, M., *Upushchennyi shans Stalina. Sovetskii Soiuz i bor'ba za Evropu: 1939–1941* (Moscow: Veche, 2000).
Miner, S. M., *Between Churchill and Stalin: The Soviet Union, Great Britain and the Origins of the Grand Alliance* (Chapel Hill, NC:

University of North Carolina, 1988).
Narinskii, M. M., Lebedeva, N. S., *Komintern i vtoraia mirovaia voina. Chast' 1: 1939–1941 gg.* (Moscow: Pamiatniki istoricheskoi mysli, 1994).
Narinsky, M., 'Le Komintern et le Parti Communiste Français (1939–1941)', *Communisme* 32–4 (1993).
Narinsky, M., Rojahn, J. (eds), *Centre and Periphery: The History of the Comintern in the Light of New Documents* (Amsterdam: International Institute of Social History, 1996).
Nation, Craig R., *Black Earth, Red Star. A History of Soviet Security Policy, 1917–1992* (Ithaca, NY: Cornell University Press, 1992).
Nekrich, A. M., *June 22nd 1941* (Columbia, SC: University of South Carolina Press, 1968).
Nekrich, A. M., *Pariahs, Partners, Predators: German–Soviet Relations 1922–1941*, ed. G.L. Freeze (New York: Columbia University Press, 1997).
Nevezhin, V. A., *Sindrom nastupatelnoi voiny. Sovetskaia propaganda v preddverii 'sviashchennykh boev' 1939–1941 gg.* (Moscow: AIRO-XX, 1997).
Nikolaevskii, B. I., *Les dirigeants sovietiques et la lutte pour le pouvoir* (Paris: 1969).
Orlov, B. M., 'V poiskakh soiuznikov: komandovanie Krasnoi Armii i problemy vneshnei politiki SSSR v 30-kh godakh', *Voprosy istorii* 4 (1990).
Parker, R. A. C., *Chamberlain and Appeasement. British Policy and the Coming of the Second World War* (London: Macmillan, 1993).
Petrov, Iu., *Partiinoe stroitel'stvo v sovetskoi armii i flote* (Moscow: Politizdat, 1964).
Pevzner, Ia., 'Zhizn' i trudy E. S. Vargi v svete sovremennosti', *Mirovaia ekonomika i mezhdunarodnie otnosheniia* 10 (1989).
Phillips, H. D., *Between the Revolution and the West: A Political Biography of Maxim M. Litvinov* (Boulder, CO: Westview Press, 1992).
'Poezdka V.M. Molotova v Berlin v noiabre 1940 g.', *Novaia i noveishaia istoriia* 5 (1993).
Pons, S. and Romano, A. (eds), *Russia in the Age of Wars, 1914–1945* (Milan: Annali Feltrinelli, 2000).
Pozniakov, V., 'The Enemy at the Gates: Soviet Military Intelligence in the Inter-war Period and Its Forecasts of Future War, 1921–41', in S. Pons and A. Romano (eds) *Russia in the Age of Wars 1914–1945* (Milan: Annali Feltrinelli, 2000).
Procacci, G., *Il socialismo internazionale e la guerra d'Etiopia* (Rome: Editori Riuniti, 1978).

Procacci, G., 'La lotta per la pace nel socialismo internazionale alla vigilia della seconda guerra mondiale', in *Storia del marxismo*, III, 2 (Turin: Einaudi, 1981).
Procacci, G., 'La coesistenza pacifica. Appunti per la storia di un concetto', in L. Sestan (ed.), *La politica estera della perestrojka* (Rome: Editori Riuniti, 1988).
Raack, R. C., *Stalin's Drive to the West, 1938–1945: The Origins of the Cold War* (Stanford, CA: Stanford University Press, 1995).
Ragsdale, H., 'Soviet Military Preparations and Policy in the Munich Crisis: New Evidence', *Jahrbücher für Geschichte Osteuropas* 47 (1999).
Rapone, L., *La socialdemocrazia europea tra le due guerre. Dall'organizzazione della pace alla resistenza al fascismo (1923–1936)* (Rome: Carocci, 1999).
Raymond, P. D., 'Witness and Chronicler of Nazi–Soviet Relations: The Testimony of Evgeny Gnedin (Parvus)', *The Russian Review* 44 (1985).
Read, A., Fisher, D., *The Deadly Embrace: Hitler, Stalin and the Nazi–Soviet Pact 1939–1941* (London: Michael Joseph, 1988).
Reese, R., 'The Red Army and the Great Purges', in A. Arch Getty and R. T. Manning (eds), *Stalinist Terror: New Perspectives* (Cambridge, 1993).
Resis, A., 'The Fall of Litvinov: Harbinger of the German–Soviet Non-aggression Pact', *Europe-Asia Studies* 52 (2000).
Rieber, A. J., 'Persistent Factors in Russian Foreign Policy: An Interpretative Essay', in H. Ragsdale (ed.), *Imperial Russian Foreign Policy* (Cambridge: Cambridge University Press, 1993).
Roberts, G., *The Unholy Alliance: Stalin's Pact With Hitler* (Bloomington, IN: Indiana University Press, 1989).
Roberts, G., 'The Soviet Decision for a Pact with Nazi Germany', *Soviet Studies* (January 1992).
Roberts, G., 'The Fall of Litvinov: A Revisionist View', *Journal of Contemporary History* (October 1992).
Roberts, G., 'A Soviet Bid for Co-existence with Nazi Germany, 1935–1937: The Kandelaki Affair', *International History Review* (August 1994).
Roberts, G., 'Soviet Policy and the Baltic States, 1939–1940: A Reappraisal', *Diplomacy & Statecraft*, 3 (1995).
Roberts, G., *The Soviet Union and the Origins of the Second World War: Russo-German Relations and the Road to War, 1933–1941* (London: Macmillan, 1995).
Roshchin, A., 'V dovoennom Narkomindele', *Mezhdunarodnaia zhizn'* 11 (1991).

Samuelson, L., 'Tukhachevsky and the Military–Industrial Complex, 1925–37', in S. Pons and A. Romano (eds), *Russia in the Age of Wars 1914–1945* (Milan: Annali Feltrinelli, 2000).

Semiriaga, M. I., *Tainy stalinskoi diplomatii, 1939–1941* (Moscow: Vysshaia Shkola, 1992).

Sheinis, Z., *Maksim Maksimovich Litvinov: revoliutsioner, diplomat, chelovek* (Moscow: Politizdat, 1989).

Shirinia, K. K., *Strategiia i taktika Kominterna v bor'be protiv fashizma i voiny (1934–1939gg.)* (Moscow: Politizdat, 1979).

Sipols, V. Ia., 'Torgovo-ekonomicheskie otnosheniia mezhdu SSSR i Germaniei v 1939–1941 gg. v svete novykh arkhivnykh dokumentov', *Novaia i noveishaia istoriia* 2 (1997).

Sipols, V. Ia., *Tainy diplomaticheskie. Kanun Velikoi Otechestvennoi Voiny 1939–1941* (Moscow: Novina, 1997).

Spriano, P., *I comunisti europei e Stalin* (Turin: Einaudi, 1983).

Stalinskoe politburo v 30-e gody. Sbornik dokumentov (Moscow: AIRO-XX, 1995).

Steiner, Z., 'The Soviet Commissariat of Foreign Affairs and the Czechoslovakian Crisis in 1938: New Material from the Soviet Archives', *The Historical Journal* 42 (1999).

Suvorov, V., *Icebreaker: Who Started the Second World War?* (London: Hamish Hamilton, 1990).

Thomas, H., *The Spanish Civil War* (London: Penguin, 1990).

Togliatti, T., *Opere*, IV, I (Rome: Editori Riuniti, 1979).

Tucker, R. C., 'The Emergence of Stalin's Foreign Policy', *Slavic Review* XXXVI (1977).

Tucker, R. C., *Stalin in Power: The Revolution from Above, 1928–1941* (New York: Norton, 1990).

Ulam, A., *Expansion and Coexistence: Soviet Foreign Policy, 1917–1973* (New York: Praeger, 1974).

Uldricks, T. J., 'Evolving Soviet Views of the Nazi–Soviet Pact', in Frucht, R., (ed.) *Labyrinth of Nationalism, Complexities of Diplomacy*, (Colombus, OH: Slavica, 1992).

Uldricks, T. J., 'Soviet Security Policy in the 1930s', in G. Gorodetsky (ed.) *Soviet Foreign Policy, 1917–1991* (London: Frank Cass, 1994).

Uldricks, T. J., 'Debating the Role of Russia in the Origins of the Second World War', in G. Martel (ed.), *The Origins of the Second World War Reconsidered* (London: Routledge, 1999).

Uldricks, T. J., 'The Icebreaker Controversy: Did Stalin Plan to Attack Hitler?', *Slavic Review* 3 (1999).

Van Dyke, C., *The Soviet Invasion of Finland, 1939–40* (London: Frank Cass, 1997).

Vishlev, O. V., 'Rech' I. V. Stalina 5 maia 1941 g. Rossiiskie dokumenty',

Novaia i noveishaia istoriia 4 (1998).
Volkogonov, D., *Triumf i tragediia. Politicheskii portret I. V. Stalina* (Moscow: Novosti, 1989).
Watson, D., *Molotov and Soviet Government. Sovnarkom 1930–1941* (London: Macmillan, 1996).
Watson, D., 'Molotov's Apprenticeship in Foreign Policy: The Triple Alliance Negotiations in 1939', *Europe-Asia Studies* 4 (2000).
Watt, D. C., *How War Came: The Immediate Origins of the Second World War, 1938–1939* (New York: Pantheon Books, 1989).
Watt, D. C., 'Who Plotted Against Whom? Stalin's Purge of the Soviet High Command Revisited', *Journal of Soviet Military Studies* (March 1990).
Wegner, B., (ed.) *From Peace to War. Germany, Soviet Russia and the World, 1939–1941* (Oxford: Berghahan Books, 1997).
Weinberg, G. L., *The Foreign Policy of Hitler's Germany. Starting World War II, 1937–1939* (New Jersey: Humanities Press, 1994).
Weinberg, G. L., *A World at Arms. A Global History of World War II* (Cambridge: Cambridge University Press, 1994).
Weingartner, T., *Stalin und der Aufstieg Hitlers. Die Deutschlandpolitik der Sowjetunion und der Kommunistischen Internationale 1929–1934* (Berlin: de Gruyter, 1970).
Werth, A., *Russia at War 1941–1945* (New York: Carroll & Graf, 1984).
Wolfe, B. D., *Strange Communists I Have Known* (New York: Stein & Day, 1965).
Zeidler, M., 'German–Soviet Economic Relations During the Hitler–Stalin Pact', in B. Wegner (ed.) *From Peace to War. Germany, Soviet Russia and the World, 1939–1941* (Oxford: Berghahan Books, 1997).
Zhukov, G. K., *Vospominaniia i razmyshleniia* (Moscow: Novosti, 1992).
Zimniaia voina 1939–1940 (Moscow: 1998).

Index

Albania, 155
Aleksandrovskii, Sergei S., 86, 91, 114, 115, 127, 129, 130, 131, 135, 147n
Almeria, 94
Anti-Comintern Pact, 58, 104, 105; Italy's membership in, 103
Antonov-Ovseenko, Vladimir A., 55, 90
Astakhov, Grigorii A., 112, 126, 129, 143, 165, 170–2; meeting with Ribbentrop (August 1939), 171, 183n
Attolico, Bernardo, 12, 87
Austria, 64, 112; Anschluss, 8, 114, 115, 126, 127, 132, 133, 141
Azana, Manuel, 57, 74n

Balkans (see also Bulgaria, Greece, Turkey), 202, 203, 204, 208, 211, 217, 218
Baltic states (see also Estonia, Latvia, Lithuania), 127, 172, 191, 160; incorporation into USSR, 200, 201
'Barbarossa', Operation, 216
Bauer, Otto, 32, 51
Beck, Józef, 12, 133, 141
Belorussia, 192
Beneš, Eduard, 86, 87, 126, 131, 135, 140, 197; and Tukhachevskii affair, 91
Beriia, Lavrentii P., 124n, 161
Bessarabia, 172, 200, 202, 208, 209, 217
Black Sea, 157, 194, 201, 202, 207–9
Blum, Léon, 36, 41n, 44, 53, 54, 57, 61, 68, 69, 91, 113, 114
Bonnet, Georges, 127, 130, 135, 136, 143, 156, 159
Brest-Litovsk, Treaty of, 3
Brussels peace congress, 49, 71

Budennyi, Semen M., 83
Bukharin, Nikolai I., 2, 31, 32, 40n, 78, 79, 84, 109, 110 124n, 125n; justifies purges, 78
Bukovina, northern, 200, 202
Bulgaria, 191, 202, 207; entry of German troops into, 217; Soviet policy towards, 208–11

Cadogan, Lord Alexander George Montague, 154
Carr, Edward H., 47
Catalonia, 93
Chamberlain, Neville, 95, 96, 103, 105, 106, 112, 115, 116, 127, 129, 130–6 passim, 141–4 passim, 150–60 passim; on dialogue with Germany, 95; meeting with Hitler, 131
Chicherin, Georgii V., 90
Chilston, Lord A., 10, 61, 75n, 87, 103
China, 99, 104; Japanese invasion of, 96, 100, 103
Churchill, Winston L., 115, 130, 135, 194, 203
Ciano, Galeazzo, 170, 172
Codovilla, Vittorio, 50
collective security, 2, 8, 15, 39n, 54, 63, 65, 91, 92, 102, 104, 116, 118, 119, 132, 133, 152, 153, 156, 162, 183n, 185n; and communist parties, 21; failure of, 114, 159, 175; and isolationism, 7, 10, 29, 35, 36, 53, 60, 68, 72, 82, 96, 106, 179; and the Munich agreement, 141, 145; and Socialist International, 40n; and the Spanish crisis, 46–9 passim, 56, 72
Comintern, 16, 30, 52, 64, 69, 72, 80,

235

187, 188; anti-fascist campaign (1937), 49; anti-Nazi activities, 211; and China, 100; and Czechoslovakia, 128, 134, 140, 143, 146; and Great Terror, 101; intent to liquidate, 220; and purges, 51, 52, 101; and popular fronts, 113; Praesidium session of March–April 1936, 17, 22, 23, 26; Praesidium session of September 1937, 100; resolution of 1 April 1936, 26, 27, 29; 7th Congress, 23; and Spain, 43, 46–9, 52, 53, 71, 97, 99; support for Soviet–German partnership, 187; and 'Trotskyism', 96, 100

Committee for Non-intervention (London), 54

communist parties, Paris conference of, 139; rift on anti-fascist struggle in, 188

Communist Party of Czechoslovakia, 140

Communist Party of France, 18, 27, 50, 57, 61, 113, 159, 191

Communist Party of the Soviet Union, 3, 17, 37, 51, 78, 83, 194, 199, 213; Central Committee, June 1936 plenum, 37; February–March 1937 plenum, 78, 79, 82, 89, 90, 92, 103, 108, 109, 120n, 146; May 1939 plenum, 162; March 1940 plenum, 194, 213n; July 1940 plenum, 199

Coulondre, Robert, 86, 91, 96, 127, 136

Cripps, Stafford, 202–6

Czechoslovakia, 45, 91, 92, 95, 112, 115, 118, 126–49; after Anschluss, 115, 126, 131; German invasion of, 150, 164, 167; pact with USSR, 127, 135

Daladier, Edouard, 86, 116, 127, 134, 136, 150, 152, 159

Danzig, 142, 171, 172

Dekanozov, Vladimir G., 200, 218

Delbos, Yvon, 91

del Vayo, Alvarez, 61

Diaz, José, 55

Dimitrov, Georgi, 17–30 *passim*, 36, 47–52 *passim*, 68–71 *passim*, 96–101 *passim*, 106, 113, 128, 134, 139, 140, 159, 162, 186–91 *passim*, 198, 199,

201, 211, 219, 220; on aid for Spain, 48, 69, 99; on the future war, 22; interview in *Pravda* (1 May 1936), 29

Draganov, Peter, 170

East Asia, 138

Eden, Anthony, 11, 38n, 61–3 *passim*, 71, 75n, 92, 95, 103, 112, 218; and Western pact, 54

Elliott, W., 194

Enukidze, Avel', 84

Erickson, John, 83, 210

Estonia, 158, 167, 192, 200, 201, 208

Ethiopia, 33, 65

Ezhov, Nikolai, 78, 83, 108, 109

Fierlinger, Zdenek, 131

Finland, 157, 163, 167, 169, 192–6, 207, 208; Soviet war against, 193–5, 198, 202

Flandin, Pierre, 5, 11

France (*see also* Communist Party of France), 6, 7, 10, 18, 23, 33, 45, 50, 53, 67, 68, 82, 91, 105, 106, 114, 116, 133, 142, 144, 151–4, 156–9, 170, 172, 178, 179, 182, 183, 187, 189, 192, 193, 195–8, 219; and Czechoslovakia, 127, 129, 132; Franco-Soviet pact, 1, 5, 10, 11, 12, 27, 91, 106, 107, 115, 129, 135, 136, 139, 142, 159, 163, 168, 169; military collapse, 199–206; and Spanish crisis, 44

Franco, Francisco, 42, 50, 54, 55, 57, 58, 94, 96, 97

Gaikis, Leonid Ia., 93

Galicia, 172

Gamarnik, Ian B., 83, 84

Gel'fand (Helfand), L.B., 170, 172, 201

Geneva, 35, 103, 111, 131, 135; peace congress, 49

Germany, 10, 22, 23, 25, 43, 49, 64, 67, 72, 81, 88, 92, 95, 102, 105, 112, 115, 126, 129, 137, 146, 151, 200; anti-Semitism in, 142; credit agreement with USSR, 173; and France, 143; pacts with France and

INDEX

Belgium, 32; with Italy, 166, 205; with Japan, 64, 205; with Latvia and Estonia, 167; Soviet assessment of military strength, 12; and Spain, 42, 58, 60, 65, 67, 71, 72; war against Denmark and Norway, 196, 198
Gero, Erno, 71
Gnedin, Evgenii A., 77, 104, 123n, 137, 161, 165, 183
Goering, Hermann, 66, 67, 75n
Great Britain, 10, 14, 30, 44, 45, 67, 82, 103, 104, 105, 106, 116, 129, 133, 200, 207; defence of France and Belgium, 61, 63; and Germany, 95, 105; guarantees to Poland, Romania and Greece, 151, 154, 156, 160, 167; and Italy, 116; Labour Party, 19; and Spanish republicans, 71; and USSR, 35, 45, 150
Great Terror, 42, 51, 77–125, 179, 180; in the Red Army, 83; second Moscow trial, 79; in Soviet foreign ministry, 89, 161; third Moscow trial, 109, 110
Greece, 156, 167, 207, 209
Guernica, 93

Halifax, Lord, 103, 104, 112, 127, 129, 135, 137, 150–9 *passim*, 166, 167, 194
Haslam, Jonathan, 78
Herriot, Edouard, 130
Hilger, Gustav, 13, 219
Hillgruber, Andreas, 221
Hitler, Adolf, 1, 6, 10, 28, 34, 45, 50, 64, 95, 125n, 126, 129, 131, 133–9, 142–5, 152, 155, 158, 163, 178–80, 186, 189–206 *passim*, 216, 217, 219, 222, 223; correspondence with Stalin, 174; denounces the Locarno agreement, 5; meeting with Halifax, 103, 104; meeting with Molotov, 207; reneges on agreements with Britain and Poland, 163, 152, 171, 174; rise to power, 2, 3, 4, 112, 179; and Spain, 67; speech on 7 March 1936, 22; on Ukraine and central Europe, 116; and USSR, 5, 9, 46, 119, 189

Howard, Roy, interview with Stalin, (see Stalin)
Hudson, Robert, 150, 151, 153, 154
Hungary, 46, 191, 209

Iagoda, Genrikh, 37
Iakir, Iona, 83, 84, 87, 88
Ierusalimskii, Arkadii, 216
Italy, 5, 12, 24, 32, 42, 44, 45, 46, 56, 58–65 *passim*, 70, 75, 81, 87, 94, 97, 102–11 *passim*, 135, 116, 121, 131, 137, 142, 147, 148, 151, 155, 163, 166, 170, 173, 178, 200–18 *passim*, 224; and Axis, 64, 94; and Spain, 42, 58, 65; war with Ethiopia, 24

Japan (*see also* China), 1, 5, 10, 23, 32, 58, 60, 64, 65, 67, 68, 75, 79, 81, 96, 100, 103, 105, 106, 168, 169, 170, 171, 173, 187, 200, 205, 206, 207, 209, 210, 214; Soviet neutrality pact with, 218

Kagan, Samuil', 54
Kaganovich, Lazar' M., 44, 45, 46, 47, 55, 108; against anti-German bloc, 1937, 47; on Spain, 55
Kamenev, Lev B., 51
Kandelaki, David N., 9, 11, 38n, 66, 67, 87, 95, 123
Karakhan, Lev M., 84
Katyn massacre, 196
Kennan, George, 77
Khlevniuk, Oleg, 78
Khrushchev, Nikita S., 199
Kirov, Sergei M., assassination of, 37, 51, 77
Knorin, Wilhelm, 29, 40n
Kosarev, Aleksandr V., 49
Kosior, Stanislav V., 37
Köstring, General Ernst, 87
Krestinskii, Nikolai N., 10, 11, 12, 47, 58, 87, 90, 109; on pact with Germany, 11; on Rhineland crisis, 15; on Spain, 44–6, 54
Kun, Bela, 28
Kuusinen, Otto Ville, 20, 21, 23, 24, 134, 195

STALIN AND THE INEVITABLE WAR, 1936–1941

Lapinskii, P., 46, 63, 64, 65, 72, 73n, 92
Largo Caballero, Francisco, 48, 70, 93, 100, 121n
Latvia, 96, 158, 167, 192, 200, 201
Laval, Pierre, 115
League of Nations, 6, 10, 11, 18, 20, 23, 30, 33, 35, 49, 53, 56, 59, 61, 62, 65, 92, 93, 97, 102, 103, 111, 114, 116, 126, 131, 132, 135, 167; expulsion of USSR, 195; Italy's withdrawal from, 111
Lemin, I., 64
Lenin, Vladimir I., 3, 18, 28, 109, 110, 181, 221
Leningrad, 196
Lensky, Julian, 19, 24, 25, 40n
Lithuania, 115, 155, 158, 159, 178, 192, 200
Litvinov, Maksim M., 2, 5–7, 9–12, 14, 31, 33–6, 38n, 41, 42, 44–7, 53–63, 65–9, 75n, 76n, 86, 87, 89, 90, 91, 93–6, 101–8, 110–12, 114–19, 121n, 123n, 124n, 125–7, 129–32, 141–4, 147n, 150–60, 166, 167, 180, 182n, 183, 199, 203, 223; on Anschluss, 114; on collective security, 2, 7, 53, 114; criticism of Western diplomacy, 56; and Czechoslovakia, 132; dismissal of, 160–5, 168; on Eastern European pact with German participation, 11; on League of Nations, 111; opposes Soviet-German détente, 87; on pacts with France and Britain, 35; on pan-European pact, 56; resignation of, 107; and Spain, 45–7, 94; support for Anglo-French mediation, 63
Locarno Treaty, 9, 10, 12, 14
London committee, 55, 59, 93–4, 102
London Peace Congress, 92

Mackensen, Hans Georg von, 201, 204
Maiskii, Ivan M., 5, 12, 33–7, 41n, 46, 55–7, 62, 63, 92, 94, 95, 103, 105, 106, 112–16, 124n, 127–9, 130, 134–7, 141–4, 150–7, 159, 161, 166–70, 176, 193–5, 202, 210, 214, 218; contacts with British diplomats, 194; on Litvinov's pan-European pact project, 57; on national security, 36; on Spain 62
Malenkov, Georgii M., 221
Manuil'skii, Dmitrii Z., 17–24, 26, 28, 31, 52–4, 69, 70, 80–2, 98, 100, 108, 113, 134, 139, 140, 146, 159, 162, 167, 187, 198, 199; on Spain, 81, 100
Marty, André, 24, 70, 100
Mekhlis, Lev Z., 155
Memel, 142, 158
Merekalov, Aleksei F., 130, 161, 164, 165
Mikoian, Anastas I., 164
Molotov, Viacheslav M., 2, 4n, 7–10, 13, 16, 19, 36, 38n, 45, 48, 66, 68, 70, 79, 80, 82, 83, 90, 106–8, 110, 113, 119, 120n, 121n, 124n, 126, 136, 138, 144, 158–63, 165–7, 169–77, 180, 182n, 183n, 186–8, 191–7, 199–211, 212n, 213n, 214n, 216–20; announces ceasefire with Finland, 196; conflicts with Litvinov, 162; and idea of collective security, 7; innovative approach to foreign policy, 68, 119; interview in *Le Temps*, 7, 13; meetings with von der Schulenburg (August 1939), 172; mission to Berlin, 205–10; on repercussions of Molotov–Ribbentrop pact, 138, 160, 169, 171, 173, 174, 192, 193, 197, 199, 200, 201, 205
Molotov–Ribbentrop pact, 77, 175, 179, 200, 202, 203, 205, 208; as cornerstone of Soviet policy on the eve of WWII, 218; impact on Soviet policy, 181; negotiations on, 173–5; secret protocol, 175
Montreux conference on the Turkish Straits, 35
Munich conference, 134, 135, 136, 138, 141, 145, 150, 165, 180
Mussolini, Benito, 33, 56, 116, 144, 158, 202

Naggiar, Paul Emile, 163
Negrin, Juan, 93, 99
Neurath, Constantin von, 112
Nikolaevskii, Boris, 31, 77

238

INDEX

Nin, Andres, assassination of, 97
Nyon Conference on Mediterranean piracy, 101

Ordzhonikidze, Georgii K. (Sergo), 55, 108

'Pact of Four' (1925), 135
Pascua, M., 54
Paul-Boncour, Joseph, 11, 114, 130
Payart, Jean, 130, 161, 166, 183n
Persian Gulf, 207, 208
Piatakov, Georgii L., 78, 109
Pieck, Wilhelm, 40
Plymouth, Lord, 55
Poland, 10, 23, 25, 67, 81, 88, 115, 127, 135, 141, 143, 150–85; attacked by Germany, 176, 198; division of, 178, 192, 209; hostility to USSR, 154; invasion by USSR, 176; non-aggression pact with USSR, 19, 133, 141; Polish-Soviet war (1920), 194
Pollitt, Harry, 24, 50, 71
popular fronts, 113
Potemkin, Vladimir P., 5, 11, 12, 61, 63, 86, 90, 91–3, 95, 106, 115, 125n, 131, 133, 136, 137, 141, 144, 147, 151, 153, 164, 167, 171
Primakov, V.M., 83
Putna, V.K., 83
purges, Stalinist (*see* Great Terror)

Radek, Karl, 12–17 *passim*, 30, 31, 39n, 43, 51, 53, 78, 80, 83, 109, 129, 190; on collective security, 15; on Franco's coup, 43; on Hitler's foreign policy, 13
Rakovskii, Khristian, 109
Rapallo, 9, 164, 171, 175
Rhineland crisis, 5–41, 97
Ribbentrop, Joachim von (*see also* Molotov–Ribbentrop pact), 112, 143, 164, 171–8 *passim*, 201, 205–10 *passim*, 219; meeting with Stalin and Molotov, 177; visit to Moscow, 174
Romania, 46, 89, 127, 143, 153–7, 160, 163, 167, 191, 200, 202, 209, 217; Italian and German guarantees to, 207

Roosevelt, Franklin Delano, 102, 158
Rosso, Augusto, 58, 65, 90, 121n, 147, 151, 173, 201, 202, 217
Rozenberg, Marcel I., 48, 57, 61, 74n, 90, 121
Rudzutak, Ian, 83, 84
Rykov, Aleksei I., 78, 84, 109

Schacht, Hjalmar, 9, 66, 67
Schnurre, Julius, 164, 165, 171, 197
Schulenburg, Friedrich von der, 34, 45, 130, 164, 165, 170–3 *passim*, 177, 197, 201, 204, 205, 210, 214n, 217, 218
Seeds, Sir William, 151, 153, 154, 159, 160, 166, 182
Shcherbakov, Aleksandr S., 220, 221
Shkvartsev, Aleksandr, 205
Shtein, Boris E., 44, 103
Shvernik, Nikolai M., 43, 49
Socialist International, 50, 57; meeting with Comintern in Annemasse, 97
Sokol'nikov, Grigorii Ia., 78
Sorge, Richard, 206
Spain, 42–76, 98, 99, 104, 112, 113, 114, 116, 128, 155; Anglo-French mediation in, 62, 63; end of republic, 155; and USSR, 69, 92, 113
Spanish Civil War, 42–76 *passim*, 93, 111; evacuation of volunteers, 96, 103, 135; and USSR, 42–4, 47–59, 63, 72, 93, 94
Stalin, Iosif V., 1, 2, 5, 7–11, 13–18, 21, 27, 31, 33, 36, 38, 39, 45–8, 54–6, 58, 61, 63, 66–8, 70–80, 82–7, 90, 91, 94, 96–101, 103, 104, 106–15, 119–21, 123–6, 128, 130, 133, 134, 136, 138, 144–52, 155–63, 165, 167, 169, 170, 173–5, 177–82, 184–91, 193–201, 203–24; and Czechoslovakia, 134; disagreements with Bukharin, 2; interview with Roy Howard, 1–7 *passim*, 14, 27, 100, 188; isolationism, 4; and purges (*see also* Great Terror), 37, 77; report to 18th Party Congress, 144, 145, 150; speech at the 17th Party Congress (1934), 31; speech to the CC plenum on fascism (June 1936),

STALIN AND THE INEVITABLE WAR, 1936–1941

37; speech to the graduates of Soviet military academies, 219, 220; support for Hitler's peace campaign, 193; telegram to Diaz, 55; on Tukhachevskii's article regarding German military strategy, 8; and war with Germany, 3, 186, 187, 190, 198, 216, 219

Strang, William, 167

Sudetenland, 131

Surits, Iakov Z., 9, 12, 45–7, 58, 67, 75n, 87, 90, 91, 94, 95, 105, 106, 111, 114–16, 121n, 125n, 127, 129, 136, 141–3, 151, 153, 154, 156, 159, 167; on French diplomacy, 91; on Hitler and Nazi regime, 9, 45, 58

Tarle, Evgenii V., 99

Thorez, Maurice, 18, 49, 50, 113, 220

Timoshenko, Marshal Semen K., 206, 220

Tippelskirch, Werner von, 205

Titulescu, Nicolae, 86

Togliatti, Palmiro (Ercoli), 19, 20, 21, 25–9 *passim*, 26, 27, 28, 29, 51, 70, 72, 97, 99, 113, 128, 139, 199, 220; on 'German spies' within Comintern, 52; speech on the 1936 Comintern resolution, 26

Trilisser, M.A., 19, 134, 140

Tucker, Robert, 77

Tukhachevskii, Marshal Mikhail N., 8, 9, 109; attack on, 82–9, 90, 91, 95, 96, 98, 109, 120n; on German strategic plans, 8, 89; Paris talks (1936), 5; self-indictment, 87, 88

Turkey, 35, 46, 84, 137, 157, 178, 201–3, 207, 208, 217; Soviet policy towards, 208, 209

Uborevich, Ieronym P., 83, 84, 88

Ukraine, 89, 116, 142, 143, 172; western Ukraine, 176, 192, 196

Ulam, Adam, 181

Uldricks, Ted, 78

Union of Soviet Socialist Republics, 6, 12, 17, 20, 23, 103, 106, 113; and Balkans, 201; and Czechoslovakia, 127, 131–3, 137; and Germany, 61; intelligence on the eve of World War II, 206, 220; isolationism, 2, 7, 10, 12, 29, 35, 53, 60, 68, 72, 96, 99, 105, 106, 179; and Italy, 61, 201, 202, 204, 217; and Japan, 168, 210; pacts with Baltic states, 158, 192; pacts with France and Czechoslovakia, 23; peace plan, 33; and Polish–Lithuanian conflict, 115; rapprochement with Germany, 66, 87, 163, 164, 170, 172–81, 197, 217; Rhineland crisis, 5, 11; relations with the West, 12, 63, 77, 90, 93, 94, 150, 156, 158, 163, 167, 168, 169, 171, 179, 199, 202, 203; treaty with Germany, 178–80, 191; and Western public opinion, 91

United States, 102, 111, 197, 198, 200, 204

Vansittart, Robert, 130

Varga, Evgenii S., 16, 17, 71, 99, 101, 108, 199, 204, 212n, 216, 217, 221; on the Rhineland crisis, 16; on Soviet security, 71

Versailles, 5, 13, 157, 186

Voroshilov, Kliment E., 53, 70, 82–5, 88, 108, 112, 121n, 126, 169, 174, 194, 197

Vyshinskii, Andrei Ia., 37, 78, 200

Weizsäcker, Ernst von, 164

Werth, Alexander, 219

Yugoslavia, 46, 209; German invasion of, 218; Soviet non-aggression treaty with, 218

Zhdanov, Andrei A., 68, 69, 78, 80, 82, 106–8, 110, 111, 124n, 127, 128, 138, 139, 141, 155, 162, 167, 168, 176, 186–9, 196, 197, 201, 218, 220, 221; on Spain, 82; on revival of isolationism, 68

Zhukov, Marshal Georgii K., 220

Zinov'ev, Grigorii E., 51